Calgary's Stampede Queens

CALGARY'S STAMPEDE QUEENS

★★★★★★★★★

Jennifer Hamblin

RMB

Rocky Mountain Books
www.rmbooks.com

Library and Archives Canada Cataloguing in Publication

Hamblin, Jennifer, author
    Calgary's Stampede queens / Jennifer Hamblin.

Includes bibliographical references and index.
ISBN 978-1-77160-003-3 (bound)

    1. Women in rodeos—Alberta—Calgary—Biography.
2. Calgary Stampede—Social aspects. 3. Beauty
contests—Alberta—Calgary—History. I. Title.

GV1833.5.H34 2014   791.8'40922712338   C2013-908262-X

Printed in Canada

Rocky Mountain Books acknowledges the financial support for its publishing program from the Government of Canada through the Canada Book Fund (CBF) and the Canada Council for the Arts, and from the province of British Columbia through the British Columbia Arts Council and the Book Publishing Tax Credit.

This book was produced using FSC®-certified, acid-free paper, processed chlorine free and printed with vegetable-based inks.

Abbreviations

ACT Magazine – The Associated Canadian Travellers' Magazine
CH – Calgary Herald
CS – Calgary Stampede
CSA – Calgary Stampede Archives

Front cover photo: Semi-finalists in the Calgary Stampede Queen contest, 1968. (GA: NA-2864-18175N)
Frontispiece: 1956 Queen Shirley Willock (centre) and Ladies-in-waiting Carolyn Schoeppe and Kay Marshall with American cowboy actor and rodeo performer Casey Tibbs. (GA: PA-3954-2)
Back cover photo: Queen Patsy Rodgers, 1946. (GA: NA-3127-1)

Photo credits: All photographs appear with the kind permission of the Glenbow Archives (GA), the Calgary Stampede Archives (CSA) and the Queens' Alumni Committee (QAC).

Contents

PREFACE — 7

SETTING THE STAGE — 11

CHAPTER 1 ★ **1946** "Once a Queen, always a Queen" — 13

CHAPTER 2 ★ **1947–1949** "Be a Booster! Help your favorite win!" — 33

CHAPTER 3 ★ **1950–1953** "To reign as Queen! Well, I'll never be the same" — 53

CHAPTER 4 ★ **1954** "A great honour for myself and all my people" — 69

CHAPTER 5 ★ **1955–1958** "This thing called glamour can get pretty exhausting" — 89

CHAPTER 6 ★ **1959–1963** "No girl can become Queen unless she's a proficient horsewoman" — 107

CHAPTER 7 ★ **1964–1966** "Rules changed: Popularity tickets out" — 131

CHAPTER 8 ★ **1967–1969** "As Stampede Queen, you are doing a job for the city" — 149

CHAPTER 9 ★ **1970–1974** "It takes ability – and plenty of it – to become Stampede Queen" — 169

CHAPTER 10 ★ **1975–1979** "There's a world of excitement for you as Stampede Queen" — 187

CHAPTER 11 ★ **1980–1985** "As good an experience as a horse-loving Cowtown girl could ask for" — 205

CHAPTER 12 ★ **1986–1989** "Stampede trio more than beauty contest winners" — 231

CHAPTER 13 ★ **1990–1994** "The riding has to become second nature" — 253

CHAPTER 14 ★ **1995–1999** "There's more guts than glamour in being Stampede royalty" — 269

CHAPTER 15 ★ **2000–2007** "An egalitarian royalty: all for one and one for all" — 285

CHAPTER 16 ★ **2008–2014** "A walking, talking poster for the Stampede" — 303

AFTERWORD Looking back and moving forward — 325

APPENDIX Stampede Royalty, 1946–2014 — 329

Notes — 332

Selected bibliography — 346

Index — 352

This book grew out of an article on the early history of the Calgary Stampede Queen contest that I wrote for *Alberta History*'s Stampede Centennial issue (Summer 2012). When editor Hugh Dempsey approached me for a topic, I immediately thought of the treasure trove of newspaper clippings on Stampede royalty that I had organized the year before for the Glenbow Library. Collector Jane Bentley, clearly fascinated with the Stampede Queen contest and its winners, had cut out almost everything on the topic that had appeared in the two Calgary newspapers from the mid-1940s to the mid-1980s. Aside from the articles in Mrs. Bentley's rich collection and another good cache of newspaper clippings in the Local History Room of the Calgary Public Library, there appeared to be very few written resources available on the topic – but that just presented an interesting challenge.

I started my research knowing virtually nothing about the contest, aside from the fact that it selected three pretty girls each year to represent the Stampede,

Queen Patsy Rodgers riding in the 1946 Stampede parade with arena director Jack Dillon. (GA: PA-3948-1)

but I quickly discovered a very intriguing history. The early years of the contest were a delightful surprise – the first queen never had to compete for her title and those who followed for nearly two decades sold votes to win their crowns – so that was the focus of my journal article, "Queen of the Stampede, 1946–1966." But my research took me far beyond that era and I soon learned that it was the twists and turns of succeeding decades that really created the modern contest familiar today. I was glad of the opportunity to tell that fascinating history but unsure at first where to end the tale. With a fresh new trio being crowned every year, it is a story potentially without end. However, I came to understand that the significant changes made to the contest and program during the late 2000s capped decades of evolution and firmly set a course for the future, so it seemed fitting to end my survey in the afterglow of the Stampede's 2012 Centennial celebration.

I am grateful to many people for helping me to research, write and publish this book. But first, I would like to thank Hugh Dempsey for initially encouraging me to delve into this neglected area of Stampede history. I appreciated his useful early suggestions and his kind reception of my completed article.

My thanks also go to Gillian Daffern for supporting the idea of producing a book on the subject, and to RMB | Rocky Mountain Books publisher Don Gorman for enthusiastically encouraging the project. Thanks also to the staff at RMB for their care in shepherding the manuscript from draft through to publication, in particular, designer Chyla Cardinal and editor Joe Wilderson.

I am indebted to Stampede archivist Aimee Benoit for allowing me generous access to the documentary and photographic collections housed at the Calgary Stampede Archives. I am also grateful for her many helpful suggestions regarding outside resources, her help in contacting individuals connected with the Stampede, her prompt answers to my many and varied queries, and her thoughtful reading of the draft manuscript. Thanks also to archives assistant Hilary Gordon and director of corporate communications Kurt Kadatz for enabling access to the Stampede archives and generously providing photographs from its collection.

With so few published sources available, an important resource for this study was the first-hand accounts provided by a number of former Stampede Queens, Princesses and Ladies-in-waiting. I am grateful to Aimee Benoit and Hugh Dempsey for helping me to connect with Patsy Rogers Henderson and Evelyn Eagle Speaker Locker during the initial phase of my research. After I decided to extend the scope of the project, Karin Kraft Benjamin and Tara Wesner Linton were helpful in determining that it would be unrealistic to attempt to arrange an interview with every former royal who had a unique and interesting story to tell – potentially all of them! We decided that a better approach would be to sample the memories of a few winners per decade and assume their experiences would be typical of the contest and program at that particular time. I am most grateful to Lisa Eastman for helping me to develop and refine this approach. She was instrumental in compiling a decade by decade listing of possible interviewees and approaching them on my behalf. Her patience and persistence with this task was invaluable, as was her assistance in obtaining copies of Calgary Stampede Queens' Alumni Committee meeting minutes. I am very thankful that she not only agreed to be interviewed for the project but also read the draft manuscript and offered a number of helpful suggestions.

Thank you to Donna Thomson Brasso for following up on our interview by sending me information regarding the history of the Queens' Alumni, and for reading the completed manuscript and offering many helpful comments. In addition to being interviewed, Tara Wesner Linton generously shared the insights she gained while producing *The Queens' Alumni Memory Book* and was invaluable in helping to locate and reproduce photographs from Alumni sources. I also wish to thank Patsy Rogers Henderson for graciously allowing access to her scrapbooks, photographs and other memorabilia, and Shirley Willock Bertoli and Margaret Powell Clark for following up on interviews by sending copies of items from their scrapbooks.

This was a personal project rather than a commissioned work, but I was very grateful for the opportunity to discuss the evolution of the queen contest and program with several members of the current Royalty Committee. My thanks go to Pat Pearson, Janelle Phillips, Sandy Young Tidswell and Dana Tremblay for generously sharing their thoughts and observations. Similarly, I am thankful for the interest and support shown by members of the Queens' Alumni Association, particularly those who participated in interviews or sent me reminiscences. In addition to those already mentioned, my sincere thanks go to the following, in alphabetical order: Frances Swann Anderson, Happy Barlow, Kari Hames Beermann, Jolene Brewster, Sherry Moore Bronfman, Barb Penner Colborne, Gwenda Marshall Davies, Peter Degenstein, Margot Turney DeMeo, Barbara Howard Denoon, Holly Dunn, Laura Godwin Dunn, Karina Tees Geleynse, Kari Griffith, June-Marie Innes, Lisa McNiven Johnsen, Cathy Robinson Ladiges, Joan Plastow Langford, Candice Lee, Eileen Beckner Lockwood, Leslie MacDonald Crowe, Jessica Manning, Marie Sharpe O'Bertos, Cindy Morres Sergerie, Inez Melby Shaver, Joan Horne Sveen, Bonnie MacGregor Thompson, Arlene Weidner, Jessica Williams and Allison Boswell Wright.

The focus of this book is the contest and program that annually selects and trains a royal trio for the Stampede, but in recent years the number of official royal representatives has grown to four with the official inclusion of the Indian Princess as part of the royal team since 2008. For this reason, and because the history of the Stampede Indian Princess intersects with that of the Stampede Queen and Princesses at many points over the past few decades, I have included a few details about the activities of Indian Princesses in the narrative whenever appropriate. Although these details necessarily are brief and do not attempt to do justice to the history and evolution of the Indian Princess contest and program, I hope they help to shed some light on why and how the four royal positions came together to share the job of officially representing the Stampede in the twenty-first century. Unfortunately, limited space for photographs meant that I could not include pictures of the Stampede Indian Princess contest winners in this book. I am grateful to Tammy Kneller and Anne Garnett of the Stampede Indian Princess Competition subcommittee for providing information relating to the Indian Princess contest and program. Although I have tried to relay accurately the information and memories contributed by all of the individuals named above, I take full responsibility and apologize in advance for any errors, omissions or inadvertent misinterpretations.

I appreciated the enthusiastic interest shown for this project by many of my colleagues at the Glenbow Library and Archives. In particular, I wish to thank to director Doug Cass and archivist Susan Kooyman for many helpful suggestions regarding resources and for generously providing photographs from the Archives' collection. Special thanks go to digital images technician Anita Dammer for her beautiful reproductions of historical photographs, and to photographer Owen Melenka for reproducing newspaper advertisements from the Glenbow Library collection. Most of all, my sincere thanks go to senior librarian Lindsay Moir for her steadfast friendship, her ongoing interest in the project, her many helpful comments and suggestions and her careful and insightful reading of the manuscript at various stages.

Finally, I wish to thank my family for their unfailing love and support throughout the duration of this project. My parents, Larry and Bunni Laidman, expressed their interest at every step of the way, having always encouraged my love of history, research and writing. In addition to offering technical advice and unconditional encouragement, my children, Lindsay and Graham, patiently listened to weekly updates for more than a year, in the process learning more about the Stampede Queen contest and program than they ever thought possible. But it was my husband, Tony, who was my mainstay during an intense year of research and writing. His calm, analytical approach to problem-solving and genuine interest in the topic made him an invaluable sounding board as my ideas developed and writing progressed. Unfailingly supportive, he generously took over on the home front, thus enabling me to complete this project while still working full time. I could not have done it without his support and it is to him that I dedicate this book.

Aside from cowboys and Indians,* horses and white hats, nothing symbolizes the Calgary Stampede quite like its royalty, the attractive young women who are its glamorous public face. As goodwill ambassadors at home and abroad, the Stampede Queen and Princesses, and, more recently, the Stampede Indian Princess, serve as a very effective

*Although modern usage usually favours more culturally sensitive and politically correct terms such as Native, Aboriginal and First Nations, the word Indian is still very much in use locally, particularly with respect to the traditional participation in the Calgary Stampede of the Treaty 7 Nations of southern Alberta. Despite shifting language and the concerns expressed by outsiders and some younger members of the First Nations' own community, the continuing use of terms such as Indian Village, Indian Princess, Indian parade, and Indian dances has the blessing of Stampede Indian Village elders and tipi owners representing the Kainai, Piikani, Siksika, Stoney/Nakoda and Tsuu T'ina Nations (known historically as the Blood, Peigan, Blackfoot, Stoney and Sarcee). See, for example, Jen Gerson, "Calgary Stampede: A defiant last stand of the politically incorrect," *National Post*, Jul 4, 2012, http://news.nationalpost.com/2012/07/04/calgary-stampede-a-defiant-last-stand-of-the-politically-incorrect, accessed Apr 22, 2013; and Zoltan Varadi, "Race, representation and the rodeo," *Fast Forward Weekly*, Jul 7, 2012, www.ffwdweekly.com/calgary-blogs/culture/2012/07/13/race-representation-and-the-rodeo-1101, accessed Apr 22, 2013.

promotional team working year round on behalf of the show and its home city. So ubiquitous is their presence in the twenty-first century that the Royal Team is considered an integral part of the Stampede image and it is difficult to remember a time when these positions did not exist. But the Calgary Exhibition and Stampede was well into its sixth decade as a fair before there was any thought of choosing a queen as a promotional figurehead, and another forty years would pass before the Stampede officially started sponsoring an Indian Princess.

The annual show now known simply as the Calgary Stampede started as two separate events: an agricultural and industrial fair, first held in 1886, and a rodeo called the Stampede, first produced by Guy Weadick in 1912. A second Stampede was held in 1919, but it was not until the rodeo joined forces with the fair in 1923 that the Calgary Exhibition and Stampede was born and became an annual event. With its high standards of judging, significant trophies and big purses, the rodeo's fame quickly spread beyond Alberta's borders during the twenties, bringing a welcome flood of participants and onlookers into Calgary each year to boost the local economy.

Encouraged by Weadick, locals supported this bonanza by wholeheartedly adopting the fair's frontier theme: dressing Western, decorating businesses with false fronts and bunting, and extending the festival atmosphere by hosting street dances, Indian parades, buffalo barbecues and pancake breakfasts. Soon, the annual celebration had become so well known that the word "Calgary" was almost synonymous in the public mind with the word "Stampede."[1]

The Calgary Stampede had its ups and downs over the next few decades, particularly during the 1930s and early 1940s when the Depression and the Second World War restricted travel and impacted tourism. Even so, locals still flocked to the show: "In a world riddled with depression and despondency, the one-week Calgary Stampede was like a ray of sunshine."[2] The war gave a big boost to the Alberta economy, and, in so doing, proved to be "the greatest thing that ever happened to the Stampede." The happy conjunction of full employment, military expenditures and good crops resulted in attendance records being broken year after year by Albertans "eager to escape wartime austerity in a week of boisterous fun."[3]

When the war finally ended, people were ready to celebrate. The 1945 Stampede attracted close to 300,000 people, nearly three times Calgary's resident population.[4] A record crowd of 55,000 watched the hour-long parade, one of the biggest ever seen. Many entries focused on veterans and the armed services, and the crowd cheered the Calgary Horticultural Society's first-prize win, a "Welcome Home, Boys" float featuring "a flower-covered cottage before which three young women welcomed a returning soldier, sailor and airman."[5]

It was during this post-war period of growth and optimism that the Stampede really began focusing on promotion. As an agricultural fair and rodeo, it had developed a loyal following in the farming and ranching community of southern Alberta but it wanted to expand beyond its natural audience. The lifting of wartime restrictions had unleashed "a wild whirl of spending and travel" that saw many Canadians and Americans take to the road, spending their holidays exploring new tourist destinations,[6] and the Stampede was eager to capture this market by broadening its appeal. In 1946 one of its key decisions was to do what many other western fairs already were doing with great success: appoint a young, pretty figurehead to go out and promote the show.

CHAPTER 1 ✸ 1946

"Once a Queen, always a Queen"[7]

In July 1945, Texas rancher Everett C. Colborn visited the Calgary Stampede to buy stock. It was a significant development for the Stampede because Colborn was no ordinary stockman: his Lightning C Ranch was co-owned by the famous singing cowboy Gene Autry, and it supplied the animals for their joint venture, the World Championship Rodeo. The WCR was a touring extravaganza that performed every fall at New York City's Madison Square Garden and the Boston Garden. The show featured all the elements of a traditional small-town rodeo – bronc busting, calf roping, steer wrestling – but on a grand scale to attract sophisticated city dwellers. To add a little glamour, the show always included five or six rodeo queens from local fairs in Texas and other western states who promoted the WCR to the public.[8] In 1945 Everett Colborn was so impressed by his visit to Calgary's fair that he offered to include the Stampede's rodeo queen in the next World Championship Rodeo, to be held that fall. It was a wonderful promotional opportunity for the Calgary Stampede, with just one problem: the Stampede had no queen to send.

Interestingly, having a queen to represent the Stampede was something arena director Jack Dillon had been contemplating for some time. He had noticed and welcomed the participation of a growing number of rodeo queens from other fairs in the annual Stampede parade. By the 1940s American fairs and rodeos of all sizes were boasting pretty royalty to help boost ticket sales by working with town promoters to attract spectators and the media. In Texas these young women came to be known as sponsor girls because of their role in representing, or sponsoring, their rodeo and community to the outside world. No matter what they were called, their role was to act as attractive goodwill ambassadors, making public appearances, bestowing trophies and riding in each other's parades. Although the rise of rodeo queens was seen by some as a negative thing, a trivializing of female rodeo participation as the number of events allowing women competitors began to shrink during the 1930s,[9] it was a trend that caught the public fancy during a period that saw great enthusiasm for festival queens of all kinds.[10]

The Pendleton Round-Up in Oregon was the first to choose a queen, in 1910, but the position only became well established there after 1923. Round-Up management saw the role of rodeo royalty for what it was, a promotional tool, so choosing a queen and two consorts was viewed as being akin to hiring a public-relations team. Candidates submitted their names and credentials and were interviewed for the job, and the successful team was "hired" during a crowning ceremony. The only inconsistency in this business-like approach was the well-known tendency of management to hire the daughters of leading local families. This actually made good sense, because leading families also tended to be big supporters of the rodeo and this forged yet another link, but it was viewed by some as unfair. When Cheyenne Frontier Days decided to have a queen in 1931, they determined to approach selection more democratically: townspeople bought tickets on queen candidates and the young lady with the most tickets won. However, this approach only lasted three years, and by 1934 they too were hand-picking their royalty, usually from among the leading families of the town and surrounding district.[11]

It was only natural that Jack Dillon followed a similar approach when Colborn prompted him in 1945 to produce a rodeo queen for the Calgary Stampede. Dillon searched his mind for a suitable young woman from amongst the daughters of his friends and others associated with the Stampede and came up with the perfect candidate: Patsy Rodgers.* Typically, rodeo queens were ranch-bred, horse-riding, pretty, young women with deep roots in their local community.[12] Descended from two noted Alberta pioneer families, 19-year-old Patsy Rodgers fit the bill in every way. Her paternal grandfather, Dublin Rodgers, had established a ranch west of Okotoks after arriving from Ireland in 1883. Her mother's family, the Hamiltons, had been pioneer homesteaders east of Okotoks, and one uncle, Johnny Hamilton, had owned an early livery stable in Calgary. Her father, William Jasper (Jappy) Rodgers, was a quarter horse breeder, rodeo competitor and former polo player working on the famed Virginia Ranch 30 kilometres north of Cochrane when Patsy was born. Six years later he had acquired his own ranch nearby, in the Bottrell district northwest of Calgary. By 1945

* For the sake of simplicity and clarity, the name under which a Stampede royal won her title will be the name used throughout the text.

he had been helping to coordinate the rodeo stock at the Calgary Stampede for many years.[13]

Patsy's western credentials were impeccable, and, being ranch-born and bred, she had been riding since age 5, and had won a number of blue ribbons in the western riding classes at the annual Calgary Spring Horse Show. Her father was associated with the Stampede, but even better, Patsy was too. By the mid-1940s, she had been living in Calgary for several years, working as a receptionist for the optical firm A. Ashdown Marshall and Associates, but she also rode in the Western section of the Stampede parade each year. She often dropped by the grounds after work during Stampede week to visit her father and exercise her pony, which he kept stabled in the barns along with his own horses. "I loved to ride around in the backfield on my pony – oh yes, it was dusty and sweaty, but I'd watch the cowboys get ready for the rodeo events and then hang on the fence and root for my favourites," she later recalled.[14] While there, she often assisted her father with grooming and watering the horses. In fact, it was his memory of seeing her on horseback on the grounds one day, leading a few horses down to the Elbow River for a drink after the rodeo was over, that brought her to Dillon's mind when Colborn inquired about a Stampede Queen.

Patsy later remembered Dillon approaching her

Queen Patsy Rodgers, 1946. (GA: PA-3930-1)

15
★

Queen Patsy Rodgers, 1946. (GA: NA-3127-1)

and saying the Stampede Board had agreed that "it would be beneficial for the Stampede and the city of Calgary to sponsor a rodeo queen… who would also serve as a goodwill ambassador." Patsy was thrilled with the prospect and grateful for the good luck that had placed her in the right place at the right time.[15] Dillon introduced her to Colborn, who explained that although he had decided it was too late for her to join the 1945 World Championship Rodeo, he would hold a place for her in the 1946 show. She had to be content with that and keep the secret all year ("I didn't dare tell hardly anyone about it in case it should fall through and I'd be disappointed"),[16] but the following spring, Dillon's informal offer was made official when Patsy attended a luncheon at the Palliser Hotel with Stampede officials.

Frank Moore, manager of the WCR at Madison Square Garden in New York City, contacted her parents and asked them to send a short biography of their daughter attesting to her rodeo queen credentials. Bursting with pride, Mr. and Mrs. Rodgers produced a fond and glowing testimonial, detailing her Western family background and describing their daughter in superlatives: "[W]hether she's at the typewriter or in the saddle she could pose as an ad for toothpaste, or shampoo or something magical in the nature of complexion care. Yes, she has curly, golden hair, pearly, even teeth, the kind of dark eyes and curling black lashes that people dream about and – believe it or not – dimples! She is five feet, four inches and one hundred and fifteen pounds in weight, all of beauty and efficiency with personality plus...." [17]

Frank Moore picked out the essentials for a press release in May but somehow the fact that Patsy was representing the Calgary Stampede at the WCR was overlooked. Perhaps New York-based Moore did not think locals would know anything about the Stampede, or even recognize the name Calgary; in any case, he seems to have decided that "Miss Rodeo Canada," or simply, "Miss Canada" would be a more appropriate and recognizable designation. Canadian newspapers coast to coast picked up the exciting news: "Alberta Girl in New York Rodeo." [18] The *Calgary Herald* ran a picture of Patsy with her horse, Starlight, and the headline, "Calgary girl is selected 'Miss Canada' in New York Rodeo." [19] The Calgary *Albertan* posed her leaning against a fence, wearing a cowboy hat and chewing on a long wheat straw, and noted that she was "the first Canadian girl to represent 'Miss Canada' at the great rodeo." [20] Only the *Canadian Cattleman* made it clear that she was first and foremost representing Calgary. After detailing her ranching credentials, the article concluded,

"No finer representative for 'Miss Calgary' could have been selected by Frank Moore, manager of the rodeo at Madison Square Garden, and Everett Colborn who manages the shows for the World Championship Rodeo Corporation." [21]

The press reported that, in addition to having all expenses paid by the WCR, Patsy would "of course be remunerated for her part in the big show" [22] and be provided with a full Western wardrobe consisting of as many as four complete Western outfits. In actuality she was given just one ensemble, a red gabardine wool western suit lavishly embroidered in white, professionally tailored by the famous Western outfitters Rodeo Ben of Philadelphia, and a new white Stetson ordered from Denver. [23] Likely wishing to put their own stamp on the image of their new rodeo queen, the Stampede Board provided Patsy with several additional outfits to wear during the upcoming Stampede. Jack Dillon, probably with the help of Stampede directors and long-time friends of the Rodgers family George Edworthy and James B. Cross, arranged for various local firms to outfit her. Calgary hat maker Smithbilt provided her with two cowboy hats in white, a colour they had just recently introduced at the instigation of local Stampede aficionado Bill Herron. Long-time Calgary-based Western outfitters Riley & McCormick provided her with two pairs of tooled leather boots, one in red and the other blue.

Since no local stores stocked the kind of highly decorated outfits deemed suitable for a rodeo queen, the Great West Garment Company in Edmonton was commissioned to tailor three Western outfits. Two were made in fine grey-green wool serge, one plain and one embroidered with roses on the yokes and cuffs. The third, less successful outfit, intended only for dress occasions, was fashioned in a gold lamé fabric. This was the first time GWG had made rodeo outfits (they mostly manufactured uniforms for the army and the police),[24] so Patsy became involved in the design, copying ideas from pictures of rodeo queen outfits that she had seen in catalogues and magazines.[25] She had to travel to Edmonton several times for fittings before she felt satisfied that the shirt and pants were tailored properly and tight enough to look trim. When all was done, GWG arranged with *Calgary Herald* photographer Harry Befus to take publicity shots at various locations around the Stampede grounds and at Patsy's aunt and uncle's ranch ten kilometres west of Okotoks.

Patsy spent a fun summer waiting to head away that fall to the World Championship Rodeo. A little nervous that she might be out of practice after having lived in the city for several years, she made an extended visit to the family ranch to brush up on her riding and roping skills. Just before the Calgary Stampede started on July 8, she was flown to Lethbridge to participate in their Victory Rally and Rodeo, July 4–6. It was a thrilling trip for Patsy, her first airplane ride and her first brush with celebrity. Air travel was still a novelty in 1946, so the *Lethbridge Herald* ran a photo of her arriving in the city, posed beside a Trans-Canada Air Lines plane with her two pilots and the stewardess. For the benefit of local readers, the reporter noted that the "diminutive saddle queen" was a niece of Mrs. J.J. Morrison of Lethbridge, with whom Patsy was staying, and that both were members of the noted Hamilton family.[26]

In addition to riding in the parade and the daily grand entry, participating in the Lethbridge rodeo provided an opportunity for Patsy to meet with Gene Autry and Everett Colborn in advance of that fall's WCR. Autry, a good friend of Lethbridge rodeo manager Herman Linder, had waived his customary fee to appear as parade marshal, "purely as a personal gesture of friendship." Colborn, who attended on Autry's invitation, and to buy rodeo stock, was

Queen Patsy Rodgers arriving in Lethbridge for the Victory Rally and Rodeo, 1946. L-R: Captain Hugh Bolton, First Officer J.L. Arnett, Stewardess Dorothy Dann, Patsy, Pat Hamilton. (QAC)

mightily impressed with the little Lethbridge fair, declaring it to be the "[w]ildest rodeo I have seen."[27] A photo in the *Lethbridge Herald*, captioned "Queen of the Calgary Stampede," showed Patsy in the cowgirl section of the parade with a rope coiled on her saddle "just as Gene Autry liked." A few days later, the *Herald* told its readers that Patsy "surely enjoyed the Lethbridge show during her three-day visit and is looking forward to returning for next year's rodeo here… After the final session at today's rodeo, she will leave for Calgary, where she will take part in the Stampede parade."[28]

Patsy's experience in Lethbridge was a good rehearsal for her bigger role during the Calgary Stampede, a six-day event held July 8–13, 1946. Her first official duty was to ride in the Stampede parade on Monday morning. Riding between Jack Dillon and director George Edworthy in the Stampede Board section, "she was thrust into a limelight she had never dreamed of," as she joined the others in acknowledging the "shouting, cheering crowds" along the parade route.[29] Before the afternoon rodeo each day, she was included in the Grand Entry, riding out of a side gate into the infield and circling the ring twice. When she came to a stop at centre field in front of the grandstand, she was announced to the crowd as the World Championship Rodeo's Miss Canada.

Introduced with that title, it may not have been apparent to most Calgarians that the Stampede also viewed Patsy as its Queen that year. Certainly, that point seems to have escaped the local media, which continued to describe her simply as "Miss Canada." But, although she was not officially identified in 1946 as the Stampede Queen, Dillon and Edworthy definitely had that in mind for her when they made it clear that her role during Stampede week was to represent and promote the Calgary Stampede.

Rodeo queens typically played a promotional role for their shows in their communities, which usually meant participating in some official capacity at social events during the fair and spreading goodwill by visiting hospitals and children's homes. With this in mind, Myrle Edworthy took on the task of shepherding Patsy around to various functions while her husband, George, was busy that week with other Stampede duties. They visited wounded and recovering Second World War soldiers at the old Colonel Belcher Hospital on 8th Avenue across from Eaton's, and children at the Red Cross Children's Hospital on 17th Avenue SW. Patsy also was the guest of the Stampede at several official events that week. Bill Linderman, a champion American cowboy who knew Patsy's family, was her escort to a party in the Sun Room on the Stampede grounds hosted by

Stampede Committee chairman Jim Cross. The pair also attended a big post-Stampede party together at Jack Dillon's home on the Elbow River, where Mrs. Dillon served large vats of chili to all the participants of the 1946 show as well as visiting rodeo queens from Pendleton, Cheyenne and Great Falls.

The Stampede Board had planned to present Patsy with a silver belt buckle to complete her western outfit, but Bill Linderman, who had competed before at the WCR, told Dillon she would be receiving a special commemorative buckle from the rodeo after she arrived at Madison Square Garden. According to him, what she really needed for completing her outfit was a pair of spurs so she could keep her horse racing around the corral at top speed day after day during the Grand Entry before the rodeo. The Board liked the idea, and also Bill's suggestion that they commission his friend, silversmith Les Garcia of Reno, Nevada, to do the job. Before the grandstand crowd on the final night of the 1946 Stampede, Board representatives Jim Cross, George Edworthy and Jack Dillon presented Patsy with a beautiful pair of silver spurs engraved with her name.

Just before the Calgary Stampede, the Fraternal Order of Eagles had capitalized on Patsy's new-found celebrity to announce her as their candidate for Queen of the Calgary Horticultural Society Flower Show, to be held later that summer. To make sure the public understood just who she was, the Eagles used pictures of her wearing her Stampede Queen outfit in newspaper advertisements for the contest. Not surprisingly, she easily won the most votes (104,000) and was crowned Queen of the Flower Show on August 24. The event was well attended, and in some ways it took the place of the official Stampede Queen crowning she never had. Piped in by a band of Scottish pipers, Patsy was carried to the flower-banked stage by members of the Fraternal Order of Eagles on a litter draped with the Union Jack, an experience she found both exhilarating and terrifying. Looking very regal in her long white dress and ermine-trimmed cloak, she was presented with a crown, mace and sceptre of flowers and then carried back through the hall by her delighted sponsors.[30]

On September 13, 1946, soon after she turned 21, Patsy headed to Dublin, Texas, to join the World Championship Rodeo show. Getting there turned out to be a long, arduous journey for the young woman, already a little nervous about heading so far away from home and for such a long period of time (two months). The first leg of her trip took her back to Lethbridge via Trans Canada Air Lines. There, she chatted "in a pleasant, friendly fashion" with a *Lethbridge Herald* reporter about her upcoming adventure before boarding a Western Air Lines flight to Great Falls, Montana. She arrived there to a modest fanfare: the *Great Falls Tribune* ran a photo of her wearing one of her GWG outfits, posed on the steps of the airplane with a stewardess presenting an orchid corsage from the airline. The caption read: "'Miss Canada' visits city en route to New York."[31]

The next leg of the journey should have taken Patsy to Denver, but a storm over Amarillo, Texas, caused the flight to be rerouted to Oklahoma City, then on to Dallas. There, she was told there was no space on the flight to Fort Worth, Texas, her ultimate destination. Stressed, exhausted, alone and somewhat fearful, never having ventured so far away on her own before, young Patsy finally became upset. With tears threatening, a seat was found for her on the flight, and she finally arrived in Fort Worth, seven hours overdue, to find no one there to meet her – an anticlimactic ending to a long day that had started with such fanfare. She felt a little scared and overwhelmed, and also very hot in her wool gabardine rodeo queen outfit, but airport officials were kind, and soon everything was sorted out. Her arrival made the *Fort Worth Star-Telegram* the next day, with a chatty article under the headline, "Airport: Cowgirl from Canada arrives in Cowtown to join Dublin rodeo." Relieved at having arrived safely, and still bubbly in spite of having been on the road for nearly thirty hours, Patsy confided to the reporter that she had resigned her job in Calgary to join the WCR: "This is all too exciting to be tied down to a job as a stenographer," she said. "Anything might happen now."[32]

She spent the night in a hotel in Fort Worth, and the next day was driven 130 kilometres southwest to Dublin, then another 30 kilometres farther south to Colborn and Autry's Lightning C Ranch, where she finally met the five other sponsor girls participating in the 1946 WCR. Chosen by their hometown rodeos for their beauty, personality and riding and roping ability,[33] Patsy's fellow rodeo queens were an impressive lot. Four represented local Texas rodeos: Ora Mae Clark from Fort Worth, Ann Tobin Riley from Bandera, Eva Mae Wilken from El Paso and Lillian Cowan from Pecos. Only Jo Ramsey had come from farther afield – Kiowa, Oklahoma – but she and Lillian were returning sponsor girls, so Patsy was the novelty as far as the press was concerned, having come from so far away and a Canadian to boot. The American media enjoyed that angle, and throughout the engagement her story and photo often figured prominently in articles about the sponsor girls.

On her arrival at the ranch, Patsy began practising right away for her role in the WCR by participating in a four-day rodeo that served as a trial run for the show.

The rodeo, already underway, was held in a newly constructed 10,000-seat arena at Dublin called the Colborn Bowl. Billed as "the 7th annual Pre-Madison Square Garden World Championship Rodeo – The roughest, toughest in the Southwest,"[34] the rodeo was the culmination of all the smaller rodeos held during the summer months "in all the greater and lesser cowtowns and cities of the sprawling West, from Texas up into Canada" where contestants had earned the right to participate in the WCR.[35] As such, the Dublin show included all the same competitors and acts to be featured in New York City and Boston: "the wildest horses, the most vicious bulls and the most talented cowboys and cowgirls" as well as daily performances by Gene Autry.[36] Patsy's late arrival meant that she only had two days to practise racing into the ring with the other sponsor girls during the Grand Entry part of the show but she was a confident and accomplished rider and quickly mastered her role.

As soon as the Dublin rodeo was over, the entire show, animals and all, was packed up and loaded onto a special 24-car rodeo train bound for New York City. In Fort Worth a reporter caught up with the sponsor girls on the eve of their September 17 departure. "Six pretty, excited young girls will leave here at 8 a.m. Tuesday for New York City, where they will be guest sponsors at the Madison Square Garden Rodeo. The girls… will make guest appearances each day of the show from September 23 through October 27. They will be guests of the rodeo association during their stay in New York City and 'will get to see all the sights,' according to Mrs. Fay Kirkwood, who will accompany them as chaperone. When the show closes, the girls will go to the Boston rodeo for 12 days, where they will be guests and make personal appearances. They will return to Fort Worth together about November 24 aboard a special rodeo train. Monday, all the girls enthusiastically agreed that they would 'have a wonderful time' and Mrs. Kirkwood also was looking forward to the trip 'with the sweetest group of girls I ever saw.'"[37]

Four days later, on Friday, September 20, 1946, the train pulled into Grand Central Station and the sponsor girls began their six-week stint as the show's glamorous promotional team. Waving their ten-gallon hats as they stepped off the train, they set to work impressing journalists with their enthusiasm. "A Big Hello to East from West: Yip-eee! The Rodeos' attractive sponsor girls arrive at Grand Central and, to put it mildly, they seem to be glad they finally have arrived in the Big Town. They want you to know the annual visit of the Rodeo to Madison Square Garden will begin Wednesday night."[38]

The sponsor girls, their chaperone and all other

female WCR performers were housed in the Hotel Paramount on 46th Street west of Broadway, conveniently close to Madison Square Garden, which at the time was located on 8th Avenue between 49th and 50th streets. The sponsor girls were all in one hallway together, sharing two to a room (Anne and Eva, Jo and Lillian, Patsy and Ora Mae) with their chaperone in a room of her own at the end. Cowboys and other male performers were in another hotel across the street and there was a strict no-fraternization rule. Several of the rodeo queens had boyfriends in the show, so activities were carefully monitored, even when the girls technically were off-duty. "We were really watched, no boys allowed," Patsy remembered.[39] She would have liked to have spent some time with Bill Linderman, the American cowboy who had arranged for her gift of spurs from the Stampede and was competing in the 1946 WCR, but the fear that she might be sent home in disgrace if discovered inhibited them both. As she later recalled, this threat usually ensured that the rules were followed – but not always. "One night we decided to duck out down the fire escape to meet some cowboys who were taking us to see the original Ink Spots. We were caught. If it hadn't been so near the end of the show we would have been sent home."[40]

The girls had a few days to settle in and do some sightseeing but their outings were strictly controlled: they went everywhere as a group and were always accompanied by their chaperone, Mrs. Kirkwood. And their contract stipulated that whenever they stepped out of their rooms, they had to wear Western attire. Just as Bill Linderman had foretold, soon after the sponsor girls arrived in New York City Gene Autry presented them with silver belt buckles inscribed "Madison Square Garden Rodeo, 1946." But Patsy soon discovered that her wardrobe was lacking, and she quickly grew tired of wearing the same three suits day after day: her new red one from the WCR and the two green ones from GWG. Being experienced in such things, the other rodeo queens were much better prepared for the six-week engagement, having come equipped with "trunkloads of designer Western outfits."[41] Luckily, they proved willing to share with the underdressed Canadian and loaned her spare pants and shirts to mix and match with her own pieces. Unfortunately, they could do nothing to help her with extra boots. To save space in her packing, she had only brought along one pair, the blue ones. Ranch girl though she was, it soon became tedious dressing Western every single day and night and she began to long for the chance to wear civvies, especially normal footwear. "I got so sick and tired of wearing boots," she later remembered with a sigh.[42]

The World Championship Rodeo opened at Madison Square Garden on September 23, and right away the sponsor girls went to work earning their weekly pay of $100 (a very handsome salary for a young woman in 1946*).[43] There were seven evening shows and four matinees each week for four weeks and the girls rode in the Grand Entry for each one. A limousine picked them up at the hotel, or they took a taxi, and they were whisked back home after the show the same way. At the Garden, they were not allowed into the basement, where the livestock was kept, except when the whole cast of the show gathered for a couple of photo shoots. Otherwise, the girls were told to keep out; it was simply too dangerous down there for performers. But Patsy later speculated that it was not just the livestock that the arena manager,

General Kilpatrick, feared might prove dangerous to the pretty rodeo queens; the livestock area was also full of lonely young cowboys and wranglers. The girls were all a little afraid of the General, so they followed his orders and waited patiently at the top of the chutes each time for their saddled palominos to be brought up to them.

The sponsor girls were the first act when the show opened. They did not do any roping or trick riding, but they did have to race around the ring as fast as the horses could go, with one hand holding the reins and the other a flag. Five of the girls waved the flags of their home rodeos but Patsy waved Canada's flag, the Red Ensign, because the Calgary Stampede did not yet have its own flag.[44] As Bill Linderman had predicted, her horse soon became bored with the routine, and she was very glad of the gift of spurs to keep him going show after show. After the Grand Entry, the girls stood their horses in a formation so the performers – the ropers, bronc busters and trick riders – could ride into the arena by weaving amongst them. After that, the girls rode around the arena once again, waving to the crowd of 18,000, and left to sit in a row in the stands to watch the show. They quickly settled into the routine but Patsy was very nervous at first. "I was scared out of my skin," she later said. "But I didn't let on."[45]

*Equivalent to about $1,300 today. According to the Government of Canada's 1946 *Census of the Prairie Provinces* (Table VII Occupations, Earnings, Employment), the weekly wage earned by the sponsor girls was roughly four times the weekly earnings of the best-paid Alberta female workers at the time – nurses and teachers – who made approximately $23–$26 per week (about $300–$340 today). As a receptionist, Patsy's regular salary would have been even lower, in line with the average weekly earnings of office clerks and stenographers (approximately $20 per week, or about $260 today). These currency conversions and all others throughout the text are based on the Bank of Canada's "Inflation Calculator," accessed Mar 9, 2013, www.bankofcanada.ca/rates/related/inflation-calculator.

At the intermission, the sponsor girls came out again, performing a crowd-pleasing act that involved driving a herd of sixteen "wild" Texas longhorn steers around the infield. The crowd loved this part of the show. Some of the steers had as much as a 16-foot spread between their horns and looked very dangerous, but Patsy soon realized that they had been driven a lot and actually were very quiet and well behaved. Even so, Everett Colborn was mounted and on hand to help the girls keep the steers corralled in a corner as the lights dimmed and a spotlight revealed Gene Autry centre stage, sitting on his horse, Champion. Autry, who had been absent from the show since 1941 while serving in the army,[46] was a huge draw in 1946. He sang a few numbers from his popular cowboy repertoire then led the way out of the arena with the rodeo queens driving the steers before them.

During the show, the girls sat in a row in what was, in effect, a press box where the media and other admirers could visit them and do interviews during the performance. Patsy had been asked by Jack Dillon and the Stampede Board to promote the Stampede whenever she could and she took her job seriously, mentioning her hometown and its show whenever the opportunity arose. Later, she recalled, with some amusement, that "few New Yorkers actually knew where Calgary was located," or had ever heard of the Stampede.[47] The local media usually relied heavily on Frank Moore's notes for details, and, rather than promoting her role as a representative of the Stampede, preferred to feature her ancestral American ties. The following report was typical:

Our good neighbor to the North, Canada, sends us attractive, vivacious Patsy Rodgers, the first Dominion girl to be selected as a sponsor girl for the annual World Championship Rodeo in Madison Square Garden. The pretty 21-yr-old blonde, blue-eyed cowgirl is a resident of Calgary and has been riding since she was six. She weighs 112 pounds and stands 5 feet 6 inches.* Patsy's father is a rancher whose hobby is breaking wild horses for polo, calf roping and saddle riding. He was once a prominent polo player. Patsy is a descendant of the noted Hamilton family whose members sailed by schooner in early 1800 to San Francisco then followed the overland trail by ox team to British Columbia. Her uncle, Johnny Hamilton, was a stagecoach driver on the famed Caribou Trail. Miss Rodgers was

*In the information he provided to the press, Frank Moore apparently improved upon the vital statistics provided by Patsy's parents for fashion-conscious New Yorkers by adding two inches to her height and deducting three pounds from her weight.

recently chosen queen of the 39th annual Calgary Horticultural Society exhibition and her ponies have taken many blue ribbons at horse shows.[48]

After the show, the girls returned their horses to the handlers at the top of the chutes and immediately headed back to the hotel. On the days when there were two shows, they had just enough time to eat something and freshen up after the matinee performance (they always did their own hair and makeup) before being whisked back to Madison Square Garden for the evening show. Those days were very tiring but three days a week the girls could spend the morning or afternoon going on outings and sightseeing before their official duties began in the evening. However, the relative freedom of those days was a bit deceptive because nearly every outing was treated as a promotional opportunity for the WCR. It even made the news when Patsy and Ora Mae tasted a new-fangled treat called a "pronto pup" (a batter-coated hot dog on a stick).[49] Just before the rodeo got underway, on September 24, they took part in the biggest publicity stunt of all, a fifteen-mile parade to City Hall, where the entire cast of the WCR was officially welcomed to New York City and certain performers, including the sponsor girls, were introduced to Mayor William O'Dwyer.

Over the next month, the WCR sponsor girls were constantly in the spotlight, making the news on behalf of the rodeo. They visited a veterans hospital with Gene Autry and Champion, went up the Empire State Building, saw the stage show *Oklahoma* on Broadway, and attended a football game at Ebbets Field and a baseball game at Yankee Stadium. They appeared on an ABC radio show, where Patsy won a $25 bond, and modelled glamorous Western wear for Saks Fifth Avenue (Patsy wore a sheriff's outfit). They met Andy Russell, star of the Lucky Strike cigarettes *Your Hit Parade* radio show, had lunch with a polo team on Long Island, and partied at famous nightclubs such as Billy Rose's Diamond Horseshoe, though Patsy later confided that this relaxation of the rules was more apparent than real. "We couldn't even leave the hotel alone. We were always under chaperone and even at the nightclubs we weren't allowed to dance or anything."[50]

During the WCR's four-week run in New York, the sponsor girls gave lots of newspaper and radio interviews and met many dignitaries. One of the most memorable experiences for Patsy was when a group of delegates from the League of Nations attending the opening night performance made a special trip to the press box to be introduced. She was especially intrigued with the Saudi Arabian delegates in full traditional dress who took turns photographing each other with the rodeo queens. Many admirers tried to arrange dates with the girls, and their hotel rooms regularly were flooded with telegrams and flowers from would-be suitors. All this male attention was quite heady for the young women and they often wished they could accept a date, but their chaperone was adamant on behalf of management that all offers were to be refused. The girls were even coached on how to handle themselves if a man got a little too pressing in his attentions. Although the need never arose, they were instructed to keep their spurs in their hands during press box interviews just in case they ever needed to ward off an overly enthusiastic admirer.

One admiring note caused particular excitement for three of the sponsor girls. Patsy, Jo and Ann had impressed RKO Pictures talent scout Stacy Keach Sr. with their riding ability to such an extent that after the rodeo on October 21 he sent them all notes inviting them to meet and talk about becoming stunt doubles for Western movies.[51] They all made appointments and attended interviews, where they were told they would be sent to a special Hollywood stunt school and taught how to do tricks on horseback such as falling from a runaway horse and fording deep water on horseback. It all sounded very exciting, but after talking things over with a trick rider in the WCR show who had worked as a movie stunt double, they realized just how dangerous the work could be and how likely it was that they would be injured. In the end, all three refused the very tempting studio offer. The studio countered with an offer for Patsy to be re-interviewed after studying dramatics in New York City, with a view to an RKO movie contract. At the same time, she was offered a job in Hollywood with Gene Autry's troupe, but she was becoming homesick for Alberta by then and turned down all offers.[52]

On October 27 the WCR finished its New York run. Just as the show was ending, Jack Dillon arrived in New York City to attend meetings and met up with Patsy long enough to take her to visit a big military hospital on Staten Island where he knew someone who had visited Calgary while working on the Alaska Highway. He also appeared beside Patsy in an official photo shoot documenting the "Cowboy and Cowgirl Contestants of the 21st Annual World Championship Rodeo at Madison Square Garden." Gene Autry provided the sponsor girls with a supply of Christmas cards to send to family and friends to commemorate their involvement in the show. Patsy's featured a picture taken at the Stampede in one of her GWG outfits. It was inscribed "Patsy Rodgers of Cochrane,

Promotional Christmas card for the World Championship Rodeo's "Miss Canada," Patsy Rodgers, 1946. (CSA)

Alberta – "Miss Canada" – Madison Square Garden – 1946 Rodeo – New York City."[53]

The arrival of the sponsor girls at Boston's South Station on October 29 generated the same kind of curiosity and excitement as in New York City. Newspaper reports featured pictures of the young ladies attractively grouped beside mountains of luggage, with headlines such as "Western Belles arrive for Rodeo: A bit of the glamorous old West arrives in Boston," "Proof that ranch girls of the World Championship Rodeo at the Boston Garden are prettier than ever," and "Winsome Westerners arrive for rodeo."[54]

The engagement at the Boston Garden was much shorter – two weeks instead of four, October 30 to November 11 – but everything else was much the same as in New York City. The sponsor girls were housed at the Hotel Touraine and again appeared in seven evening and four matinee shows each week. Dutifully performing their prime function as walking advertisements for the rodeo, they gave interviews and visited local hospitals and sites such as Plymouth Rock. Patsy liked Boston, finding it to be "a quaint old place" and friendlier than New York City.[55] On opening day the rodeo queens were featured at a special luncheon at the Manger Hotel hosted by Gene Autry and his horse Champion. It was one of the few occasions when Autry actually mixed with the show people, though Patsy gained fleeting impressions over the course of the show that he was "a real nice person."[56]

The Boston media was especially interested in Patsy the Canadian, because two hockey players with the Boston Olympics team were from Canada (Armand (Dutch) Delmonte and Pentti Lund), and Pat Egan from Blackie, Alberta, whom Patsy knew from Calgary, was playing with the Boston Bruins. The press, assuming that Patsy, being Canadian, was a skater and a hockey fan (she was neither), featured her twice at the hockey arena on her own without the other sponsor girls. The caption under one photograph that showed her watching as a pair of ladies' skates were being sharpened, read "Versatile, pretty Patsy Rodgers of Calgary, Canada, who is appearing with the Rodeo at the Garden, finds time each day to skate at the Arena. Here she's having her skates sharpened. She hopes to be able to see part of the Olympics' games." Another showed her powdering her nose while perched atop a hockey net between Delmonte and Lund, both in full game attire and smiling broadly at their countrywoman. Doing double duty, promoting both the rodeo and an upcoming game, the caption read, "Range Beauty on Ice: Patsy Rodgers, Calgary, Canada, Boston Garden Rodeo cowgirl, poses atop goal cage with Dutch Delmonte and Pentti Lund of the Boston Olympics, who met Washington Lions last night at Boston Arena and face them again tonight there. Both are in the starting lineup and both are natives of Canada, like Patsy."[57]

The Boston run of the WCR ended on November 11 with a gala farewell luncheon hosted by Gene Autry and Champion at the Manger Hotel. The show returned by train to its winter headquarters in Dublin, Texas, but Patsy flew directly to Calgary. After a busy two months on the road, she was tired and ready to head back to Alberta. She had a sweetheart back home and also missed her parents, the family ranch and her horse, something her father had predicted when her mother had worried that she might stay on in New York City and never return. He had faithfully kept and numbered her biweekly letters detailing her first trip away from home. She also shared some of her adventures with an *Albertan* reporter who met her return flight in Calgary. Under the headline "Patsy Rogers back from Cinderella trip," the reporter expressed great surprise in seeing the young cowgirl arrive dressed "in a New York-designed black suit and Paris model hat." Why? She had been paid well for her two-month stint with the rodeo and had enjoyed the novelty of shopping in New York City. Also, and perhaps more import-antly, she said, "I never had a dress on all the time I was there – just cowboy clothes." The reporter was pleased to tell readers that, "[d]espite the night clubs, the movie stars, the open-armed welcome and the flashy cowboys, the 21-year-old Calgary miss was still 100 per cent a booster of Calgary and the Stampede. 'Even the top-notch cowboys down there said there was nothing to beat the Calgary Stampede,' she said." But Patsy had no illusions and realized that she had been performing in more of a stage show than an authentic rodeo: "The show was much more artificial than the Calgary Stampede. All the performers were sort of professionals. It wasn't quite as western as the Calgary Stampede," she told the interviewer. And she was disarmingly frank about her decision to turn down RKO and Hollywood: "I still think Calgary's tops."[58]

Patsy told the *Albertan* reporter that she planned to spend a quiet winter at her family's ranch, then pick up the threads of her life by finding another job, marrying and settling down in Calgary. As a thank you from the Board for her work the previous year, she was invited to ride in the Stampede section of the 1947 parade, this time between the recently retired Jack Dillon and Stampede Committee chairman Jim Cross. Thus began a long tradition of Patsy riding in the annual parade until she retired some fifty years later.

Her experience as queen led to a lifelong involve-ment with the Calgary Stampede. In 1972 she was a founding member of the Stampede Queens' Alumni Association. In 1984 she was made a Special Honorary Associate of the Stampede and became an Honorary Life Member in 2008, the same year she was named Parade Marshal. It was a thrilling conclusion to her long association with the Stampede. But an honour that proved to be just as significant personally was one she had received a decade earlier, in 1996, when she had been named Honorary Parade Marshal. Seventy years old, and riding in the parade for the last time, the "Queen Mum" led a large contingent of former royals in celebration of the 50th anniversary of her appointment as Calgary's first Stampede Queen.

CHAPTER 2 ★ 1947–1949

"Be a Booster! Help your favorite win!"

When Patsy Rodgers rode in the 1947 parade, she was not identified as the 1946 Stampede Queen or even recognized as the show's first queen. That distinction went to Doreen Richardson, an aspiring young Calgary actress riding on a lavishly decorated float in the Community section of the parade. Doreen had come to be queen in an entirely different way from Patsy's quiet Board appointment, and the public fanfare surrounding her selection meant it was she, not Patsy, who was celebrated by the press and public for many years as the first Stampede Queen.

Even before Patsy had headed off to Dublin, Texas, in mid-September 1946 to join the WCR, Jack Dillon had retired as Stampede arena director. The Board liked having a rodeo queen representative for the 1946 show, but it is possible that the idea might have died had not a local service club come up with a scheme to capitalize on the enthusiasm in postwar Calgary

Queen Doreen Richardson, 1947. (CSA)

for all things Stampede by proposing to sponsor a contest to choose the Queen of the Stampede.

The Associated Canadian Travellers (ACT) was a social club and fraternal benefit society for travelling salesmen that formed in Calgary in 1918. Originally called the Associated Commercial Travellers, the club grew quickly and the name soon changed. By the late 1940s, there were three dozen local branches in Western Canada and Ontario but the founding group remained dominant and Calgary functioned as headquarters for the national club even after its 1993 amalgamation with the United Commercial Travelers of America.

Men's social clubs in mid-twentieth-century Canada were very popular and usually exhibited service club tendencies; that is, members combined their social activities with fundraising initiatives to support a variety of charities or projects beneficial to their local communities. Although the Calgary ACT was relatively inactive during the early years of the Second World War, in 1944 the group began supporting Girls Town, a newly organized social club for underprivileged girls in Calgary's east end directed by the City's Children's Aid Department.[59] They held a Christmas party that year for 180 girls ranging in age from 6 to 14. Buoyed with having given pleasure to young people who were, in the words of the club newsletter, "through no fault of their own, less fortunate than our own children,"[60] club members decided to support Girls Town by raising funds. With the help of their Ladies Auxiliary, they ran very successful carnivals over the next two years which enabled them to sponsor ten-day summer camps for 75 girls in 1945 and 107 in 1946. Wanting to do even more, they tried hosting greyhound races in the fall of 1946 but the results were disappointing.[61]

As the ACT was casting about for a better fundraising opportunity, someone must have pointed out the great success of the Kinsmen Club's annual Stampede street dance, introduced in 1942 to raise funds for various charities including the Milk for Britain fund and the Junior Red Cross Crippled Children's Hospital. With an admission price of just 25 cents, the Kinsmen's 1946 Cowboy Street Ball on the Friday night of Stampede week had attracted more than 5,000 people.[62] That level of public participation seemed to indicate that a second street dance held earlier in the week might prove successful.

While this idea was under consideration, a member of the Ladies' Auxiliary, Helen Abercrombie, suggested that the club host a contest to elect a queen to reign over the dance.[63] The novelty of this approach might give the ACT dance an edge in attracting participants, an important consideration for a fundraising initiative. The committee which formed under the chairmanship of Jim Hannah decided to go one step further and approach Stampede directors for permission to advertise the ACT queen as the "Queen of the Stampede" for all of Stampede week. This was easily done at the time because the heads of local service clubs, like Calgary ACT president George Camden, also served as associate directors of the Stampede.

The timing of this request suited the Stampede. The ACT proposal would perpetuate Jack Dillon's rodeo queen idea without the expense and effort of the Stampede actually having to find and support a likely young woman for the position. There was to be nothing official about the ACT's queen, but directors saw no problem in allowing her to be known as the Queen of the Stampede. Luckily, the Calgary Exhibition and Stampede had a very loose and inclusive perception of its brand. Ever since the show became an established annual event in 1923, Guy Weadick had fostered a sense of local ownership for the Stampede by encouraging Calgarians to dress Western and decorate their storefronts. Despite his urban background, in 1923 Mayor George Webster had "happily duded up and set the tone for Cowtown, allowing Calgary's downtown to be closed off for two hours every morning for street dancing."[64] Coincidentally, what may have been the very first Stampede pancake breakfast was served to the public from a chuckwagon that year.[65] By 1947 just about anything that generated local excitement for, and participation in, the annual fair could be promoted as something "Stampede," so the Board readily granted permission to the ACT to use the Stampede name in promoting its contest.

In deciding to run a Stampede Queen contest, the Calgary ACT had hit upon a brilliant fundraising idea. Queens as mascots for various events and attractions were very popular during the middle years of the twentieth century. Starting in 1910, but gathering momentum after the Pendleton Round-Up re-established the role in 1923, western North America had a long tradition of rodeo queens.[66] However, these ladies were chosen for specific skills such as riding, roping, and public speaking, so it is likely that the craze for hometown fair and festival queens owed more to the rising popularity of beauty contests during the post-war period. The biggest and best known of these was the Miss America pageant, first

introduced in 1921. By the 1940s its influence was widely felt , even north of the border, where the Miss Canada pageant was launched in 1946.[67]

Searching as they were for the ideal representative of a nation's femininity, these national beauty contests had a patriotic flavour. Similarly, local queen contests were viewed "as a form of community pride and boosterism."[68] Unlike rodeo queens, who had to prove certain desirable skills such as riding and public speaking, carnival queens, festival queens, flower show queens and the like rarely had to perform demanding or skill-testing public duties, so their selection usually was based on personality and appearance. Thus the contests often became community events that allowed for direct public involvement in choosing winners. A very common template was for groups to generate votes for a candidate they had sponsored by selling tickets on her behalf at various promotional events. Part beauty contest, part popularity contest, the competition would culminate in the candidate with the most votes or ticket sales becoming queen while the runners-up in those tallies would become her attendants or ladies-in-waiting.[69] Because of its fundraising potential for sponsors and communities, this form of contest was very popular. For example, in April and May of 1947 the Calgary *Albertan* reported on the crowning of many local small-town queens, including the Fort Macleod Lions' Carnival Queen, the Red Deer Rotary Street Carnival Queen and May Queens for Bellevue, Alberta, and Cranbrook, BC.

Since fundraising was the whole point of the ACT's decision to hold a queen contest, this was the model the Calgary club adopted in the spring of 1947.[70] It invited local community groups and service clubs to get involved by sponsoring candidates and selling tickets to the ACT's Mammoth Outdoor Ball to be held in Calgary on Monday, July 7. Whether or not one planned to attend the dance, each 25-cent admission (about $3 today) entitled the purchaser to twenty-five votes in support of their favourite candidate for queen. As an incentive to come, attendees also had a chance to win numerous prizes. As the organizer and main sponsor of the contest, the ACT announced that it would share ticket sales proceeds fifty-fifty with sponsoring organizations but would take all responsibility for contest coordination and promotion. As the only branch in southern Alberta, the Calgary ACT naturally thought beyond Calgary in designing the contest, and so, as club members travelled on business during the winter and spring of 1947, they promoted their novel fundraising idea among groups and clubs in the southern half of the province.

Meanwhile, chairman Jim Hannah's committee fine-tuned the idea by contacting the Pendleton Round-Up and proposing that its queen come to Calgary during the Stampede to crown the new Calgary queen. This was a brilliant marketing ploy, using the queen of the show with the longest tradition of rodeo royalty to lend an aura of legitimacy to the proceedings marking the beginning of a new tradition for Calgary. In exchange the Calgary club suggested that its royalty could attend the Pendleton Round-Up that September. Once Pendleton had agreed to send three queens to the Stampede (one current and two former), George Camden attended a Stampede Parade Committee meeting to request and be granted space in the parade that featured them riding with Calgary's new royalty.[71]

The contest was kicked off on April 18, 1947, with the following announcement:

The 1947 Calgary Stampede will have its own official "queen" for the first time in the history of the annual show, directors of the Calgary Exhibition and Stampede announced today. The queen will be crowned during Stampede Week and will participate in Stampede ceremonies. Her election will be based upon the number of tickets purchased to a cowboy dance in downtown Calgary during

MISS DOREEN RICHARDSON (left) was crowned Queen of the Calgary Stampede with a cowboy hat for a crown Monday evening, when Miss Patti Folsom, queen of the Pendleton Round-Up in Oregon, officiated at the coronation. Miss Richardson was accompanied by her lady-in-waiting, Miss Eva Brewster, of Macleod, and three queens from Pendleton.

Top First Associated Canadian Travellers Queen of the Stampede contest ad, *Albertan*, May 31, 1947.

Left Doreen Richardson being crowned Queen of the Stampede by Pendleton Round-Up Queen Patti Folsom, *CH* July 8, 1947.

Stampede Week. Each admission ticket purchased for the dance will entitle the buyer to cast 25 votes for the candidate favored. The queen and her lady-in-waiting, the runner-up in the contest, will also go to Pendleton, Oregon, in August, as official guests of the Pendleton Round-Up. The contest is open to any Alberta girl, 18 years of age or more, and any organization in Alberta is invited to sponsor a candidate. The Stampede Queen competition is being conducted by the Calgary Club of the Associated Canadian Travellers. Organizations wishing to sponsor a candidate should write James L. Hannah, chairman of the Stampede Queen Committee. Proceeds of the project will be donated to Calgary's "Girls Town" and to other community work.[72]

As of May 1, the Calgary club began sending out short updates to the press about the contest. To keep interest high, these press releases usually featured a photograph and description of a pretty, young candidate and details about her sponsoring organization. Response was enthusiastic, and by the end-of-May closing date there were eleven candidates for queen, who were featured in a big newspaper advertisement advising the public to "Be a Booster! Help your Favorite Win!" Despite contest advertising that specified 18 as the minimum age, one candidate was only 16. The contestants included high school and university students, young women who worked or had served during the war in the CWACs and WRENs, and one horse show winner. Interestingly, only four of the candidates were from Calgary. Thanks to ACT members' promotional efforts, the majority of hopefuls were sponsored by organizations from all over southern Alberta: Fort Macleod, Drumheller, Hanna, High River, Brooks, Strathmore and the Crowsnest Pass.[73]

As the votes came in, frequent updates appeared in the *Calgary Herald*. "Drumheller girl leads contest" (June 25); "Stampede Queen contest is close" (June 28); "Drama 'Queen' leads contest" (June 30). The excitement finally came to a head on July 3 when the media were invited to witness vote counting at the ACT office. To emphasize its impartiality in choosing a winner, the club had invited Calgary city clerk Jack M. Miller to supervise the count. "Keys were removed from the office safe, and the seals on the [ballot] boxes were broken in the presence of a dozen members of the association." After counting the votes, the ACT announced that the candidate from the Calgary theatre group Workshop 14, Doreen Richardson, had won with 238,025 votes. With the Calgary location and focus of the contest, it was not really very surprising that a Calgary candidate won. What was more surprising, and a testament to the hard work done jointly by the Fort Macleod Junior Chamber of Commerce and the Macleod Lions Club, was that their candidate came in a relatively close second. Eva Brewster, a high school student who had won in mid-April as the Macleod Lions Carnival Queen, had generated 208,100 votes. Doreen was declared the Stampede Queen and Eva her Lady-in-waiting.[74]

When she won as queen, 19-year-old Doreen was close to graduating from Western Canada High School, where she had begun acting several years earlier under the direction of Workshop 14's founder, drama teacher Betty Mitchell. Doreen was well known in Calgary, having played the lead in a recent school production of *I Remember Mama* and having been voted the Sat-Teen Club Queen in 1946. At the beginning of an acting career that would see her win a best actress award at the 1951 Dominion Drama Festival, Doreen was thrilled with the publicity generated by winning the title of "Calgary's First Stampede Queen." Modern-day feminist sensibilities not yet having influenced the press, the *Albertan* photographer had no qualms about placing her in a cheesecake-style pose wearing a bathing suit and high heels, telephone receiver in hand. The caption read: "The curvaceous miss can wear a bathing suit, as shown above, but was getting into the mood for a

cowgirl suit with a cowboy hat perched on her shoulder." Doreen was quoted as saying, "I'm so thrilled and shaking so badly I can hardly stand at the telephone" as she took calls congratulating her on her victory.[75]

The *Calgary Herald*'s report focused on the winnings of the "tall, slim… brown-eyed, brown-haired" young queen and her attendant, an important consideration since Doreen and Eva would receive no other compensation for their week of representing the Stampede. "Miss Richardson and Miss Brewster will have a free trip to the Pendleton Round-Up in Oregon September 10 to 13 as their prize, as well as two smart cowboy outfits each. [They have] also been offered a free pack pony trip by C.B. Brewster of the Kananaskis ranch near Banff." It also reported that Workshop 14 planned to use its share of the winnings to build a small theatre.[76]

While Doreen and Eva awaited the start of the Stampede, they were fitted for their new outfits. Even though the history and culture of the Canadian West bore little resemblance to the mythologized American West portrayed by Hollywood Westerns during the 1940s and 1950s, the enormous popularity of these movies dominated public perceptions and strongly influenced the image projected by the Stampede during this period.[77] With cowboys increasingly viewed

39
★

1947 Queen Doreen Richardson and Lady-in-waiting Eva Brewster at the Trail Riders of the Canadian Rockies camp on Simpson Summit, CH August 4, 1947.

as romantic figures, it is not surprising that the trend was to dress rodeo queens in the kind of glamorous, highly decorated outfits seen on movie cowgirls like Dale Evans, Jane Russell and Barbara Stanwyck.[78]

With this image in mind, the ACT happily spared no expense outfitting its first royalty. "Stampede Queen will wear bright western costume," announced the headline.

[Both] will wear colorful embroidered western outfits in the Stampede parade Monday morning and at all social functions during the week. Two complete costumes, tailored in Philadelphia and New York, will be given to each of the girls. They are similar to outfits worn in Hollywood screen productions. The "first" suits were designed in Philadelphia by a firm which specializes in Western suits [Rodeo Ben] and the "second" costumes are made by a New York firm and feature bolero jackets… [Doreen] will wear a wide, hand-tooled leather belt which features a buckle and tip of gold set with rubies. The band of her wide, white Western hat is the same, with "Queen Calgary Stampede 1947" tooled in it and a smaller buckle in the same design… There will be boots and belts for both from Riley and McCormick Ltd.[79]

Doreen and Eva were an eagerly anticipated attraction of the Stampede parade which took place on the morning of Monday, July 7. The *Herald* noted that "Stampede Queen Doreen Richardson and her court of beautiful ladies-in-waiting evoked admiring cheers. There never was a better parade. There never were such large crowds to see it. It was a great success."[80] In fact, Eva was the only Stampede Lady-in-waiting on the ACT's float; the other western beauties were the three Pendleton Round-Up Queens, who had arrived in the city several days before, accompanied by their chaperones, Mr. and Mrs. Lester King of Pendleton. That evening, with Eva and the Pendleton guests in attendance, Doreen was crowned by reigning Pendleton Queen Patti Folsom with the specially prepared cowboy hat. Reminiscent of Patsy Rodgers's experience the year before at the Calgary Flower Show, Doreen was carried to the stage before the grandstand show on a floral throne, but made her departure after the ceremony "on a spirited pony."[81]

The five young royals immediately headed from the Stampede grounds to the General Supplies parking lot at 6th Avenue and 1st Street, where they presided over the ACT's Stampede Queen's Ball. According to the ACT newsletter, Doreen was introduced to the crowd by Calgary club president George Camden and then drew tickets for the attendance prizes: a Coolerator, won by someone from Fort Macleod; a radio, won by someone from Nanton; and a Toastmaster, won by someone from Calgary. ACT members and their wives served hot dogs and drinks to happy guests who danced and enjoyed the evening's entertainment until "the small hours of the morning [when] a perfect day was brought to a close by the orchestra playing 'God Save the King.'"[82]

Officially, Doreen and Eva had no other duties to fulfill after the Stampede ended, but several weeks later they attended the Cardston rodeo. They rode in the parade on July 22 and made a number of public appearances over the next few days, including visits to several local hospitals.[83] Several days later, they took up the prize offered by C.B. Brewster. A newspaper photograph showed them mounted on horses with a teepee in the background, guests of the Trail Riders of the Canadian Rockies at their 24th annual camp on Simpson Summit, 28 kilometres from Banff.[84]

In early September Doreen and Eva headed to Pendleton, Oregon, to ride in the Round-Up parade and attend the fair. They were accompanied by Mr. and Mrs. J.L. Hannah and Mr. and Mrs. F.E. Abercrombie. The two couples went along as representatives of ACT, which was sponsoring the trip, and to act as chaperones for the Calgary queen and her lady-in-waiting. During the Round-Up, as her last official act on

behalf of the Stampede, Doreen presented Pendleton Queen Patti Folsom with a pair of hand-stitched riding boots from Riley and McCormick and a jewelled, silver-mounted bit from the ACT and the Calgary Stampede.[85]

The 1947 Queen of the Stampede contest was a good money-maker for the Calgary ACT, so the club ran it again in 1948 and every year thereafter until they finally turned everything over to full Stampede control after the 1966 contest. In the intervening years, the Calgary club made many small changes and improvements to the contest, and members devoted an enormous amount of time and energy to making a success of this, the club's main annual fundraising activity. Ultimately this hard work over twenty years resulted in the Calgary ACT making donations of well over $175,000 (well over $1-million today) to a wide variety of worthy local groups and charities.[86]

But in 1948 they had no idea this scheme would prove to be so long-lived, and they simply repeated the successful format devised the year before. On February 14, to kick off the contest, they placed advertisements in major newspapers. These were aimed at the all-important sponsoring organizations rather than potential candidates themselves. The advertisement, which contained an entry form and a graphic of a cowgirl waving her hat, read:

"Attention… Service clubs and community organizations. Are you looking for a project? Sponsor a candidate in the contest for "Miss Calgary Stampede 1948." Applications will be received from any girl complying with the rules and regulations set down, sponsored by a responsible organization in any community.[87]

A month or so later, when all the candidates had been chosen, the newspaper ads showing their pictures and sponsor names advertised that proceeds were in aid of community projects rather than specifying a single group such as Girls Town. Another change was that two ladies-in-waiting were to be chosen this time (to stimulate competition by increasing candidates' chances of winning), and some nice prizes were announced for the winning threesome: a seven-day all-expenses-paid trip to Banff for the runners-up (or a $100 cash equivalent) and a ten-day all-expenses-paid trip to Victoria for the winning queen (or a $300 cash equivalent). These were considered at the time to be very desirable prizes, worth about $1,000 and $3,000 today.[88]

To pump up excitement for the contest and generate a few more candidates, other prizes were announced as the June 19 entry closing date drew near. As in 1947 the winners would ride on the ACT float in the Stampede parade on the morning of July 5, and be crowned that evening before the grandstand show, but it was revealed that during the afternoon they would be treated to an airplane ride by Cal-Air Ltd. The *Calgary Herald* reported that "The queen will have her choice of routes, and if she is an out-of-town girl the pilot will fly over her home town if she wishes." The paper also revealed that "'Miss Calgary Stampede of 1948' will be made an Indian princess of the Sarcee [Tsuu T'ina] tribe Thursday, July 8, when the Associated Canadian Travellers will hold a chuckwagon dinner at the Sarcee reserve for all the contestants."[89] Although local tribes occasionally named honorary chiefs or Indian princesses during the Stampede, most likely this was another publicity gambit copied from the Kinsmen Club, which had hosted a similar ceremony as part of their Cowboy Street Dance during the 1944 Stampede. On that occasion, Corporal Betty Ward, the Air Force's candidate for Flower Show Queen, had been made an honorary Indian princess with the name Princess Skylark by Duck Chief and the Siksika.[90]

The promise of wonderful prizes attracted sixteen sponsors and candidates from a wide circle around Calgary. In this year, and in fact most years, fewer than half of the contestants were from the city; the rest in 1948 were from Bowness, Bassano, Didsbury,

Lethbridge, Drumheller, Banff, Olds, Beiseker and Edmonton.[91] Having a candidate from as far away as Edmonton surprised Calgary organizers, but the Edmonton branch of the ACT had played up the contest in their city and the local Federation of Community Leagues decided to add to its fundraising by fielding a candidate. The Edmonton media were delighted to play on the traditional rivalry between the two cities. With a note of glee, the *Edmonton Journal* reported:

> An Edmonton beauty has Calgary worried. Citizens of the southern centre fear that an Edmonton girl may be named Queen of the Calgary Stampede. The capital city charmer who has Calgarians plotting against her is a blossoming brunette, 17-yr-old Joan Farley of the Highlands… Calgarians, perturbed at the thought that Edmonton might quite possibly score another victory in the inter-city rivalry of long standing by supplying their Stampede queen, are frantically buying votes in support of southern candidates. [92]

A second report advised that the Federation of Community Leagues was planning to stage a mammoth parade in downtown Edmonton that weekend, the highlight to be a royal float with Miss Farley

enthroned amid banks of flowers. "Accompanying 'Miss Edmonton' in the parade will be representatives of the 26 community leagues selling votes in the [S]tampede queen contest.[93]

This friendly rivalry only served to boost local ticket sales, so the Calgary club was delighted. Finding it a little more difficult to interest the press in a contest that was no longer a novelty, it explored other ways of attracting media attention. One such scheme occurred on June 18. It involved parading 1947 Queen Doreen Richardson and the seven 1948 queen candidates from Calgary on a chuckwagon from the CJCJ radio studio on 9th Avenue, east to Centre Street, north to 8th Avenue, and west to the Palace Theatre, where a new short film called *Calgary Stampede* was set to debut later that evening. The film, shot in Technicolor by Warner Brothers the previous summer, featured "action shots taken during the whole of Stampede week, accompanied by a commentary" and promised shots of the parade with "closeups of the Stampede Queen, as well as the more colorful bands, Indians and chuck wagons." Only twenty minutes long, it was the added attraction preceding the main feature, a Warner Brothers western called *Silver River*, starring Errol Flynn and Ann Sheridan. The local candidates for Stampede Queen were introduced

Queen Gloria Klaver after her adoption into the Tsuu T'ina tribe as Princess Glorious Mountain Echo, 1948. (GA: PA-3435-1)

1948 Queen Gloria Klaver (second from right) and Ladies-in-waiting Margaret Forsgren and Shirley Kemp with 1947 Queen Doreen Richardson (second from left). (GA: PA-3435-10)

from the stage of the Palace Theatre at 8:45 p.m. during the interval between two showings of the short and the feature.[94]

When the 1948 contest closed on June 19, city clerk Jack M. Miller was prevailed upon once again to count the ballots. The threat of an Edmonton winner had proven to be an effective spur to local ticket sales; all three winners were Calgary residents: 20-year-old Queen Gloria Klaver with runners-up and Ladies-in-waiting Margaret Forsgren and Shirley Kemp.

Although Gloria was an accomplished horse-woman, she and her attendants rode on the ACT float in the parade. As in 1947, the trio presided over the ACT's Mammoth Outdoor Ball on July 6 after being crowned with cowboy hats before the grandstand show, then enjoyed several more days at the Stampede as guests of the ACT. As promised, on July 8, Gloria was adopted by the Tsuu T'ina as an honorary Indian princess with the name Glorious Mountain Echo. The only other commitment the ladies had after presiding at the Stampede was to attend the Medicine Hat Rodeo.

The financial success of the Stampede Queen contest in its first two years guaranteed that the Calgary ACT would continue organizing it year after year. But it was its success in generating widespread public interest and support that convinced the Stampede Board in 1949 to acknowledge that the crowd-pleasing contest and resulting royalty were valuable symbols that were fast becoming an integral part of Stampede celebrations. In July 1949 the ACT club newsletter reported with satisfaction, "This year the lucky winner will rule supreme with the complete sanction of the officials of the show and will initiate proceedings by leading the mammoth parade which opens the biggest rodeo of them all." It also noted that the Stampede had suggested that the winning

queen should be "an accomplished horsewoman,"[95] but it would be many years before this wish became an absolute requirement.

The Calgary sweep in 1948 had raised some criticism that contest results were skewed in favour of Calgary candidates. As a result, advertising for the 1949 contest promised:

No one knows who will win: Only one official of the Association knows how many tickets have been issued, how many have been returned, or the exact number of votes any individual contestant has at a given time… It is absolutely impossible for anyone to know in advance how many votes will be necessary to elect the Stampede Queen.[96]

This assurance must have worked, because, once again, eight of the fifteen contestants came from outside Calgary (including another attempt by an Edmonton candidate).

To make the contest more exciting the ACT issued updates to the media as tickets were returned, giving candidates' relative standings (though not their actual vote count). These reports could be misleading, however, and the final result a surprise, because clever sponsoring organizations held a certain number of tickets back until the very end to obscure how well

Top Queen Merle Stier, 1949. (GA: PA-2807-3641)

Right Lady-in-waiting Marion Birchall, 1949. (CSA)

their candidate was doing relative to her competitors. Furious ticket selling in the final few days of the 1949 contest saw an exciting finish to "a particularly hard-fought contest"[97] which saw the two front-runners see-sawing back and forth in the standings for first place. The St. John's Ambulance brigade's candidate, Merle Robinson Stier, was declared the winner after votes were counted on June 15, but 20-year-old Marion Birchall's sponsor, Girls Town, demanded and got a recount after it was informed that there had been a difference of only eight ticket books between first and second place. Another five days elapsed before Merle's win was confirmed: she was Queen with 820,700 votes, a convincing 4,500 lead over the first runner-up, Marion.[98] The third-place finisher was the Calgary Trades & Labour Council's candidate, 23-year-old Inez Melby, who garnered 502,506 votes despite an earlier rumour that ticket sales on her behalf at the CTLC national convention held in Calgary that spring might result in an unfair stuffing of the ballot box by "easterners."[99]

Merle was an interesting choice for queen because she was 34 years old when she won and was a married woman. For the first few years of the contest, the ACT did not place any restrictions on candidates but most tended to be young and single. Although Merle was childless at the time, her age and marital status meant that her time was more committed and sometimes she found it difficult to juggle her disparate roles of wife, employee and Stampede Queen. When her reign was over, she recommended to ACT Queen Committee chairman Bill Pollard that it would be easier for winners to fulfill their queenly duties if candidates were single and between the ages of 17 and 24. These new regulations were put into place for the next contest.

Merle was described in newspaper reports as a "Calgary housewife and horsewoman," but she was much more than that. Like many so-called Calgary candidates, she lived and worked in the city but had strong rural ties. She was an instructor with the Calgary branch of the St. John's Ambulance brigade, had been a volunteer nursing sister at the Colonel Belcher Hospital from 1944 to 1948 and was currently employed at the Medical Arts Building as a receptionist for Dr. Gordon Duncan. But she spent most of her free time at her parents' ranch northeast of Calgary and at the ranch near Priddis that she owned with her husband of eight years, Pat Stier, a travelling salesman with Merchant Hardware Ltd. An ardent horsewoman, Merle raised palominos and Tennessee walking horses. When she learned she had won a trip to Victoria, she announced she would take the $300 cash equivalent instead and buy another horse.

Lady-in-waiting Marion Birchall, 1949. (CSA)

INEZ MELBY, Lady-in-Waiting

Lady-in-waiting Inez Melby, *ACT Magazine*, July 1949.

In any case, Merle felt she could not take more time off work to visit Victoria. She was planning to take a week of vacation time during the Stampede to fulfill her duties as Queen and had already used her other week the preceding November travelling to Toronto with her husband to cheer on the Calgary Stampeders football team in their bid for the 1948 Grey Cup.[100] Merle had responded to organizer Bill Herron's call for riders in the Grey Cup parade, so the Stiers had joined 250 other riders, square dancers and football fans on the "Stampeder Special," a train chartered by Herron to send a little sample of Western hospitality east for the event.[101] The Stampede had thrown its support behind the excursion, "kicking in one thousand dollars to pay the freight on the horses," and quietly covering the $900 deficit once the event was over. "The rationale for these subsidies," according to Stampede historian James Gray, "was that a group of rambunctious Calgarians in gaudy western costumes riding in western saddles in a football parade in Toronto would be easily identified with the Calgary Stampede. Such identification was super advertising."[102]

In effect, Merle's involvement with that storied excursion had been her first experience of promoting the show, an appropriate precursor to her role as Stampede Queen. During her campaign, she had worn the large white cowboy hat supplied to her, and all Calgary fans during that trip, by Herron, and had reminisced with a reporter about being offered $125 for it while in Toronto.[103] No doubt the friendships made with other Calgary boosters during that week in November helped to push her ticket sales over the top the following spring. As Queen, she welcomed a return cavalcade of 263 Torontonians who had been intrigued with the cowboys, Indians, chuckwagons and square dancers during that boisterous Grey Cup week and decided to pay Calgary a goodwill visit to experience the full Stampede for themselves. Led by Toronto mayor Hiram (Buck) McCallum, the group chartered a train called the "Toronto-on-to-Calgary Stampede Special," which arrived on July 11, just in time for the group to participate in the Stampede parade with a float called "Toronto the Good." That year's parade also featured a little train called the "Stampeders' Special" containing football players and others who had made the trip East the previous fall. The Grey Cup trophy itself occupied an honoured spot behind the locomotive. Later that evening, Mayor McCallum officially opened the Stampede before the grandstand crowd.[104]

Merle's horse-riding skills were put to good use during the parade because, for the first time, Stampede royalty rode horses instead of being seated on the ACT float. As promised, she and her ladies-in-waiting rode near the head of the four-mile-long parade, "all attired in Western habits and riding matching ponies."[105] Lady-in-waiting Inez was relieved when the parade was over and she was not required to ride again during Stampede week because, unlike Merle, her riding skills were a very recent accomplishment. Prior to the contest, she had never ridden before, but thanks to a few lessons from her husband-to-be's uncle, and the fact that she had been given "a nice old horse who didn't care about anything or get excited by crowds," she was able to get through the parade without incident.[106]

Although Merle's horse wore a serape announcing that its rider was "Miss Calgary Stampede 1949," and her ladies and 1948 queen Gloria Klaver were identified in a similar manner, some observers among the record crowd of 70,000 watching the parade were disappointed. In a letter to the *Calgary Herald*, Naomi Barenholtz complained that "the parade, like everything else, is not without fault. For instance, why no float for the Stampede Queen? After careful concentration we finally spotted her and her attendants on horses immediately following a chuckwagon,

and not even a sign anywhere to identify her. Don't you think she deserves better treatment?"[107]

The Calgary ACT may have been secretly disappointed not to have the royal court on its float, but now that the ladies had received official recognition from the Stampede, it was deemed unsuitable for them to be on a float advertising a specific club, even though the contest itself still was very much under ACT control. Queen Committee members made up for the loss by making sure that their connection was obvious when the ladies visited children's and seniors' homes and hospitals, and by doing "a splendid job escorting the Stampede Queen and her beautiful Ladies-in-waiting around the high spots of the city, to the Stampede performances, and introducing them to the crowds and to the many stars who made up the entertainment at the end of the big show."[108] The club scored something of a coup by having Toronto mayor McCallum open its street dance on July 12 and distribute prizes of $500, $300 and $200. In just three years, the ACT Hoedown and its presiding queen had grown so popular that the club newsletter was moved to predict that they might become "as traditional as the Calgary Stampede."[109]

CHAPTER 3 ★ 1950–1953

"To reign as Queen! Well, I'll never be the same"

After the excitement of the 1948 Grey Cup and its aftermath, both Calgary and the Stampede entered the 1950s flying high. Promotional efforts had paid off and Stampede attendance increased by 100,000 in the years following the war; by 1949 it was 407,000, nearly four times the population of Calgary. During the 1950s, attendance records were broken nearly every year, and by the end of the decade overall attendance had increased by 200,000.[110] It was at the beginning of this golden age that the Calgary Stampede began promoting itself as the World's Greatest Outdoor Pageant. By 1952 this slogan had evolved to become the Stampede's very recognizable brand, The Greatest Outdoor Show on Earth.[111]

With the discovery of oil at Leduc, Alberta, in 1947, followed by the development of other important oilfields, Calgary became the oil capital of Canada and a magnet for business and professional immigrants

1950 Queen Eileen Beckner (seated) in the Stampede parade with Ladies-in-waiting Ann Dutchak and Gussie MacDonald. Standing behind Eileen's throne is 1949 Queen Merle Stier. (GA: PA-2807-34)

with money to spend carving out a new life in their adopted city. Many of these newcomers were Americans from the south and southwest who were already familiar with rodeo as entertainment. Thus primed to embrace the Stampede, they threw themselves into the week of festivities, dressing Western, eating pancakes, hosting barbecues and promoting the Stampede by inviting friends and relations back home to come to Calgary on their vacations so they too could join in the fun.[112]

The ACT's fundraising queen contest and street dance benefited enormously from this influx of money and support for all things Stampede. In 1950 the club decided to revert to giving the bulk of the contest proceeds to one worthy cause, the Red Cross Crippled Children's Hospital. After a very successful campaign, the club reported it had donated $4,600 to the hospital.[113] Also that year, to maintain interest in ticket buying for the fourth year in a row, the club advertised that each ticket would give the holder a chance to win a 1950 Meteor sedan.[114] And to encourage ticket selling and sales by ACT members, the contest committee, under the chairmanship of Lyle Lebbert, introduced an annual Stampede-themed spring luncheon to kick things off. The 1950 event featured a number of notable guests, including newly elected Calgary mayor Don Mackay.[115]

Ticket sales in 1950 were good on behalf of the fifteen candidates, and this time a winner from small-town Alberta was triumphant: 22-year-old Eileen Beckner from Carstairs. Eileen's sponsor, the Junior Farmers' Union of Alberta, garnered huge support for its candidate by staging community dances all over the southern half of the province. Although she was not a farm girl, Eileen was a horsewoman and so was very disappointed when she learned she would not be allowed to ride in the parade. Bowing to criticism expressed in 1949, the ACT reverted to placing the Stampede Queen and her court on a float in the 1950 parade so that they would be highly visible to the crowd. Accompanied by 1949 Queen Merle Stier and 1950 Ladies-in-waiting Ann Dutchak and Gussie MacDonald (both of whom were non-riding Calgary girls who were very relieved to be on a float rather than a horse), Queen Eileen was presented sitting on a throne on a special horse-drawn float sponsored by the City of Calgary.[116] It featured a giant white cowboy hat, which was fast becoming one of Calgary's most recognizable symbols thanks to the

promotional efforts of mayor Don Mackay. A former radio personality and alderman, Mackay had accompanied the 1948 excursion to Toronto's Grey Cup festivities and followed up on the popularity of Bill Herron's white-hat initiative by introducing the custom of honouring visiting dignitaries with the presentation of a white hat. The float on which Eileen and the other royals rode promoted the city and its 75th anniversary with a banner reading "Welcome to Calgary – Ten Gallon Hospitality for 75 Years."

As usual, the official crowning took place the next evening before the grandstand show. This time, Eileen got to show off her equestrian skills. She rode into the infield on a palomino pony and was crowned with the traditional white hat by Merle Stier and Stampede Board vice-president George Edworthy "before a background of colorfully dressed Indians." To soften the blow for unsuccessful candidates, the club had announced that "[a]ll of the fifteen entrants in the contest will be guests of honor in the city for two days at the expense of the A.C.T., and will receive cowboy hats and neckerchiefs in addition to other awards." The three winners received the customary prizes and performed the official duties now

1950 Queen Eileen Beckner (far right) and Ladies-in-waiting Gussie MacDonald and Ann Dutchak with 1949 Queen Merle Stier (second from left). (CSA)

expected of royalty during Stampede week, including visits to local hospitals and various city-wide events.[117] Highlights for Queen Eileen included meeting the 1950 parade marshal, Prime Minister Louis St. Laurent, and visiting the Indian Village at the Exhibition grounds, where she was made an honorary princess by the Tsuu T'ina with the name Star Woman.

During the early years, royal duties mostly were confined to Stampede week, but not surprisingly the official recognition of the queen and her consorts by the Stampede led to an increasing expectation that these pretty mascots could be called upon anytime during their year-long reign to represent the show. Over the years, joint promotional efforts had so blurred the distinction between the Stampede and its home city that almost anything representing the show could be viewed as an envoy for the city as well. Mayors during the 1940s had praised the Stampede's success in advertising Calgary throughout North America; those who followed in the 1950s and 1960s – Don Mackay, Harry Hays, Grant MacEwan and Jack Leslie – actively cultivated Calgary's Cowtown image, reasoning that "what was good for the Stampede was also good for the city."[118]

Calling on Stampede royalty to represent the City of Calgary occurred only occasionally during the 1950s, but the queen and sometimes the ladies-in-waiting could expect to attend an additional half-dozen or so functions after Stampede week was over. Interestingly, the City seemed to take the approach that "once a queen, always a queen." In April 1952 it sent the 1950 Queen, Eileen Beckner, as its representative to the opening of Spokane's Ridpath Hotel. The local media, naturally assuming she was the reigning queen, reported: "It was a festive occasion and one which even reached across an international border. Bringing the greetings of neighbors to the north was John Loader, president of the Trail, British Columbia, Chamber of Commerce. Two Canadian beauties also were on hand for the occasion – Eileen Beckner, Queen of the Calgary Stampede, and Betty Rae, Queen of the Banff Winter Carnival. With other queens and princesses, they arrived in open cars as the ceremony got underway." The city had rounded up a bevy of queens for the auspicious occasion, and Eileen and Betty were joined by Miss Spokane, the Queen of the Spokane Lilac Festival, the Queen of the Portland Rose Festival, the Seattle Seafair queen, Miss Walla Walla, Miss Yakima, Miss Pasco, the Ellensburg Rodeo Queen and the Lewiston Roundup Queen.[119]

The success of a Carstairs candidate in 1950 must have given heart to rural organizations, because the

1951 contest saw eleven of eighteen candidates come from small-town southern Alberta: Black Diamond, Magrath, Rocky Mountain House, Lacombe, Innisfail, Red Deer, Bowness, Brooks, Lethbridge, Alix and Stettler, even a candidate from Kinnaird, BC. But, for all that, it was a Calgary candidate who won in 1951: 17-year-old Marion McMahon, sponsored by the Windsor Park Ratepayers Association. It was a close win and reports earlier in the contest had another local candidate consistently in the lead, the Hillhurst-Sunnyside Community Club's June Dewhirst. June's mother, another June Dewhirst, had been a popular annual participant in the Stampede parade for nearly twenty-five years, dazzling spectators with "costumes which glitter with hand-worked designs in sequins" and a saddle decorated with more than one hundred silver dollars. Equally enthusiastic about the Stampede, daughter June had won the award for best-dressed cowgirl in the parade in 1949.[120] Magrath Junior Farmer's Union of Alberta candidate Shirley Clark was another close contender in the 1951 contest, but she and June ended up finishing second and third respectively.

Marion was an accomplished horsewoman who had been riding since the age of 8,[121] but there were mutterings that, in the end, her wealthy family had pushed her ticket sales over the top. Her father Frank and her uncle George McMahon were well-known Calgary oil entrepreneurs and owners of the Calgary Stampeders football club. Their financial contributions and significance to the community were recognized when McMahon Stadium was named in their honour when it opened in 1960. It must have only confirmed the cynics' views about the privileges of wealth when Queen Marion drew the winning ticket for the 1951 Meteor car at the ACT Hoedown during Stampede week and the lucky winner was none other than her sister-in-law, Mrs. Frank McMahon Jr. of Windsor Park![122]

Presiding over the ticket draw was just one of many duties expected of the Queen and her ladies. To give the boys in the Calgary club a sense of what else the girls did during Stampede week that justified all their hard work promoting the contest and selling tickets, a committee member submitted a Dear Diary-style article to the club newsletter in August 1951. Presented as if written by the teen-aged Queen Marion, it is written in a breathless, girlish style but still provides an interesting look at the activities and expectations of Stampede royalty during this early period:

Dear Diary: I hope I am the lucky girl when Mr. Lebbert steps out with the results.

Yes, I made it.

The ACT boys are nice, and getting my picture for the papers kind of gives you a tickly feeling. My ladies-in-waiting are cute, and that chaperone is strict but a good sport.

Monday. Will it ever quit raining? What a place and time to be riding a horse! The rain will ruin my beautiful costume. The meals and whirl have been fun all day and the Stampede is terrific.

Tuesday. What a thrill the crowning ceremonies were – beautiful. The weather must have heard my prayer. Thanks, dear God, for helping me make that speech to all those wonderful people.

Wednesday. The street shows, chuck wagons etc., are fun but I cried today. Imagine a Queen crying, but only inside. Those wonderful guys at the Colonel Belcher Hospital who fought for us and their country were glad to see me. But it was the crippled children at the Red Cross Hospital that started it all, and they didn't even want to let me go, and the little gifts that my ladies-in-waiting helped me distribute. You would think I had taught them to use those withered limbs and twisted backs.

Thursday. The Mayor, Don Mackay, had us out

1951 Queen Marion McMahon (centre) with Ladies-in-waiting June Dewhirst and Shirley Clark. (GA: PA-2807-2588)

to dinner today. The Lions Club dinner was really something also. Our two ACT escorts seem to get nicer with each change – nothing appears too good for us.

Friday. Today we took in the midway. My head is still spinning from the rides and color of the shows.

Saturday. Today I was named Princess White Eagle Plume by the Stoney Tribe – another beautiful ceremony. Running Bull performed the crowning and said all kinds of nice things about me. I hope they are true. Those ACT escorts assured me that they are.

It seems to me I've square danced a million miles this week, eaten a thousand banquets and met a billion wonderful people. Like John Fisher and the American ambassador to Canada, the ACT boys etc.

The Calgary Stampede was always a thrill to me but to reign as Queen! Well, I'll never be the same.[123]

By 1952, the closing date for the queen contest had been backed up to June 20 to allow more time for the queen and ladies-in-waiting to be fitted for their outfits and groomed a bit for their upcoming public role. In addition to providing updates about the relative standing of the fourteen candidates every few days throughout May and June, the ACT also attempted to pique interest in the contest by announcing that "[a]mong the many honors which will be extended the winner will be a week-long visit to the Minneapolis Aquatennial, which opens July 18. As guest of the National Grain Company Ltd. of Calgary, she will attend luncheons, dinners, civic events, aquatennial events, and will ride in a banner-covered convertible in two parades."[124]

Although only five of the fourteen contestants in 1952 were from Calgary, once again a Calgarian was the winner: 17-year-old Sherry Moore, candidate of the Elks Club No. 4 of Calgary. Unlike most previous Queens, and her own Ladies-in-waiting, Donna Christie of Calgary and Helen Smith of Bittern Lake (near Camrose), Sherry was not a horsewoman, but it was not an outright requirement at the time, so that fact was overlooked. She was given a few lessons so she could get on and off her palomino with dignity, but she remained nervous and so riding was played down in 1952. As Sherry later recalled, most of her time on horseback was to pose for photographs. When she had to ride during daily downtown appearances and into the infield each day before the rodeo, she "just held on for dear life and hoped the horse knew what he was doing." She was very glad to be allowed to ride in the parade on the back of a convertible.[125]

In any case, the media focused on Sherry's real talent and popular draw, which was the fact that she was a well-known local dancer and baton twirler with children's dance studios in Calgary and Lethbridge (her "little army" of queen contest ticket sellers). She was used to performing and happy to do so many times during the contest. Wearing a costume in the Elks colours (purple and white), she and her student dancers helped the club earn money on behalf of the Alberta Branch of the Canadian Cancer Society, and their share of her ticket sales came to a very impressive $3,153.75 (about $27,500 today).[126] Sherry also performed on several occasions during Stampede week. At the annual ACT street dance, attended by a crowd of nearly 10,000 people in colourful Western outfits, she "delighted the spectators with an exhibition of dancing and [a] spectacular baton demonstration."[127] When she and her ladies-in-waiting appeared at a street event featuring Tsuu T'ina drummers and dancers, she was more than willing to be drawn into the performance. The resulting newspaper headline, typical of its time, read "Heap big time for all – Stampede Queen Sherry Moore and Sarcee Chief – Cameras keep clicking, Indians keep dancing – A Mardi Gras with feathers."[128]

1952 Queen Sherry Moore (centre) with Ladies-in-waiting Helen Smith and Donna Christie. (GA: NA-2864-18115A)

The Stampede Queen contest was so well established by 1953, and making such good money as a fundraiser, that the Calgary ACT decided to increase ticket prices for the first and only time. Ever since the contest had started in 1947, tickets worth twenty-five votes had been priced at 25¢ each and sold in books of twenty-five for $5. It is an indication of how hard several dozen ACT members worked every year to attract sponsoring organizations – and sign up local clubs and groups to sell tickets on behalf of the ACT in a sort of pyramid scheme – that these low prices were able to generate such big donations for local charities. Between 1947 and 1953, over $40,000 was raised in this manner (about $354,000 today). Half the money earned had gone to organizations sponsoring contest candidates, but the half retained by the club had been used to benefit many local organizations, including Girls Town (more than $3,000, or about $26,000 today), the Alberta Crippled Children's Hospital ($4,600, or $40,000 today), the Community Chest ($1,500, or $13,000 today), the Salvation Army ($1,000, or $9,000 today) and an impressive $7,900 ($70,000) to the Calgary Fire Department for the purchase of a rescue truck.[129]

But, as a group of professional salesmen, the natural inclination of members of the ACT Queen Committee was to find a way of increasing profits year over year, so in 1953 the club decided to change the rules and save money by having just one winner, a queen with no ladies-in-waiting. They also raised ticket prices to 50 cents for fifty tickets worth fifty votes. Unfortunately, this turned out to be a big marketing mistake. Although the club announced that all proceeds would go to the Southern Alberta Cerebral Palsy Association, participation in the contest plummeted to just seven candidates, exactly half the number of the previous year, and soon after the contest began one of the seven dropped out. With so few contenders, sales and profits fell accordingly.

However, the contest itself was as exciting as usual for those involved. The winning candidate was 21-year-old Edith Edge, a third-generation cowgirl from a local ranching family who had been sponsored by the Cochrane Light Horse Association. Mayor Don Mackay was present for the ballot counting and presented the "five pretty girls [who] bowed out of the picture" with tooled leather belts with silver buckles, a gift of the ACT. He congratulated the candidates, saying, "None of you has lost the race. Whether you were at the top or at the bottom, you are a winner. You have all contributed to a good cause."[130]

Queen Edith Edge, 1953. (GA: NA-2864-18116D)

Although they had only one young lady representing them, Queen Edith was a good figurehead for the Stampede because of her riding skills and ties to the local ranching community. Her family had long been involved in the Stampede and all three of her brothers competed in the rodeo that year. Edith herself was an exceptional horsewoman and barrel racer who would become first runner-up in the Miss Rodeo Canada contest in 1955.[131] When she won the Stampede Queen contest, the *Calgary Herald* reported admiringly, "The tall, quiet-spoken queen has lived all her life on her father's ranch and for her it is the only life there is. Riding is second nature to her and she wears her frontier pants and fringed calfskin jacket with jaunty ease. Edith doesn't remember when she first learned to ride a horse; she's been around horses and cattle all her life."[132]

The Stampede capitalized on Edith's horsemanship by having her ride in the parade. To short-circuit complaints about her lack of visibility, ACT past president and former Queen Committee chairman Lyle Lebbert rode beside her holding up a sign that read, "Miss Calgary Stampede 1953."[133] She performed all the usual duties expected of a queen over the week following the parade, greeting Prime Minister Louis St. Laurent at the airport and helping him to award prizes to the champion cowboys on the final night

of the Stampede. The following week, the Stoney/Nakoda made her an honorary Indian princess during the opening of Banff Indian Days. In a ceremony performed by tribal councillors Tom Kaquitts and Eddie Hunter in the presence of the chiefs of the three bands comprising the Stoney/Nakoda Nation, Edith was presented with a feathered headdress and declared an adopted daughter of the tribe with the name Princess Good Eagle Girl.[134]

Typical of the times, when Edith became queen one newspaper reporter described her physical charms for readers. "Queen Edith stands 5 feet 8 inches and weighs 130 pounds. She wears her light brown hair in a long bob. Her other attributes include green eyes, a wistful smile and measurements that stack up very nicely with… Hollywood lovelies… They are: bust 34, waist 26 and hips 36."[135] As intrusive and repugnant as this kind of reporting seems today, Edith's physical description was very interesting to *Herald* readers at the time because they had learned there was every possibility

Queen Edith Edge after her adoption into the Stoney/Nakoda tribe as Princess Good Eagle Girl during Banff Indian Days, 1953. The ceremony was performed by Councillors Tom Kaquitts and Eddie Hunter in the presence of Chiefs Jacob Two Young Man, David Bearspaw and Tom Snow. (GA: NA-2864-3901B)

that their Stampede Queen might be compared to a "Hollywood lovely" during her reign.

In later years, the Queen Committee would become quite adept at approaching local businesses for prizes and donations, but during this period the ACT was still the main supporter of the royalty program. However, in 1953 a valuable prize unexpectedly came its way. Ken Leach, the owner of several Famous Players movie theatres in Calgary, conceived the idea of sending the Stampede Queen to Hollywood as a goodwill promotional stunt that would advertise his own local theatres while providing publicity for the Calgary Stampede. It seemed like a natural partnership, as movie Westerns and cowboy performers were all the rage in Calgary at the time and many locals had adopted a showy Hollywood Westerns look for Stampede week in preference to the more practical attire worn by real working cowboys and cowgirls.

Leach was joined in this prize offering by Abe Schiller, flamboyant public-relations director of the newly expanded and refurbished Flamingo Hotel in Las Vegas, Nevada. Resplendent in "a specially-made cowboy outfit patterned with large pink flamingos," Schiller attended his first Stampede in 1953 and the *Calgary Herald* reported he was "so impressed with the big show so far that he has already decided to make his Stampede visit an annual one. Not only that, he is going to make sure that every queen of the Stampede in forthcoming years has a trip to Las Vegas."[136] Schiller saw his involvement in Leach's scheme as good advertising aimed at luring wealthy vacationing Calgary oilmen and their wives to the luxury hotel and casino famous for attracting movie stars and other celebrity entertainers to its lounge – "everyone who was anyone."[137] Similarly, it was hoped that the Stampede Queen's visit to Las Vegas and Hollywood would pique the interest of wealthy Americans and promote travel to Calgary to see the famous show.

Schiller and Leach outdid themselves describing the delights awaiting Queen Edith. "We'll see that she's feted in fine style," they promised as she was presented with a key to the royal suite at the Flamingo Hotel. Schiller assured her that she would see all the floor shows in the resort hotels and Leach promised she would tour the big Hollywood movie studios and meet all the stars.[138]

Edith decided not to go to Victoria, preferring to take the $300 cash equivalent and later applying it toward a business course, but there was no question of giving up the trip to Las Vegas and Hollywood. It took some time to organize, but she and her chaperone, Marion Boothby, finally left Calgary for Las

Vegas via Vancouver and Seattle on November 1, 1953. Arriving first in Hollywood, they visited several movie sets, including *A Star is Born* and *White Christmas*, where Edith was photographed with stars Bing Crosby and Danny Kaye. She also appeared on television's *Queen for a Day*, a popular game show where female contestants competed by telling "sob" stories, the winner being the one who received the most sympathy based on audience applause as measured by a machine with a dial that registered sound volume.[139] As a guest Queen on the coast-to-coast show, Edith admitted to feeling "a bit nervous," but she presented the winner, Mrs. Mildred Churchill of Compton, California, with a cup and saucer and later claimed it was one of the highlights of her trip.[140] After four days in Hollywood, the women flew to Las Vegas, where they stayed a week at the Flamingo Hotel. While there, Edith "[took] time off from her gay, cowboy princess life, to play the role of goodwill ambassador" when she presented the mayor of Las Vegas with a big white cowboy hat, a trademark gift from Calgary mayor Don Mackay.[141]

Queen Edith Edge riding in the Stampede parade, 1953. ACT past president Lyle Lebbert rides alongside holding her sign. (GA: NA-3127-2)

CHAPTER 4 ★ 1954

"A great honour for myself and all my people"

While Edith Edge was enjoying her trip to Las Vegas and Hollywood in the fall of 1953, members of the ACT Queen Committee were busy analyzing the disappointing financial results of that year's contest and making plans for 1954. They were well aware that changing the rules and raising ticket prices in 1953 had been a disaster. To get the contest back on track, Lyle Lebbert, who had been chairman in 1951, agreed to come back and head the committee. Not surprisingly, one of his first decisions was to revert to former rules (choosing a queen and two ladies-in-waiting) and former ticket prices (25 cents for 25 votes).

Realizing that it might take some work to rekindle enthusiasm for attracting sponsors and selling tickets, Lebbert promised members in the February newsletter that "the 1954 contest will be held with the glamor and color and promotion of [the] 1951 and 1952 contests."[142] To generate a little excitement and encourage the ACT boys to get out early selling tickets, the club's annual Stampede luncheon was held in March, two months earlier than in previous years. A few of the early contest entrants attended along with Stampede Board president Maurice Hartnett, vice-president W.A. Crawford-Frost and mayor Don Mackay.[143]

This re-energizing effort worked well and 1954's contestant numbers rebounded to former levels. There were fourteen candidates, half from Calgary and the rest from East Coulee, Drumheller, Banff, Hanna, Nanton, High River and Rocky Mountain House. Contest ads promised prizes similar to previous years, including trips to Victoria and Banff for the winners and Hollywood–Las Vegas for the queen, and announced that net proceeds from the contest would go to the Council for Retarded Children. In almost every way, the contest looked to be shaping up the same as every other year except for one important difference. In 1954, for the first time ever, one of the sponsoring organizations asked an Aboriginal girl to be its candidate for queen.

1954 Queen Evelyn Eagle Speaker (centre) with Ladies-in-waiting Kay Dench and Peggy Fisher. (CSA)

From the first show in 1912, Guy Weadick had insisted that local Indian tribes be an integral part of the Stampede. Since that time there had been a strong tradition of local native participation in the Indian Village set up on the Exhibition grounds during Stampede week. Most years, the reigning Stampede queen was made an honorary Indian princess by one of the five tribes living in the Indian Village. For the first seven years, that was as far as it usually went in terms of native participation in the queen contest. While there was nothing in the rules preventing a girl from any racial background or ethnicity from competing, the Calgary contest seems to have been viewed by interested parties as an exclusively white activity, with the result that candidates and winners almost uniformly were white, middle-class girls from Anglo-Saxon backgrounds.

Interestingly, this was not the case for some of the big American rodeos, which appointed native girls as rodeo queens and attendants a number of times during the first half of the twentieth century. In fact, by 1954, the Pendleton Round-Up had been represented five times by royalty courts (i.e., queen and attendants) comprised entirely of Aboriginal girls: in 1926, 1932, 1948, 1952 and 1953.[144] But there had never before been a native girl in the Calgary Stampede

Queen contest and this resulted in a very exciting race in 1954.

The Calgary Elks Club No. 4 had sponsored queen candidates before and had even produced a winner in 1952 (Sherry Moore). Hoping to win again, they searched for a novel idea and came up with sponsoring an Aboriginal girl. It went without saying that they wanted a candidate who was pretty and smart, but in choosing a native girl it was important that she lived in the city rather than on a reserve so she could participate in all the fundraising activities the club planning. Sponsoring organizations often turned to social, cultural and riding clubs as well as local high schools and post-secondary institutions to find young ladies who fit their requirements and were in the right age range, so it was natural for the Elks to contact a couple of the local business colleges to find a suitable candidate. After interviewing two young women suggested by the head of the Henderson Secretarial College, and gaining the approval of the federal Department of Indian Affairs[145] (which oversaw and controlled the movement and activities of all native people in Alberta at the time), the club offered the candidacy to Evelyn Eagle Speaker.

Nineteen-year-old Evelyn was from the Blood Reserve near Cardston (now called the Kainai First Nation), some 230 kilometres south of Calgary. At the time, she was one of the few young people from her reserve to attend and complete high school in Cardston. When she graduated with honours, her father, Chief Mike Eagle Speaker, who was a strong proponent of education, encouraged her to enhance her job prospects by getting further training in Calgary. There were not many jobs considered suitable for young women in the early 1950s; Evelyn was not interested in nursing or teaching, so she chose secretarial training. When the Elks contacted her, she was within months of graduating from Henderson's with top marks in every subject.

At first, Evelyn turned down the Elks' offer but they asked her to think it over and reconsider. She was a modest, shy young woman who disliked the idea of being in the limelight and shrank from the thought of competing with a college friend who was very excited about having been chosen as a queen candidate by another organization. But she thought it over, talked to her family and eventually said yes, "not for any personal glory," as she put it, but "to be an example to my own people," to show Calgarians, whose views often were affected by stereotypes, "that an Indian could progress and succeed just the same as any white person."[146] After the Elks announced her candidacy in mid-April, she told the press: "my one thought on accepting this honor is for the good

it can do my people. Sadly enough, the large majority of persons still think of the Indians as an illiterate people. Perhaps, now, I may get the opportunity to inform the thousands of tourists visiting Calgary during the Stampede that the Indian of today is well educated and a good-living Canadian."[147] Interestingly, historian Patrizia Gentile found that Indian princess pageants popular a decade later were predicated partly on the anticipation of achieving this same kind of positive outcome. "Aware of negative Aboriginal stereotypes and images… [the] winner of the Indian Princess contest became the spokesperson for all things noble, good and dignified… an advocate against racial discrimination… [u]sing beauty… to help promote racial pride… [and] show that Aboriginal people are good, trustworthy and 'beautiful' even if they are not white."[148]

After Evelyn accepted the Elks' offer, there followed a busy two months of fundraising, mainly on weekends, since she was still in school until the end of June. She was living with a family in the Mount Royal area of Calgary, earning her room and board and tuition money by looking after the family's three children in her free time. But they were excited about her candidacy and there was no problem getting time off during the queen campaign. She had no car, so every time there was a fundraising function, and there were many, an Elks member would pick her up and drive her there and back. As she later recalled, the Elks "had her going all over" promoting the contest and "worked so hard to get her elected." She found club members invariably kind and supportive, gently providing on-the-job training with little hints that stood her in good stead whenever she found herself the centre of attention ("always acknowledge the crowd and smile").[149]

At the club's request, she wore a native dress and a single feather in a headband whenever she appeared on their behalf. She was the star attraction many times at Friday night socials at the Elks Lodge. She also was in an Easter parade, went to Edmonton to open a speedway, helped to welcome a baseball team visiting from Spokane and appeared at the Western Canadian Sportsmen's Show held in Calgary that June. The public was invited to meet and vote for her at an Indian village set up at the show, while another queen candidate, Kay Dench, held court at the nearby Russell Sporting Goods booth. Dressed in cowgirl garb, Kay demonstrated her expert horse-riding skills each evening during the event. In the words of historian Susan Joudrey, "This was a common dichotomy – the cowgirl and the Indian Princess, a feminized version of the dominant cowboy/Indian binary made popular by American Wild West shows,

dime novels and Hollywood movies."[150] Although Evelyn too was an accomplished horsewoman, she was never portrayed by the Elks as a rider, but rather as an "Indian maiden." The juxtaposition and costuming of the two main rival candidates for queen at the 1954 Sportsmen's Show served to highlight in a very obvious way the choices available to the voting public.

Soon after the Elks decided to have a native girl represent them in the 1954 contest, they came up with a brilliant advertising scheme to promote her candidacy. They proposed to the chiefs of the Treaty 7 Nations in southern Alberta, which also happened to be the five Nations that participated in the Stampede each year (Kainai, Piikani, Siksika, Stoney/Nakoda and Tsuu T'ina), that all five tribes come together to adopt their candidate as an honorary Indian princess. If Evelyn became Stampede Queen, she would represent them all to the world. This novel idea appealed to the chiefs and gained the blessing of the Department of Indian Affairs, which could have scuttled the project had it disapproved.[151] Someone came up with the clever idea of bestowing on Evelyn the name "Princess Wapiti" in honour of her sponsors, the Elks (*wapiti* being the Cree word for elk). After the fact, it might seem rather ironic that the chiefs allowed the Elks to choose a Cree name with which to honour Evelyn, as the Cree lived mostly in the central and northern part of the province and were not part of the Treaty 7 confederacy proposing to adopt the young Kainai woman.[152] But according to Evelyn, the group had considered a Blackfoot word for elk, *ponokhka* and rejected it as less recognizable and more likely difficult to pronounce by the largely Caucasian population living in southern Alberta at the time.[153]

The Elks submitted a request to the Stampede Board, asking if they could hold Evelyn's Indian princess naming ceremony in the Stampede Corral after one of the hockey games, but the executive committee, fearing that it might be interpreted as showing favouritism for a particular candidate, turned down the request.[154] After scouting around for another venue big enough to hold what was expected to be a very large crowd, the Elks chose the Cinema Park Drive-In on Bowness Road. It was a great choice for attracting drive-in and car-mad Calgarians of the mid-fifties. When the drive-in had opened the previous summer, it had been described as "the largest theatre of its kind in Canada," with a screen 65 feet wide and 48 feet high. Cinema Park itself covered 45 acres in all, with 20 acres for parking.[155]

On April 22 the Elks placed a big ad in the *Calgary Herald* that featured a photograph of Evelyn in her native outfit and announced "Tonight Only! Special Indian Tribal Ceremony: Featuring the recognition of Princess Wapiti by the following Indian Nations: Stoney – Sarcee – Peigan – Bloods – Blackfoot* – as candidate for Stampede Queen. Sponsored by the Calgary Elks' Lodge, BPOE No. 4 – Entire ceremony filmed by CBC-TV cameraman." Gates to the park would open at 6 p.m. as usual and the naming ceremony was to be the pre-show entertainment at 8:00 before the main attraction started half an hour later. Ironically, it was a Western starring Alan Ladd and Shelley Winters that had been filmed in Alberta the year before but was called, for some reason, *Saskatchewan*. As if the promise of an exciting double feature (*Mexican Manhunt* was to play later that evening) and the special Indian ceremony were not enough, the ad also promised the Canadian Legion pipe band, the Elks Patrol, a giant fireworks display and that "8 lucky kiddies" would win "a repeating cap gun revolver."[156] To add legitimacy and importance to the event, special dignitaries included Calgary police chief Larry Partridge and mayor Don Mackay.[157]

---

*These were the historical names in use at the time for the following First Nations: Stoney/Nakoda, Tsuu T'ina, Piikani, Kainai and Siksika.

With the promise of such an exciting evening of entertainment, the Elks had no trouble attracting a sellout crowd for the event. The press took a great interest, featuring photographs of Evelyn surrounded by Treaty 7 chiefs and wearing a new five-feathered headdress symbolic of her adoption into the five First Nations of southern Alberta. Evelyn's parents had hoped to present their daughter with a new outfit to wear at the ceremony but it was not quite ready so she wore the same dress she had worn to most previous functions. The outfit that Mrs. Eagle Speaker and Evelyn's aunt and sister were preparing was of the type typically associated with Indian princesses: a milk-white deerskin dress, moccasins, belt and necklace, fringed and beaded with traditional Kainai patterns in purple, red and white. Chief Eagle Speaker had ordered the special deerskin from British Columbia when the family learned that a ceremony was planned but there had not been enough time to finish the elaborate beading.[158]

Even before Princess Wapiti was introduced to the voting public, interest in Evelyn's candidacy had been high simply because of the novelty of her being the first-ever Aboriginal contestant. Now, as a result of the Elks' brilliant marketing ploy, her local popularity soared. Her campaign also benefited from the support of native people living in southern Alberta,

Stampede Queen candidate Evelyn Eagle Speaker after her adoption by the Treaty 7 Nations as Princess Wapiti, 1954. (GA: NA-2864-18117A)

who were pleased with their co-operative venture and proud to see one of their own competing on an equal footing with more traditional candidates. It was not really surprising to learn that Evelyn had won the contest when ACT Queen Committee chairman Lyle Lebbert announced that fact to the media after votes were counted on June 21.

The press was delighted with the precedent-making novelty of the situation: "First time in history of Western show: Indian girl is voted 1954 Stampede Queen." Well aware of the significance of her win, a "quietly nervous" Evelyn said, "It is a great honor for myself and for all my people." She impressed reporters with her quiet dignity and with the fact that "[h]er first thoughts were for those who helped her reach a goal that has never before been sought by an Indian girl." She said, "I should like to thank all the members of the Calgary Elks Lodge who sponsored me, the ladies of the Royal Purple and all the others who supported me with their votes." Her family had not been able to come to Calgary for the vote counting, but she told the *Herald* that she knew her parents would be very happy to hear the news of her win. "They will be right at the radio listening," she said, as would her four siblings.[159]

As usual, Evelyn had worn her native dress and feathered headdress to the vote counting so the public's first glimpse of the new Stampede Queen was of an Indian girl surrounded by cowgirls (Ladies-in-waiting Kay Dench and Peggy Fisher, in traditional Western garb). This was not the usual visual for winners of the annual queen contest; traditionally, contestants tried to reinforce their suitability as cowgirl representatives of the Stampede by wearing Western-style clothing during the competition. As overall sponsors of the contest on behalf of the Stampede, the ACT had only ever conceived of the royal trio as cowgirls dressed in a Hollywood Western style. Accordingly, they assured the public that "[t]he Indian princess turned queen will exchange her Indian finery for Western garb for her reign"[160] and proceeded to have the winners measured for their prize outfits. But the Elks had been very successful in portraying Evelyn as a "typical" Indian maiden, and many supporters were by now firmly convinced she was in fact also a hereditary Indian princess. Some began voicing the opinion that it would be a travesty to make her wear a cowgirl costume, and so began a public controversy that was in many respects more apparent than real.

Two days after it was announced that Evelyn would wear the usual cowgirl attire as Stampede Queen, a media campaign began in the *Calgary Herald* pushing for her to be allowed to wear her native costume instead. Later it was discovered that this campaign was precipitated by Philip Godsell, a former fur trader, adventurer and writer who considered himself a friend to native people and was a regular judge of Indian events during the Calgary Stampede. Six months later he told Evelyn's father that he had "worked very hard to help get her elected, and got over 500 votes for her from one firm alone." When he had read that Evelyn was to wear a cowgirl outfit as Stampede Queen, he had set to work, determined to change that decision. He felt strongly that she should be allowed to appear as she was, as an Indian girl, and a princess at that, rather than as something that she was not, a cowgirl. Although he acted from the best of intentions, his reasoning may have been faulty in that there was no reason why Evelyn could not be both a cowgirl and an Indian at one and the same time, especially since being a cowgirl for the Stampede was just playing a role, not the real thing. Only a few Stampede Queen contest winners had ever been real cowgirls. In any case, the glamorous outfits that winners wore as representatives of the Stampede bore very little resemblance to the clothing worn by real working cowgirls.[161] Finally, as a modern young woman who had been raised in a ranching area and was accustomed to riding horses, Evelyn frequently wore casual Western wear during her free time when she was not working or playing the role of Indian maiden for the Elks' contest campaign.[162]

However, Godsell, sincerely believing he would be righting an incipient wrong, "really got busy on the telephone." He gave the details in a letter to Mike Eagle Speaker the following January:

> I phoned Alan Bill, editor of the *Herald*, who's an old friend of mine, and then, at his request, wrote him the enclosed letter, and phoned up a whole bunch of my friends and got each of them to write in to the *Herald* insisting that Evelyn be allowed to wear her Indian costume in the Parade. Bill promised he'd run the letters, and also an editorial along the lines I suggested, which he did – see Editorial Page enclosed. This did the trick all right!!![163]

In his resulting editorial, headlined "She should wear her native dress," Alan Bill penned a cogent and compelling argument in favour of Queen Evelyn appearing in her deerskin outfit. After describing Evelyn's background and saying she was "a credit to her race," Bill continued:

> There can be no doubt that the fact she was an Indian girl appealed to many who bought tickets.
>
> However, she has been informed that for her

reign as Queen, she will dress in the cowgirl costume that Stampede Queens traditionally wear. It seems remarkably short-sighted and senseless.

During Stampede Week all sorts of Calgarians, who never get closer to the range than the one in the kitchen, will be wearing cowboy clothes, in a form of masquerade that helps create the Stampede atmosphere in the city. The queen's ladies-in-waiting will be wearing the ten gallon hats, colored shirts, cowboy boots, etc. Why should the Indian princess not wear the clothes which are her native costume? Surely the Indian dress is as typical of the Stampede as "western" outfits. However colorful these may be, they can be matched and will be matched in every city holding a rodeo this year from Madison Square Garden to Gopher Gulch. Miss Eaglespeaker* is naturally disappointed, not only because she regards the honor of being Queen as an honor for her race, but because her mother has been making a new Indian dress for her.

The election of a Stampede Queen normally is of little interest other than to those immediately concerned in Calgary. But this year Miss Eaglespeaker's winning has already caused great interest outside the city and this will be more marked when the Stampede is on. It is excellent publicity for the Indians of Alberta. Not only that, but Miss Eaglespeaker, in native dress, is going to attract more attention from newspaper editors and readers and the public in other parts of the country than will any stampede [sic] Queen in a ten gallon hat.

This newspaper has already received indications that people, many of them supporters of the contest for queen, are disappointed at the suggestion she will not be wearing her Indian dress. The sponsors of the Queen contest and Stampede officials should think again and make sure that the Queen is dressed as the Indian princess she rightfully is. There are enough ersatz cowboys around here as it is.[164]

Bill implied that letters had been pouring in to the *Herald* regarding the issue, but only one appeared in that day's paper:

Princess Wapiti's dress: We are two native teenagers, who are very disappointed to learn that Princess Wapiti will wear western garb during her reign. We feel that Indians are as much an attraction at the Stampede as cowboys, that their own dress is very

*Although Evelyn and her family spelled their name Eagle Speaker, the media occasionally followed a convention popular at the time and combined the two words into one to create a single last name, Eaglespeaker.

spectacular and that it would be a great honor for the Princess to appear as she actually is, an Indian Princess.

—Puzzled, Calgary[165]

On June 28, when no additional letters had been submitted – at least, none that it printed – the *Herald* raised the issue again with an article headlined "Wapiti costume debated." Telling readers that it had received "several letters and telephone calls from persons who believe Princess Wapiti should wear her native garb," the *Herald* stated that Stampede Board officials "favor the Indian costume and plan to confer with ACT officials on the dress problem."[166]

Disconcerted, but standing on its dignity, and determined not to be dictated to by the *Herald*, the ACT announced a concession on June 29. Evelyn would be allowed to wear her native dress on two occasions, for the parade and for the crowning ceremony, but would wear the traditional cowgirl outfit worn by all Stampede royalty for the rest of the week. Queen Committee chairman Lyle Lebbert explained the ACT position to the *Herald*:

Because Evelyn Eaglespeaker (Princess Wapiti) is an Indian girl is not going to make any difference to the ACT queen contest regulations…

It has been the practice through the years that the Stampede Queen wear cowboy costumes which have been specially tailored for her at the ACT expense, and therefore we cannot see a reason why such a practice should be altered this year. Miss Eaglespeaker saw the costumes as they were being made and she was exceptionally pleased with them.

We do not feel we are mixed up in a controversy on the subject. We are only carrying out what has been done in other years.[167]

Determined to force the ACT to allow Evelyn to wear her native dress for her entire reign, the *Herald* printed another editorial the same day as the ACT announcement. Most likely written by Alan Bill at Philip Godsell's urging, the ACT was the target. Under the headline "Not part way: Indian dress all week," it continued:

Displaying an attitude almost inconceivably stubborn, the sponsors of the Stampede Queen contest agreed to go part way on the question of allowing Princess Wapiti to wear her native dress during her reign next week. Part way is not enough; it is time they woke up.

Evelyn Eagle Speaker is a native Indian. Her tribal dress is as symbolic of the history of this province,

Stampede Queen candidate Evelyn Eagle Speaker after her adoption by the Treaty 7 Nations as Princess Wapiti, 1954. The five chiefs who placed symbolic feathers in her headdress were Jacob Two Young Man (Stoney/Nakoda), James Starlight (Tsuu T'ina), Joe Crowfoot (Siksika), Michael Eagle Speaker (Kainai), and Percy Creighton (Piikani). (GA: NA-5600-7771A)

to let her wear her native costume in the big parade, but after that she will preside in western dress (typical of nothing any ranch woman ever dreamed of) the same as that worn by her attendants.

Talk to almost any citizen and you will find that they heartily object to putting Miss Eagle Speaker into Hollywood Cowgirl dress. The Indian people, whose contribution to the Stampede each year is of the utmost importance in giving the big show the color that sets it apart from ordinary, routine rodeos, all of which have a "western" queen, may well be indignant that this representative of their race is not to be allowed to wear the ceremonial clothes of her people…

Under ordinary circumstances dressing the queen as a cowgirl is in keeping with the Stampede atmosphere. But these are not ordinary circumstances. It will be probably only once in a lifetime that an Indian "princess" (so honored by five Alberta tribes) will be Queen. It is insulting to the Indian people and unfair to the public who support the ACT and the Stampede, not to mention downright shortsighted, to take the stand that she must conform to a "tradition" of dress which, in her case, is completely foreign.

It is a pity that the only time a real native of Alberta has been selected to reign over an event

and the spirit of the West which the Stampede seeks to recapture, as could be hoped for. For some foggy reason, the Associated Canadian Travellers officials feel that cowgirl dress, and only cowgirl dress, is suitable attire for a queen of the Calgary Stampede. They have decided, doubtless under public pressure, which is famous far beyond our borders the happy incident should be marred by a ridiculously narrow outlook.[168]

By June 29 public sentiment finally had been aroused – or at least appeared to have been aroused, judging by the *Herald*'s letters to the editor section. Curiously, no letters on this issue ever appeared in Calgary's other daily newspaper, the *Albertan*. A sampling of letters to the *Herald* includes the following:

I have just finished reading Puzzled's letter and I agree… Princess Wapiti should wear Indian dress during her reign as Stampede Queen. It would be a great attraction to the many visitors who will visit the Stampede. There is nothing more beautiful than Indian dress, so I say again, let's have a Stampede Queen in her native dress, one that is fitting to a real Princess.

—DAR, Calgary

I for one gave three cheers when an Indian girl, Princess Wapiti, was voted this year's Stampede Queen, and a nice warm feeling flowed inside of me at this display of real Western fraternity. What a drawing card. Thousands will come to Calgary to see the lovely Indian girl we picked to be our Queen all rigged out in her native dress, surrounded by her cowgirl attendants. What a lovely touch!

However, my feeling of elation was short-lived when I read that she would have to wear a cowgirl outfit. Could anything be more ridiculous or out of harmony! In fact, in all fairness, it should be the other way round: the Queen's attendants should dress in Indian costume out of deference to the Queen…

—William D. Dowell, Midnapore

Your editorial in connection with the costume to be worn by the Stampede Queen is timely and it is to be hoped that ere now those responsible have changed their minds…

The day may come when genuine full-blooded Indian maids are as scarce in Calgary as genuine cowgirls are now and by that time we may have to resort to make-believe substitutes, but while we have them to show to our visitors in their own beautiful outfits, let us do so…

—Harry Hutchcroft, Calgary[169]

And finally, Godsell himself publicly joined the discussion:

I, in common with many others, was delighted to learn that Calgarians had this year acknowledged the great part taken by our Western Indians in making the Calgary Stampede a continued success by electing a charming Indian girl, Miss Evelyn Eagle Speaker, as Stampede Queen.

A daughter of the proud and progressive Blood tribe, she had looked forward to representing her people in the beautiful white, beaded doe-skin costume which she had a traditional right to wear, and which becomes her so well. Now she finds to her disappointment that instead of being permitted to continue to wear this native dress, which would give her the poise and dignity she needs to maintain her position as Stampede Queen, she must relegate it to obscurity and don a cowgirl outfit which does not suit her and would cause her to be eclipsed by those attendants who could carry it to better advantage.

Indians have a natural dignity which is greatly enhanced when they don their own distinctive and picturesque raiment; and it can hardly be considered a compliment to the Indians as a whole, whom this young lady represents, to have her native dress jettisoned for one that will be all but duplicated in every hole and corner of Calgary.

The officials of the Calgary Elks Club showed rare judgement and originality in sponsoring an Indian Stampede Queen. So, why let the public and their protégé down now by insisting on this anachronism which will not only prove a disappointment to the girl but to the general public and many outside visitors as well?

—Philip Godsell, FRGS, FRES, Calgary[170]

As an aside, it is interesting to note that the comments made by Godsell and others purporting to champion Evelyn's right to wear her native dress reveal, in fact, a certain acceptance and reinforcement of the traditional stereotypes held by the dominant white population regarding how Aboriginal people were expected to look and act. In "The Expectations of a Queen: Identity and Race Politics in the Calgary Stampede," Susan Joudrey argues that

according to the non-Aboriginal public, it would be incongruous if she were dressed as a cowgirl and not an Indian because it would be inauthentic… markers of race, such as clothing, were important to affirm the authenticity of one's racial identity… for her to wear cowgirl attire would be inappropriate, deceptive and even less attractive... [A]s an Aboriginal woman, Eagle Speaker was considered a piece of living history... The belief that authentic Aboriginal culture was vanishing influenced how the public expected [her] to perform her race.[171]

It was a confusing issue. By insisting that Evelyn be dressed identifiably as an Indian, supporters professed to be acknowledging and celebrating the important partnership of native people in the success of the annual Stampede. But by making her conform to a racial stereotype – wearing a traditional native dress instead of the uniform customarily associated with the title Stampede Queen – they risked devaluing her achievement by turning her into a tourist attraction and undercutting her own stated goal of dispelling long-held stereotypes by serving as an example of a modern native person competing on an equal footing with members of the white community.

Perhaps suspecting that the dress problem originated as a manufactured controversy rather than a genuine public issue, the *Albertan* made no comment until an entire week had gone by and the *Herald* had printed half a dozen letters to the editor, all of which appeared to support the idea of Evelyn wearing her native dress for the duration of her reign. Deciding that it was time to get in on what had by then become a topic of public interest, the July 3 *Albertan* published an editorial cartoon by John Freeborn captioned "1954's Miss (Poor-little-mixed-up) Calgary Stampede." Although Evelyn is shown wearing cowgirl clothes, her racial identity is made clear by her long braids, the fact that she is riding a horse pulling a travois, and the tall feathers poking through a hole in her hat. In spite of the caption, she seems calm and collected, but the public, as represented by the horse and a dog on the travois, look mightily confused. The horse sports a feather in its mane but the brand is a question mark. The dog, which is wearing a cowboy hat with a feather, looks bewildered, a point confirmed by a hovering question mark.[172] Interestingly, in depicting Evelyn as somewhat impassive, Freeborn accurately portrayed her deliberate detachment as she let others discuss the clothing issue. But she never viewed his "mixed-up" caption as applying to her; rather, she saw it only as the media's perception of her situation. Although the press and certain members of the public may have been confused – "could the Stampede Queen be both a cowgirl and an Indian Princess?" – Evelyn herself never relied on clothing to define her identity and never experienced any confusion about her role as Stampede Queen.[173]

The same day the newspaper ran Freeborn's cartoon, an *Albertan* reporter decided to find out what the man on the street was thinking, and discovered opinions on both sides of the argument. Peter Martinson said, "This is a real cowboy week and I think the Princess should dress in cowboy costume. But I'd give in and let her wear her special robes for one appearance." W. Pullar said, "Follow the cowboys. She'll look better, it's cooler, and besides much more practical for riding a horse." Danish visitor Ove Ahm thought that an Indian maiden winning as queen was "one of the great, truly great, examples of Canadian democracy" and said, "Of course, by all means, let her wear her Indian garb." Interestingly, the one native person they consulted, Tsuu T'ina elder Daisy Crowchild, supported the ACT's compromise solution: Indian dress for the parade and cowgirl clothes the rest of the time, for the very practical reason that "the costume is too heavy to wear all the time."[174]

Somewhat bewildered by the passionate and unexpected nature of what appeared to be a public outcry, the ACT was slow to respond, but ultimately it was goaded into defending its position. On July 3 the *Herald* printed a rebuttal from long-time ACT member W. Gordon Cochrane:

The ACT Viewpoint: As a member of the Associated Canadian Travellers for some years, I take great exception to your editorial of June 29, also to your previous one, for reasons as follows: First the Stampede Queen Contest is a project to raise funds for ourselves, and also for all other organizations sponsoring candidates in this contest, for local charitable purposes only. It is not a popularity or beauty contest in any way, shape or form. Inquire of… many… local charities who have received benefits from our efforts. The Calgary Exhibition and Stampede, of which we are all very proud, has received a large amount of good advertising which is almost province-wide, from this source. Regarding the costumes which you berate so much… when the Princess Wapiti was elected, she was shown her cowgirl costume and was delighted with it. Later, when she had her picture taken with it on, she was greatly thrilled with everything. Now, sir, I suggest that instead of casting unfavourable and slurring remarks about a body of men and their actions, you should give them a slap on the back and a great big "well done!" These men have worked for years on this project, giving of their time and efforts without thought of personal gain. They deserve the thanks of the whole community, not knocks. They, as the sponsoring body, have a perfect right to decide what type of costume should be worn by the Queen and her attendants…

—W.G. Cochrane, member, Calgary Club, ACT[175]

That same day, the *Albertan* announced:

Stampede Queen's costume settled: The "costume controversy" surrounding Evelyn Eaglespeaker (Princess Wapiti) was apparently settled Friday to everyone's satisfaction when Calgary Stampede officials announced that the new Queen would wear her royal Indian robes in the opening day parade and at the crowning ceremonies Tuesday night – and cowboy regalia for all other occasions.[176]

After many days of heated discussion in the media, this was exactly the same solution that had been suggested by the ACT nearly a week before, on June 29. The club, and very likely the Stampede, was willing to appease popular sentiment and acknowledge the Aboriginal background of their new queen by allowing her to be portrayed as a traditional Indian princess on two occasions, but aside from that, they asserted their right to dress the royalty representing the Stampede as they saw fit, in other words, as traditional rodeo queens dressed in cowgirl attire.

Evelyn had remained silent during the week of debate, content to let others settle the issue of her costuming as Stampede Queen. It was the end of June and she was busy with final exams, but, more importantly, she did not want to take sides.[177] She loved the dress her family had created, but, in common with most observers at the time, she had long associated the Hollywood cowgirl look with Stampede royalty and loved the fancy cowgirl outfits the ACT had provided. In spite of wearing native dress for the Elks' contest promotions, she had always assumed she would be dressed as a cowgirl if she were one of the winners, and that had not bothered her at all. She was an intelligent, sensible young woman who realized that no matter what outfit she wore as Stampede Queen, she would be dressed for a very specific role. She no more customarily dressed as an Indian princess than as a rodeo queen, but she was happy to assume those roles and dress accordingly when required, both to fulfill expectations and to make everyone happy. For example, upon request, she obligingly wore her new deerskin dress when she helped to lead the Waterton Lakes Jamboree parade the weekend before the Stampede.[178] She wore the dress on many occasions after that but was not willing to make it an issue during the Stampede. So she kept out of the controversy, prepared to abide by whatever was decided. But there is no doubt that she was happy when the compromise solution allowed her to please

MANY THANKS

. . . to all the kind friends of Calgary and from Alberta, British Columbia, and Saskatchewan, who were instrumental in electing m e Stampede Queen for 1954.
. . . And to the B.P.O.E. No. 4, may I express my sincere gratitude for selecting me as their candidate.
. . . You're choice has brought great honour, through me, to all my people.

PRINCESS WAPITI

(Honorary Princess of the Blood, Blackfoot, Peigan, Stoney and Sarcee Indian Tribes)

Queen Evelyn Eagle Speaker's thanks to supporters, *CH*, July 3, 1954.

both sides by making a final few appearances for the Elks Club as Princess Wapiti while doing the expected promotional work for the Stampede as Queen Evelyn.

Shortly after the dress controversy was resolved, Evelyn thanked her supporters by placing an ad in the *Albertan*:

Many thanks… to all the kind friends of Calgary and from Alberta, British Columbia and Saskatchewan who were instrumental in electing me Stampede Queen for 1954… And to the BPOE No. 4 may I express my sincere gratitude for selecting me as their candidate… Your choice has brought great honour, through me, to all my people.

—Princess Wapiti[179]

And then everyone relaxed and simply enjoyed the annual spectacle known as the Stampede. On July 6 the *Albertan* included in its front page coverage of the parade a close-up of a waving Evelyn in Indian dress on the Elks Club float. The accompanying article recapped for readers what many had seen for themselves the day before:

The parade took about two hours to pass and paraders and spectators alike suffered somewhat from the 90 degree heat of Calgary's hottest day of the year… The surreys came, the chuckwagons, gaily attired cowboys and cowgirls on cantering mounts. And then came the Elks band, bringing with it the moment many had been waiting for. Wearing her white native dress which had been the centre of so much discussion, smiling delightedly, waving cheerfully, holding herself proudly as the first member of her race to be chosen queen – Princess Wapiti, the reigning monarch of the 1954 Calgary Stampede. The crowd cheered, the crowd clapped, and the crowd was just as happy as she.[180]

Evelyn and her ladies-in-waiting went from the parade to the opening ceremonies of the afternoon rodeo and were by then all wearing the new cowgirl duds provided by the ACT. "Calgarians on Monday saw Princess Wapiti, Stampede Queen, in a cowboy outfit for the first time. The young Blood Indian received a tremendous ovation from the large first-day crowd as she appeared in front of the grandstand riding a palomino."[181] The grandstand crowd was equally charmed the next evening:

An estimated 20,000 spectators at the Stampede grandstand were hushed Tuesday night as a shy, 19-year-old Indian girl, Evelyn Eaglespeaker – Princess Wapiti of five southern Alberta Indian tribes – was crowned Queen of the 1954 Stampede by last year's queen, Edith Edge of Cochrane. The young Indian girl… is the first member of her race to be so honored.[182]

"'This is one of the proudest moments of my life,' beamed Princess Wapiti."[183]

Contrary to the ACT's stated intention, Evelyn did not wear her native dress for the official crowning, probably because the crown was a white cowboy hat. Officials, concerned about what to do with her feather headdress during the crowning, and worried that a cowboy hat might look inappropriate with her deerskin dress, quietly decided to dress her in Western wear for the event: her new gold and white queen's outfit. No one seemed to mind or even notice the change of plan; there were no comments or criticisms in the daily newspapers from journalists or members of the public.

The rest of Stampede week went by much as usual for Evelyn, Kay and Peggy, ably chaperoned throughout by two wives of ACT members, Bea Fowler and Myrna Pollard. Perhaps the media showed a little more interest than usual in the trio's activities, accurately sensing that readers enjoyed the novelty of having an Indian princess for Stampede Queen. The situation attracted nationwide attention and Evelyn was invited to attend the Miss Canada Pageant in Windsor, Ontario, as an honoured guest. After she returned, Princess Wapiti also attended a Kainai chieftainship ceremony on the Blood Reserve.

After the Stampede parade, Abe Schiller, back in Calgary to take in the big show for a second time, had announced that Evelyn would be the second Stampede Queen to enjoy an all-expenses paid trip to Las Vegas and Hollywood care of himself and Ken Leach. A three-day stop in Hollywood was to be followed by a week in Las Vegas, timed so that Evelyn could take part in the Helldorado Days parade. Schiller, ever the showman, told the press: "We want her to wear her Indian Princess dress in this one. It will be the first time we've had a real Indian Princess in the show."[184]

The long-anticipated trip finally occurred the following May, 1955. Just before takeoff, Evelyn and her chaperone, Ken Leach's daughter Kaye Marks, posed for reporters on the aircraft steps with ACT Queen Committee chairman Lyle Lebbert and Maurice Hartnett, manager of the Calgary Exhibition and Stampede. Both young women were dressed in Western outfits, and although Kaye told the press that Evelyn would be wearing "her authentic Indian dress during much of the southern visit,"[185] in actual fact she only wore her native dress on a few occasions because her ACT cowgirl garb was so much more comfortable and practical for touring.[186]

Evelyn had a marvellous two weeks in Hollywood and Las Vegas doing all that was promised and more. Just days after she returned to Calgary, it was announced she would be starting work as a stenographer in the City of Calgary's planning department. She was still a media darling a year after her win as Stampede Queen, with newspapers describing her as "Calgary's most glamorous ambassador" who would add "a touch of glamor and color to the city's headquarters," although they also were quick to point out that there had been no favouritism involved; she had won the job "on merit alone," having been, in terms of technical qualifications, "far and away above her competitors."[187]

The dignified and reserved young woman, who had made such a strong impression on the city during her year as queen, continued to interest Calgarians long after her reign was over, although media reports about her subsequent career and activities invariably focused on the romance of her transformation from Princess Wapiti to Stampede Queen. Evelyn herself was proud of her unique achievement, that she had overcome local stereotypes about Aboriginals to give the Stampede exactly what it always wanted in a regal representative: "a horsewoman from a Western tradition that was proud of her... heritage."[188]

CHAPTER 5 ★ 1955–1958

"This thing called glamour can get pretty exhausting"

During the booming 1950s the Stampede was determined to grow beyond its natural audience of "cattle country people"[189] and attract onto the grounds the growing number of urban Calgarians who enjoyed downtown attractions such as square dancing and Indian parades during Stampede week. By mid-decade, the Board had realized that one sure way of attaining this goal was to offer popular entertainment. The Stampede Corral had opened in 1950, the Big Four Building in 1959. Service clubs were authorized to raffle coveted prizes: new-model cars starting in 1952 and a "dream home" starting in 1958. Fireworks shows became a nightly occurrence. And, according to Stampede historian James Gray, the Board took to examining "what was pleasing the crowds in the biggest shows south of the line" and followed suit, "bringing in the best acts it could find as special crowd attracters."[190]

Queen Mary Ellen Jones receiving a white hat from Calgary mayor Don Mackay while ACT chaperone Elizabeth Cope and Stampede president Maurice Hartnett look on, 1955. (GA: PA-2807-2038B)

The buoyant decade between the mid-1950s and the mid-1960s "marked a significant change in the Stampede," according to historian Max Foran, "one in which the authenticity of the Canadian frontier experience disappeared and was replaced by Hollywood's 'Wild West.'" He believes that "the American western myth took hold, especially among the younger generations due to the enormous popularity of westerns on television." For the Stampede, cowboy performers were high-profile drawing cards who were "feted and honoured for being what they represented: a mythologized embodiment of a West that never existed in Canada or, according to American scholars, in the United States."[191] Leading American stars such as Duncan Renaldo and Leo Carrillo (The Cisco Kid and Pancho) received so much adulation in Calgary that they came back to the city over and over. They proved to be such popular goodwill ambassadors for the show that inviting other Hollywood stars was a logical next step. By the early 1960s, having celebrities such as Gene Barry (Bat Masterson), Jay Silverheels (Tonto), Bing

Crosby, Bob Hope, Phil Harris and Walt Disney as special guests and parade marshals had become a regular and expected part of the modern Stampede experience.[192]

By the mid-1950s, the ACT had found a winning formula for its Stampede Queen contest and simply applied it every year, only making minor changes occasionally to attract participants or boost ticket sales. The Stampede naturally was delighted to have the club manage this very successful annual event on its behalf, but the ACT did not continue sponsoring the contest year after year simply to oblige the Stampede. It took an enormous amount of work for the Queen Committee to pull off a successful contest, but it was such a good and dependable money-maker that club members agreed it was worth the effort. And the local community benefited greatly from this steady commitment.

In the advertising for the 1955 contest, the ACT announced that net proceeds from ticket sales over the first eight years of the contest had been donated to well over a dozen charitable and worthy causes, including Girls Town, the Sisters of Providence Crèche, the Council for Mentally Retarded Children, the Winnipeg Flood Relief Fund, the Community Chest, the Salvation Army, the Junior Red Cross Hospital, the Cerebral Palsy Association,

the Canadian Cancer Society, the Grace Hospital, the Colonel Belcher Hospital, the John Howard Society, the Victorian Order of Nurses, The Home in Youngstown, Lacombe Home, Woods Christian Home and the City of Calgary Fire Department.[193] In advertising the 1956 contest, the ACT drove the point home by revealing that in the nine-year history of the contest it had raised $52,000 for local charitable groups (about $450,000 today).[194]

In fact, the ripple effect of the ACT's fundraising effort was even greater than this list implied, because these groups were just the ones that benefited from the ACT's portion of the proceeds. The sponsoring organization behind every young lady who ever ran in the contest over the years had earned funds for its own projects too, because these groups were allowed to keep half of all that they raised on behalf of their candidates. Because of this, the contest reliably attracted fifteen to twenty entries each year from within the city as well as outlying districts.

The population of Alberta experienced a dramatic shift from rural to urban after the Second World War. Prior to that time, some 60 per cent of the population had been rural. At the beginning of the 1950s, the rural–urban split was fifty–fifty. By decade's end, 60 per cent of Albertans lived in urban areas. Even so, the Stampede Queen contest typically attracted more rural and small-town contestants than Calgary candidates during the 1950s. In 1955 only five of the nineteen girls entered in the contest were from Calgary. This did not really matter – it was up to sponsors to sell enough tickets to put their candidate over the top and a little rural–urban competition was always good for sales. But it was much harder to sell sufficient tickets in a small town or rural area, so city candidates often won. In fact, two of the five Calgary candidates in the 1955 contest were winners: runners-up Joan Johnston, sponsored by the Calgary Old Age Pensioners Association, and Elaine Kent, sponsored by the Oddfellows and Rebekahs of Calgary. But the Stampede Queen that year was Mary Ellen Jones, a farm girl from west of Ponoka who had been supported by the Junior Farmers' Union of Alberta. This group had the ticket selling advantage of being a province-wide youth organization. Mary Ellen's win was the fourth time the Junior FUA had fielded a successful candidate: they had sponsored Queen Eileen Beckner (1950) and Ladies-in-waiting Shirley Clark (1951) and Helen Smith (1952).

The headline announcing Mary Ellen's win said she was just "the second country girl in nine contests to win the title,"[195] but in fact she was the third, following Eileen Beckner from Carstairs and Edith Edge from the Cochrane area (1953). Even that was a

1955 Queen Mary Ellen Jones (centre) with Ladies-in-waiting Joan Johnston and Elaine Kent. (GA: NA-2864-18118B)

bit misleading. Mary Ellen was only the third queen to be living outside Calgary at the time of her win, but a number of others had been very recent imports to the city and had deep rural roots: Gloria Klaver (1948), Merle Stier (1949), and Evelyn Eagle Speaker (1954). But because they were living in Calgary at the time of their sponsorship by a local organization, the media considered them to be city candidates.

Mary Ellen was a Grade 11 high school student when she won as Stampede Queen and her youth generated a lot of media interest. "The thought of facing flash cameras, microphones and throngs of people would frighten most 17-year-olds, but Mary Ellen is ready to take it in her stride. 'I've had to make so many speeches in the past two months, I think I'm getting used to it,' she laughed." Reporters made much of the fact that the confident young horsewoman had spent all her life on the family farm, her hobby was raising and showing palomino horses, and she would be able to handle "any steed the Stampede officials provide for her Stampede travels." When they told her she would be travelling to Las Vegas and Hollywood representing the Stampede, they were amused when "a look of amazement crossed her face. 'It can't really be true, can it?' she questioned." [196]

Much to the delight of winning queens like Mary Ellen, who travelled south the following May, this trip was offered year after year throughout the 1950s. Although it was a prize with strings attached, very much a working holiday for the queens who won it, it was an exciting travel opportunity during a period when airline travel was still something of a novelty and the image of Hollywood and Las Vegas still had an aura of glamour. Not every queen was able to go – several declined for personal reasons – but those who did enjoyed the trip enormously and the possibility of winning it definitely helped to attract contestants. So too did the other travel prizes: the trip to Victoria for the queen and to Banff for the ladies-in-waiting (although in fact most winners took the cash equivalents, or "scholarships" as they were termed).

Since 1953 the ACT had been treating all contest participants to the fun and excitement of a full round of activities for the first two days of the Stampede. This was a significant reward for unsuccessful queen candidates, an acknowledgement that their ticket sales represented a valuable contribution to the club's charitable fundraising. Assuring the public (i.e., the parents) that the girls would be chaperoned at all times and covered for insurance purposes by the ACT,[197] their participation was built right into the queen's official Stampede week schedule, which by this time was becoming a demanding merry-go-round of public events:

Monday – the queen and her ladies-in-waiting will

ride in the parade in an open car while the former Stampede queens and western riders participate in the parade on horseback. The queen and the 19 contestants in the 1955 event will be at the grandstand Monday afternoon. In the evening they will attend "Holiday on Ice" at the Stampede Corral.

Tuesday morning they will be busy making public appearances and in the afternoon the entire group will be at the exhibition grounds to take in the midway rides and sideshows.

A dinner will be given for the contestants at the Palliser Hotel. Tuesday evening at the night grandstand show Mary Ellen will be crowned by the former Stampede queen. After watching the evening performance the girls will attend the ACT street dance downtown at 2nd Street West between 8th and 9th Avenues.

Wednesday the queen and her attendants will distribute cigarettes at the Colonel Belcher Hospital and toys at the Alberta Red Cross Crippled Children's Hospital. Wednesday evening the three girls will watch the chuck wagon races from a choice spot in the infield.

A visit to the city hall is slated for Thursday morning and the girls will sign the visitors' book at that time. In the afternoon they will visit the Stampede exhibits and that night they will be at the grandstand.

Friday, Children's Day at the Stampede, the queen and her attendants will appear on horseback to say hello to the thousands of youngsters who will turn out for the special occasion. In the afternoon, Friday, they will take part in a ceremony in which Abe Schiller of the Flamingo Hotel at Las Vegas will be made an Indian Chief. The Kinsmen street dance on the lot at 1st Street West and 6th Avenue will end their day.

Saturday they will appear at the special events program at the grandstand.

During the week they will be guests at luncheons sponsored by the Calgary Women's Press Club, the Calgary Lions' Club, the Calgary Active Club and by Mayor D.H. Mackay.[198]

Public interest in the clothing and appearance of the Stampede queen and her attendants was always very high. This was a period when the media considered the physical description of people, especially women, de rigueur, so readers learned that "in the statistics department" Mary Ellen Jones was "5 foot 6 inches tall, has light brown hair and very, very blue eyes,"[199] that 22-year-old Lady-in-waiting Joan Johnston was blonde and that 18-year-old Lady-in-waiting Elaine Kent had "large brown eyes with eyelashes that bat a mean average."[200]

Turning to the trio's apparel, the journalist noted that "the young queen certainly does justice to the cowboy uniforms which have been elaborately designed for Alberta's 50th Jubilee year," then described the outfits in detail:

Mary Ellen's dress uniform is of white English gabardine with gold trim. Her other uniform is a royal blue serge with white piping and she has two cowboy hats, one in white and one in gold. Her cowboy boots of white leather are trimmed in gold.

The ladies-in-waiting will wear dress uniforms of yellow gold serge and grey. Their boots are in green leather.

Mr. [Ed] Hendel, who has been designing the Stampede Queen costumes for the past five years, said, "These are the best yet." They have concealed zippers in the pockets for a snug fit and tassels of gold silk are all hand-made.

Mr. Cecil Sheinin, manager of Westmount Manufacturing, made special efforts to have the gabardine and serge flown from England in time for the Stampede.

The final touches completing the ensembles are hand-tooled leather belts with sterling silver buckles and colorful hand-painted ties.[201]

By the mid-1950s the cowgirl queen and her ladies-in-waiting had become firmly entrenched in the public mind as symbols of the Calgary Stampede, so it is not surprising that there was such interest by the public, and by the Stampede itself, in the image projected by the young women who won the job of representing the Greatest Outdoor Show on Earth. But aside from the fact that contestants had to be single young women between the ages of 17 and 24, and the stipulation that the winners were those who sold the most tickets, there were no rules governing the contest. There were no guarantees that the young women who won would be credible representatives of the Stampede, but by the mid-1950s there certainly were expectations. After chatting with Lyle Lebbert, Rosemary Wood of the *Calgary Herald* told her readers in 1955 that "good deportment, a passing appearance and personality, and the ability to appear in public in Western dress are the necessary qualifications for a Stampede queen to make her regal debut." Since there were no stated rules to this effect, the ACT had to depend on sponsoring organizations to field only those candidates who already fit the bill. Luckily that was usually what transpired.

During the 1956 contest, a reporter decided to see just what was involved in being a queen contest candidate, and concluding that it was "a gruelling grind," came away with a new respect for those who competed:

There were no complaints about late hours, constant smiles, endless pressing jobs, and lumpy pin curls every night…

This thing called glamor can get pretty exhausting… How does a Stampede queen contestant do a job all day and then step out at night looking like a sleek model pictured in a magazine?

She works at it. You can bet… the list of activities is shaking… Almost every night there is something to do. The girls attend meetings, sports events, dances, any gathering where there is an opportunity for an accompanying member of their sponsoring organization to introduce them. Naturally, they ask for support and, naturally, this requires a little speech-making.

Sometimes they sell tickets to aid the sponsor and sometimes they distribute pamphlets about themselves and their supporting organization. But mostly they look pretty, which they are, and act charming, which they are too…

Despite the gruelling grind and the shortened hours of beauty sleep, the queen candidates are learning something. In meeting new people of all ages, they must project their thoughts beyond themselves. They can't be too disturbed about the little things, and [even though]… they've smiled so much their faces ache, they must continue to sparkle stoically. Youth is wonderful. The fun they have, and the new excitement in their lives, is repaid by the help they give their supporting organization…

The buildup is exciting, the climax is next door to nerve wracking, and it takes good sportsmanship to enter and stick with the competition.[202]

Fourteen young women competed in the 1956 contest and the winner was the Calgary Booster Club's candidate, Shirley Willock. At 23, Shirley was a little older than some of the previous winners had been, but the future model and actress was a natural with reporters, who told readers that she was "mighty easy on the eyes."[203] The infectiously bubbly Boosterette and Quarterbackette posed for a cheesecake-style photo in her short-skirted uniform, accompanied by the following information: "The queen has blue-green eyes and dark brown hair, is five foot five inches tall, and distributes 118 pounds over 35–24–36 measurements, reading down."[204] It was probably a coincidence, but 1956 was the first year that one of the queen's official outfits included a skirt instead of pants.

"For pete's sake!" Shirley was quoted as saying

Queen Shirley Willock, 1956. (GA: NA-2864-18119A)

when she learned she had won the contest and a trip to Las Vegas and Hollywood.[205] The Edmonton Cerebral Palsy Association had the satisfaction of producing the contest's first winning candidate from Edmonton, 19-year-old Kay Marshall. Shirley's second attendant, 18-year-old Carolyn Schoeppe, was a Calgarian who had been sponsored by the Bow Valley Lodges Foundation.[206] The three young women enjoyed their week at the Palliser Hotel at ACT expense with chaperone Mabel Sherman, and they did all the usual things expected of them during a busy Stampede week. In addition to winning $300 and some nice prizes such as luggage and jewellery, Shirley received a few modelling lessons, mainly instructions on how to walk and smile. There was no riding requirement, so the ladies rode on the back of a convertible in the parade and were driven up to the grandstand stage every night in a chuckwagon.

Shirley was very nervous about speaking before a crowd of approximately 20,000 each night before the grandstand show, and rejected the stiff, formal speech supplied by the ACT in favour of one that sounded more natural because she had written most of it herself. She later remembered feeling "just petri-fied" before making the first speech but it became easier and easier as the week went on and by the

1956 Queen Shirley Willock (centre) with Ladies-in-waiting Kay Marshall and Carolyn Schoeppe. (GA: PA-3954-4)

end she had gained so much confidence that she was sorry the Stampede was over.[207]

As fun as the Stampede had been, Shirley later recalled the trip south as the highlight of her year-long reign. Accompanied by chaperone Kaye Marks, she spent the first week in Las Vegas and ended the trip with four days in Hollywood. She was a devoted Hollywood movie fan, so the Las Vegas portion of the trip felt more like work to her. She spent much of that week representing Calgary and the Stampede at Helldorado Days. Even her arrival was framed as a publicity stunt: when it was discovered she was not yet sporting a Helldorado Days button, she was "arrested," whisked off to "jail" by two police officers and "bailed out" by Abe Schiller. Although Shirley could ride, having grown up visiting family members on farms and ranches, she was by no means a horsewoman and was "a nervous wreck" wondering how she would acquit herself riding a strange horse in the Helldorado Days parade, which was being broadcast coast to coast on television in the United States. Nerves may have been the culprit when her face started to swell and she broke out in a rash just an hour or so before the parade was scheduled to start. She was rushed back to the hotel, "stuffed full of pills," and, after an hour's rest, rejoined the parade wearing sunglasses. "I don't think anybody noticed," she later recalled. "Everyone wore dark glasses."[208] Shirley rode in a group with Miss Helldorado, Miss Rodeo America and Abe Schiller, and there were no incidents, although her horse shied every time it heard the big loud drum in the marching band following closely behind.

Shirley spent the rest of the week riding in the Helldorado Days Grand Entry each day with Miss Rodeo America, and since she was over 21, being taken to see floor shows at the local clubs and casinos. Never having travelled outside of Alberta, she was overwhelmed by the glamour and luxury she saw around her and by meeting so many "beautiful people," including entertainer Liberace. Even the plane ride from Las Vegas to Hollywood was eye-popping: she found herself seated in the row behind well-known movie actors Debbie Reynolds and Eddie Fisher. This continued in Hollywood with visits to the sets of *Queen for a Day* and *Teacher's Pet*, where she had lunch with stars Doris Day and Clark Gable and was introduced to other famous names such as Gig Young and Anthony Quinn. The star-struck young woman enjoyed these experiences so much that it did not feel like she was performing official duties of a promotional nature even though she was required to wear her Stampede Queen outfit to each and every one. Ken Leach had important connections in Hollywood, so the media provided excellent coverage, even noting that she would be "quartering with movie notable Judy Garland" when it was discovered they were registered at the same hotel in Las Vegas.[209]

While Shirley was enjoying her prize trip, back in Calgary the 1957 Stampede Queen contest was underway. After the results were announced, there was a little controversy when it was learned that the winner, 18-year-old Marquitta Elton, had been the personal secretary to Calgary mayor Don Mackay during his unsuccessful quest for the Calgary South riding during a federal election. The media questioned Marquitta's win but let it go when chairman Harold Lee and his Queen Committee "declined to give the number of votes polled by the winning queen, but hinted that it was a comfortable margin to win by." In this era of ticket sales, it was considered a plus to field a candidate from a wealthy family or one associated with a well-known name. As a matter of interest, the Mount Pleasant Community's candidate in the 1957 contest was Heather MacEwan, daughter of Grant MacEwan, a Calgary alderman who later became mayor and then Alberta Lieutenant Governor.

In any case, the Calgary Junior Chamber of Commerce could prove that it had worked hard on behalf of the "striking blue-eyed blonde, with all the

1957 Queen Marquitta Elton with 1956 Queen Shirley Willock. (GA: NA-2864-18120B)

vital statistics apparently in order." Another potential sore point that was raised at the time – Marquitta's lack of horsemanship – also went nowhere as reporters focused on her five years of calling square dances during Stampede week and gave her credit for making a special point of learning to ride especially for the Stampede and falling off a few times in the process. One reporter even opined, "Although the winner of the annual queen competition is chosen on the basis of the number of tickets sold on her behalf, Miss Elton might have won anyway had the judges also taken into consideration beauty, personality, poise, talent and brains."[210] This media focus on the new queen's personal appearance continued when she was featured a week later as the *Albertan*'s July Calendar Girl. Photographer Ron Meigh posed her sitting on a rail fence and holding onto a horse's reins. Wearing a neckerchief, cowboy hat and boots, she looked like a typical rodeo queen except for one discordant note: her very short shorts.[211]

After their win was announced on June 25, Queen Marquitta and her Ladies-in-waiting, Karen Downey and Kay Larsen, were measured for two outfits each, to be crafted by the design manager at Westmount Manufacturing, Ed Hendel. Now in his sixth year of creating royal outfits, Hendel told *Herald* reporter Joy Van Wagner that having only two weeks in which to produce the garments was a challenge, and indeed the ladies received their clothing just hours before they registered at the Palliser Hotel for Stampede week. For the benefit of readers, Hendel described the outfits in detail, estimating the total value to be between $300 and $400 (about $2,500 to $3,300 today):

Queen Marquitta Elton has a formal outfit of white English gabardine trimmed with blue and red fringe, and a semi-formal costume featuring a frontier skirt and matching shirt of grey melange.

Ladies in Waiting Kay Larsen and Karen Downey have formal outfits of navy blue sheen gabardine trimmed with white fringe, and semi-formal outfits of gambler stripes and shirts with white reversed yokes. All feature the latest in diamond-shaped pearl snap buttons.[212]

Instead of riding on the back of a convertible in the Stampede parade, the three young women rode on a large float, a "mammoth bronze Indian head capped by brilliant white feathers" that captured first prize in the parade's commercial float section for the Calgary Brewing and Malting Company.[213] Unusually, the ladies were joined on the float by the contest's twelve unsuccessful candidates for queen, who then joined the winning trio for first two days of the Stampede

1957 Queen Marquitta Elton (centre) with Ladies-in-waiting Karen Downey (far left) and Kay Larsen (far right). (CSA)

at ACT expense.[214] As had been the case with Queen Shirley in 1956, Marquitta and her ladies were not required to ride during Stampede week but instead were conveyed to the grandstand stage each night in a chuckwagon.[215]

After the 1957 contest, the ACT presented the Salvation Army with a cheque for $1,300 (about $11,000 today) to help furnish a two-bed ward in the new wing of the Grace Maternity Hospital.[216] This was just one of several organizations to benefit from the club's generosity that year, and a fairly typical amount to be donated, but the 1958 contest saw a huge increase in donations. A total of $12,113 (about $99,000 today) was given out that year, a whopping $10,293 ($84,000 today) to the Alberta Crippled Children's Hospital alone to equip a new operating room. Smaller amounts were given to five other worthy organizations: $500 each to the Calgary Community Chest and the Canadian National Institute for the Blind (each gift worth about $4,000 today); $200 each to the Western Canada Epilepsy League and the Alberta Rehabilitation Society for the Handicapped (about $1,600 each today); and $120 the Shriners' Crippled Children's Hospital in Winnipeg (close to $1,000 today).[217] This amazing increase in donations was entirely due to two unforeseen circumstances: an unexpected increase in the number of contestants, and, more importantly, the unique circumstances surrounding the winning candidate.

When the ACT placed their regular contest announcement in the May 17, 1958, edition of the *Calgary Herald*, there were so many candidates pictured that there was no room to identify sponsoring organizations. Thirty-three young women were vying for the crown that year, more than double the number in most previous contests. There is no identifiable reason why competition was so keen in 1958; perhaps contest chairman Les Gainor and his committee simply outdid themselves in talking organizations into participating. But the really interesting development that year was the participation of a non-Caucasian candidate for just the third time in the history of the contest. Mindful of the Elks' 1954 success in fielding atypical candidate Evelyn Eagle Speaker, in 1955 the Taber Lions Club had sponsored a young Japanese-Canadian woman, Fumi Setoguchi. Her run at the crown was unsuccessful, but the novelty of sponsoring an ethnic candidate appealed to the Calgary Fire Department's Toy Campaign when they decided to enter the contest in 1958. With Firehall No. 1 located directly across from Calgary's Chinatown, a Chinese candidate seemed the obvious choice.

The firemen approached the Calgary Chinese Council, which suggested Jennie Chow as a suitable contestant. Twenty-two-year-old Jennie was a second generation Chinese-Canadian whose parents had come to Calgary from China in 1933. She had been born in Calgary but had lived with her family in San Francisco and Vancouver before returning to Calgary for the bulk of her schooling. According to media reports, she "never spoke a word of English until she started school," but by the time she entered the contest the "pretty and disarmingly friendly" secretary for a local oil company was described as being "a typical young Canadian."[218]

After Jennie was declared Stampede Queen, a sympathetic reporter said she had "won the hard way, taking part in car washes, a Firemen's Ball, the Fire Chiefs' convention and countless public appearances to sell tickets."[219] That no doubt was true – the firemen and Jennie herself worked very hard on her campaign – but the comment likely was in response to a slight feeling of resentment amongst other participants that Jennie's campaign had benefited from the support of a very large single-interest group, namely the Chinese community. In addition to Calgary, ticket books were sold on her behalf in Vancouver, San Francisco, Montreal, even Aklavik, NWT. There was no criticism from the ACT on that account – Jennie's huge ticket sales not only guaranteed her win but also provided an enormous boost to the Calgary Fire Department's Toy Campaign and enabled the ACT to make that year's very generous donations to the Red Cross Crippled Children's Hospital and other organizations. But Jennie may have felt the need to mollify critics by donating her $300 scholarship winnings to a local charity.[220]

The media across Canada picked up on the novelty of a Chinese-Canadian Stampede Queen. Newspapers all across the Prairies and even as far away as Montreal featured a photograph of Jennie in Western wear posed beside a horse with an accompanying article detailing her win.[221] Interestingly, no question was raised about the suitability of a Chinese-Canadian girl being required to wear cowgirl clothing for her reign as Stampede Queen. Unlike with Evelyn Eagle Speaker's win, there was no suggestion that Jennie might be more appropriately attired in a traditional Chinese costume.

Jennie was a vivacious young woman who charmed the media with her warm personality and engaging public speaking ability. She enjoyed being Stampede Queen and seemed well-suited for the role, fulfilling all duties conscientiously even after Stampede was done, although she declined the trip to Hollywood and Las Vegas. The only problem, and unfortunately it turned out to be a big one, was that she was not a horsewoman. She was athletic, having

Queen Jennie Chow, 1958. (CSA)

Top 1958 Queen Jennie Chow with Ladies-in-waiting Isabelle Hamilton and Beverly Haeh. (GA: NA-2864-18122B)

Left Queen Jennie Chow, 1958. (GA: NA-2864-18122A)

dabbled in other recreational sports – swimming, golfing and skiing – but had not had much experience riding a horse, as rural pursuits and horseback riding were not promoted much in the urban Chinese community. When she won as queen, she admitted that, in spite of growing up in Stampede-obsessed Calgary, she had never actually attended the rodeo.[222]

Although riding was not a requirement at the time for entering and winning the Stampede Queen contest, Jennie felt the pressure of representing a horse-based show, particularly when her qualifications as a rider were overstated in national media reports. Rather rashly, she assured ACT and Stampede officials that simply by brushing up on her skills, she would be ready to ride during Stampede week.[223] Unfortunately, she was kept far too busy in the lead-up to the Stampede to focus on riding lessons, but, not wanting to let everyone down, she did not reveal her lack of confidence. When she fell during her first Grand Entry before the afternoon rodeo, the idea of having her ride during Stampede week was dropped.[224] Many previous royals, being acknowledged non-riders or novices, had gotten through Stampede week successfully without riding and without controversy. But, unluckily for Jennie, the two runners-up that year, Ladies-in-waiting Beverly Haeh from High River and Isabella Hamilton from Okotoks, were countrywomen and excellent riders, so the contrast between their performance and hers was all the greater. Ultimately this served to coalesce official opinion that proven riding ability should be made an absolute requirement for all future candidates who wished to serve as Stampede royalty.

CHAPTER 6 ★ 1959–1963

"No girl can become Queen unless She's a proficient horsewoman"

Jennie Chow had been an excellent Stampede Queen in every way but one: her lack of riding ability.[225] Unfortunately she was the third queen in a row whose riding skills were questionable; the last true horsewoman to be queen had been Mary Ellen Jones in 1955. Lack of skill in that area may have seemed like a minor objection; after all, even if the queen and her ladies-in-waiting were competent horsewomen, paradegoers seemed to prefer seeing royalty on a highly visible float (although substituting a convertible had resulted in criticism that the queen was not being presenting in a "Western style").[226] Aside from the parade, a large part of the queen's job involved non-riding duties such as making public appearances at street dances, pancake breakfasts, charitable events and the like. However, the Stampede was first and foremost a horse-based Western show, and the tradition was for rodeo queens to be competent

Queen Julie Akkerman after winning her title at the Calgary International Horse Show, 1959. (GA: NA-2864-18124A)

horsewomen who could ride in other fairs' parades and wow rodeo crowds by racing into the infield during the Grand Entry. No matter how excellently they performed every other aspect of their job, it was a potential embarrassment for the show to have non-riding royalty as its representatives.

And so, for the 1959 contest, the Stampede Board insisted that the ACT add a rule requiring all candidates to prove their riding ability before being declared winners. The early months of the contest would look the same as usual, with sponsoring organizations selling tickets on behalf of their candidates, but before announcing a winner and two runners-up, the top candidates would be assessed on their riding ability by judges watching them perform standard riding exercises. Under the new rules, an official told reporters, "Even if she has 10,000,000 votes… no girl can now become queen unless she's a proficient horsewoman."[227] For good measure, since they were introducing new requirements anyway, the minimum age for candidates was raised to 18, and officials announced that contestants would be assessed for their suitability as Stampede ambassadors by judges looking for desirable qualities such as personality, deportment, appearance, public speaking and "the ability to appear in public 'to advantage' in costumes suitable to Stampede events."[228] Thus, in one fell swoop, the whole orientation of the Stampede Queen contest changed from its original concept and first decade as a competition based on the popularity of contestants, as shown by their volume of ticket sales, to one that more closely resembled its future as a competition based solely on judging candidates for proven ability.

Undeterred by the new rules, eighteen candidates for the 1959 contest were announced at the end of March: nine from Calgary and the rest from Banff, Springbank, Innisfail, Sundre, Red Deer, Elk Point, High River, Oyen and Forest Lawn. To generate a little excitement just as the ticket sales portion of the contest was ending, nine of the candidates were paraded through Calgary streets on Saturday, May 18, perched on the back of convertibles driven by members of the Calgary Sports Car Club.[229] The motorcade, billed as "the first time the contest has begun with one official coordinated event," also took in opening ceremonies at several new Dairy Queens.[230]

Two days later, the votes were counted and the ACT announced the top seven ticket sellers, those who would be judged during phase two of the competition. A reporter from the *Calgary Herald* attended the final day of judging, on June 24, and filed this report:

Tension mounted steadily at Fort Calgary House Wednesday evening as the clock ticked towards 10 p.m. and some fifty persons anxiously awaited the judges' final decision...

The judges took about one-half hour to make their decision ... [after an] ... 8-hour judging session running throughout the afternoon and evening.

First performances began at 2 in the afternoon when the girls each gave two demonstrations of their ability as horsewomen at the Stampede Grounds after drawing lots for their respective mounts.

The other two judging items – attractiveness and personality – were judged at Fort Calgary House prior to the announcement with a buffet dinner sponsored by the Associated Canadian Travellers and attended by members of the Exhibition board, the press and parents of the seven contestants.

At the reception which preceded the dinner, the girls mingled with guests, after which each gave a short speech telling of hobbies, interests, a brief history of childhood.

Judges on this occasion were Roy Chown, Mrs.

Merle Stier and Carl Nickle. Auditor of all the judges' reports was Vic Price, who conducted, along with the judges, a private interview with contestants following their speeches.[231]

The winning Queen was Julie Akkerman, 21-year-old daughter of the mayor of Forest Lawn, a separate village on the eastern outskirts of Calgary at the time. Sponsored by the Canadian Citizenship Council, Julie was judged to have been "by far the best horsewoman of the contestants. Besides that, she's a sweet, talented girl."[232] She was a barrel racer, a charter member of the Canadian Girls Barrel Racing Association and runner-up in the Miss Rodeo Canada contest held in Calgary later that same year.[233] Starting a new tradition, 1958 Queen Jennie Chow crowned the 1959 Queen at the Stampede Arena right after the contest results were announced and then again before the grandstand show on July 7.

Julie's two Ladies-in-waiting were 18-year-old Doreen Wynne, sponsored by the Canadian Picture Pioneers, and 22-year-old Margaret Powell, sponsored by the Hillhurst-Sunnyside Community Association. As usual, the queen was given the choice of $300 or a ten-day trip to Victoria and each of her attendants had the choice of $100 or a seven-day trip to Banff.

Over the next few years it was a little disappointing for unsuccessful contestants who had big ticket sales, knowing that they might have been winners had the new rules not been introduced. If ticket sales had been the sole requirement for winning in 1959, Margaret Powell certainly would have been Queen instead of second Lady-in-waiting because she sold far and away the most tickets that year. A smiling picture of her in uniform accompanied a little notice in the Hillhurst-Sunnyside Community newsletter:

Let's help make this a "winning" smile! Let's pitch in and help this stunning young lady, Miss Margaret Powell, take top honours in the Calgary Stampede Queen contest. Marg is a stewardess with T.C.A. and is being sponsored by the Hillhurst-Sunnyside Community Association. Naturally, all fliers will want to give her a hand in capturing the title and prizes. Tickets are on sale in the office, and any member who would like to take a few to sell can get them from Sylvia.[234]

Regular customers on Trans-Canada Air Lines' Calgary–Edmonton commuter run bought tickets every time they flew with Marg that spring.[235] A similar thing happened in the 1961 contest when first Lady-in-waiting Lynn Puckett's employer,

British American Oil sold "vast numbers" of tickets for her through their BA service stations all across Canada.[236] Both young women became ladies-in-waiting instead of queen simply because, by the time they competed, ticket sales had been declared of secondary importance to horsemanship.

However, Margaret Powell's super ticket sales did earn her a place among the top seven finalists in 1959. During the ticket campaign, she had received a few riding lessons from a Mountie who was a TCA customer but her skills were too newly acquired to allow her to win. So she swallowed her disappointment and worked with first Lady-in-waiting Doreen to support Queen Julie throughout Stampede week. Having chosen its winners at least partly on the basis of horsemanship, the ACT decided to feature the queen and her attendants riding horses in the Stampede parade for the first time since Queen Edith Edge had ridden in the 1953 parade. Waving their hats, they also were introduced from their horses each night in front of the grandstand crowd.

As usual, the threesome lived at the Palliser Hotel with their chaperone for the week and did everything

1959 Queen Julie Akkerman (centre) with Ladies-in-waiting Margaret Powell and Doreen Wynne. (GA: NA-2864-18124B)

together during the Stampede, including being presented to Queen Elizabeth II at a barbecue hosted by Mr. Justice Marshall M. Porter and his wife, Lillian. In honour of this special occasion, the girls had been requested to don their Western skirts instead of the usual pants. Strolling about the grounds, the Queen and Prince Philip had stopped to talk with the trio, the Prince reputedly saying to Margaret, "You are very beautiful," and asking Julie, "What duties does the Stampede Queen have to perform?"[237]

Margaret later recalled that, what with being treated equally by everyone all week and receiving an equal share of the attention, all three girls came out of the experience feeling as if they had been Queen. In an unusual move, Abe Schiller and Ken Leach even invited all three to travel as a group to Las Vegas and Hollywood the following spring. The young ladies were photographed with Schiller during the Stampede when the trip was announced, but in the end not one of them was able to take the time to travel south. By then, Margaret's thoughts were far from the Stampede, but she credited her experience as a Stampede royal with helping her to win the Miss Calgary and Miss Canada contests the very next year.

From 1959 on, the Stampede always had horse-riding royalty, but it took another few years to work out how best to manage the contest so that the right candidates for the job of ambassador emerged victorious. The ACT's contest had been successful as a fundraiser, since it was based on ticket sales, but that structure produced a very random selection of candidates. It was only by chance that winners had the right combination of personality, poise and public speaking ability to handle what was fast becoming an important public-relations job on behalf of the Stampede. With the introduction of new rules in 1959, the ACT tried to select for those qualities, but after the fact and only from among those candidates whose sponsors had been most successful in selling tickets on their behalf, a limited field to be sure. The only solution was to drop ticket sales and open the contest to any young woman who considered herself capable of taking on the job. But with fundraising having been the only goal behind the ACT's long sponsorship of the contest, the club understandably was reluctant to let ticket sales go.

Accordingly, the 1960 contest was run along the same lines as in 1959, with ticket sales followed by judging of the top half-dozen candidates. Continuing the previous year's successful partnership, the fourteen candidates for queen were introduced to the public during an hour-long "Pageant of Queens" at the Southern Alberta Jubilee Auditorium on May 28, the final night of the third annual Calgary Sports Car Show. Jack Gow, the 1960 Queen Committee chairman, was MC for the event, and Merv (Red) Dutton, chairman of the Calgary Exhibition and Stampede Board, spoke on behalf of the Stampede.[238] In another publicity gambit, the candidates were featured during an all-day event on June 11 when ACT members performed all announcing and advertising duties over twenty-four hours at Calgary radio station CFCN.[239]

For the first time since Evelyn Eagle Speaker had competed in 1954, a native woman entered the queen contest: Joan Big Throat from the Blood [Kainai] Reserve at Standoff, south of Fort Macleod, who was sponsored by the Foothills Riding Club. The next year, Violet Runner was sponsored by the Sarcee [Tsuu T'ina] Reserve on the southwestern edge of Calgary. Both of these young women were accomplished riders but without a brilliant marketing scheme such as that devised for Evelyn by the Elks, their ticket sales were insufficient to put them into the top six for the riding portion of the contest, so neither of them successfully competed for the crown.[240]

After ticket sales had identified six finalists, judging at the Stampede grounds on June 29, 1960, proceeded along the same lines as for the previous year: six hours of competition where candidates were judged on their riding and such intangibles as

Queen Margot Turney with Silver, mascot of the Calgary Stampeders football team, 1960. (GA: PA-2807-3874)

personality, intelligence, poise and appearance. The winning queen, 21-year-old Margot Turney, had been sponsored by the Calgary Ski Club, which her stockbroker father, Alan H. Turney, had helped to form in 1933.[241] A horse-loving city girl whose family was part of the wealthy business elite in booming postwar Calgary, Margot had attended private schools in Canada and finishing school in England. She had come out at debutante balls in Calgary in 1955 and London in 1956, where she was presented to Queen Elizabeth II.[242] Appropriately, just before the 1960 queen contest commenced, she played the lead in a play called *The Reluctant Debutante*, presented at the Jubilee Auditorium by the Calgary Players.[243] But she was equally well known in Calgary as a trophy winning horsewoman and her ticket sales were supported by her two riding clubs, the Pony Club and the Alberta Light Horse Association, as well as the Junior League of Calgary.

An accomplished and confident young woman, Margot easily "swept all three sections of the judging – horsemanship, personality and public speaking."[244] She was delighted with her win. "I was born here, and for a Calgary-born girl this is the ultimate," she said upon receiving her white hat crown from 1959 Lady-in-waiting Margaret Powell (Queen Julie Akkerman having been unable to attend the 1960

1960 Queen Margot Turney (centre) with Ladies-in-waiting Gail Leonard and Judy Taylor. (GA: NA-2864-18127E)

judging and crowning ceremony).[245] Runners-up in the contest were 18-year-old Judy Taylor, sponsored by the Scarboro Community League, and 19-year-old Gail Leonard, sponsored by the Elks Lodge No. 1.

Although the media naturally assumed that the 1960 Stampede Queen would be offered a trip to Las Vegas and Hollywood, 1959 turned out to be the last time that the trip was offered. For various reasons, no winner had taken the trip since Queen Shirley Willock in 1956. Abe Schiller continued to make his annual visits to the Stampede for another half-dozen years, but the seeming lack of interest in the prize by queens during the late 1950s apparently led to the quiet retraction of Schiller's 1953 promise that all future queens would visit Las Vegas. Luckily, Margot had travelled overseas many times so was not disappointed.

In addition to the usual gifts, the 1960 winners received white fringed leather jackets. Margot's was decorated with glitter to indicate her status as queen. She rode into the infield each evening on a beautiful grey parade horse loaned especially for her use during Stampede week. Each night, she made a short speech before the grandstand show. The first few times, she felt very nervous facing such a huge crowd and was happy for the support of one of the show's special guests, Bing Crosby,* who whispered encouragingly each time it was her turn to go up, "C'mon, Margot."[246]

Stampede attendance had climbed steadily during the booming 1950s, so organizers were confident it would ring in the new decade by topping 600,000 in 1960. Instead it dropped 60,000 from the year before to 527,000, a level not seen since the mid-1950s. It would be another six years before the 600,000 threshold was broken, in 1966. The reason for the drop in 1960 was that the Stampede doubled its admission prices that year, from the long-standing 25 cents for adults to 50 cents (about $4 today). Since "all other western fairs had long since gone to that figure and the state fairs below the border were up to one dollar in some places," the increase did not seem unreasonable to Stampede officials but locals were unhappy and many stayed away for the next several years.[247]

To counter value-for-money criticism, the Stampede began providing free entertainment on the grounds – bands, animal acts and the like – to supplement the sideshows and other offerings of the midway.[248] Some were critical of this move, which they feared would hasten the Stampede's alteration from something authentically based on the Canadian frontier experience into a Wild West movie version of history that bore little relation to historical fact.[249] Many felt that the focus on entertainment and reliance on the drawing power of stars such as Bing Crosby, Bob Hope and Bobby Curtola was accelerating the Hollywoodization of the show. But in 1960 the new offerings were received so well that free daily outdoor shows became a regular feature of the Stampede.[250] Even the daily visits of the Stampede Queen and her Ladies-in-waiting to the Exhibition grounds were deemed to have entertainment value and the young ladies were mobbed by youthful autograph hunters every time they appeared.

However, most of the trio's promotional time was spent off-park during Stampede week, attending pancake breakfasts and other attractions downtown in the morning, visiting hospitals, schools and seniors' residences in the afternoon, and appearing at dinners and other special events hosted by local clubs and organizations in the evening. Although the role of Stampede royalty gradually was expanding, the focus still was very much on the queen. Ladies-in-waiting tended to end their reign with the end of Stampede but invitations for the queen often continued long after that. Naturally, the ACT expected the ladies to

*Crosby had been parade marshal in 1959 and enjoyed the experience so much that he returned to the Stampede as a special guest in 1960.

attend several club functions over the year, to help bestow donations or publicize the upcoming contest, but often the queen was invited on her own to attend local rodeos, ride in parades, open exhibitions or be an attraction at a convention or other special event. It was a feather in her cap to have won the contest, but increasingly the queen found she had to put in extra time for her higher status and the extra $200 in prize money. Generally, it was just for a few extra days per month, but representing the Stampede had become a volunteer job that now required a year-long commitment.

With the growing popularity of the queen and her ladies as a symbol of the Stampede, the City of Calgary began to make more use of the trio's public-relations potential. It became the custom for winning trios to visit City Hall during Stampede week to sign the guest book and receive small gifts as a token of appreciation, usually engraved silver bracelets and/or sterling silver makeup compacts. The City started including the queen in delegations of municipal and chamber of commerce representatives to events in other cities. An early example was when 1950 Stampede Queen Eileen Beckner represented Calgary at the grand opening of the Ridpath Hotel in Spokane, Washington, in April 1952. But the practice of using the queen as a city figurehead accelerated

during the 1960s. As Margot Turney later recalled, winners quickly discovered that "[w]hen the excitement of Stampede finally died down, the Queen still had official duties and was part of the civic life of the city for the year."[251]

In May 1960, reigning 1959 Queen Julie Akkerman christened a West Coast Airlines prop-jet with the name "U.S.–Canada Friendship" in ceremonies at the Calgary airport before the plane took its inaugural flight from Calgary to Spokane. Passengers included newly elected Calgary mayor Harry Hays and the president of the Calgary Chamber of Commerce, Charles Kennedy.[252] Similarly, Queen Margot Turney was present at the Calgary airport in January 1961 when a crowd of 15,000 watched as Trans-Canada Air Lines' massive, four-engined DC-8 jetliner touched down with passengers from Toronto, including that city's mayor, Nathan Phillips. According to news reports the event "usher[ed] in for Calgary the commercial jet age."[253]

Certainly, the most exciting public-relations event Queen Margot attended on behalf of the city and the Stampede was the 1960 Grey Cup football game, played in Vancouver. Although the Stampeders had not made the finals, the Calgary Grey Cup Committee sent a promotional team to participate in the festivities, and for the first time the team included the Stampede Queen. The city's Grey Cup parade entry featured three chuckwagons and "a noisy delegation from Calgary mounted on matching black horses."[254] Margot rode alongside Charles Kennedy and Harry Hays. Successor to the ebullient Don Mackay, mayor Hays had been well known as a city booster and Stampede supporter ever since 1952 when he had introduced the iconic and wildly popular annual pre-Stampede shindig known as the Hays Breakfast. The following spring, Margot represented Calgary and the Stampede at the Spokane Lilac Festival, where one of her duties was to decorate the derby winner.

Jack Gow returned as queen contest chairman in 1961. It was a big job, as it was becoming harder to talk organizations into sponsoring candidates. Ticket selling was hard work and it was discouraging for organizations to realize that no matter how hard they worked on behalf of a candidate, she could win only if she outperformed all other contestants in the subsequent riding and other tests.

As well, the financial impetus for sponsoring organizations to become involved in the contest was becoming less pressing during the 1960s. The ACT still shared the proceeds of ticket sales with sponsors fifty-fifty, but other sources of funding for community groups and charitable organizations were becoming available. The Federation of Calgary Communities, officially incorporated in 1961, had become very active coordinating the social and financial needs of community associations. The Calgary Community Chest, a body first active in the early twenties, had been resurrected at the start of the Second World War to coordinate fundraising for member social agencies. By 1962 it had grown to become the United Fund and was renamed the United Way in 1973. With these big organizations sourcing and distributing grant money, there was far less need for community and charitable groups to undertake big fundraising initiatives. In the words of ACT Queen Committee member Peter Degenstein, "Suddenly communities were able to get some money on their own and they weren't that interested in sponsoring queen candidates."[255]

The ACT was well aware of the decline in participation – they could see it in the reduced number of contestants (only eleven in 1961) and in declining fundraising totals. Advertising for the 1961 contest claimed that the ACT had helped to raise $175,000 for charitable organizations over fifteen years of running the contest (well over $1-million today).[256] The club had presented "a very worthy $3,500" (about $28,000 today) to the Canadian Mental Health Association,[257] but it was a far cry from donation levels during the mid- and late 1950s. At the conclusion of the 1961 contest, Jack Gow reported with relief, "The Stampede Queen contest came to a satisfactory conclusion and we found, despite certain apprehension, that we ended up on the black pages of the ledger."[258]

The winning Queen in 1961 was 22-year-old Marie Sharpe, described in the press as "one of the most ardent horsewomen ever to hold the title."[259] Another city girl, but from a distinctly more modest background than her predecessor Margot Turney, Marie had learned to ride "by hanging around the riding academy on 14th St. at the bottom of Nose Hill," earning riding time in exchange for doing odd jobs. As a teen, she had bought herself a horse by becoming the neighbourhood babysitter, and as a result her community of West Hillhurst got behind her candidacy even though her official sponsor was the Calgary and District Soccer Association. One of her favourite campaign memories was rounding up high school girlfriends for a big wiener roast held in honour of a soccer club visiting from England.[260]

In addition to her outfits, Stampede week expenses and a $300 bursary, Queen Marie won a decorated "Queen of Hearts" saddle in white and turquoise leather. Crafted by Eamor's Saddlery of High River, it had been donated by Simpsons-Sears. Not as exciting as the Las Vegas–Hollywood trip

that it somehow replaced, it was nevertheless a very desirable and valuable gift, reputedly worth $1,000 ($8,000 today).[261] Saddles became a standard prize for the queen from then on, even after Simpsons-Sears discontinued its involvement in the mid-1980s, but it was many years before saddles were gifted to other members of the winning trio as well. Unlike the Vegas trip, which usually had occurred long after Stampede and was acknowledged to be something of a double-edged gift in that it was a working holiday, the saddle was an immediate and ever-present reminder of the queen's superior status. It must have gone a long way toward recompensing the winner for the extra time she spent over the year performing queenly duties, but it also served to make the distinction between the queen and her attendants more explicit. Ladies–in–waiting in 1961 were 20-year-old Lynn Puckett, daughter of local Stampede enthusiasts Jerry and Alice Puckett and candidate of the Westgate Community Association, and 19-year-old Sharon Taylor, sponsored by the Calgary Canadian Citizenship Council. As the queen's attendants, they simply received the standard prizes that had been in place for runners-up for well over a decade: two

1961 Queen Marie Sharpe (centre) with Ladies-in-waiting Lynn Puckett and Sharon Taylor. (GA: NA-2864-18128B)

outfits each, expenses during Stampede week and a $100 cash scholarship.

Before the 1962 contest, committee chairman Bill Ouellet reminded participants of the ground rules: "Cost of the tickets, prizes, organization, costs for winners and major publicity will be borne by the ACT. Organizations sponsoring candidates will pay for miscellaneous expenditures such as posters and ticket distribution."[262] Optimistically, he set the goal of realizing $10,000 for charity ($77,000 today). The club had seen that kind of profit and more during the late 1950s but it was an ambitious number in 1962. Ticket prices were raised to 50 cents for 50 tickets to help meet the fundraising goal, even though the price increase in 1953 had proved disastrous. In the club newsletter, Ouellet exhorted ACT members to get involved. "Let's get those books of tickets out of the drawer and sell them, remember this is our one and only major project for the year. Let's make this the best contest ever, so sell the two books and then get some more and keep selling."[263]

In 1962 the Calgary Stampede celebrated its Golden Jubilee. The queen contest benefited from the festivities because participation in the Stampede was on everyone's mind that year. With organizations in some of the smaller communities south of the city fielding candidates as a way of taking part in the celebration, Calgary contestants were joined by hopefuls from Lethbridge, Medicine Hat, Pincher Creek, Turner Valley, Crowsnest Pass, and Cranbrook, BC.

In a process that was by now becoming very familiar, the public was informed that once ticket sales were done, judging would commence at the Victoria Park Agriculture Building on the Stampede grounds.

The city's seven leading queen contestants will appear before the committee at 9:30 am Thursday at the Stampede grounds. In the morning, they will be judged for horsemanship, and at 1:30 pm, they will be given a general knowledge test in the agricultural building. At 5:30 pm, contestants will attend a buffet meal where they will be under observation as to deportment, personality and appearance. At 7 pm, each girl will speak for five minutes on a subject of her choice, and at approximately 8 pm, the selection committee will announce the queen for the 50th anniversary of the Calgary Exhibition and Stampede.[264]

It was an intense day of judging for the seven finalists, who "spent a hard day riding and being interviewed by three teams of judges."[265] The three winners were "only fractions of points apart" according

DONNA THOMSON

UN ⌒ +Y-

Candidate for
CALGARY
STAMPEDE QUEEN

Sponsored by the
TURNER VALLEY OILFIELD CURLING
ASS'N

Don't Forget Our
CURLING CARNIVAL and DANCE
at Black Diamond · August 3rd and 4th
Your Queen Ticket admits you free   CASH DOOR PRIZES

Stampede Queen candidate Donna Thomson's campaign poster, 1962. (CS)

to Ouellet, but a ranch girl from Black Diamond, 19-year-old Donna Thomson, emerged as Queen. Appropriately, she was the daughter of champion cowboy Don Thomson, who had won the North American title in 1937 as all-round cowboy and twice won North American honours as top bareback and Brahma bull rider. Even more appropriately, her mentor during the contest had been close family friend Patsy Rogers, the Stampede's first queenly representative, in 1946. Donna's sponsor was the Turner Valley Curling Club, and with a local girl in the running, everyone in the area became involved in her campaign. Her sales received a boost because she spent May and June working in local schools as a student teacher. Often accompanied by Patsy, she was "hauled all over the country" that spring selling tickets at little rodeos, auctions and dances. It was worth the effort: not only did she win, but the Curling Club was able to build a new rink with its share of the proceeds.[266]

After the crowning, Donna was presented with a Queen of Hearts saddle, again crafted by Eamor's and provided by Simpsons-Sears. Made of milk-white latigo leather, it was trimmed with red valentines. In the start of a new tradition, all three winners received distinctive striped blanket coats from the Hudson's Bay Company. In honour of its Golden

Queen Donna Thomson wearing her golden jubilee outfit for the Stampede parade, 1962. (CSA)

and other official occasions. With the Stampede raffling a $50,000 gold bar for a dollar a ticket, and Stampede president H. Gordon Love sporting "a frontier suit… made out of 10 carat gold cloth," 1962 truly was a golden year for the Calgary Stampede.[268]

When she won, Donna was in her first year of studies at the Calgary campus of the University of Alberta. As a student she was off for the summer, and although she was still expected to help out on the family ranch whenever possible, there was no question she would be able to find the time to be Stampede Queen. But her Ladies-in-waiting – 18-year-old Linda Rennells, sponsored by the Britannia Community Association, and 22-year-old Frances Joan Reeder, sponsored by the Boosterettes of the Calgary Booster Club – were city girls with jobs at local oil firms. For the first time, a journalist thought to inquire about how young women who were employed managed to fit in the duties expected of Stampede royalty. He reported that receptionist Linda had arranged for her two weeks of vacation time to coincide with the Stampede and its buildup, but "although [Frances] will be taking holidays from her secretarial position next week, this week she must squeeze fittings and other events into her lunch hours and coffee breaks."[269]

As the newspaper article implied, official duties began for the trio a few days before the Stampede

Jubilee, the Stampede announced that Queen Donna would be mounted on a golden palomino and wearing an "all-leather, all-gold outfit"[267] for the parade

1962 Queen Donna Thomson (centre) with Ladies-in-waiting Frances Reeder and Linda Rennells. (CSA)

airfield, judging a local fashion show, riding in the Grand Entry at the All-Girl Rodeo in High River and attending the Press Club's Double B Barbecue at Happy Valley. But the parade was the big thrill as far as Donna was concerned, because she got to meet and ride near her childhood hero, Roy Rogers and his wife Dale Evans, headliners for the Jubilee show. For the first and only time, the Stampede royals all wore leather: Donna's second outfit was in white leather appliquéd with red roses, and her ladies-in-waiting had two leather outfits too, one in peach and the other in pale blue. Parade day was very hot, and afterwards Donna discovered that her golden leather pants required emergency tailoring; they had stretched so badly that they resembled jodhpurs.[270]

To keep their focus on the job and ease the logistics surrounding scheduling and transportation, queens and their ladies-in-waiting were sequestered at the Palliser Hotel with their chaperone during Stampede week and discouraged from visiting with family members and friends. Some young winners found this restriction difficult, especially if it was their first experience being away from home and living in close quarters with virtual strangers. In later years, the situation was eased somewhat when parents were invited to meet with their daughters midway through the busy week, but Queen Donna was

actually started, with a busy weekend of appearances that included greeting "Aunt Jemima" at McCall one of the lucky few to see a parent daily. Since her father was a chuckwagon backstretch judge and had to ride with the wagons in every race, she was able to visit with him each evening as she waited on horseback to be introduced to the grandstand crowd.

After the Stampede, both ladies-in-waiting announced they were resigning, one to marry and the other to attend school out-of-province. This was not an unheard of decision during a period when the focus was very much on the queen, particularly once the busy Stampede week was over. It was not a requirement that all three ladies had to make themselves available all year long but it had become an expectation, so this development was a surprise to Donna and the ACT. Luckily, there were very few additional engagements over the rest of the year (just one or two per month), so Donna was able to continue representing the Stampede single-handedly with ease. One of the most interesting opportunities to arise from being named Stampede Queen occurred that fall when she was invited to compete as Miss Rodeo Canada* in the Miss Rodeo America contest in Las Vegas.[271]

*Although she had not won a competition, Donna was asked to compete under that title because the Miss Rodeo Canada contest was in hiatus from 1961 to 1974. Several years later, the same invitation was extended to 1965 Stampede Queen Donna Israelson.

Bill Ouellet and his Queen Committee did not meet their ambitious fundraising goal in 1962 and that prompted a rebellion of sorts. In late February 1963, Ouellet and vice chairman Jack Gow advised the Stampede Board that "it is the intention of the Associated Canadian Travellers to discontinue judging for the Stampede Queen Contest and to revert to their former rules on which the Queen is chosen entirely on the basis of ticket sales." After a brief discussion, the Stampede Executive Committee rejected this proposal, recording in the minutes that it had advised the Board that "the Company should not recognize a Stampede Queen chosen in this fashion."[272] It looked like a stalemate, but a compromise of sorts was reached over the next few weeks.

On April 1, the *Calgary Herald* announced:

Ticket sales, not ability, to decide Stampede Queen: "Beauty, charm and horsemanship will have nothing to do with the final outcome of the 1963 Stampede Queen Contest." That statement was a bit misleading; those qualities still were very much a deciding factor in choosing Stampede royalty but the ACT and Stampede officials had agreed that judging for them would come into play much earlier in the process. On April 21, before ticket sales even began, candidates chosen by sponsoring organizations would assemble at Ken Paget's Cochrane-area ranch "to convince a panel of judges… that they are pretty, personable, intelligent and amply endowed with horsemanship, without which no girl can succeed in the contest. Once they qualify, the girls and their sponsoring organizations will have to sell 25-cent tickets on themselves, and the one selling the most automatically becomes queen and is featured in the Stampede Parade."

Continuing to explain the reversal in rules, the *Herald* reminded readers:

For the past four years, a panel of judges appraised the six girls with the top ticket sales and chose the winner from them. Officials said that proceeds of the contest, which used to be in excess of $10,000 per year, fell badly in the past four years because there was less incentive for the girls and their campaign organizations to sell the tickets. [Last year's] 50-cent ticket price also cut down sales, officials felt.[273]

The ACT predicted to the *Herald* that twenty candidates would likely attend the pre-judging event at Ken Paget's ranch and, of these, 75 per cent would qualify to move on to stage two of the contest, namely ticket sales.[274] The response was better than that: twenty-eight candidates applied and nineteen were chosen to vie for votes during the ticket sales portion of the contest, shortened that year from fifteen weeks to nine, May 1 to July 3. To provide a little incentive for ACT members signing up organizations to sell ticket books on behalf of the club, the Queen Committee announced that club members would earn $5 for every organization they brought in. Five dollars was a nice motivator in 1963 (worth close to $40 today) and ACT member Peter Degenstein remembers making a tidy sum by signing up seventeen clubs.[275] Similarly, to provide incentive to ticket buyers, ticket prices reverted to 25 cents for 25 votes and the ACT announced that a compact car would be offered as first prize in a draw to be held during the club's popular street dance on the Tuesday of Stampede week.[276]

Ticket sales were hard-fought and there were some mutterings about ticket skulduggery,[277] but in the end "a trio of 5 foot 4 inch blondes" emerged victorious in the 1963 contest. The new Queen was an 18-year-old Calgarian, Frances Swann. Officially sponsored by the Banff Trail Community Association, Frances received strong support from Job's Daughters, whose Queen she had been, and from the students at William Aberhart High School, from which she

graduated just days before winning the Stampede Queen title.

Like Queen Marie in 1961, Frances was a horse-loving city girl who had learned to ride at local stables and had worked part time and done lots of babysitting to earn the money to buy a horse of her own, a half-Arabian called Mandy. After her win, she told reporters that she "began riding as a child, but polished up her horsemanship at Happy Valley this spring in readiness for the queen contest," a common practice among city candidates. Her Ladies-in-waiting, both aged 19, were countrywomen and seasoned riders: Beryl Edge of Cochrane, candidate of the De Winton Community Association and cousin to 1953 Queen Edith Edge, and Dixie Mae Girletz of Midnapore, sponsored by the Calgary and District Boys Pipe Band.[278]

Stampede officials tried to talk Frances into riding a bigger, showier horse in the parade but she told them she felt more confident riding a "bombproof" horse, her own dependable Mandy.[279] When the trio dashed out into the infield during the Grand Entry before the first afternoon rodeo, she was glad to be riding little Mandy instead of a big, barrel-chested

1963 Queen Frances Swann riding in the Stampede parade. (GA: PA-2807-3714)

quarterhorse, because she was the only one of the three not to rip the back seam out of her tightly fitted and lined wool pants! Frances chose to take the $300 scholarship instead of the trip, applying the money toward tuition when she started at the University of Alberta at Calgary that fall. For the third year in a row Simpsons-Sears presented the queen with a saddle, this time a more practical, but still beautifully tooled, stock saddle on the advice of 1962 winner Donna Thomson. The young women all received silver compacts and inscribed bracelets from the City and classic blanket coats from the Hudson's Bay Company.

To provide a little human interest, a *Herald* reporter decided to trail after the trio through one long day in the middle of Stampede week 1963. At the time, it was considered an exhausting schedule, but the pace was relatively relaxed compared with that demanded of future royalty. For Frances, Beryl and Dixie, the royal day started at the Palliser Hotel before 7 a.m. and ended there late that same evening:

Their official guardians, Mr. and Mrs. Jack Gow, drove them to City Hall, where they were greeted by Calgary's mayor J.W. Grant MacEwan. Signing the official register, the girls were shown the signatures of many former Stampede Queens. The mayor

Queen Frances Swann signing the guest book at City Hall while Calgary mayor Grant MacEwan and Ladies-in-waiting Dixie Girletz and Beryl Edge look on. (GA: NA-2864-18130C)

presented them with silver bracelets engraved with their names and titles, and the royal party was off to its next appointment… introduced at a street show and stayed to join the merrymakers. "We had our first square dance of the week," said Frances… Returning to their home base, the three girls had time to take off their boots and relax for a few minutes… Discussing their whirlwind round of activities, Beryl said, "We do have a pretty rough schedule to maintain, but it is all fun." "Boots on!" cried Mrs. Gow, their chaperone, and the Queen and party were off for lunch with the downtown Lions Club… Another quick spruce-up in their suite found the girls on their way to the Alberta Children's Hospital. Waiting in the solarium were more than 100 tots, on beds, in wheelchairs and on stretchers. The girls charmed the children. They talked with them, laughed with them and signed autographs for them… Leaving the hospital, the trio of blondes returned to the Palliser for a short break before dinner and the evening events. Chuckwagon races headed the schedule at the Stampede grounds. A touch of stage fright set in before their introduction on stage, but few in the audience would have guessed. Official duties over, the girls, their chaperone and crew headed back to their site with only one problem left to solve: "which late show should we watch tonight?"[280]

Unfortunately this happy description of the royal trio performing their duties masked a couple of real problems with the 1963 contest. Jealousy and a lingering feeling of ill will among misguided supporters of a rival candidate had resulted in an ugly incident that never made the news but caused a certain amount of disenchantment for its victim, Queen Frances.[281] Inadequate supervision of the trio's horses on the Exhibition grounds had allowed an intruder to enter the barns unobserved and slash a stirrup nearly off the Queen's new saddle. If this spiteful damage had not been detected and repaired, it might have resulted in a nasty fall for an unwary Frances the next time she mounted her horse.[282]

More importantly, the rumour that there had been underhanded ticket dealings by an ACT member on behalf of a favoured candidate simply would not go away. This issue caused so much dissension in ACT ranks that newspaper columnist Johnny Hopkins mused in print that all had not been "sweetness and light" in the 1963 campaign.[283] The rule changes made for that contest – judging preceding ticket selling – had not led to an increase in sales or a return to previous fundraising levels. However, it was not the financial shortfall but the other problems associated with that year's campaign that changed the Stampede Queen contest forever.

CHAPTER 7 ★ 1964–1966

"Rules changed: Popularity tickets out"

As an active member of the Calgary ACT, Peter Degenstein had done his share of signing up organizations and selling ticket books, but the 1963 contest was his first experience on the Queen Committee. Shocked and dismayed by the reports of ticket "skulduggery" and other irregularities he witnessed that year, he went to Irv Parsons, manager of the Calgary Exhibition and Stampede, and suggested it was time for ticket sales to go and for the Stampede to take full control of the contest.[284] With such lacklustre ticket revenues over the past four years, Degenstein figured the ACT was more than ready to hand over the reins, but in 1964 the Stampede was not yet ready to assume control. In the end, Parsons and the Board talked the ACT into dropping the contentious ticket sales and continuing to manage the contest for a few more years. But that decision really spelled the end of the ACT's interest in running a contest that was quickly becoming a liability rather than the fundraising bonanza it had been for its first dozen years or so.

After the ACT agreed to drop ticket sales, it took a little negotiation to hammer out a new framework that would give the Stampede its royal trio while still allowing the ACT to make money for its charitable projects. In an opening salvo on January 31, 1964, the ACT suggested the following new rules:

1. Ticket sales shall no longer have a part of electing the Stampede Queen.

2. The Queen shall be chosen by an impartial board of judges on a basis of horsemanship, intelligence, personality and appearance.

3. Any girl of the age of 18 or over, unmarried and with the exception of previous Stampede Queens, shall be eligible to enter the contest upon payment of a $5 entry fee.

4. After an extensive elimination trial the few remaining contestants must put up a further $50 entry fee for the final judging by the Stampede Queen selection committee.

1964 Queen Sharon Patterson (centre) with Ladies-in-waiting Gail Henry and Gwenda Marshall. (GA: NA-2864-18132A)

5. There will be a Stampede Queen with no ladies-in-waiting.

6. The Stampede Queen will be awarded a $500 scholarship, a $1,000 saddle from Simpson Sears plus an extensive wardrobe.

7. We propose to have the final judging done at the Spring Horse Show (or like event) and the winner of The Calgary Stampede Queen Contest announced on the final evening.

8. Extensive publicity will be given throughout Southern Alberta inviting girls to be contestants…

9. As this contest will no longer produce a revenue for charity, The Calgary Club, ACT, propose to hold 3 Stampede Queen Street Dances in downtown Calgary. These will be held on the Saturday prior to Stampede week and on the Monday and Tuesday evenings of Stampede Week.

10. It would be appreciated if the Stampede Board would give favourable consideration towards the Calgary Club, ACT and allow us to conduct a money raising project on the Stampede Grounds, by a money raising project we mean a "Jitney Dance"* or similar function.[285]

*Jitney dances were pay-as-you-go. Instead of charging admission, organizers sold tickets on each dance.

These proposals were reviewed by the Stampede at both executive and board levels in early February and a number of objections were raised: the Stampede did not want the ACT to run additional fundraising dances, either downtown or on the grounds; it wanted to continue with two ladies-in-waiting; and it did not want entrants to be charged a $50 fee.[286] It seemed like a stalemate – the ACT simply was not prepared to continue organizing the queen contest without generating funds for its own projects. Luckily, the Board liked the idea of running the contest during the Calgary Spring Horse Show, an annual event that was held on the Exhibition grounds every May, and that led to some creative thinking. By mid-March the two sides had come to the following agreement, as recorded in the Stampede Executive minutes:

The ACT is prepared to sponsor and operate the Stampede Queen Contest with no ticket sales involved, at a cost to the ACT of between $3 & $4,000, and with the finals of the contest to be judged on a horsemanship basis at the Spring Horse Show. In return the ACT has requested that they be provided with 2,000 vouchers, each worth $1.50 toward the purchase of a Horse Show ticket, which ACT members will sell to provide revenue for the club. All vouchers in excess of 2,000 to be sold to the ACT at

75¢ each. Moved & seconded that the proposal be approved if the ACT will agree to provide 2 ladies-in-waiting as well as a queen for Stampede Week, with the Horse Show to be subsidized for $1,000 out of Stampede expense to compensate for the loss of revenue from ticket sales. Horse Show Committee to work out final arrangements. Carried.[287]

After finalizing details, 1964 chairman Bill Ouellet and his Queen Committee got to work publicizing the new rules. The *Calgary Herald* alerted the public about the changes on March 26:

Stampede Queen rules changed – Popularity tickets out: A new method of selecting the Queen of the Calgary Stampede, with the emphasis firmly fixed on horsemanship, was outlined Wednesday by the ACT. The winner will be decided at the Calgary Spring Horse Show, May 6 to 9. The system of selecting candidates through the sale of ballots has been abandoned. Since the new method entails a loss of revenue, the sponsoring ACT organization will try to make it up by selling tickets to the horse show, the money to be used to defray the cost of the contest.[288]

A few days later, the *Herald* printed a contest entry form featuring a graphic of a pretty cowgirl and the following instructions:

1964 ACT Stampede Queen contest – NO ticket sales: Open to a single girl 18 years and over. No previous Queens are eligible. Entries must be received prior to April 17th. April 18, preliminary judging of horsemanship will be held at the Two Rivers Ranch west of Cochrane (on 1A Highway). Horses and saddles will be provided and entrants must use these horses. From the judging a maximum of 25 girls will be selected. The girls will then be judged on Personality, Appearance, Poise, Intelligence. A maximum of 12 girls will then compete in the Spring Horse Show. The girl receiving the most points for horsemanship will be declared Queen and two runners-up will be 'Ladies in Waiting.' Judging will be on Western Equestrian Style. Judges will be appointed by The Horse Show Committee. The Stampede Queen will receive a $300 scholarship and the two runners-up $150 scholarships each.* Suitable costumes will be provided to the successful contestants.[289]

*The ladies-in-waiting had received a $50 raise in scholarship money in recognition of the new requirement for proven riding skills.

Although the queen competition was never publicized as a beauty contest, entrants were asked to provide, along with their $5 entry fee, a few details about their personal appearance: age, height and weight, together with a recent photo.[290]

As the Calgary contributor to the ACT club newsletter put it, "Quite a change from previous years isn't it?"[291] But it turned out that the new contest structure worked very well. After initial equestrian trials at Two Rivers Ranch, a panel of five judged the twelve successful horsewomen on their personality, poise, appearance and intelligence. A *Herald* reporter present for the event was highly amused by some of the answers given by the young contestants:

Wild replies fail to unfreeze poker faces of "Queen" judges: A poker-faced attitude was undoubtedly the prime requisite for the panel of five judges… Their oriental inscrutability was tested to the limit, particularly when the contestants were asked for the population of Calgary. The answers ranged from a meagre 7,000 to a whopping 17,000,000… the audience could almost hear an audible gasp from the judges when one pert young lady suggested Edmonton had a larger area than Calgary… The greatest disappointment of the evening came when several of the shapely misses blandly suggested

their interest in life was "mainly in horses and riding."[292]

Surprisingly, the question that stumped most of the candidates was to name the featured attraction at that year's grandstand show (singer Juliette).[293] It was the first year that the Stampede had opted out of the western fair circuit and developed its own show and there had been much hype and excitement in the media. The Rockettes were coming from New York and young local dancers had been auditioned to participate in the show. The Calgary Kidettes so charmed and impressed the audience that by 1968 they had evolved to become a star attraction, The Young Canadians of the Calgary Stampede, under the direction of show producer Randolph Avery.[294]

Two weeks after the interviews, eight remaining competitors competed in a series of tests showing off their western equitation skills before a panel of judges each day of the horse show. The final eight, all good riders, liked the fact that they were competing on an even playing field in the 1964 contest. Although he did not speak for every ACT member, Peter Degenstein agreed, telling reporters that ticket sales had created hard feelings amongst losing candidates who sometimes suspected that the winners' families or friends had "bought her in."[295] Now that contestants were judged on their own merits, with no possibility of wealthy connections or a single-interest group influencing the final decision, the result was closer relationships among those competing and a general feeling of harmony during the competition.[296] As one contestant observed during the judging, "There is more spirit put into this year's competition. If the contest continues to be run in this manner, the complete city will become more enthusiastic about it."[297]

On the closing night of the horse show, the eight finalists put their mounts through a reining pattern in the show ring. Marks were tallied with earlier results and placed in sealed envelopes. ACT president Don McKinnon announced the three winners and crowned 20-year-old Sharon Patterson from Irricana as Stampede Queen. Interestingly, Sharon had competed in the 1963 contest, sponsored by the Irricana Chamber of Commerce.[298] As such, she was probably the only candidate for Stampede Queen ever to compete in both versions of the contest, both with and without ticket sales.

There was no problem with Sharon competing for queen a second time, because contest rules were simple and straightforward in the early 1960s, having stayed basically the same for nearly fifteen years. "A contestant must: be acceptable to the Committee; be 18 years of age; be single; not be one who has previously been selected and acted as Stampede Queen." Only one new rule had been added, in 1964, because of a few problems in previous years: "be free to enter a contract respecting her services while Queen or alternate." Although ACT members were discreet about details, *Herald* columnist Johnny Hopkins had learned that some previous royals had attended privately arranged events that had not been sanctioned by the ACT. Since the club was responsible for the program, it wished to maintain control over the kind and quality of public appearances made by the royal representatives it had chosen on behalf of the Stampede. Hopkins tried to spell it out for *Herald* readers without pointing any fingers:

This year the contestants must sign a form stipulating that they will make appearances as Stampede Queen only with the approval of the ACT. Some girls in the past did sign contracts with individuals, although no particular conflict arose. But the ACT has plugged this loophole so that the queen won't appear at any "image-hurting" affair.[299]

Winner of a number of horse show and all-girl rodeo trophies, Queen Sharon shared her hopes for the 1964 Stampede royalty: "I'd like to see the girls out on their horses more. That's where we belong. And this year we can all ride well enough. I don't know if it can be arranged, but I'd like to see us associated with the infield events, or at least riding horses more instead of convertibles."[300] Sadly, Sharon did not get her wish. As had been the custom ever since proven horsemanship had become a requirement in 1959, the 1964 trio rode horses in the parade and into the infield each evening to be introduced to the grandstand crowd, but aside from that, there was little call for them to be on horseback the rest of Stampede week. Instead they were shuttled from place to place on the back of a convertible while making the usual community visits and attending other functions.

The 1964 Ladies-in-waiting were 19-year-old Gail Henry from Burns Lake, BC, and 18-year-old Gwenda Marshall, the young lady who had so amused the press during the preliminary interviews by suggesting that the population of Calgary was a whopping 17 million. Gwenda was another in a long line of horse-loving Calgary girls who had learned to ride despite of having a city upbringing. Her first instructor at the Pony Club was 1961 Queen Marie Sharpe, a direct influence on her decision to run for Stampede Queen in 1964. She was a good rider but had learned English style, so once she knew she was in the finals, she went to Wilbur Griffith's Pinebrook Ranch to practise riding Western on a variety of horses and to nail down proper reining patterns for the final competition. She made it through to be chosen as second Lady-in-waiting but was teased good-naturedly forever after by expert Western riders Sharon and Gail for her English riding style (they called her a "flat-ass saddle rider").[301]

All three girls received silver bangles from the city of Calgary, silver compacts from the ACT, belt buckles engraved with their titles, and two western outfits. Sharon was given $300 and a black, nickel-plated parade saddle donated by Simpsons-Sears. Gail and Gwenda were given $150 each. Although it was termed a scholarship, there was no restriction placed on how their prize money was to be used, so young Gwenda bought a dog with hers.

The Calgary *Albertan*'s Linda Curtis provided more details about the new queen's ensemble: "Her boots will be of desert sand ostrich skin; her belt, hand-tooled by patients at the Colonel Belcher Hospital and the silver buckle engraved with the ACT crest. The crest will also adorn her cufflinks." ACT member Jack Gow's wife, Orpha, had been designing the royal outfits for six years but the disaster during the first day of the 1963 Stampede (when both ladies-in-waiting had split the back seams of their pants while racing into the infield during the Grand Entry)

Queen Sharon Patterson (centre) with Ladies-in-waiting Gwenda Marshall and Gail Henry riding in the Stampede parade, 1964. (CSA).

meant that this year she had to keep in mind "the fact that what might look beautiful on the girls as they stand on a platform might fall apart when they start riding."[302]

Even so, there were a few hitches in 1964. Mrs. Gow had created a "light wool crepe and brocade outfit featuring slim-fitting, bell-bottomed frontier pants, white ruffled sissy-front shirt and a white bolero edged vest with pearls and silver fringe. The outstanding feature was considered to be the appliquéd

Alberta rose motif that extended down the front of the slims and curved around the bolero bodice." The problem was that the pants seemed not to have been designed with riding in mind, so the young ladies had to unpick the hems and lengthen the pant legs to cover their boots properly. The other unforeseen problem was that the black dye on Sharon's new saddle rubbed off every time she wore the white wool pants, so they had to be dry cleaned after each time she appeared on horseback.[303]

In February 1965, Irv Parsons advised the Stampede Board that the ACT was willing to run the queen contest again along the same lines as in 1964. However, he added that the club had "suffered a substantial loss in the running of the contest last year" and that "suitable arrangements were being made to offset the deficit this year."[304] Clearly, profits from horse show ticket sales were not sufficient even to cover the cost of running the contest, let alone provide the ACT with funds for their charitable projects. The Stampede voted the club a grant of $1,000 to help cover its losses in 1964. To help guarantee a better fundraising return next time, it authorized the club to sell Stampede merchandise and souvenirs at two booths on the grounds during the 1965 Stampede.[305]

Once again, contestants were charged a $5 entry fee. That may have dissuaded some; others may have felt intimidated by having to compete in front of horse show judges. In any case, only fifteen candidates applied to compete in the first round of judging, on April 10 at the Two Rivers Ranch indoor arena. Even so, the level of horsemanship was very high and onlookers did not envy the judges their task.[306] Using horses supplied by the ranch, the candidates took turns demonstrating a general walk, a jog and a lope around the arena and coming to a sudden stop. They performed figure eights, dismounted, led the horses up to one of the three judges and then remounted. To prevent the possibility of anyone being favoured, all were given two chances, each time on a different horse. Interestingly, one of the judges for this event was 1958 Lady-in-waiting Isabella Hamilton.[307]

ACT contest chairman Peter Degenstein and his able assistant Jack Gow were pleased with how well the new contest model was working. They were proud of the three-step judging system that had been developed: weeding for basic riding skill, then evaluating for people skills, then judging once again for horsemanship. Focused as they were on avoiding the problems of non-riding royalty, it was understandable that the ACT and the Stampede put a lot of effort into finding good riders, but they were also aware of the importance of finding a balance. "We want an all-around queen, not just the best rider," claimed

Degenstein. And retiring Queen Sharon Patterson knew why: for all that she had been chosen because she was the best rider, in actuality much of her time over the year had been devoted to public-relations work. Claiming she had enjoyed every minute, she nevertheless warned, "Whoever is this year's queen should be prepared to devote much of her time to the role. It involves not only appearing at rodeos throughout the district all summer but also attending banquets and special luncheons during the winter."[308]

Although competition was stiff in the 1965 contest, the final night of the horse show saw 20-year-old Donna Israelson from Didsbury emerge as Queen, with 20-year-old Frances Chamberlain of Calgary and 18-year-old Mary Elizabeth MacDonald from Balzac as her Ladies-in-waiting. The contest emphasis on horsemanship had paid off: for the first time, all three winners were competitive riders, members of the Canadian Barrel Racers and Rodeo Association. The Las Vegas–Hollywood trip was no longer being offered, but with the blessing of the Stampede Board and a grant of $300, Donna competed in the Miss Rodeo America contest in Las Vegas the following

1965 Queen Donna Israelson (far right) and Ladies-in-waiting Frances Chamberlain and Mary MacDonald after winning at the Calgary International Horse Show, 1965. (GA: PA-2807-1955)

year as Miss Calgary Stampede 1965.[309] Aside from that, the trio was given the usual prizes, this time including luggage from Simpsons-Sears for the Ladies-in-waiting to help offset the Queen's saddle prize. They met all official visitors and dignitaries during Stampede week, including parade marshal Walt Disney, but were unanimous that the thrilling highlight was meeting pop singer Dave Clark, whose group the Dave Clark Five performed at the Stampede Corral. The envy of the 7,000 fans who attended the show, the lucky young women reported breathlessly, "He's an absolute doll."[310]

All through 1964 and 1965, the ACT continued reminding the public that the contest had changed and ticket sales were no more, but that was not true, strictly speaking. Although tickets were no longer being sold on individual candidates, the ACT was relying on horse show ticket sales for funding and they no longer had community sponsor organizations to help with that task. Asking all ACT members "to get behind this first big project of the year," returning contest chairman Peter Degenstein and his committee announced in the club's April 1966 newsletter that the chore of ticket selling itself had become a contest. "Any member selling ten or more books will receive an ACT blazer and crest free. The member selling the most tickets will also

get a matching pair of slacks free."[311] The promise of this prize must have been only moderately successful, because the next newsletter saw Degenstein still pleading, "Fellows, let's get out and push these tickets for the horse show so we have the Corral bursting at the seams every night."[312]

In July the newsletter reported, "A tip of our ten gallon hats to Pete Degenstein, Jack Gow and Lyle Isman, who sold over 10 books of horse show tickets and were tireless in their efforts towards the Queen Contest,"[313] but it was not enough. In spite of earning revenues of approximately $1,800 from ticket sales and the sale of Stampede souvenirs, Irv Parsons reported to the Stampede Executive that the ACT had lost $1,400 on the queen contest. Once again the club was granted $1,000 to partially offset this loss.[314] Agreeing to run the contest once again, the club was given the right to operate a food concession on the grounds during the 1966 Stampede.[315]

But the chairman for 1966, a returning Peter Degenstein, could see that it was time for the Stampede to take over the contest completely. ACT sponsorship had been predicated upon it being a good fundraiser for the club, but the change from ticket sales to an ability-based contest had turned it into a losing proposition. Jack Gow's review of recent ACT contest budgets following the 1966 contest told the tale. The budgeted amount for contest revenues had dropped from $10,000 in 1962 and 1963 (when ticket sales were still in effect) to $5,000 in 1964 (when the ACT still was optimistic that selling horse show tickets would offset the loss of sponsors and traditional ticket sales) to approximately $2,500 in 1965 and 1966 (once they realized that running the queen contest in conjunction with the horse show would never be a decent fundraiser).[316] Not surprisingly, club members were not interested in working hard for something that gave so little return. Even by supplementing with other Stampede-related sales ventures, the club could no longer support local charities at the level it wished. If the Stampede wanted to continue finding its royalty through holding a contest – and it did – the feeling among ACT members was that it should take over the task and allow the club to develop new sources of revenue or concentrate on better Stampede-oriented money-makers such as the street dance.

Discussions along these lines between the ACT and the Stampede began soon after the 1965 contest ended, but it would be another year before the official handover occurred. In the meantime, the ACT geared up in 1966 to run the contest one last time. It chose Calgary Boys Town to be the final recipient of funds raised that year, a very fitting choice considering that the original recipient when the club first introduced the contest in 1947 had been Calgary Girls Town.

Aware that the handover was now inevitable, Degenstein and his committee worked with Irv Parsons and the Stampede to hone rules and procedures, making sure that the contest framework the ACT handed over would be as perfect a vehicle as possible for identifying goodwill ambassadors for the Stampede. While the 1966 contest may have looked much the same as those held in 1964 and 1965, the committee actually introduced a number of improvements that helped to ease the transition from ACT to Stampede control in the fall of 1966.

A minor change was the timing of crowning the winners. For the past few years, winners had been announced on the final night of the horse show, in late May, but their reign had not officially commenced until their crowning in front of the grandstand on the Tuesday night of Stampede, a gap of nearly two months. Starting with the 1966 contest, winners were to be crowned when their win was announced, and their reign would start immediately. This change only formalized what had been happening informally for several years, but it meant that Stampede royalty could make an official appearance at the growing number of pre-Stampede events. To allow for ongoing public involvement, a small ceremony would still take place before the grand-stand crowd on the Tuesday night of Stampede week, when the queen and her ladies would be introduced to the crowd and officially presented with their prizes.[317]

After years of basing the number of finalists and semifinalists on the number and quality of candidates competing any given year, the committee decided to standardize by setting the number of semifinalists at ten and finalists at five. The ten contestants who passed the first riding test were to be invited to a public dinner introduced to allow secret judges to circulate and evaluate contestants' personality, poise and facility in meeting the public in a real social setting. Contestants were to be given a break from wearing Western wear in that they would be invited to wear "informal feminine dress" to this event for the one and only time in the contest. The five candidates who passed this stage of the judging would compete at the horse show, a different candidate demonstrating her riding ability each night during the five-day event.[318]

Finally, after several years of discussing the topic, the minimum age of candidates was raised from 18 to 19. The committee felt that with more mature young women they would have a better field from which to choose and more likelihood of ending up with more suitable representatives for the Stampede.[319] As Peter Degenstein explained, "We discovered girls of 18 didn't have the same chance. They didn't have enough experience or poise, particularly in public speaking as older girls… This had an adverse effect on future contests, as the younger girls would be discouraged from entering subsequent contests."[320]

The ACT announced these changes when they rolled out the 1966 contest. Everything ran smoothly but organizers were thrown a curve when a young lady from Edmonton entered the contest and won. There were no rules specifying that candidates must come from south of that invisible provincial mid-point at Red Deer, but over the years most had been from communities within the Stampede's orbit, traditionally the southern part of the province. Bold Edmonton organizations had fielded candidates seven times during the contest's twenty-year history, but five years had elapsed since the last attempt, and this bid for the Calgary crown appeared to be much more determined and better organized. Surprised Calgarians first heard the news in early April when Peter Degenstein announced that "the Sheriff's Posse of Edmonton may send as many as four girls to Calgary to vie for the Stampede Queen title."[321]

As it turned out, 19-year-old Betty Wright was the only Edmontonian to enter, but, as Degenstein had foreseen, her progress throughout the contest was watched by the media with a great deal of interest. Betty was an excellent rider – she rode as a flag girl with the Edmonton Klondike Posse – and easily passed the first riding test at the Two Rivers Ranch on April 17. She then sailed through the next level of testing (the dinner, interviews and public speaking events), competing with nine other semifinalists to emerge as one of five finalists to compete at the horse show in early May. Speaking a little defensively to the media after it was announced she had reached the finals, Betty said she did not feel that her Edmonton heritage would be a hindrance in the final competition. "I am aware that my being from Edmonton will cause quite a bit of controversy in Calgary. However, Guy Weadick, one of the founders of the Calgary Stampede was not a Calgarian. He was not even a Canadian. He was an American from New York. Every contestant should have a square deal. The square deal in Stampede competition – like Calgary friendliness – is traditional," she ended persuasively.[322]

"Stampede Queen title won by Edmonton girl" trumpeted the *Herald* when the contest ended three weeks later. Public protest soon followed. One letter to the *Herald* was typical of the reaction of many Calgarians to the unexpected news of Betty's win.

Queen Betty Wright with Edmonton's Klondike Kate at the Hays Stampede breakfast, 1966. (GA: NA-2864-18135E)

Editor: I have never been so disgusted. To think that the Calgary Stampede would pick its queen from Edmonton. I cannot see, for one minute, Miss Toronto Maple Leaf coming from Montreal, Western Canada High School choosing its queen from Henry Wise Wood High, the Hamilton Tiger Cat queen being picked from Vancouver, or the Queen of England being selected from France. Somebody has got to be sick.

—A Calgarian[323]

Degenstein and the ACT immediately set to work to smooth things over. Queen Betty was quoted in the *Herald* as saying she had

taken on her task with the hope Calgarians and Edmontonians will form a stronger friendship between them. "I hope everyone in Edmonton will feel much more a part of Calgary and Calgarians will have the same attitude towards us. From what I have seen of Calgary, working with the other contestants and officials, everyone is just wonderful."[324]

But it was Betty's voluntary move to Calgary several weeks later that really did the trick. Although contest rules at the time did not require winners to live in Calgary, Betty's employer, Shell Oil, facilitated her reign by transferring her to their Calgary office so that she could continue working as a stenographer while fulfilling her queenly duties. The *Herald*, immediately recasting Betty as a Calgarian, framed the move as a victory: "The Stampede Queen title is being returned to Calgary,"[325] it announced with glee.

Edmonton almost pulled off the biggest steal since the gold bars disappeared at the Winnipeg Airport when it got its hands on the 1966 Calgary Stampede Queen title. However, its grasp was only temporary, as… Betty Wright decided to move on a permanent basis to Calgary from the northern outpost early in June.[326]

By the time the Stampede was over, the *Edmonton Journal* could report with satisfaction Betty's complete infiltration of the northern city's traditional rival:

Stampede Queen contest finalists, 1966. After final judging, Betty Wright (far right) was crowned Queen with Ladies-in-waiting Ann Neilson (far left) and Lorraine McLean (second from right). The other finalists were Gwen Backs (centre) and Carol Burns (second from left). (CSA)

144

Calgary getting over Miss Stampede shock: There may have been some objections at first, but Calgarians have forgotten their Stampede queen is an Edmonton girl… Betty… said she was thrilled with the Stampede – and with the reception she has received in Calgary. "She's a beautiful girl," an admirer said. "We couldn't have found a better queen." She rode behind parade marshal Red Adair in the Stampede parade Monday morning, charmed the guests at the Harry Hays breakfast Sunday and is appearing each evening at the grandstand show.[327]

The article went on to note that many Edmontonians savoured the irony when Betty returned to her roots later that month to ride as Stampede Queen in the Klondike Days parade.

Once Calgarians had accepted Betty Wright as queen, there were no other issues and the 1966 trio enjoyed the usual excitement and perks of being Stampede royalty. Although the ACT was no longer making money on the contest, the trio received all the same gifts as usual: two complete outfits, scholarships, engraved belt buckles, Hudson's Bay blanket coats, a tooled saddle for the queen and luggage for the ladies-in-waiting. Queen Betty's white hat was fitted with a sparkly silver tiara* while the Ladies-in-waiting, Calgarians Lorraine McLean and Ann Neilson, sported rhinestone hat bands. As promised, the three young ladies were crowned after the horse show but received public recognition and their gifts during a ceremony before the grandstand show on the Tuesday night of Stampede.

In addition to fulfilling all the usual duties, including visits to Flare Square, newly created on the grounds as part of the Stampede's 1966 Salute to the Petroleum Industry, Betty was the first queen to represent Calgary and its western show in the Tournament of Roses Parade in Pasadena, California, on January 1, 1967. Doug Johnson, first general manager of the Calgary Tourist and Convention Association and originator of the Calgary white hat ceremony made famous by mayor Don Mackay, was an enthusiastic Stampede booster and supporter of the Stampede Queen program (and was recognized

---

*Although Betty's hat sported a tiara, there was no consistency in the jewellery used to designate the queen prior to the introduction of official crowns in 1979. During the 1960s, some early queens wore a pin on their hats bearing the ACT logo and some later ones sported sparkly brooches. During the 1970s, most queens wore a removable tiara or had a hat beaded with crystals in the shape of a crown.

for this support by being made an honorary associate of the Queens' Alumni Association during the 1980s). Johnson invited Betty to join the delegation when the CTCA decided that Calgary's third entry in the annual Parade of Roses would have a Stampede theme. The ambitious float was highlighted by a giant branding iron.

> The 40-ft-long iron will be held 17 feet above the ground and will give off real smoke, provided by a smoke generator inside the float. About 400,000 flowers will be used in the float, which will have an overall length of 55 feet. A miniature chuckwagon will be located at the front of the float and Linda Fraser, Princess Starlight of the Indian Friendship Centre, and Betty Wright, Miss Calgary Stampede, will ride the float.[328]

No one was surprised when Irv Parsons reported to the Stampede Executive on November 2 that the ACT had lost money on the 1966 contest. The club had spent $2,700 in conducting the contest and financing the subsequent activities of the queen and her ladies but had received revenues of only $1,300 from the sale of horse show tickets. Parsons requested and received another $1,000 grant to help offset the club's losses but also announced formally: "The ACT are not prepared in the future to carry on with the Queen Contest if they are to operate at a loss." The Executive, and later the Board, officially agreed that the Calgary Exhibition and Stampede would take over the Stampede Queen contest. Parsons then suggested that a committee to operate the contest be formed under the chairmanship of Frank Finn and recommended that "two members of the ACT, who are very interested in this contest, be asked to act on this committee, namely Mr. Jack Gow & Mr. Peter Degenstein."[329] These suggestions were approved, and with that the ACT relinquished control after nearly twenty years of sponsorship. The Stampede Queen contest was poised to start a new chapter as a full-fledged part of the Calgary Stampede.

CHAPTER 8 ★ 1967–1969

"As Stampede Queen, you are doing a job for the city"

Just a few weeks after the Calgary Exhibition and Stampede took control of the queen contest, chairman Frank Finn met with his new committee to assess where things stood and to start working on the 1967 contest. The inaugural Stampede Queen Committee consisted of just a dozen people, including Finn, Alex Bailey, Jerry D'Arcy, Dale Main, Irv Parsons, Don Welden, Wilf Baker, Tom Hall, Ian Brown, Jack Gow and Peter Degenstein. As historian Max Foran has noted, association with the Stampede is so highly regarded in Calgary that there is never any difficulty filling positions with volunteers drawn from "exclusive business, ranching, social, and civic circles."[330] Membership in the new Queen Committee was no exception: Brown and Main were successful local businessmen, while Finn, Bailey and D'Arcy were oil industry executives with ranching connections. Most of the others were directly

Queen Patsy Allan (centre) and Princesses Candace Smith and Bonnie MacGregor receiving official gifts from Calgary Stampede president Albert T. Baker, 1967. (CSA)

connected with the Stampede: Parsons was general manager; Hall, assistant manager; Baker, secretary; and Welden, publicity director. Degenstein and Gow had worked on the ACT Queen Committee for years and provided much-needed continuity as the contest transitioned from ACT to Stampede control. Several of the new members, notably Alex Bailey and Dale Main, quickly became devoted to the queen program and served on the Stampede Queen Committee for many years.

An unnamed twelfth member of the original committee was Welden's assistant in the public-relations department, Joan Plastow.[331] Unofficially a member of the Committee because she was a Stampede employee, Joan sat in on every meeting and quickly became involved in all aspects of the Committee's work. She continued to serve on the Committee after she became public-relations manager, then corporate secretary, and only resigned in 1977 because she left her position with the Stampede to marry director Harry Langford. Missing Stampede involvement, she returned as a volunteer in 1980 and served another half-dozen years as a royalty chaperone. Joan and a number of other original Stampede Queen Committee members were rewarded for their devotion to the program by being made honorary associates of the Queens' Alumni Association after it formed in 1972: Peter Degenstein, Jack Gow and Alex and Amy Bailey during the 1970s; Joan Plastow Langford in 1983; and Doug and Jeanne Main in 1986.[332]

The first Stampede Queen Committee meeting, on December 14, 1966, mostly just confirmed the contest framework that had been fine-tuned over the past few years by ACT Queen Committee members Degenstein and Gow working with Stampede officials.[333] The first order of business was finance, but after Jack Gow reviewed the variable nature of the ACT budgets over the past five years the group decided it was too early to draw up a proper budget; 1967 would be a test year in which they would create a budget as they went along and expenses were revealed. Right away, members thought they spotted several hundred dollars of savings by eliminating paid contest advertising in favour of targeted news releases, but this penny-pinching scheme proved short-lived. Disappointed with the discreet announcement of the 1967 contest buried on page two of the *Calgary Herald*'s City section, the

Stampede Queen contest poster, *CH*, February 18, 1967.

Committee placed an eye-catching ad the following week featuring a gun-waving cowgirl in a very short, fringed skirt.[334]

The group discussed timelines and delegated responsibility for the many jobs essential to running the contest: D'Arcy and Gow would organize the preliminary equestrian judging; Degenstein and Main would handle the personality contest; Hall and Baker would make arrangements for the buffet supper; and the final riding contest would be the responsibility of Alex Bailey. Each subcommittee would line up its own judges, Welden would handle press releases and publicity, and Degenstein and Gow would contact previous donors to see if they would carry on sponsoring prizes for the winners. Finally, Jack Gow informed the group that his wife, Orpha, who had been coordinating costumes for the winners for many years, was prepared to carry on. Jerry D'Arcy stated that his wife, Patty, would be happy to assist.

Determined to put their own stamp on the brand, Committee members felt strongly that the queen and her ladies "should be utilized on the grounds more during Stampede Week rather than making appearances off the grounds," although they conceded that the trio should continue visiting "the necessary Service Clubs and Children's Hospitals as much as possible."[335] Anticipating that the role of these goodwill ambassadors would continue to expand, the Committee decided that a change of name for the runners-up was in order. According to Peter Degenstein, members found the title Lady-in-waiting to be old-fashioned sounding. The runners-up were not waiting on the queen, or waiting for her job, so it seemed only fair to give them a more important sounding title. Henceforth, ladies-in-waiting were to be known as princesses in recognition of their growing importance in supporting the queen in what was rapidly becoming a year-round public-relations job too onerous for a single volunteer. Not only did the title Princess have a better ring, it more accurately expressed the modern view of the near equivalency of the three positions.[336]

The Queen Committee set down a few basic rules regarding the behaviour of Stampede royalty: no smoking or drinking in public and no interactions with boyfriends or other male admirers while on duty.[337] It also confirmed that contest eligibility rules would remain the same, although the flap caused by Edmontonian Betty Wright's win in 1966 prompted the addition of a new rule aimed at out-of-town winners.

In order to compete for the Stampede Queen Title,

applicants must be: (1) A resident of Alberta for one year prior to the closing of entries. (2) Be prepared to reside in Metropolitan Calgary by June 1 following the Horse Show if she is chosen Queen or Princess. (3) Must be 19 years of age and under 24 years of age on the closing date of entry. (4) Single and must remain single during her reign as Queen or Princess.[338]

Although it was not articulated as an official rule on the contest entry form until the early 1980s, it was during this period that the custom evolved of not allowing finalists to run again. Previously, only former winners had been disallowed from re-entering. After a final riding competition at the horse show was introduced in 1964, organizers began to suspect that participation in this public event gave previous finalists an unfair advantage over new, untried contestants. When the Stampede took over the contest, this suspicion led to a rule barring any young woman who had finished in the top five (later the top six) from ever competing again.[339] Although its assumptions and validity were questioned occasionally, this restriction on eligibility would stay in effect for the next 35 years.

The ACT's $5 entry fee was retained and it was decided that

The selection of Queen will be made on the same basis as in 1966, whereby the Queen will enter the finals at the Horse Show carrying 20% on personality, poise and appearance, which will be added to her marks attained on her riding ability at the Horse Show, which will account for 80%.[340]

The scoring for the horse show itself was based on riding ability (55 per cent), personality and poise (40 per cent), and something called "barn conduct," a category that actually appeared to rate attitude (5 per cent).[341]

The second Stampede Queen Committee meeting, February 9, 1967, showed that contest arrangements were well in hand. Enough work had been done to allow chairman Frank Finn to present a budget of $3,300 (about $22,400 today).[342] Interestingly, the new Committee's budget request came in very close to the ACT's last budgeted figure, 1966's $2,660 plus the $1,000 granted afterward by the Board to help offset the club's losses. The Committee decided to continue the long-standing tradition of giving scholarships to the winners – $300 to the queen and $150 to the two runners-up – although right from the beginning there seems to have been some disagreement among members regarding the purpose of this money. Generally, in the late 1960s and early 1970s, it seems to have been viewed as an outright gift, but starting in the mid-1970s it came to be considered more of a stipend to cover expenses, to be doled out to winners over the course of their reign at the discretion of the Committee.

The ACT had outfitted the royal court mainly from the proceeds of its fundraising efforts, supplemented by a few donations from local businesses and private citizens. As part of the Stampede organization, the Queen Committee would receive a budget from the Board, but it realized that it could supplement these funds by adopting the ACT's approach and forming partnerships with sponsors to help offset the cost of goods and services required by the trio during its reign. Peter Degenstein reported to the February meeting that previous donors had agreed to continue sponsoring gifts for the winners, notably a saddle for the queen and luggage for the princesses care of Simpsons-Sears and blanket coats for all three from the Hudson's Bay Company. Jack Gow generously volunteered that his company, Gow's Transport, would take over the ACT's role of supplying winners with engraved belt buckles, and Frank Finn arranged for the Stampede to take over from the City of Calgary in presenting a small silver token of appreciation to each member of the royal trio (bracelets, cufflinks, makeup compacts and the like).[343]

The ACT had thanked Simpsons-Sears and The Bay for their donations by having the royalty attend their Stampede week events as featured guests – a win-win situation in terms of advertising. The Stampede Queen Committee was to adopt this same approach, starting in 1967 with donors' items being identified and displayed in the concourse of the Corral during the horse show.[344] Donors were to be given special consideration when they requested the attendance of the queen and princesses for corporate events or photo shoots. Over time, as the number of donors mounted, much of the Stampede trio's time was spent making appearances as a means of thanking donors and other supporters.

The last two ACT queens, Betty Wright and Donna Israelson, were invited to attend and give input to the second Committee meeting in February 1967. One of their recommendations was that Sibyl Butler be appointed chaperone for the 1967 royalty. Sibyl had served several years in that capacity under the ACT and both young women had enjoyed her company. Donna also offered to donate the hat she had been crowned with in 1965 to be used by the Committee as the "Official Hat for Crowning Purposes." This gift was accepted with thanks.[345]

Because of the hard work done by the ACT Queen Committee in refining the contest prior to handing it over to Stampede control, the transition was so smooth that the 1967 contest looked almost interchangeable with 1966, and ran like clockwork. Twenty-one candidates applied by the March 31 closing date; one was eliminated right away and the remaining twenty competed in the first riding test on April 16 at Wilbur Griffith's Pinebrook Ranch. To make the point that this first event was about basic skill and not glamour, the entry form stipulated that "girls must be dressed in suitable Western riding dress, not in Western costumes." As a group, the candidates put their horses through standard reining patterns, first walking, then cantering, finally trotting before a panel of three qualified judges (Stuart McRae, Ralph Rowe and 1949 Stampede Queen Merle Stier).[346]

The ten who survived this first competition went on to the second eliminations in the Stampede's Brand Room on April 21 and 22. The personality and poise part of this trial was conducted by three secret judges (Maria Hagan, Harry Cohen and Doug Johnson) hidden among twenty-five couples invited to a buffet dinner attended by the candidates, who were encouraged to mix and mingle to demonstrate their social skills. Although they could wear cocktail dresses to the dinner, contestants were back in Western dress the next day for the public speaking part of the competition. This event, which involved personal interviews and the presentation of a two-minute speech, was open to the public but most in the audience were family or friends of the ten young competitors.

The five who made it through phase two demonstrated their riding ability once again at the Calgary International Horse Show, May 2–6. Each young lady was required to ride a different horse each night to perform a modified version of a quarter horse Western riding pattern as determined by Alex Bailey and Jerry D'Arcy. Before a panel of three qualified horse show judges, the riders were instructed to

Enter at the in-gate, circle at a slow lope, line up at the east end facing the centre. The first girl will then move out, proceed halfway down the north side to judges' box at walk, trot to corner, lope, then flying changes around stakes, wide open lope, sliding stop and back up a few paces. Each girl will follow in turn. The girls will enter on a rotation basis during the five nights of the Horse Show.[347]

Although the final competition was a serious test of riding ability, the mark distribution reveals the Committee's awareness that other qualities were of almost equal importance in choosing a queen: nearly half of the final mark was based on the assessment of personality, poise, public speaking, and attitude.[348]

The winning trio was crowned before a crowd of more than 6,000 at the Stampede Corral on the final night of the show: 21-year-old Queen Patsy Allan and Princesses Bonnie MacGregor and Candace Smith, both 19. Queen Patsy limped into the dressing room after acknowledging her win because a horse had stepped squarely on her toe while she was presenting a ribbon during the afternoon show.[349] Interestingly, Bonnie MacGregor was a former Edmontonian who had gone through high school with Betty Wright and had roomed with the 1966 queen after moving to Calgary. In view of the fuss made in 1966, the Committee kept Bonnie's Edmonton origins quiet.[350]

As in the past, the young ladies each received two nicely styled western suits in autumn colours designed by Orpha Gow, one in a fine wool crepe and the other in a heavy "sofa" brocade, both lined and very hot to wear, especially in July during the Stampede. One suit or the other, and sometimes both, was picked up late each evening for dry cleaning and returned fresh and ready to wear by the next morning. They received two pairs of boots and a little purse to match. Princess Bonnie had short hair and the others pulled theirs back for a neat and tidy look completed by wearing white gloves. Instead

Queen Patsy Allan after winning her title at the Calgary International Horse Show, 1967. (GA: NA-2864-18139B)

of neckties, the girls wore a rhinestone brooch at their collar. Queen Patsy had a star-shaped rhinestone brooch on her hat in lieu of a tiara, and her Princesses wore hatbands consisting of a little strip of rhinestones. A little bit jealous of Patsy's prize saddle, Bonnie used her $150 scholarship to buy a saddle of her own.[351]

In keeping with their determination that the trio would spend more time on the grounds during Stampede week, and perhaps to save a little money as well, the Committee briefly considered housing the 1967 royalty and their chaperone at the nearby Elbow Lodge Motor Hotel, but in the end they decided to stick with tradition and the group stayed in a two-bedroom suite at the much nicer and more centrally located Palliser Hotel.[352] Stampede "week" went to nine days from seven that year, a rather odd arrangement because it ran from Thursday until the next Friday, with Sunday as a day off because of Lord's Day Act restrictions. The parade occurred midway through the festivities on the Monday morning. Sometime between their crowning at the horse show and the start of the Stampede, the threesome attended a self-improvement training course which taught them about etiquette, makeup, walking properly and getting in and out of cars in a ladylike manner.[353]

As part of the transition process, there were a number of special events in 1967 celebrating the ACT's long association with the Stampede Queen contest. The ACT donated pictures of all past winners to the Stampede; in April the club newsletter announced with satisfaction that these would be displayed, along with an ACT crest and plaque, "in a prominent position along with all noteworthy celebrities of the past."[354] On April 1, seven former queens attended the club's last-ever Stampede Queen luncheon at the Westgate Hotel. Merle Stier (1949), Marquitta Elton (1957), Julie Akkerman (1959), Marie Sharpe (1961), Donna Thomson (1962) and Frances Swann (1963) joined 1966 Queen Betty Wright and her Ladies-in-waiting, Lorraine McLean and Ann Nielson, in an enjoyable afternoon reminiscing about their individual reigns and comparing notes about contest changes over the years.[355]

As a link between past and present, from the old system of choosing Stampede royalty to the new, the Committee invited all former queens to ride in the 1967 parade. The original intention had been to have all past winners ride but that idea was dropped when the Committee realized that including all previous ladies-in-waiting would make the section too big. In the end, fourteen former queens either rode behind 1967 Queen Patsy and Princesses Bonnie and Candace or cheered from the sidelines: Patsy Rodgers (1946), Doreen Richardson (1947), Gloria Klaver (1948), Merle Stier (1949), Eileen Beckner (1950), Edith Edge (1953), Mary Ellen Jones (1955), Julie Akkerman (1959), Margot Turney (1960), Marie Sharpe (1961), Donna Thomson (1962), Sharon Patterson (1964), Donna Israelson (1965), and Betty Wright (1966). Many of these women had married and changed their names but they were identifiable to parade watchers because the horses they rode sported red and white serapes announcing the name under which they had won and their year of winning.[356]

Since 1967 was Canada's centennial year, the biggest event for the trio, aside from the Stampede itself of course, was their attendance at Expo '67 in Montreal. The highlight was their participation in the Alberta Day parade held on October 7. It was a mammoth extravaganza that featured, in addition to the Stampede Queen and Princesses, six chuckwagons, eight marching bands, twenty Indians in full dress, 200 horses, a mule train, floats from Calgary and Edmonton, and Wilf Carter and his Midnight Ramblers.[357]

Unfortunately, the trip to Montreal proved to be one of the last functions the 1967 group attended as a trio. On November 9 the Stampede Board was informed that Princess Candace had married, and as a result was no longer qualified to represent the Stampede.[358] Although there was as yet no written contract requiring winners to remain unmarried for the year, the expectation certainly was there. Contest rules stated quite clearly: "Single and must remain single during her reign as Queen or Princess."[359] The heaviest period of Stampede promotion was over for the year but the Committee was disappointed at having its trio become a duo mid-reign. This development led to a stronger statement of contest rules (candidates were required to be "single, promising to remain so for the year of their reign"[360]) and the introduction of a preliminary meeting for applicants before the contest officially began. The informal introductory meeting was an opportunity for potential candidates to ask questions and for Committee members to outline contest procedures and expectations.[361] As such, it proved to be a very good tool for weeding out applicants who were not prepared to follow the rules or make the year-long commitment.

In a promotional piece leading up to the 1968 contest, the *Calgary Herald*'s Vern Simaluk speculated that a "ranch-girl turned 'city slicker'" was likely to be Stampede Queen. He had looked at past winners and noticed a trend. "Twenty years ago, Stampede queens generally came from rural communities, but recently city girls have been riding off with most of the queenly crowns since industrialization of the provincial economy started in earnest in the 1950s." Simaluk's research had revealed that Calgary's dominance was somewhat deceptive, as most past "city" winners had been born in rural areas and had "saddled their first horse at a ranch corral instead of a riding stable." However, "the lure of urbanization [had] caused the country girls to trade in their jeans for mini-skirts," an explanation, in his opinion, for the fact that twenty of the twenty-five application forms issued to young women wishing to enter the 1968 contest had been sent to Calgary addresses.[362]

Unwilling to tamper with its first successful contest, the 1968 Queen Committee simply duplicated all that had been done in 1967. Based on a year of actual experience, it increased its budget request to the Board to $4,000, broken down as follows:

General expenses:
Publicity $300
Queen's Western dress outfits $850
Gifts and honorariums $650
Meeting expense $50
Sundry and contingencies $225

Special expenses:
Preliminary judging $100
Buffet reception (Personality, poise judging) $250
Final judging (Appearance & ability) $65
Care of horses (Horse Show and Stampede) $200
Hats $40
Stampede Week accommodation $725
　　Stampede tickets:
　　Presentation night $70
Serapes $60
Cleaning and transportation allowance $300
Chaperone, Stampede Week $140
Photographs $75
　　　Total $4,100 [less entry fees of $100]
　　　Net $4,000.[363]

Although there was a budget line for publicity, the amount was used mainly for advertising the contest; the Public Information Committee's budget covered the cost of giveaways such as souvenir postcards of the queen and princesses.[364]

In 1968 the Lord's Day Act restrictions were lifted, allowing the Stampede to fill in the Sunday gap and

1968 Queen Diane Leech (centre) with Princesses Arlene Weidner and Heather Lawrence. (GA: PA-2807-2265A)

Queen Diane Leech being fitted for her official outfit by dressmaker Elfreda Holtkamp, 1968. (GA: NA-2864-18175K)

become a ten-day event, a relief with attendance numbers continuing to climb. By decade's end, the figure had exceeded 800,000, more than double Calgary's resident population.[365] However, the parade kept to the Monday morning tradition, only switching to the first Friday of Stampede in 1976. Once again, an invitation was issued to former Queens to ride in the parade.[366] Seven accepted and rode behind the royal convertible that had been supplied by Maclin Motors and featured the 1968 Queen, 21-year-old Diane Leech and her Princesses, 19-year-old Heather Lawrence and 21-year-old Arlene Weidner.

All three winners were announced as Calgarians, but Heather was a very recent arrival from Edmonton and Arlene had only come into the city from the Didsbury area to train as a nurse. The Queen Committee often suspected that word of mouth was the most effective approach for attracting contestants and that suspicion was confirmed in 1968. Both princesses had been encouraged to enter the contest by previous winners: Arlene's neighbour on the family farm had been 1965 Queen Donna Israelson, and Heather was a cousin of 1967 Princess Bonnie MacGregor.[367]

With the contest now operating in such a straightforward and predictable manner, reporters turned to other aspects of the royal experience to enliven their columns. In June 1968, Beth Raugust of the *Calgary Herald* produced a piece on Mrs. Herman W. Holtkamp, a dressmaker who had worked with Orpha Gow since 1963 designing and creating official outfits for Stampede royalty. The article featured pictures of Elfreda Holtkamp fitting Queen Diane for one of her two prize outfits, one made in heavy brocade and the other in the traditional wool crepe. "We stick strictly to western wear because this is custom and tradition for Calgary and the Stampede," she said. "But each year I try to make the costumes a little different either by an unusual piping or by varying the type of yoke. And each year the color of the outfits must also be different. The girls' suits must be interchangeable in case they soil one during the events." Mrs. Holtkamp confided to Raugust that she had been secretly grateful when the ACT had dropped ticket sales and shifted the contest conclusion to the horse show in early May. Prior to that, "the queen selection was made so late we had to work day and night to finish the costumes," but now she and her staff had a few extra weeks to create the outfits before they were needed for Stampede duties.[368]

Another *Herald* reporter searching for a human interest story in 1968 interviewed royal chaperone, Sibyl Butler. "Ten hectic days of chaperoning the Stampede Queen is Mrs. Sibyl Butler's idea of a holiday" began the article. The widow of an ACT member, she had become involved in the contest in 1962 when she chaperoned unsuccessful candidates during their two-day on-the-town consolation prize. In 1964 she graduated to chaperoning the queen and ladies-in-waiting, and the Calgary stenographer had spent every vacation since doing the job she loved, chaperoning Stampede royalty:

> It is her duty to be at the side of the Stampede queen and princesses for the entire Stampede. This means checking into the Palliser with the three girls for the duration and attending all the functions. Everything from getting the girls out of bed in the morning to sewing buttons on Western outfits comes into the chaperone's domain… By the end of the day, all four women fall into bed and "die."[369]

It was not hard to discover why Sibyl was such a favourite with winning trios. "She had high praise for the girls who become Stampede 'royalty' each July. 'Every year you meet three nice girls and you think you could never meet nicer ones, but the next year, three more lovely girls come along.'"[370]

More than forty years later, Princess Arlene gave Butler a lot of credit for how well the 1968 trio got along during their intense week at the Palliser. Diane was an easygoing queen, and all three went into the experience with a good attitude, determined to make it work, but little disagreements were inevitable. "It's quite a strain," Mrs. Butler told a reporter. "By the end of the second week the girls are tired and a lot of tension has built up."[371] But, with the help of their den mother, the girls "learned how to work around it or through it and talk about it." Confident and experienced, Sibyl was firm and consistent, a stickler for rules and but also a lot of fun, and she never wavered in her message that it was a team effort. The girls found her presence very grounding. She treated them all the same and never played favourites but did not hesitate to take them down a peg if she felt they needed it, reminding them "not to let their heads get too big for their hats."[372] She served as a royal chaperone for a decade and was one of the first to be made an Honorary Associate of the newly formed Queens' Alumni Association in 1974.

One of the exciting perks enjoyed by Queen Diane, though not her princesses, unfortunately, was being among the first to meet federal Liberal leader Pierre Elliott Trudeau when he made a brief campaign stop in Calgary just a week before his party won a majority and he became Prime Minister of Canada. On behalf of the city, Diane joined officials and a crowd of 4,000 excited local citizens at the Calgary airport just before midnight on June 18, 1968, to greet Trudeau with the ubiquitous white hat. She must have been the envy of many a swooning Canadian woman in the throes of Trudeaumania that spring when she had the opportunity to kiss the dashing and sexy new leader.[373]

The 1968 trio was the first since 1960 to attend the Grey Cup. They travelled to Toronto as part of the Calgary delegation supporting the Stampeders football team against the Ottawa Rough Riders. Typically the Calgary Grey Cup committee ensured that the city's parade entry promoted its most identifiable product, the Stampede, as well as the city itself and the concept of Western hospitality.

Following the banner proclaiming Calgary will be the city float, a giant white hat counterbalanced by a huge football, proudly announcing "Here's Calgary." Then will follow Pat Cooper, Miss Stampeder, in a sports car flanked by the marching Stampettes. Immediately behind them will ride the horsemen led by Mayor Jack Leslie and Mrs. Leslie… Preceding the rumbling chuckwagons will be Stampede Queen Diane Leech and her princesses Arlene Weidner and Heather Lawrence… Bill Herron's western car with its mounted guns, rifles, silver dollars and hand-tooled leather upholstery will follow.[374]

As lovely as Mrs. Butler had found each new crop of royalty, after several years of running the contest, the Stampede Queen Committee began to wonder if its focus on finding the best possible riders might not be narrowing the field in the search for the best possible representatives for the Stampede. In 1968, Committee member Jerry D'Arcy suggested reversing the order of judging to effect a change in emphasis. The Committee, agreeing unanimously to try D'Arcy's approach, followed through in the 1969 contest by testing for personality and such before, rather than after, the first riding elimination. It was hoped this would ensure that the ten semifinalists had the right soft skills for the job, even if better riders ended up being eliminated. In any case, poorer riders would be given time to improve their skills before the first riding test pared numbers down to five finalists.[375]

This new approach was very obvious when Committee chairman Alex Bailey met the media in January 1969. "Applications are being sought for young women between 19 and 23 who like meeting celebrities from all over the world and have the stamina to attend at least 100 functions and parties in one year. In addition, they have to be beautiful, be good at speaking in public and show fine form on a horse." Bailey predicted that about twenty young women would "take a shot at being the city's top glamor girl."[376] The rewards were spelled out in newspaper advertisements:

> What it means to be the Stampede Queen: You will be in the newspaper, on television and radio, and make personal appearances on behalf of the Calgary Exhibition and Stampede. You will meet hundreds of fascinating people – celebrities, civic officials and dignitaries. You will also receive many valuable prizes including: $300 Scholarship for the Queen and $150 for each Princess, plus complete western outfits from the Calgary Exhibition and Stampede; Queen's saddle and luggage for each Princess from Simpsons-Sears; Hudson Bay coats for Queen and two Princesses from The Bay; cowboy boots from Woodward's; plus many other valuable prizes.[377]

The winning trio were all from Calgary: 21-year-old Queen Carol Burns and Princesses Patricia Johnston, 20, and Winnifred Reid, 21. Patsy and Winn were university students, but Queen Carol, who had won after a previous attempt at the crown, was an assistant sales manager at The Bay, likely an important consideration in "hiring" her to lead the team in what was now being described in the media as "a full year of public-relations work for the world's greatest outdoor show."[378]

Among their many other activities (some 200 over the year), the 1969 trio was the first to attend the Quebec Winter Carnival. As one perceptive reporter observed, "Calgary is willing to do almost anything to promote itself and the Stampede. So sending the Stampede queen and princesses to the Quebec Winter Carnival in Quebec City is not unrealistic. In return, Bonhomme Carnaval, symbol of our sister city's winter festivities, comes here for the Stampede." While enjoying the winter festival, the girls "blew Calgary's horn and drummed up interest in the city and the Stampede."[379]

In recognition of the trio's wider public role, a more sophisticated look was deemed desirable, so the group was given a crash course in queenly appearance and deportment courtesy of John Cox, a volunteer in charge of makeup and onstage training for The Young Canadians. Cox was also a friend and former colleague of Joan Plastow, who had encouraged him to extend his expert advice and services to the Stampede royals. After several years of volunteering in this capacity, he officially joined the Queen Committee. Joan hosted many fondly remembered evening sessions in her apartment, where Cox

worked with the girls on their public image. After several years, local actor Gary Dan began attending the sessions to relieve Cox of coaching deportment and public speaking, but in the beginning Cox did it all.[380] According to a reporter who shadowed the 1969 trio through one of their sessions, he had spent nineteen hours over many evenings "coaching the girls on makeup techniques, camera poise, how to wave gracefully and how to smile… and smile… and smile." The young women, clearly enjoying their sessions, had ready explanations for why the Committee had felt it necessary to enhance the public image of the royalty:

165
★

> The emphasis has moved away from the cowgirl image. "We have to be 'sophisticated Western ladies' this year," explained Carol… We can't waggle our hands in front of our faces when we wave. And we can't just stand there and smile when someone is taking a picture – we have to line up in three-quarter position."
>
> The girls demonstrated the stance, as Mr. Cox murmured, "Chin up. Don't clench your fist. A little bit more this way, girls. There."
>
> Winnifred… laughed as she said, "When we stand this way, nobody knows we're bowlegged from riding too much." …

1969 Queen Carol Burns (centre) with Princesses Winnifred Reid and Patricia Johnston. (GA: PA-2807-379B)

The Stampede Queen look has changed this year. "For the first time, we're wearing earrings," [Carol] said, pointing to the delicate pearls all three girls will wear.

"Our hair will always be worn back, with a postiche [chignon], so it doesn't fly around in the convertibles or when we're riding. And we never take our hats off in public at any time during Stampede. Our outfits have little pearls sewn on to match the earrings; I wear a new jewelled pin in my hat."

The outfits have become more tailored and sophisticated. The skirts will be quite mini – "because the girls don't have maxi legs," laughed John Cox. And instead of leather or suede, the matching vests will be in fine brocade.

The final subtle sophistication has to be the boots the girls will wear. They're cowboy boots, all right – but they have been sent to Montreal, metropolis of Eastern culture, to be dyed to match the pant suits and dress outfits. And the color is not good old Western brown, either – it's blue…

[The ladies] are worried not so much about nervousness as about being tired. No matter how hot the sun is, or how hard it's raining, they will have to maintain a bubbling enthusiasm and a ready smile.

Mr. Cox has given them a word to say very quietly whenever they're tired and yet another photographer

1969 Queen Carol Burns (far left) and Princesses Patricia Johnston and Winnifred Reid posing with Bonhomme Carnaval at the Quebec Winter Carnival, 1970. (QAC)

is shouting, "Hold it!" It is a common word, short, which expresses frustration well yet lends itself to a pretty smile. But that word is a secret. We couldn't print it here.[381]

Queen Carol's team approach, very much a result of her job experience, was just right for the times, a period when the Committee was transitioning the royalty from local goodwill ambassadors into a well-packaged modern promotional tool for the Stampede. Although many previous trios had achieved a harmonious relationship through goodwill or good management, the concept of the threesome functioning as an interdependent team all working toward the same goal only emerged during the late 1960s after the Stampede committee took over from the ACT and changed the emphasis from a queen with two attendants to a royal trio. Even so, because there was a competition, which of course had a winner, the queen, it was all the more important to select this individual wisely in order to promote rather than hinder the team effort.

A media interview near the end of Carol's reign made it clear how significant her leadership had been in helping to facilitate this transition.

Unlike other years, when the Stampede queen has made numerous public appearances on her own,

this year's "royalty" is a trio. "I felt we should be a threesome at all times and I told the queen committee so," says… Carol. "I hope queens in the future will insist on this too, and not steal all the glory for themselves." Carol is firm about this; she knows she could not have done the job without her princesses. "Patty sets the pace. She is always in a good mood. Winnifred has the dry sense of humor and is always making us laugh." During the 12 days they lived together during Stampede – up at 6 am and never to bed much before 2 am – there was never a blow-up. "Any problems we had we settled among ourselves."

The article's concluding statement confirmed the new direction for all future royalty: "As Stampede queen, Carol attributes her effectiveness to the fact she was pushing a product – Calgary and the Stampede – she believes in. 'I hope next year's queen has the same idea. As Stampede queen, you are doing a job for the city.'"[382]

CHAPTER 9 ★ 1970–1974

"It takes ability – and plenty of it – to become Stampede Queen"

With Calgary's population continuing to expand and oil fuelling the local economy, the 1970s were good years for the Stampede. Attendance, which was hovering around 800,000 going into the decade, hit the one million mark in 1976.[383] After the success of the Stampede's Salute to the Petroleum Industry in 1966, annual themes helped to attract new audiences to the show. The Board, sensitive to 1960s criticism that the fair had been Hollywoodized, turned more often to Canadian politicians, sports heroes and international celebrities as parade marshals and special guests, although it still relied on popular actors, entertainers and musical groups to entice crowds to the grounds. With the ongoing participation of The Young Canadians, the evening grandstand show grew to become a more polished, professional offering. The old grandstand was replaced with a modern structure in 1974, the same year the Exhibition grounds

Queen Vicky Hayden (centre) and Princesses Lynn Boake and Cheryl Going with members of the Tsuu T'ina First Nation entertaining downtown during Stampede week, 1970. (GA: NA-2864-5878-4)

were renamed Stampede Park. By 1976, when the parade was moved to the first Friday of Stampede from its traditional Monday slot, the ten-day fair had achieved the modern structure still evident today.

The decade also saw the rise in Canada of what later came to be termed second-wave feminism, a movement that pushed for equal rights for women and the liberation of women from social and media objectification. These new attitudes had started percolating in Calgary during the previous decade but were much more in evidence in the 1970s with the rise of local feminist groups and the well-publicized push for equal pay, access to birth control and abortion and an end to sexual stereotyping.[384] The Stampede Queen contest had never promoted itself as a beauty contest – in fact, in the early years of ticket sales it was more of a popularity contest – but winners in the 1940s and 1950s rarely had qualms about posing for cheesecake-style photographs or sharing personal information with reporters. This would become unheard of in the more enlightened decades to follow, but the 1970s was a curious period of contrasts for the Stampede as attitudes evolved: early in the decade, the Calgary Jaycees (Junior Chamber of Commerce) were still advertising a beauty contest to choose Miss Pot o' Gold and two Gold Diggers to promote their Stampede Jackpot lottery, but by 1979 the Stampede Board had appointed its first female director, Eleanor Bailey.[385]

The fact that winners were called queens and princesses, and that candidates were judged on appearance and other traditionally feminine qualities such as poise, grooming and manners, made the queen contest an obvious and easy target for feminist criticism. Organizers and winners held fast to the line that skills and ability were more important considerations than personal appearance, but few trios escaped insinuations, even outright assumptions, that they had participated in a traditional beauty contest. Although the occasional dismissive or derogatory comment stung or made them feel angry, winners were well supported by chaperones and Committee members who taught them to anticipate and deflect negative statements by gracefully ignoring, correcting, or redirecting the conversation in a more positive direction. Luckily, the Stampede was such a good tourist draw, and so strongly identified with Calgary's well-being and economic development,[386] that the publicity department had little difficulty in garnering media support and overt criticism of the contest and its winners rarely made the news.

In 1970, *Herald* reporter Edythe Humphrey attempted to bolster the contest's public image by issuing a warning to potential candidates. "If she thinks it's a beauty queen contest, with cheesecake to the fore, she's in for a rude shock and might as well forget the whole idea. It takes ability – and plenty of it – to become Stampede Queen." Humphrey then gave a detailed overview of the judging process for those encouraged to persist:

At the first go-round… the girls have three functions to attend… judges meet and talk with them and consider their general poise, grooming and social sense… second… each give[s] a 3-minute speech on a subject of their choice… third… [a] private interview at which each candidate is asked the same set of questions by the judges, and is judged on her awareness and spontaneity. The marks are totalled and ten girls are chosen from the initial entries, as semifinalists.

The ten semifinalists are given about five weeks in which they must improve their riding skills. At the end of April, they are judged on their equestrian ability, and the marks for this are added to their previous scores.

From this group, five are selected to compete at the horse show. Not only are they marked by international equestrian judging, they are given points for barn cleaning and punctuality as well. The girl with the highest score wins the honors.

There is no voting, but by the time the contest ends, 15 judges have looked the contestants over.

Once the queen is chosen it isn't all glamour either. This year's queen and attendants will have filled 75 to 80 engagements other than their Stampede appearances by the time their reign is over.[387]

By 1970 that hard work on behalf of the Stampede consisted of being on the go for up to fifteen hours a day for twelve days straight during the show and being present at an average of two additional functions per week for the rest of the year.[388] Journalist Elaine Seskevich decided to do a "day in the life" piece on the 1970 royalty, trailing after them on Children's Day when they not only participated in some of those activities but also made appearances at a Stampede breakfast, the Foothills Hospital, an economics convention luncheon, a reception at Fort Calgary House, the Elks Golf Club and a Rotary Club barbecue, as well as making their usual appearances at the afternoon rodeo and before the evening grandstand show. Aside from a one-hour rest break to change clothes

and freshen up their hair and makeup, the trio was zipped from place to place all day long in the royal convertible, accompanied by faithful chaperone Sibyl Butler with her white vinyl "diaper bag" full of supplies for quick repairs. And through it all, despite nursing blisters and sunburns, the trio observed the golden rule: "Ya gotta keep smiling." At the end of the day, an exhausted Seskevich concluded, "It's a job that requires the endurance of a stevedore, charm of Dale Carnegie, good looks of a starlet and equestrian know-how of Gene Autry. Few men could keep up with the hectic pace."[389]

After this long and relatively rigorous judging process in the spring of 1970, Vicky Hayden, a 21-year-old Calgary nurse from Rimbey, was crowned Queen with two 19-year-old University of Calgary students as her Princesses: Cheryl Going of Black Diamond and Lynn Boake of Acme. When they accepted their crowns, a reporter noted they had committed themselves to "a dizzying round of functions throughout the year. The queen and her princesses work hard for their royalty."[390] But, with the 1969 trio as a model, Queen Vicky promised that the queen and princesses would act as a unit. "If I can't attend a function, Lynn and Cheryl will go together… Nobody [will] ever go alone. We'll give each other moral support and help hold each other up when we're tired."[391]

Queen Vicky Hayden and Princesses Lynn Boake and Cheryl Going dancing with members of the Tsuu T'ina First Nation during Stampede week, 1970. (GA: NA-2864-5878-13)

1970 Queen Vicky Hayden (far left) with Princesses Cheryl Going and Lynn Boake. (CSA)

Relying on the same advertisement that had proven to be an effective hook in previous contests – the

ad that promised "a world of excitement for you as the Calgary Stampede Queen" – the 1971 contest attracted twenty-five competitors, the largest group since 1959's record thirty-three. One of the judges for the personality and poise segment was 1967 Queen Patsy Allan. The topics chosen by the hopefuls for their three-minute speech provide a illuminating glimpse at the times. "They talked on themselves, drug abuse, Bobby Orr, recreation, the Stampede and horses, what is a teacher, the Canadian Forces Naval Reserve, highway deaths, oil industry, fashion and hair, friendship, spelunking (cave exploration), reputations, prejudices."[392]

On the final night of the Calgary International Horse Show, 23-year-old Calgarian Leslie MacDonald, a hostess in the Air Canada Maple Leaf Lounge, was crowned Queen with the traditional white hat by Stampede president Ed O'Connor and outgoing Queen Vicky Hayden. Once again, word-of-mouth communication had been at work in encouraging participation in the contest. Leslie knew several former queens through the Saddle Club and the Calgary Pony Club (including Margot Turney and Patsy Allan), but it had been her immediate supervisor at work, Queen Committee volunteer John Cox, who had encouraged her to enter the contest.[393]

Leslie had been riding and showing horses for

years, so she was delighted with her main prize, a beautiful hand-tooled quarter-horse saddle sponsored by Simpsons-Sears and crafted by Eamor's Saddlery of High River. The winning princesses were two 19-year-olds, Wendy Copithorne, a student nurse in Lethbridge, and Calgarian Shirley Inkster, a student at the University of Calgary. Wendy, from a long-established Cochrane-area ranching family, was an excellent horsewoman, but self-proclaimed city girl Shirley had learned to ride simply to enter the contest. Remembering her lessons at Art Anderson's local stables, she said "I cried a lot but I learned."[394]

A photo shoot on the Exhibition grounds reinforced the sophisticated Western lady style that the Queen Committee had been striving for since 1969. The trio was shown wearing white gloves and outfits specially designed by "The House of Everal" (Mrs. Everal Jones of Priddis). Red-and-white cowboy boots and crushed-velvet handbags completed the look.[395] But the girls ended up supplementing their outfits with a few tricks of their own. As later recalled by Princess Shirley, on chilly days they

Queen Leslie MacDonald (far left) and Princesses Shirley Inkster and Wendy Copithorne receiving official gifts from Stampede president Ed O'Connor, 1971. (CSA)

wrapped blankets under their Hudson's Bay coats, and they learned to put Vaseline on their teeth to prevent their lipstick from coming off during the many hours of being under public scrutiny.[396]

Just as the Stampede was ending, Queen Leslie surprised a reporter by suggesting that the show should consider having a rodeo king to help the queen and princesses through the busy week. "He could be chosen in the same manner as we are," she said, with a public speaking contest, a riding elimination and a banquet with judges and officials. She envisioned him to be more than simply the queen's escort, adding that "his role would have to be kept very masculine, just as ours is kept feminine although we wear Western garb." After examining the trio's Stampede week duties, the reporter concluded that there was one job a rodeo king might not do as well as his female counterparts: "escorting winning cowboys all [Saturday] afternoon."[397]

During the late 1960s, the Queen Committee had experimented with advertising the Stampede beyond Alberta borders by sending queens and princesses to big national and international events in addition to little local parades and rodeos. Royal trios had gone to the Grey Cup festivities in 1960 and 1968, the Tournament of Roses parade in 1966 and the Quebec Winter Carnival in 1969. All three forays were judged to have been successful in promoting the Stampede, so the 1970s saw a continuation of this trend, although there was no consistent policy and suitable destinations were chosen year by year depending on finances and the best use of the Stampede's promotional resources. Some trios travelled to one or another of these big events, some went to all three and some also attended events in neighbouring British Columbia and the northwestern United States.

In 1971 the Stampede Board vetoed the Queen Committee's request to send the trio to Pasadena for the Tournament of Roses parade because the Promotion Committee was already paying half the cost of the city's float and that was considered to be a sufficient contribution. But, in compensation, they agreed to let the girls represent the Stampede at the Grey Cup, being held that year in Vancouver.[398] The group also travelled to Wyoming to attend Cheyenne Frontier Days. That particular outing ended prematurely for Queen Leslie after the trio and their chaperone, Joan Plastow, stopped en route in Fort Collins, Colorado, to look at an unusual statue consisting simply of a pair of legs topped by a loin cloth. Examining the statue a little too closely, Leslie received "a giant bloody gash across her nose." While flying to Denver for plastic surgery, she baffled a fellow passenger with the explanation, "Oh, I cut myself on an Indian's loincloth."[399]

In the fall of 1971, a small group of long-retired Stampede Queens who were personal friends came up with the idea of forming a social club for former queens and princesses so that these women with common interests and experiences could stay in touch and provide mentoring support for current royalty. Merle Stier (1949) suggested the idea to friends Patsy Rodgers (1946) and Donna Thomson (1962), and the three approached Queen Committee chairman Alex Bailey, requesting permission to form an alumni association using the Stampede Queen name.[400] Bailey was excited by the idea of tapping into the expertise of generations of capable women who had been trained specifically to support and promote the Stampede. He suggested taking the idea a step further and forming an official Stampede committee so that the social group could give back within the recognized structure of the Stampede. Realizing what an integral part of the Stampede they could be, Stampede president Ed O'Connor was enthusiastic and took the idea to the Board on November 8, 1971, gaining approval for the alumni group to use the Stampede Queen name and for the formation of a full-fledged Stampede committee provisionally called the Women's Committee.[401]

In January 1972 the Women's World Committee was created as the Stampede's first all-female committee. The Board specified that Committee members "would be drawn from the women who have reigned since the Stampede took over the contest in 1964."[402] One of the Committee's first activities was helping Donna, Merle and Patsy to locate former queens and princesses, a job made more difficult because so many had moved away from Calgary or married and changed their names.[403] The response from those they contacted was overwhelmingly positive, so, in the spring of 1972, more than twenty former queens, princesses and ladies-in-waiting met to form the Calgary Stampede Queens' Alumni Association. The first executive consisted of Merle Stier (chair), Donna Thomson (vice-chair) and 1959 Lady-in-waiting Doreen Wynne (secretary-treasurer).

As directed by the Board, the main focus of the Women's World Committee was public relations, so during the 1972 Stampede, members hosted Tourist and Convention Association functions and the annual Hays Breakfast and presented mini western fashion shows. It also established a Women's World display in Flare Square on the Exhibition grounds that featured three kitchens: historical, modern and futuristic.[404] The following year, the group took over running the annual Stampede handicraft competition and display and began riding together in the parade as a colour party. In 1975 it added the Western Art Display and Auction to its responsibilities. In all of these activities, the Committee was assisted by volunteers from the Alumni Association, and as the commitment grew larger, volunteers from the wider community, including men. In 1978 the name was changed to the Creative Living Committee to better reflect this broader community involvement.[405]

Many alumni chose to volunteer on this Committee as it evolved, but those who declined still enjoyed the social benefits of belonging to the alumni group. In 1976 the Association introduced an annual luncheon where royalty from the previous year were officially inducted into the alumni and the reigning queen and princesses were introduced to the group. That year also saw the alumni host the first Stampede Stomp, a pre-Stampede party for the fair's hundreds of volunteers. By the end of the decade, the group had added a service dimension, with a commitment to sponsor Stampede-related activities for special-needs children that started with the first Stampede Special breakfast and morning on the grounds during the 1979 Stampede.[406]

In the meantime, the annual contest to choose a queen and princesses took place as usual in 1972, but at Rodeo Royal, an indoor rodeo held at the Stampede

Corral which that year had replaced the International Horse Show as Calgary's premier springtime riding event. The horse show had been held in early May but Rodeo Royal opened in late March, so the 1971 trio's reign ended some six weeks earlier than usual. The timing of the new event suited the Queen Committee quite well, as now there would be more training time for new royals before Stampede activities began. However, the change necessitated an earlier contest closing date, mid-February, and a quicker, early January, start to contest advertising in the new year. It also prompted the Committee to re-evaluate contest organization and introduce a few new rules. Experimenting with lowering the upper age limit, the rules for 1972 read: "Contestants must be residents of Calgary or surrounding area, be between 19 and 23 years of age inclusive, and be single, promising to remain so for the year of their reign."[407]

Everything else about the contest stayed the same. Ever since judged events had been introduced into the proceedings in 1959, community volunteers had been involved in helping to judge various aspects of the competition. In 1972 *Calgary Herald* columnist Johnny Hopkins joined Martha Cohen, Bob Jenkins, Mona Cozart and 1962 Queen Donna Thomson to rate the contestants on poise, decorum and public speaking. Reporting on the experience, Hopkins joked, "It's not an easy job – looking at and talking to 17 fine girls, all the while being lavishly entertained by the Stampede board." Before they served as hidden judges for the buffet dinner, event organizer Joan Plastow and committee chairman Alex Bailey gave the judges a few pointers. Hopkins learned that young women who used incorrect grammar (words like "ain't") or foul language were to be eliminated immediately. He was worried that judging during the buffet dinner might prove to be an impossible task, but found, to his surprise, that "the five judges were almost in complete accord as they were the next day for the public speaking." Moreover, the young candidates were surprisingly impressive.

The judges, if I may speak for the rest of them, quickly learned that age bracket has a lot of poise and, for lack of a better word, class. They're radiant. They're articulate... It was also pointed out [by Donna] that most of the queens and princesses over the years have been superb – maintaining their good humor throughout the year and their poise in moments of chaos.[408]

Patti Girling, a 19-year-old Calgarian and receptionist, was crowned Queen on March 25 on the final night of Rodeo Royal. Princesses for the year were

Queen Patti Girling (centre) and Princesses Dawn MacLean and Diane Wallace celebrating the Calgary Stampede's 60th anniversary, 1972. (CSA)

19-year-old Diane Wallace of Brooks and 21-year-old Dawn MacLean of Calgary. After a decade of chaperoning royalty, Sybil Butler had retired, to be replaced in 1972 by 1949 Lady-in-waiting Inez Melby.[409] The

next year, 1971 Queen Leslie MacDonald took over as main chaperone for the royal trio and coordinator of their activities. She served in that capacity on the Queen Committee for a decade before resigning in

1983 to serve another thirty years as a queen contest horsemanship judge.[410]

As her reign was ending, Queen Patti reminisced about her year. The trio had done all the usual things, including riding in the Grey Cup parade in Hamilton, but for Patti the two highlights had been "Meeting Chief Dan George – he's just a lovely man [and]… going through the Stampede midway with [Olympic] skater Karen Magnussen… I'll never forget that. She's just a wonderful person." As Queen, Patti was several years younger than her immediate predecessors (the last five of whom had been 21 or older. Betty Wright in 1966 had been the last 19-year-old to be queen). Therefore, it was not surprising that Patti reflected that she had "grown up a lot" and "learned a lot" over the year of leading the royal team. But, in a plug for the 1973 contest, she emphasized that it was a job any enthusiastic and motivated young woman could do. "I'll bet there's a lot of girls who don't think they have a chance to be Stampede Queen. But they really do… You don't have to be a ravishing beauty, a model or [even] a great rider… All you have to do is be able to stay aboard a horse and manage it."[411]

This column may have encouraged a few more girls to enter the contest (twenty in 1973, as opposed to just seventeen in 1972), but the Queen Committee had a slightly higher standard of applicant in mind

than Patti's rather offhand comments implied. After their public three-minute prepared speech, 1973 hopefuls had to face another panel of judges "in a closed test of their ability to speak spontaneously on an unexpected subject." The emphasis on public speaking reflected the Committee's oft-repeated intention and hope, as expressed by Stampede public-relations manager Jack Sirrs, that "this year the girls may be used more as public-relations people than in the years past, when they were mainly Stampede symbols."[412]

Even so, Patti had accurately portrayed the Queen Committee's reduced emphasis on riding ability during this period. At the second elimination, an equestrian trial held at Committee member Randy Dunham's arena south of Calgary, the ten semifinalists chosen in 1972 competed in a riding test that consisted of "a half-hour warm-up period on quarter horses with about 15 minutes of show riding. The girls rode at basic gaits, mounted, dismounted and did basic reining patterns." A *Herald* reporter noted that "the five finalists were not necessarily the top riders," because points gained for poise and speech earlier in the competition were added to the riding test points to determine the standings going into the finals. As one official remarked, "Poise and speech are actually more important… since the queen and her two princesses will speak at public functions and engage in public relations for the Stampede." Confirming this attitude, the same simple riding manoeuvres performed during the second elimination were repeated by finalists during the nightly competition at Rodeo Royal.[413]

With this structure in place, the Committee did not expect winners to be good riders, merely adequate, as Patti had indicated. The feeling was that as long as finalists had some degree of riding competence, they could be taught the skills specifically needed by royalty – queenly presence and the ability to ride fast with one hand while waving to the crowd with the other – in a series of group lessons during the month leading up to Rodeo Royal. These lessons, and all things horse-related during the 1970s and early 1980s, were superintended by Randy Dunham and Percy Alexander (husband to 1951 Lady-in-waiting June Dewhirst). The sterling efforts of Dunham and Alexander on behalf of Stampede royalty were recognized by the Queens' Alumni Association in 1986, when both gentlemen became Honorary Associates.

Despite the de-emphasis of horsemanship during this period, after the 1973 contest, the Committee was glad to discover that all three winners were good riders. The Queen, 19-year-old Suzanne Randle, had served as a Calgary Jaycees Gold Digger the year before[414] but she also was a barrel racer from Blackie. After she was crowned, Suzanne waved at the crowd with her right wrist encased in plaster, the result of an accident several weeks earlier during a rodeo competition.[415]

Working with Suzanne in her role of helping to publicize the Stampede were two other 19-year-olds, who owned their own horses and were accomplished riders: Calgarians Bettie Knight, a junior accountant, and university student Joan Horne. Like Leslie MacDonald, Joan was friends with a past winner (1972 Queen Patti Girling) but had been encouraged to enter the contest by a supervisor, a gentleman who had volunteered for years with the Stampede Rodeo Committee.[416] Since all three were horsewomen, and the old grandstand was still in place for one last season, the 1973 trio was the last able to ride "full tilt" down the racetrack to be introduced before the afternoon rodeo each day. With that in mind, Princess Joan later observed that few royals who were horsewomen agreed with the Committee's approach to riding during this period. Although royalty had to meet and greet and speak far more often than they had to ride (riding was required 10 to 15 per cent of the time, according to one estimate), many felt it was crucial for winners to be skilful at handling horses

Queen Suzanne Randle (centre) and Princesses Joan Horne and Bettie Knight riding in the Stampede parade, 1973.
(GA: NA-2864-23332-7)

for their own safety and for the sake of credibility in representing the horse-centred Stampede.

As a princess during a period when there was still a distinction made between the different roles, with the queen often singled out for more attention and better gifts, Joan frankly admitted that sometimes, in the beginning at least, she was disappointed not to have gained the top job.[417] Her bugbear was the fact that the queen had been given a saddle and the princesses had received only luggage. But she was glad of the $150 prize money – she used it toward her education – and could see that Queen Suzanne had more pressure on her because of her position and she did not envy her that. More importantly, the three girls got along well – "one of the easiest groups to work with" according to chaperones Leslie MacDonald (Queen, 1971) and Mary MacDonald (Princess, 1965) – and once they got going doing the job they had been selected to do, they became a solid trio and any small distinctions of rank were forgotten.

Instead, Joan remembered the fun of attending the Quebec Winter Carnival as the Stampede's first representatives after that city and Calgary became twin cities in 1973. Even better was her memory of zipping through city streets from function to function during Stampede week perched on the back of the royal convertible (and once, landing in a heap on the floor when a driver took a corner too sharply). It was during times like those, and on hot days when they were "cooking" because of their wool suits and grizzly hats (long-felt hats decorated with rhinestone beadwork), that the trio was very glad to be wearing the neat little false hair buns known as postiches, chignons or simply hair "bunnies."

In a bid to enlarge the field of applicants, the Queen Committee reinstated the upper age limit to 24 in 1974 after just two years of restricting it to 23.[418] In spite of the change, just eighteen young ladies entered the 1974 contest. After the usual six-week period of tests and trials, the three winners chosen on the final night of Rodeo Royal were 20-year-old Queen Happy Barlow, who was a college student from Carseland, and two 19-year-old Princesses who were already in the work force, Karin Kraft from High River and Sis Thacker from Red Deer. Unusually, the 1974 trio received two belt buckles because it was a transition year. Gow's Transport, which had been sponsoring buckles for more than a decade, presented one last set of buckles before withdrawing its sponsorship after former owner Jack Gow left the company to pursue other business interests. The Stampede, which had been giving the ladies a small silver gift since 1966 – usually a bracelet, cufflinks or a makeup compact – used this opportunity to start

184

⋆

1974 Queen Happy Barlow (centre) with Princesses Sis Thacker and Karin Kraft. (CSA)

a new tradition and presented them with buckles crafted by the Olson Silver and Leather Co. of High River.[419]

Queen Happy was living in Calgary, studying at the Southern Alberta Institute of Technology and working part-time. Shortly after winning, however, she realized just how heavy and unpredictable the demands on her time as Stampede Queen would be, so she decided to quit her job rather than be the cause of a scheduling nightmare for her co-workers. She moved back to Carseland to work on the family farm for the duration of her reign, a financial solution that often saw her scrambling to change from farm labourer into glamour queen before zooming into Calgary in response to some last-minute request for a public appearance. Since her metamorphosis included time-consuming routines such as applying makeup and false eyelashes, she was grateful for several short cuts: white gloves and the bunny that tidied and hid her long hair under her hat.

More than a decade later, Happy reflected on the sometimes challenging experience of representing the Stampede.

Being queen or princess for a year is not an easy position for anyone. It means putting your best foot forward at all times, even when you may be experiencing personal problems or tragedies. They work as a trio and with three different personalities thrown into hundreds of situations they learn a lot about themselves and life in general. It's exciting, glamorous and fun and a year of experience that no money on earth can buy.[420]

That part of the job was easy to see – in addition to the Quebec Winter Carnival and the Grey Cup in Vancouver, the 1974 trio had gone to New York City with the Calgary Tourist and Convention Association and to Spokane for the World's Fair – but Happy felt that the challenging parts, though less obvious to outsiders, also should have been acknowledged. During a demanding and exhausting Stampede week, she had seriously considered quitting her job as queen and wondered how many other royals had felt the same.

As it turned out, her mother had talked her into following through on her commitment, but when her reign was over, Happy shared some of what she felt that she had learned in a meeting with the Queen Committee. Mainly, she thought that potential candidates should be made more aware of the expectations, rules and heavy time commitment expected of winners – that being a royal was not just about fun and glamour, as implied by the advertisements; it actually took a lot of hard work and personal sacrifice. She suggested that last-minute requests for public appearances should be discouraged or at least regulated in some way because they were so difficult for those who worked or lived out of town. And she felt very strongly that it would be much easier for trios to function as a team if all members were treated equally so that petty jealousies and resentments could be avoided. She felt bad that, in addition to receiving a saddle, while the princesses got luggage, she had also been given a colour television while they only got transistor radios. Although Happy had the impression at the time that some Committee members were uncomfortable, even annoyed, with her criticism, many of her observations and suggestions were taken into consideration as royalty rules and procedures evolved over the next few years.[421]

CHAPTER 10 ✳ 1975–1979

"There's a world of excitement for you as Stampede Queen"

In 1975 the City of Calgary celebrated its 100th anniversary and the Queen Committee joined the celebration by designating that year's winner the Centennial Queen.[422] Perhaps that was what attracted more contestants that year – twenty-six, up significantly from 1974's eighteen – but the contest also benefited from some unexpected but very welcome publicity just as it was getting underway in mid-November 1974. *Calgary Herald* reporter Barry Nelson spotted a curious loophole in the contest rules and ran with it:

> The rules of the contest bar anyone who has ever been married or had a marriage annulled, but they do not bar men. Stampede officials explained at a news conference that banning men from the contest would violate human rights legislation, which forbids discrimination on the basis of sex… Asked what would happen if some gay blade entered the

competition, Don Postlethwaite, chairman of the Stampede Queen Committee, replied, "If we've got judges that are doing a proper job, they're going to eliminate him."[423]

Still reporting tongue-in-cheek in a followup story in mid-January, a *Herald* journalist warned: "The young men of Calgary may have missed their only chance to become Stampede Queen [as] the rules could be changed to exclude men when Stampede officials review them later this year." The contest had closed "without a single guy throwing his hat in the ring." On the other hand, twenty-six young women had taken the bait and rushed to submit applications.[424] Unfortunately, six dropped out after attending the preliminary meeting where candidates were briefed on the rules, expectations and time commitment entailed by the job.[425] The lucky winners chosen from among those who had persisted were 22-year-old college student and Calgarian Barbara Howard as Queen and Princesses Stacy Kirk from High River, also 22, and Chris Wigle, 20, from Calgary.

Queen Barbara Howard (centre) with Princesses Chris Wigle and Stacy Kirk, 1975. (CSA)

Palliser was busy and tiring, but chaperone Mary MacDonald kept them on schedule and on an even keel. After several years of chaperoning trios, she "could defuse any tense situation with her sense of humour."[426] In common with the other main chaperone of this period, Leslie MacDonald, Mary had been a Stampede royal herself (Princess in 1965) so she knew what the girls were going through physically and emotionally, and, just as important, knew when to let them bend or break the rules and when to hold firm. She encouraged them to take turns speaking at the grandstand and other functions to share the workload and the fun of being in the limelight. The Grey Cup was in Calgary in 1975 but the group still got in lots of travel: to Toronto for the Canadian National Exhibition, to Pasadena for the Tournament of Roses parade and to Quebec for the Winter Carnival.

The 1975 trio was the last to have a police escort during Stampede week. Organized about a half-dozen years before by staff inspector Mel Bestwick, a policeman who reputedly loved the Stampede, the escort had consisted of three motorcycles surrounding the royal convertible – one in front and two behind – that alerted the public to the presence of the waving royals and cleared the way ahead. It added immeasurably to the fun and drama of being ferried from function

The 1975 trio attended about twelve functions each day for the ten days of Stampede. Their week at the to function over the busy week and was remembered fondly by royals who served during the early 1970s. According to Queen Barbara, Mayor Rod Sykes had been angry when he learned that the police motorcycles parked outside a function that he and the royal trio were attending had been deployed for no more important reason than to escort Stampede royalty around the city. Confirming his reputation as a mayor antagonistic to all things Stampede, Sykes had cancelled the service immediately.[427] Similarly, Princess Joan Horne recalled Sykes commenting disparagingly when he saw the 1973 trio's rhinestone-studded cowboy hats. Apparently, he had told the young ladies rather contemptuously that their hats made them look like they were from Vegas.[428]

The new rule that prohibited widows, divorcées and married women from taking part in the contest was not the only change in 1975. To allow more time for testing, the contest closing date was moved forward three weeks to mid-January (hence the start of the advertising campaign the previous November), and, for the first time since it had been introduced in 1948, the $300 scholarship traditionally given to the winning queen was increased to $400. The princesses' scholarships, which had been raised in 1964 to $150 from the original $100, also were increased, to $250.[429]

In 1976 those amounts increased by $100 again, to $500 for the queen and $350 for each of the princesses, and also that year, the term "honorarium" was substituted for "scholarship."[430] After that, contest advertising which promised "a world of excitement" for winners referred only to valuable prizes, with no mention of scholarships or honorariums. Although the money still was advertised as a prize in 1976, the change in terminology marked a shift in thinking that had been brewing for several years. Even in 1968 the Committee's budget line item for the money given to winners as scholarships had read "Gifts and honorariums."[431] Although the 1976 princesses still were allowed to use their honorarium money to buy saddles, 1975 Queen Barbara felt that the Committee already was viewing her scholarship money as more of a stipend. She remembered feeling subtle pressure to use it to cover the cost of transportation, dry cleaning, makeup and the like – even white gloves and false eyelashes – as well as extra expenses incurred on out-of-town trips. Since these things were deemed essential for projecting the right image and performing the job, she considered her scholarship to be a double-edged gift with strings attached.[432] The Queen Committee was working very hard during this period to line up an impressive list of valuable gifts from donors for its royalty, so this move away from awarding scholarships was understandable, but there must have been some confusion about expectations during the transition period. As late as 1979, Committee minutes recorded that "All agreed that the purpose of the honorarium and 'walk around money' for the Queen and Princesses should be clearly defined at the beginning of their year."[433]

The rise in honorarium amounts reflected the increasing cost of living in Calgary during the 1970s but also the Queen Committee's increasing budget as the role of royalty grew and expanded. In the early 1970s, it was receiving around $5,000 annually from the Stampede, an amount that had doubled by mid-decade and trebled by 1980.[434] Those figures were supplemented each year by several thousand dollars of cash donations and prize goods from local sponsors. This approach, initially copied in a small way by the Stampede Queen Committee from the ACT model when it took over the contest in 1966, had become a Stampede-wide funding strategy after Bill Pratt was appointed general manager in 1971.[435] Accordingly, reliance upon donors and sponsors to supply Stampede royalty with everything from makeup to airline flights increasingly became the norm from the mid-1970s on. In 1976 some two dozen sponsors were gratefully acknowledged on queen contest flyers; six years later the number of sponsors had climbed to forty, and suitably thanking them for their generous support had become an important Committee preoccupation.

A Committee expenditure that had been rising over the years was "uniforms," the outfits worn by the royal trio. By 1976 that figure was $1,700 (close to $7,000 today), even after generous discounts from suppliers. One reason for the increase was that more clothing was being provided for the young ladies in recognition of the expanding nature of their job – several hundred appearances in 1975, 111 during Stampede week alone. The 1975 trio had done all that with just three outfits apiece – one formal, one informal and one for riding. In 1976 the number of complete outfits was increased to four and several coordinating pieces were added to create a more realistic and flexible wardrobe to support a year of public appearances.

The outfits created in 1976, and for many years thereafter, were supplied by the Hatchwear Uniform Company of Calgary but they were designed by Margaret Fraser, a newcomer to the Stampede Queen Committee who worked at Bradley's Western Wear and Saddlery Ltd. in High River. She had competed unsuccessfully in the 1968 queen contest and only became involved with the Committee because of a chance encounter with one of the 1976 candidates.

The young contestant, a horse-loving Calgarian, had been nervous about not having suitable Western wear for the Rodeo Royal portion of the contest, so she had visited Bradley's with her mother to buy an outfit for the competition. Margaret had so much fun advising and dressing this young woman, who turned out to be a winner, that it prompted her to offer her services to the Committee as a designer and coordinator of royal outfits.[436]

The Queen Committee, lacking a strong vision of its own at the time with respect to the royal image, accepted her offer, and her practical, traditional approach to Western wear dominated the royal look for the next two decades. Soon after she joined the Committee, Margaret also began serving as a chaperone for the royal trio during Stampede week, sharing duties with Marg Markus for the first few years, then taking over leadership of the job in the 1980s. A strong personality utterly dedicated to the Stampede and the queen program, Margaret ended up serving on the Queen Committee as clothing designer and coordinator, royal chaperone and in many other capacities for the next thirty years, much of it, as time went on, as chair or de facto chair.[437]

In a feature article for the *Herald* a few years later, journalist Catherine Butlin accompanied the royal party to Hatchwear for one of their fittings. As Margaret cut trimmings to embellish the outfits, she talked about interpreting authentic Western style in dressing queens and princesses. "The western suit has a distinctive, tailored cut… which is practical and has clean, flowing lines," she told Butlin, who noted that Marg's designs featured

long, fitted jackets and flare-legged pants decorated with lots of fancy "yoking" as Fraser calls the leather edging, embroidery and piping bedecking the stylized yokes, cuffs and flares of her suits. Cowboys and girls prefer close-fitting, tailored clothing. It's safer because there are no loose ends flapping. And it's also flattering to a cowgirl's figure, according to Fraser. The jacket is cut close at the waist but fits long and full over the hips which Fraser says tend to be well developed on cowgirls skilled at staying in the saddle. "The pants are cut tight right to the knee to keep them from riding up in the saddle… Below the knee they flare to make room for cowboy boots." And the pants are cut longer than average to cover the foot and make an uninterrupted line in the saddle.[438]

In addition, Margaret had to consider the unique circumstances facing Stampede royalty. "They attend so many functions it would be very easy for them to

Princess Brenda Warden being fitted for one of several official outfits by Margaret Fraser, 1979. (GA: NA-2864-35640-10)

gain weight… Their suits are made of stretchy polyester material… just in case."[439] In 1976 she provided each young lady in the royal trio with four suits (pants and jackets), an evening skirt, five blouses and one vest, all in coordinating colours to mix and match. A complicated listing she produced that year directed who should wear what and when for every event each day during Stampede week. Several changes of clothing were required each day, but every time, Margaret made certain the outfits to be worn by the princesses contrasted but coordinated with those worn by the queen.[440]

The larger number of applicants in 1975 proved to be a blip; the number returned to normal in 1976 with just eighteen. Pre-contest advertising stated that candidates would be examined by at least twenty-nine judges, and chairman Postlethwaite stressed that "there is no chance for favoritism in the judging. Each judge works independently and none of them are directly associated with the Stampede organization."[441] Ever since judging had become part of the contest in 1964, officials had been aware of the importance of eliminating any hint of bias in the process of selecting winners. For the first decade or so, judges' marks were tallied and placed in sealed envelopes in a vault after each event, the final tally by the Committee chairman occurring at the end of the contest, just before the crowning ceremony.[442] By the late 1970s, the Committee had removed itself entirely from the process by sending all marks out for tabulation by an independent accounting firm. Although Committee members usually glanced over the results and queried any obvious inconsistencies in marking, this hands-off approach to determining winners remained standard practice from then on.[443]

However, although the Queen Committee may have maintained a distance technically speaking, they provided very specific guidelines for the judges which could not help but influence the outcome of their decision in a manner considered acceptable to members of the Committee. In a 1976 document entitled "Information for Judging Interviews," judges were reminded:

> As discussed… we are looking for a personable, outgoing young lady. The winning three girls are required to accept a reasonable amount of discipline and therefore will find the job easier if they are not too radical in their outlook. We are not too concerned about the extent of the girls' knowledge about a certain issue but it is important that there be a reasonably intelligent reply to the question. An indication that the girl is aware and interested in what is going on should be of great help to them during their reign.[444]

The same mark distribution was to be used in evaluating candidates on four occasions – interviews, public speaking, buffet dinner and informal dinner: "25 points each for 'beauty' ('natural attributes'), 'queenly presence' ('charm, poise and posture (class)'), 'personality' ('alertness, aliveness and intellect'), & 'communication' ('voice quality and tone, grammar and vocabulary, effectiveness of delivery')" for a total of one hundred points. The emphasis on qualities such as co-operation, poise and presence over riding ability was clearly evident in the mark distribution for equestrian judging: "rail work, 45 points; reining pattern, 20 points; dismount/mount, 10 points; 'queenly presence,' 25 points" for a total of one hundred points.[445]

The young ladies who fit the bill in 1976 were Queen Cindy Morres, the 20-year-old Calgarian who had consulted Margaret Fraser about what to wear for Rodeo Royal, and 19-year-old Princesses Wynne Anderson from Calgary and Carol Ovans from Cochrane. After years of watching the royal job expand, *Herald* columnist Johnny Hopkins commented drily: "It's doubtful if the girls really realize the exhausting year that they have ahead, and

193
★

1976 Queen Cindy Morres (left) with Princesses Wynne Anderson and Carol Ovans. (CSA)

hopefully all have understanding employers."[446] As it turned out, Cindy had to quit her full-time secretarial job and move back home that year to save money, and her princesses also had to put their lives and schooling on hold in order to fulfill royal obligations.[447]

In what had become an annual rite by this time, the young ladies went to the Quebec Winter Carnival as well as the Grey Cup, but they had the most fun that year right at home during the Stampede. In honour of the Stampede's salute to the U.S. Bicentennial, Margaret Fraser dressed them in an outfit of red, white and blue polyester and even included little American flags on their boots. Steven Ford, son of the U.S. president at the time, Gerald Ford, represented his father at the Stampede celebrations and thoroughly enjoyed being taught the two-step by the royal trio at the Golden Garter Saloon.[448]

Queen Cindy had been encouraged to enter the contest by her mother's best friend and work colleague, 1946 Queen Patsy Rodgers. A shy girl, Cindy disliked the media focus on the queen, especially when asked, as she invariably was, "Why did you come out on top? What makes you better than the other two?" Although she did not feel very confident at times, she realized she "had to step up to the plate and lead the team," making sure, if she could, that everyone was included in media interviews and speaking opportunities. Although the young women in her trio ended up becoming friends and functioning well as a team, Cindy worried that the distinction in prize levels "sometimes made a sadness between them," especially when she was the one to win a saddle even though she was the only one who did not own a horse. Wynne and Carol very sensibly solved the problem by purchasing saddles for themselves with their prize money, but when the Queen Committee asked for feedback at the end of her reign, Cindy did not hesitate to tell them that the sponsorship approach of distinguishing the queen had an adverse effect on team building, "driving the girls away from each other" as they struggled with a mixed message about their value as supposedly equal members.[449]

For the sake of convenience, the queen, princesses and their chaperone were housed at the Palliser Hotel each year during Stampede week, but the rest of the year they had to get themselves from wherever they lived, worked or went to school to functions in scattered locations across Calgary and the surrounding area. To help facilitate this, the Queen Committee added a new rule for the 1977 contest: all candidates were required to have a valid Alberta driver's licence. The number of rules and expectations relating to winners was starting to mount, as were timelines and guidelines for organizing the annual contest, so Committee member John Cox offered to create a manual to outline rules and regulations for the girls,

the Committee, and Stampede support staff.[450] Over the years, this manual, which came to be called the Red Book, grew to be many hundreds of pages as details were added and rules clarified and updated.[451]

Hoping to attract more applicants for the 1977 contest, the Queen Committee specified in its promotional material some of the prizes 1976 winners had been given: "belt buckles, chaps, boots, purses, hats, leather coats, watches, cameras, saddles, halters, luggage and four complete outfits – from more than 25 donor businesses." In case applicants might feel intimidated at the thought of being judged, it described judges as "a cross-section of our society," everyday Calgarians who were "businessmen, housewives, members of the news media," and reiterated the fact that "Stampede Queen hopefuls don't have to be expert riders."[452]

Talking to the *Herald*'s Johnny Hopkins that year about the evolution of the contest, former chairman Don Postlethwaite said:

Naturally the girls have to be able to ride. But what can't be overlooked is that they are meeting everyone from the prime minister to girl guide groups to foreign dignitaries. They have to be able to express themselves well, they have to be presentable, they have to be knowledgeable. Considering the important role they play, we can't have girls who are stuck for an answer when someone says hello to them. We want at least a touch of class, and I think the judging format has given us that… while it might need revisiting from time to time, I think the concept is the right one.

For the benefit of applicants who might be hesitating, Postlethwaite added:

The girls all get a lot of help. If they can't ride too well, then Randy Dunham can help them out. John Cox works with them on makeup. Marg Fraser and Carol Brooks provide clothing tips. They are also assisted throughout the year by a chaperone. It's now Leslie MacDonald, who was a queen herself a few years ago.[453]

The young ladies who survived this rigorous examination to emerge as winners in 1977 were 20-year-old Calgarian Gillian Newman as Queen with Princesses Brenda Orr and Sylvia Wittmoser. In the start of a new tradition, the 1977 trio was featured at pancake breakfasts in the parking lots of some of the city's larger shopping centres. The Stampede Caravan Committee had formed the year before with the goal of bringing downtown attractions to Calgary's growing suburban population, hoping thereby to increase city-wide involvement and attendance on the grounds. After a positive reception in 1976, the Caravans quickly grew bigger and better. In addition to flapjacks and coffee, the 1977 version promised country and western bands, marching bands, animals, characters such as Ponderosa Chuck and Conko the Clown, visits by Indians and professional cowboys and appearances by the Stampede Queen and Princesses.[454]

The 1977 threesome attended the usual out-of-town functions, but undoubtedly their most exciting moment occurred in Calgary when they met "two of the world's most eligible bachelors." Prince Charles and Prince Andrew were in the city because the former had been asked to serve as Stampede parade marshal. After meeting the royal brothers, the trio told reporters that they had found them to be "very natural and not at all stuffy," and agreed that "they wouldn't mind dating either one of the princes."[455] According to Queen Gillian, after meeting them, 28-year-old Prince Charles had teased his younger brother by saying "Look at those gorgeous girls, Andrew. What are you standing around for?" To everyone's amusement, this so embarrassed 17-year-old Prince Andrew that he replied, "Shut up, Charles."[456]

1977 Queen Gillian Newman (centre) with Princesses Sylvia Wittmoser and Brenda Orr. (CSA)

By the late 1970s the Queen Committee had determined that a good advertising campaign was crucial

to attract enough candidates to run an exciting competition. Pat Pearson, a former radio announcer teaching broadcasting at the Southern Alberta Institute of Technology, was brought on board to help with publicity and media relations and to give pointers to contestants during a speech clinic offered before the public speaking event. As he became more involved, Pearson served as a judge for the interview and public speaking events and began helping the royal trio prepare for media interviews. Around 1980 he officially joined the Queen Committee, serving in many capacities, including chairman, for more than thirty-five years, but he focused mainly on helping royalty with his first love, publicity and public speaking.[457]

Advertising for the contest usually started in the second week of January with a media blitz. Local newspapers, radio and television stations co-operated well, often featuring individual members of the reigning royalty or the group as a whole in promotional pieces. At the same time, there was a massive poster campaign targeting local educational institutions, employers and other places where eligible young women might be found: "major oil companies, banks in the city, Mount Royal College, the Southern Alberta Institute of Technology, the University and the five major hospitals, as well as shopping centres."[458]

Committee members from outlying districts took posters for distribution in their area, but the focus of the campaign was Calgary, so it was not surprising that all three winners in 1978 were city girls: 20-year-old Queen Dawne Van Wart and Princesses Judy Shaw and Patti Stephens, both 21. *Albertan* columnist Eva Reid was impressed when she discovered that Dawne, fittingly, was the great-granddaughter of I.G.S. Van Wart, an early Calgary town sheriff who had served as president of the Calgary Exhibition from 1907 to 1913.[459]

Given the focus of the advertising campaign, and the 19–24 age range required of contestants, most winners were students or employed in their first jobs. Generally, students were off school for the summer, so there was no problem fulfilling royal duties during the most demanding period of the reign. But young women who worked faced a trickier situation, with very few having sufficient holiday or flex time to cover the year-round time commitment that was in addition to Stampede week. By the late 1970s the committee had developed a strategy of contacting winners' employers right after the contest, "to [explain] the duties and requirements with regard to time off in the coming year."[460] Although most employers tried to be co-operative, occasionally there were problems. "It's really a very demanding role," said

1978 Queen Dawne Van Wart (centre) with Princesses Judy Shaw and Patti Stephens. (CSA)

Princess Judy as her reign was ending. "You have to dedicate yourself to the job. It's a good thing we have understanding employers. I work for my father and even he's beginning to lose patience with my erratic schedule. Few people really understand how much time is involved in fulfilling our duties."[461]

In spite of their demanding schedule, the 1978 trio had a fun year with lots of travel. They attended the Grey Cup in Toronto and the Quebec Winter Carnival, but it was during the Commonwealth Games in Edmonton in early August that they had their biggest adventure. They were attending an official dinner – "a very posh and impressive affair" as a newspaper story put it – and Dawne was introduced to Queen Elizabeth. According to Dawne, the Queen had said, "You must be very busy being the Stampede Queen," to which Dawne replied, "Oh yes. We're going to a rodeo at the Eden Valley Indian Reserve tomorrow. Would you like to go with us?" Blushing with embarrassment when she related the story to the reporter, Dawne confided, "I don't know what made me say that. It just popped out. But the Queen said she thought she would enjoy such an informal gathering very much. She said she was especially fond of watching cutting horses at work. She is such a gracious lady."[462]

Prime Minister Pierre Trudeau also attended the dinner. He remembered square dancing with the royal trio during an earlier meeting at the Stampede, and befriended them again in Edmonton. Perhaps that connection explained why, as the official dinner was concluding, one of the trio

finally mustered up enough courage to ask a member of the royal entourage if it would be possible for the young prince [Andrew] to go disco dancing that evening. "We really didn't think he'd turn up," said Dawne, "but when we were back at the hotel, dressing for the dance, a message came that Prime Minister Trudeau and Prince Andrew were waiting for us in the lobby!" A section of the dance floor was roped off for the group, where they swirled and twirled the evening away.[463]

By 1978, the young prince had overcome his former shyness around Stampede royalty and reputedly ended the evening by exchanging kisses with Queen Dawne.[464]

Throughout all their adventures, the 1978 trio got along extraordinarily well. This may have been due to the fact that Dawne and Patti had been lifelong friends before entering the contest, but they happily welcomed Judy to the fold and bonded very quickly as a group, perhaps because they shared a ready sense of humour that helped them to get over the rough spots that were inevitable with spending such an intense period of time together. As well, Patti had come into the trio "[knowing] something of the publicity routine" because of her experience as a Jaycees Gold Digger during the 1977 Stampede. The group presented a more casual and carefree image to the media than was usual with royal trios, even revealing glitches that had occurred during their reign. Dawne had spilled hot chocolate all over her white suede outfit just as the Toronto Grey Cup parade was about to start, and Patti experienced ongoing struggles with hiding her own hair ("pinned up on top like two little horns") so that only the hair bunny was visible under her hat. Their informal charm endeared them to media old timers like the *Albertan*'s Linda Curtis, who wrote, "A happier trio would be hard to find... they never lose their sense of humor." Even tough-minded chaperone Margaret Fraser paid the ultimate compliment: "This is one of the best groups I've ever worked with. They all get along well and even when they're dog-tired, they sparkle."[465]

After a second in-depth interview with the young women as their year was coming to an end, Linda Curtis said they had "formed a happy and colorful ambassadorial trio for the Stampede and for Calgary."[466] That may have been true, but the Queen Committee had struggled with a weakness in the 1978 trio that few outsiders noticed, although it had

worried the Committee right from the start. After years of de-emphasizing riding ability in the advertising campaign, the inevitable had finally happened in 1978: all the semifinalists, those who had survived the initial tests for personality, poise etc. to participate in the first riding competition, were discovered to be novice or nearly novice riders. The least confident riders were eliminated but that still left five finalists who could by no means be described as horsewomen. Of the three winners, Dawne and Judy had done some riding prior to entering the contest, but Patti had not, and only learned to ride during the six weeks between the first and second eliminations. Luckily, she "caught on to the riding pretty fast," well enough to become second runner-up.[467]

Even so, there was no escaping the fact that all three winners in 1978 were relatively inexperienced riders. After the contest, Rodeo Royal officials had protested at the low level of riding ability show-goers had witnessed during the nightly Stampede Queen ride-off, and the Queen Committee was forced to acknowledge that riding ability, or lack thereof, had once again surfaced as an issue. In their first post-contest meeting, "the problem of the lack of riding experience in the five finalists was discussed, particularly [with] respect to Rodeo Royal. It was agreed that Rodeo Royal was an excellent place to wind up the contest but that the contestants must be able to put on a better riding exhibition." To achieve this, Committee members realized that contest rules would have to be revised. Various strategies were discussed: "(1) remove the reference on the application form… that riding experience is not a necessity; (2) consider a riding event early in the contest before the first cut; (3) arrange for more riding time between the selection of the five finalists and Rodeo Royal."[468] Over the next decade, the Committee would implement all of these practical strategies.

To deal with the pressing immediate problem – the lack of riding experience in the 1978 trio – the committee directed that "regular riding lessons be arranged for the three girls so that they will be prepared for the upcoming riding functions."[469] It was a challenge for the three to maintain their regular working schedules while fitting in a sufficient number of riding lessons at two local stables, along with makeup lessons from John Cox, speech and deportment with Gary Dan, and media sessions with Pat Pearson, but some ten weeks later Queen Dawne reported to the committee that everything was on track in the lead-up to Stampede. Still a little nervous about fulfilling their equestrian duties, Dawne asked that the girls be allowed trial runs with the horses they were to ride in the daily Grand Entry so that

they could get acquainted with them.[470] This strategy proved effective and became standard practice, even after 1993, when the Queen Committee finally acquired horses for the exclusive use of royalty.

To address the problem of poor riders being discovered only after they had already advanced some way into the contest, the Queen Committee once again revised the order of elimination events. For the 1979 contest, forty candidates demonstrated their riding ability in a basic series of tests before those who passed were interviewed and presented formal speeches. Ten semifinalists were chosen and attended two dinners, one formal and one informal. This group was cut to five finalists who competed on horseback during three nights of Rodeo Royal. The changed contest order had the desired effect and all three winners in 1979 were competent riders: 24-year-old Queen Pam Jonassen and Princesses Shauna Harrington and Brenda Warden. With just a little tweaking now and then, this successful format remained constant in the decades that followed.

After completing her reign, Princess Shauna recalled several disconcerting but amusing experiences that had enlivened her year. Like many other royals during the 1970s, she appreciated the hair bunny for the good job it did keeping her hair looking good in the worst circumstances, but it was not up to the task on the last night of the Stampede when one of her colleagues "accidentally" nudged her into a swimming pool set up by the grandstand stage for a performance by the local Aquabelles Synchronized Swim Club:

> Her false eyelashes dislodged themselves and mascara blackened her face. Worst of all, the chignon came free of [her] natural dark locks, floated around the pool a short while, then sank. The audience, remembers Harrington, went wild. If nothing else had been scheduled for the evening grandstand show, the incident would have ended when [she] climbed out of the pool. No such luck – the Aquabelles were slated to perform a short while later. Noticing how odd the chignon looked down there and worried it would disrupt the Aquabelles' act, Harrington dived in and retrieved the soaking mass.[471]

At first, chaperone Margaret Fraser had been furious about the group's final-night shenanigans, but her temper cooled when Stampede president Les Blackburn chose to pass off the incident as a huge joke.[472]

The following spring, when Queen Dawne was unable to go, Princess Shauna and chaperone Val Longmoor travelled to Australia at the invitation of the Sydney Spring Show. At the beginning of an on-air interview, a radio announcer unexpectedly introduced her as a "female bullrider from Calgary, Alberta, Canada." Wishing to support "the only female radio announcer in the country," an astonished but amused Shauna played along, maintaining a straight face while replying, "Yes, I have broken a few bones, nothing serious though."[473]

The 1979 trio was the first to wear permanent crowns specifically designed for queens and princesses to wear on their hats for the year of their reign and then hand over to their successors. Most queens during the Associated Canadian Travellers period had worn no special jewellery on their hats to denote their position, although a few in the early 1960s had worn a pin sporting the ACT club logo. After the Stampede took over the contest in the mid-1960s, queens had worn rhinestone brooches or diadems pinned to their hats, attached small rhinestone tiaras or worn hats with crystal designs beaded onto them.[474] Usually, princesses had not been distinguished in any way, although a few in later years had worn narrow rhinestone hatbands.

In the fall of 1978 the Queen Committee raised the idea of crowns that were "perpetual and supplied by the Stampede," but, even by the following April, they were still just "looking into the cost of a permanent tierra [sic] for the Stampede Queen." It was not until January 1979, when Committee member Leslie MacDonald reported that the Queens' Alumni Association was "willing to buy a tierra [sic]… and is willing to spend up to $800 for it" (providing that they could be involved in its design), that the idea finally took off.[475]

In the end, the Queen Committee and the Queens' Alumni collaborated on the cost and three crowns were created. They were etched with the Stampede brand, a large C for Calgary and a lazy (or sideways) S for Stampede. The queen's crown, made of sterling silver and 14-karat gold, was set with seed pearls and a synthetic amethyst. When it was created in 1979 it was estimated to be worth $2,000 (about $6,000 today). The princesses wore a smaller version, made of silver and minus the jewels.[476] In keeping with the thinking of the times, the queen's crown was bigger and showier, but the provision of three crowns went a long way toward improving the status of princesses. After 1979 every member of the trio was readily recognizable to the public as being a member of the royal party.

1979 Queen Pam Jonassen (right) with Princesses Brenda Warden and Shauna Harrington. (CSA)

CHAPTER 11 ★ 1980–1985

"As good an experience as a horse-loving Cowtown girl could ask for"

The 1980s saw ups and downs for the Calgary Stampede that echoed the ups and downs of a local economy dependent on the price of oil. The decade started and ended well, with the Stampede sharing in the celebration of Alberta's 75th anniversary in 1980, and celebrating its own 75th anniversary in 1987 and the XV Winter Olympic Games in 1988. However, a recession from 1983 through 1985 saw Stampede income and attendance plummet as locals lost jobs and tourists stayed home. Several iconic buildings opened on Stampede Park during this period – the Roundup Centre and the Saddledome – but committees occasionally had budgets trimmed and were told to get creative and do more with less.[477]

The Queen Committee operated on a relatively small annual budget, heavily supplemented by donations and donated products or services, so the recession had very little impact on the contest or program. Nevertheless, the Committee faced a number of challenges over the decade. During the early 1980s the focus was on fine-tuning rules and procedures, trying to find just the right balance of requirements to produce credible, well-rounded winners who could ride reasonably well and handle the increasingly demanding promotional end of the job while maintaining the Stampede's public image and getting along well enough to function as an effective team. During the latter half of the decade, the Committee faced media criticism for some of these very same rules and requirements and a challenge to its formerly exclusive marketing position within the Stampede family.

During the 1980s the main difference from the decade before was in the number of contest applicants. During much of the 1970s the contest had attracted fewer than two dozen contestants, but forty had responded to the call for entries in 1979. In 1980 a record sixty-six applied. This surge of interest was a sign of the times. The wave of feminist thinking that had decried beauty contests and the like during the 1970s as shallow and insulting to women had subsided by the 1980s as women made strides socially and

1980 Queen Jodi Merriman (left) with Princesses Audrey Collins and Dawn Pringle. (CSA)

economically. There was a new interest in contests like Miss Calgary, which had some success in repositioning themselves as being more about accomplishments and self-confidence than physical beauty, and, as such, could be marketed as a positive, empowering opportunity for young female competitors. However, this triumph was short-lived: by the end of the decade, public opinion had turned against beauty contests once again, and even the Miss Canada Pageant was struggling (and ultimately ended in 1992).

The Stampede Queen contest avoided this fate, despite occasional media criticism, because of its success in advertising the annual competition not as a beauty contest, but as a search for a public-relations team, and not just for the annual show, but for its host city, as well. As Max Foran has noted, the historic importance of the Stampede to Calgary as a tourist draw, and its ongoing contribution to the city's economic well-being, cannot be overstated and has led to an unshakeable belief in some quarters that what is good for the Stampede must be good for the city and vice versa.*[478] Although city officials never

have become involved in the queen contest or program, except indirectly as members of the Stampede Board, the relationship between the city and the show traditionally has been so close, and distinctions so blurred, that officials never have hesitated to make use of the Stampede's royal ambassadors to help promote Calgary's Cowtown image locally, nationally and internationally. Similarly, provincial marketing schemes and promotional efforts often have relied on the highly recognizable symbolic value of Stampede images and representatives, including Stampede royalty, to promote tourism and attract foreign investment to Alberta.[479]

The local press understood the mutually beneficial relationship between the city and the Stampede very well and usually tried to support it. A long piece on the 1980 queen contest penned for the *Calgary Herald* by Dave Margoshes was subtitled "Judges seek salesperson for the city." Observing that the contest was "more of a personality hunt than a beauty pageant," one Committee member told Margoshes that "the judges look for women who are 'reasonably attractive'... "but really, it's personality we're interested in, and that sort of queenly presence you can't really pin down but know when you see." Margoshes added:

Of course, being able to sit straight in the saddle

---

*This perception continues today, and with some merit. As Foran notes, the Calgary Stampede's 2003 Report to the Community stated that for every dollar of revenue generated from Stampede activities, another $2.60 was spent elsewhere in the city in 2003.

helps too. The queen, whoever she winds up being, will be more than just a smiling presence at the big whoop-up in July. During her year-long reign, in fact, she'll wind up travelling thousands of miles, shaking hundreds of hands and doing a non-stop selling job not only for the show whose name she carries, but for the city that spawned and nurtured the Stampede. It's a big job, but also a lot of fun and as good a piece of experience as a horse-loving Cowtown girl could ask for.[480]

As Margoshes's article makes evident, despite coming into the decade resolving to give the Stampede royal representatives who could ride well enough to make the show proud, the Queen Committee during the early 1980s was still soft-pedalling the level of riding ability required, for fear of scaring off girls who had all the other qualifications essential to winning. However, there was some attempt to attract better riders. Although a riding test for semifinalists would not be introduced until the end of the decade, the 1980 contest brochure alerted candidates that change was on the way. The wording "riding experience is not a necessity"[481] was replaced with "riding ability would be an asset."[482] The *Herald* picked up on the change of emphasis and warned that winners would be "chosen on the basis of their performance on horseback as well [as] the standard beauty queen attributes of appearance and speech."[483]

Although the 1980 contest received sixty-six applications, the actual number of contestants dropped to forty-four after the initial meeting revealed the rules and the time commitment required of winners.[484] The winning three were native Calgarians: 19-year-old university student Jodi Merriman as Queen, with 24-year-old Audrey Collins and 22-year-old Dawn Pringle as Princesses. Before the Stampede, the Committee had discussed the increasing demands on the trio's time, observing that the number of Caravan breakfasts alone had doubled from the previous year. With that in mind, they decided that requests for appearances that were not Stampede-related were to be given lower priority or declined altogether.[485] Even so, the 1980 trio made some eight to ten appearances each day during the Stampede and another 200 or so over the year, both locally and out of town, including the Grey Cup in Toronto, the Tournament of Roses parade in Pasadena and the Quebec Winter Carnival. Although they admitted that Stampede week had been a "treadmill of activities," the trio said afterward that the best thing about competing and winning, meeting people and making small talk had been the boost to their self-confidence, an asset that

Queen Jodi predicted "will be helpful to me the rest of my life."[486]

As had become the custom, when the 1980 royalty finished their year, they were invited to join the Queens' Alumni Association. It had been an important year for that group. Even though many members had continued to volunteer with the Creative Living Committee, by the late 1970s this body had evolved to become a community-based group no longer associated with the Alumni. Hoping to recapture something of the esprit de corps experienced during the early Women's World Committee years, members began investigating the idea of bringing the Alumni into the formal Stampede volunteer system so that members could volunteer as an identifiable group. In 1980, under the leadership of 1966 Queen Betty Wright, 1976 Princess Wynne Anderson and 1977 Queen Gillian Newman, a new Stampede committee was formed, the Queens' Alumni Committee. The first executive of this new group consisted of chair Wynne Anderson, vice-chair Gillian Newman, secretary Patsy Rodgers (Queen, 1946) and treasurer Julie Akkerman (Queen, 1959).

As before, retiring royalty automatically became members of the Alumni Association, but now those who wished to volunteer with the Stampede also could join the Alumni Committee and qualify for the benefits associated with being an acknowledged Stampede volunteer. Committee membership grew slowly – just twenty-nine members by 1984 – but over the next few years, the Committee proved its usefulness to the Stampede by assisting many other committees. In addition to participating in well-established Association activities such as the parade and the Hays breakfast, members became involved in many new activities, including organizing and overseeing public participation games in the original Weadickville, assisting with corporate judging, staffing an information booth and hosting in the Stampede volunteers' lounge. Meanwhile, Alumni interest in enabling special-needs children to experience Stampede-related activities remained high with an ongoing commitment to the annual Stampede Special visit to the grounds and the introduction of the first Rodeo Royal Special in 1987.[487]

Almost every year during the early 1980s, the Stampede Queen Committee made a few small revisions to the contest entry form based on the previous year's experience before sending it out to advertise the next contest. In 1981 the rule "you must be single and never married, divorced or had a marriage annulled" was replaced by a simpler statement: "You must be single and never married."[488] But almost as soon as the 1981 contest got underway, the Committee was faced with an application from a young woman who had a child but otherwise fulfilled the stated entry requirements in every way, as she had never been married. This was a first, and Committee members suddenly realized that "nowhere in our application does it state that the applicants must not have any dependents." Taking a vote "as to whether she should be given consideration," the committee decided to let her enter, but noted that "she will be strongly discouraged to carry on with the contest, as it is very difficult for a person with a dependent to have enough time to devote to her duties as Queen or Princess."[489] As a result of this discussion, the 1982 brochure was modified to read: "You must never have been married nor have had a child."[490] This wording would cause problems for the Committee later in the decade because it implied something more judgmental than simply not having a dependent competing for one's time and attention.

The other non-traditional candidate in 1981 was a British citizen. This question was easier to resolve. After some discussion, the Committee decided to reject her application, reasoning that "because the Stampede is a Canadian-based event and stepped [sic] in western tradition, it would be only proper for the royalty of the Stampede to be Canadian citizens."[491] As a result of this discussion, a rule that contestants must be Canadian citizens was adopted.

Two other basic eligibility rules were added or contemplated during the 1980s. Mid-decade, the Committee established the rule "must not have a criminal record."[492] In 1989 they rejected a proposal that would have required entrants to have a high school diploma, saying, "It could cause problems and… we have the judges who are able to make qualified decisions."[493] This requirement finally was added two decades later.

By specifying that riding ability would be an asset, the 1980 contest had identified three "particularly good riders," but judges had had to weed through an extraordinarily large number of initial applicants with little or no riding experience to find them.[494] This gave the Committee the push it needed to state the requirement in slightly stronger terms, a change it made in 1981 when it revised the brochure to read "previous riding experience would be a definite asset."[495] In case entrants failed to grasp the significance of that statement, the Committee decided that the importance of good riding skills would be emphasized in the introductory meeting before testing began.[496]

Despite these safeguards, one winner in the early 1980s required several months of extra lessons to bring her riding ability up to an acceptable level before the Stampede began, and a trio mid-decade experienced so many difficulties managing a variety of unfamiliar horses over the course of their reign that Marg Fraser requested a change in the rules for equestrian judging to give "actual riding ability and confidence on a horse" heavier weighting than "queenly presence and look while riding." Marg's request sparked a long debate regarding "how we can get 3 good riders who can jump on a horse and look good even if they haven't ridden for a while?" Committee member John Finn, who had taken over handling the horses and riding issues after the retirement of Randy Dunham and Percy Alexander, convinced the others to leave the weighting the same but suggested that judges be told "to look for girls who they can see fulfilling the duties that are required of them – which includes knowing how to handle a strange horse and riding in totally new circumstances."[497] But because the Committee left the weighting in favour of appearance over skill, hardly a year went by during the 1980s that did not see John Finn arranging extra riding lessons for some member of the royal team that he judged to be "in need of a lot of work."[498]

At the suggestion of the 1980 trio, the Queen Committee experimented with changing from five finalists to six in 1981, with two girls demonstrating their riding ability on each of the three evenings of the show. The Committee was pleased with the result, so the change was made permanent. The three winners in 1981 were 20-year-old Queen Cathy Robinson and 23-year-old Diane Hamilton and 19-year-old Barb Penner as Princesses. All three young women lived in Calgary, but media reports made much of the fact that Queen Cathy had owned horses for ten years and could even shoe them herself, having been certified as a farrier in 1979 after a four-month course at Olds Agricultural College.[499] Cathy had developed a friendship with 1971 Queen Leslie MacDonald while they were riding and showing horses together. Always on the lookout for potential queen candidates, Leslie had given 16-year-old Cathy a piece of advice she had never forgotten: "Don't get married or pregnant 'til you're over 20 so you can run for Stampede Queen!" Cathy followed in Leslie's footsteps after her reign as well, serving for many years in many different capacities as a Stampede Queen contest judge.[500]

Barb Penner came into the contest from an entirely different angle, as a practice run for the Miss Calgary contest. A city girl, she was a very inexperienced rider but made up for her shaky horsemanship skills during the contest (she later recalled that she had "nearly trampled a judge") by exhibiting other

1981 Queen Cathy Robinson (left) with Princesses Barb Penner and Diane Hamilton. (CSA)

queenly qualities given more weight in the marking scheme at the time. She was a quick study, and a month of riding practice with the other finalists, "to learn how to ride like queens" (i.e., waving while cantering),[501] enabled her to capture third place at Rodeo Royal, although she was one of the winners judged to be in need of additional lessons. Later she wondered just how necessary those had been, since her trio spent most of its time doing public-relations work and very little time on horseback.[502]

Interestingly, their different backgrounds and motivations for entering the contest resulted in Cathy and Barb having very different experiences with Margaret Fraser. Coming from small-town southern Alberta cattle-country herself, Marg tended to favour royals with a similar background, or at least a rural or small-town upbringing. Sometimes she ended up connecting well with a city girl, but she was notoriously cautious, only accepting them after they had proven to have "appropriate" Western values or some interest in common. She could be very straitlaced, even old-fashioned in her thinking, had strong ideas about the role and image of Stampede royals, and could be very strict and stern as a chaperone. Whereas Barb and some others found her manner to be cold, critical and occasionally intimidating, many others, including Cathy, saw a different side of

"Mother Margaret," and loved her for the support and encouragement they felt they had received during their reign, and for her dedication to the Stampede Queen program.[503]

Shortly after winning, the lucky 1981 trio was part of a fifty-three-member delegation from Calgary that made a whirlwind tour of England and Scotland, designed "to pique the interest of Britons in the Stampede and Western Canada." The tour had been conceived by Stampede officials after British Airways announced the inception of direct flights between Calgary and London, England. A Stampede employee contacted the airline about doing a joint promotion, and the idea met an enthusiastic response. As noted by Joanne Blain of the *Calgary Herald*, "[F]rom modest beginnings, the tour mushroomed into an extravaganza… The Alberta government got involved, with the idea that what was good for the Stampede was good for the whole province." Instead of the original idea of "10 or 20 people [putting on] a little show," the tour, which ran from May 21 to June 7 and visited London, Birmingham, Glasgow and Edinburgh, included a number of volunteers from the Stampede Caravan Committee, the Stampede royalty, five Indians, a number of professional

Princesses Barb Penner and Diane Hamilton, 1981. (CSA)

cowboys and cowgirls, a complete western village, a chuckwagon, two horses, 4,000 pounds of Canadian bacon and two-and-a-half tons of pancake mix.[504]

The 1981 winners were very young, and the trio did not have much time together before being thrown into such an important international event. Most threesomes had months of time to form a good working relationship and settle into their role as Stampede representatives before taking on the added stress of an outside promotional appearance such as the Grey Cup, the Rose Bowl or the Quebec Winter Carnival. Insufficiently prepared for what they would face, the group felt the strain and (in the opinion of some members of the delegation) displayed an occasional lack of judgment during their so-called free time. The Committee, alerted to the criticism by a member of the Board, called chaperone Leslie MacDonald into a meeting to explain. Having been a queen herself in 1971, she understood the situation from both sides, and loyally defended the girls: "Leslie agreed that there were a few occurrences that were uncalled for but in general, the girls were very co-operative, congenial, and tried very hard to fulfill the duties expected of them." The Committee, worried about Board censure, decided there should be no distinction between on-duty and off-duty behaviour whenever the trio represented the Stampede away from home, and that, "in the future… the girls should above all behave in a fashion suiting to their titles."[505]

But no matter how much the Committee focused on finding just the right candidates and dictating acceptable behaviour, there were many intangibles that could never be controlled. Often, luckily, the three young women who won had just the right chemistry to result in a smooth, harmonious year, but other years, unpredictably, the Committee had to deal with a trio whose relationship was strained and fractious. Heading into a new decade, the 1980 Queen Committee had decided to deal with this problem by adding group dynamics as a judging category. "Judges should be instructed to watch the areas of co-operation among the contestants, as the ability of the girls to get along with each other in close co-operation is important." Hoping to avoid potential problems by doing more troubleshooting along the way, the Committee tried better monitoring, asking for regular updates from chaperones, offering advice and occasional mediation. It decided to start touching base with reigning royalty several times a year, around day four of the Stampede, "to go over any problems they may be facing," and near the end of their reign, to review all problems and difficulties they had encountered. Problem areas would

then be incorporated into the interview questions for the next year's contestants with the hope that similar situations might be avoided in future.[506]

Although trios rarely allowed their personal dynamics to colour their public performance, a group that was experiencing difficult interpersonal relationships was hard to chaperone and sometimes in danger of tarnishing the Committee's carefully nurtured public image of three smiling young ladies with a single harmonious purpose, that of being goodwill ambassadors for the Stampede. It could not force three different personalities to get along, but the Committee hoped that by more clearly spelling out duties and expectations, it might ease areas of conflict. Accordingly, in the early 1980s it began asking chaperones to give the young women more guidelines and detailed instructions before making appearances.[507] After experiencing problems with royals who flouted dress requirements or refused to attend certain functions they viewed as distasteful or boring, the Committee began asking contestants to provide a brief explanation on their entry form as to why they wanted to become Stampede Queen, and added attitude as a new judging category.[508]

Coming at it from a slightly different angle, for more than a decade applicants had been advised of rules and expectations at an introductory meeting before competition began, in the hope that those who could not see themselves abiding by the strict rules of behaviour for an entire year would drop out early.[509] Most winners willingly complied, but, over the years, a few challenged the seemingly old-fashioned rules of conduct that prohibited smoking or drinking in public and regulated relations with the opposite sex. As long-time substitute chaperone Joan Plastow Langford observed, usually it was problems with men rather than public behaviour that caused discipline headaches. And the problem was not confined to boyfriends pressing girls to break the rules; often it was male admirers or volunteers from other Stampede committees involved in an out-of-town trip who hustled the young women. The young ladies were warned about certain known offenders, coached on how to deflect unwelcome attention, and knew they could call on the greater authority of a chaperone to give an excuse for escaping a situation without giving offence. But over the years, a few girls were flattered into flouting the rules. This kind of behaviour inevitably affected a trio's harmony and group dynamics, and it was that knowledge, rather than a desire to enforce the rules blindly, that usually motivated royal chaperones to be vigilant about preventing breaches of conduct. According to Joan, by travelling and staying with the girls, experienced chaperones quickly developed a sixth sense about who they could trust and give more leeway, and who required more careful oversight.[510]

Social mores governing the behaviour of young women generally had relaxed with the advent of feminism and modern birth control methods, particularly the taboo against engaging in premarital sex. But, with the Stampede's public image in mind, the Queen Committee felt justified in demanding that reigning royals behave at all times in a manner considered to be above reproach. By the end of the decade, a review of problem areas prompted the introduction of much stricter guidelines for chaperones supervising out-of-town trips, a time when discipline problems typically arose if they were going to. Hoping to impress upon winners their role in upholding a positive public image for the Stampede, the Committee spelled out the consequences of misbehaviour:

All breaches of conduct MUST be reported by the chaperone. Serious cases such as defying the chaperone, being intoxicated, being absent from the room at night – or having male friends in the room, should result in the girl being sent back to Calgary as quickly as possible. It will be understood the girls could be forced to relinquish her title on decision of the committee and the Board.[511]

In the early 1990s the Queen Committee followed up on this discussion by requiring that there be at least one female chaperone on all out-of-town trips, and by introducing a letter of understanding for winners to sign indicating they understood their commitment and obligations and the possible consequences of breaking the rules.[512] Later, a simplified version of this letter was introduced for all candidates to sign prior to the contest to ensure there were no surprises for winners.[513]

Aside from the obvious difficulty of dealing with three often very different personalities, a big problem for some trios was jealousy. Some princesses felt cheated at coming second or third in the contest, and that resentment burned brighter as the year went on if they felt, rightly or wrongly, that their queen was not performing as they would have done had they won top spot. Looking back, more than one queen remembered thinking that learning to handle crowds and drunken cowboys had been easy compared to the challenge of handling the disparate personalities in their trio and learning the fine art of leading without causing alienation.[514]

Sometimes, interfering parents caused a problem in this regard. The parents' cocktail party was introduced in 1980, partly as an opportunity to impress upon the families of finalists the role of the parent during the royal year. Discontinued briefly in the mid-1980s as a cost-cutting measure, its absence was felt and it was reinstated once finances improved. As Marg Fraser so aptly observed, it was an "excellent time (90 minutes) to tell parents to butt out and back off."[515]

Ever since the late 1960s the Committee had encouraged trios to function as a unit, with all three attending as many functions as possible together. In 1980 the Committee finally formalized this expectation by stating, "If requests come in for the Queen only, they will not be accepted."[516] But attempts to convince trios that all three women played an equally important role in representing the Stampede had variable success during the 1980s. When time was short, the queen often was an organization's chosen spokesperson, and she usually was the one the media wished to focus on. Aware that there had been a competition, and that the queen had won the top position, the media assumed, not illogically, that she must have been the best candidate and therefore was worthy of special attention. No matter what the Committee said, in the public mind, the use of the titles queen and princess implied a pecking order and a focus: the queen.

Sometimes it was a challenge for a queen to deflect and redirect this attention, and some queens were more adept than others in getting the message across. Event organizers and reporters did not always co-operate, but over the decade, the Committee made progress in encouraging a more even-handed approach that did not leave princesses feeling like "excess baggage."[517] In the earnest words of 1983 Queen Shannan Leinweber, "It's very important that people know that we work as a threesome. People often forget that I have two princesses and that they were very close competition or else they wouldn't be in that position. They should be recognized for their efforts as well; everything I do, they do, and everywhere I go, they go. They give up the same amount of time as I do."[518]

That said, the Queen Committee was giving a mixed message to the media, and to the girls themselves, by insisting that the queen's position as top winner be acknowledged: she always led the way in parades and grand entries, with the other two placed together and several steps behind, and she always was featured in the centre of group photographs. Easygoing, team-playing princesses accepted these distinctions with equanimity, but it was always easier when the queen too had a generous, team-playing approach and the self-assurance to say she would prefer a different arrangement or distribution of duties. When the queen lacked self-confidence, or was reluctant to challenge the status quo, or her leadership was challenged by a discontented princess, group dynamics fell apart and the trio suffered.

The Committee approached the problem from both angles at once, attempting to recognize and reward princesses for their crucial support role while at the same time trying to guarantee that the winning queen was up to the job of providing leadership for the team. For the 1982 contest, it instructed judges to keep leadership qualities in mind, that the "ability to lead or head a group should be examined before [winners] are chosen and [deciding] which one should then be selected as queen." Committee members believed in the concept of independent judging and tried hard not to be seen as influencing results, but they also realized that the only way to get winners who would perform well in the job was to give very clear instructions to community-based volunteer judges. "What we want out of the contest winners should be voiced prior to their judging so the judges have an idea of what we expect in the successful girls."[519]

Meanwhile, in a bid to strengthen the bond between the girls, and head off jealousies by sending a clear message that all three winners played a significant and equal role in the eyes of the Committee, it was decided to even things up in terms of cash prizes and gifts from sponsors. In 1982 *Calgary Herald* journalist Kate Zimmerman reported that "sterling silver and 14-karat gold belt buckles, luggage, radios, cameras, free photo developing for a year, free dry cleaning for a year, coats, and trips to Vancouver are just some of the prizes the young women will get over the course of the year." Even more importantly, she noted that, for the first time, "Each girl will receive a saddle, and for the three riders that's a pretty terrific gift." Simpsons-Sears, which had been donating a hand-tooled saddle for the queen ever since the prize had been introduced in 1961, continued to sponsor the queen's saddle, while Associated Grocers came on board as the sponsor of saddles for the princesses.[520]

The rise in the number and importance of donors during the 1970s had resulted in the Committee dropping scholarship prizes in the mid-1970s. Renamed "honorariums," the money was issued to the young ladies to cover extraordinary expenses incurred in the performance of their duties. In 1976 the honorarium total had been $1,200: $500 for the queen and $350 for each princess.[521] By 1981 the total had risen to $1,500, but the queen still was entitled to receive nearly half that, although generally speaking her costs were the same as the princesses'. This uneven split reflected the origin of the honorarium as a scholarship prize. In the past the queen had received

a bigger share of the prize money to acknowledge her win and the greater demands on her time as queen. By the 1980s all three royals were expected to spend the same amount of time on the job, and the Committee could see that the uneven distribution was outdated and unfair. At a meeting on September 23, 1981, they voted to split the honorariums equally in three, giving the 1982 winners $500 each.[522] Although there still were a few distinctions – the queen's saddle was worth nearly double those given to the princesses, and she got some nicer gifts, such as a television to their radios – from 1982 on, all three members of the royal trio were compensated more or less equally for their volunteer effort.

While the Queen Committee tinkered with rules and processes during the early 1980s, trying to get entry requirements and judging just right, the contest itself continued to run relatively smoothly year after year. In 1982 fifty hopefuls applied. That number was reduced to thirty-nine after the first riding test and interview; ten semifinalists were selected after the public speaking event; and six remained after the formal and informal dinners. Finally emerging as Queen was 22-year-old Michelle Williamson from Bragg Creek, with 20-year-old Jenny Baillod from Calgary and 22-year-old Penny Watt from Balzac, as Princesses.

Queen Michelle Williamson (centre) with Princesses Penny Watt and Jenny Baillod riding in the Stampede parade, 1982. (CSA)

This was the first trio after changes had been made to ensure that a focused and harmonious group would be chosen, and the positive dynamics of the group were helped along by the fact that Jenny and Penny had been long-time 4-H and Saddle Club friends before entering the contest. The Committee must have given a collective sigh of relief when *Herald* reporter Kate Zimmerman found them to be "fresh, positive and fun to be with… a healthy, happy trio [who] seem to have a good time together."[523] Later that year, a Stampede director told the Committee that "the Board is pleased with the girls and they find them particularly refreshing in front of a microphone. They do a super job of representing the Stampede."[524] As well as being on the go for fifteen hours a day for the ten days of Stampede, the group had impressed Board members by serving as ring clerks at the fourth annual chuckwagon canvas auction held that May.[525] Incidentally, this group was the first to abandon the sometimes contentious hair bunny and sport the more feminine, curly-haired look popular during the 1980s.

The 1982 trio narrowly missed the impact of a global economic recession that affected Stampede finances for the next few years. On the assumption that additional revenues would come from nearly forty donors, the Board approved a modest increase to the Queen Committee budget but decided to cancel the trio's projected trip to Portland, Oregon, to participate in the Rose Festival because of a lack of funds.[526] Sponsors stepped in and the trip was made as planned, as were trips to the Grey Cup in Toronto and the Quebec Winter Carnival. However, a shortfall in funds did force the Queen Committee to make a cut that it later regretted when it trimmed the parents' cocktail party from the 1983 contest.[527]

In 1983 the contest winners were 19-year-old Shannan Leinweber from Balzac as Queen, with 19-year-old Sharon Dacen and 22-year-old Marlie Milne, both from Calgary, as Princesses. After she won, Shannan gave *Alberta Rural Month* reporter Phyllis Leppa an insider's look at the judging process:

The first test was on riding alone; a Stampede Queen who couldn't ride would be a definite no-no. Contestants drew a horse's name out of a hat and rode for five equestrian judges as if they were in a Western equestrian class. Then they were interviewed by a panel of three lawyers, a stockbroker and TV person. "They asked questions like if you were one of the three girls and you couldn't get along, how would you go about getting along? You have three different personalities and you have to combine them as a unit. What do you like about

Calgary? What don't you like about Calgary? How would you promote Calgary and the Stampede?" After a 3 to 5 minute speech in front of a panel of five judges, the group was cut down to ten finalists. The ten girls then attended two dinners: one was informal where they knew the five judges and talked with them; and the second was a formal dinner with 150 people and five hidden judges… After the formal dinner the group was cut down to six finalists, who began three weeks of riding lessons at Elkana Ranch in Bragg Creek, given by the '82 Queen, Michele Williamson. "That to me was the hardest pull," says Leinweber. "Everything went so quickly and then all of a sudden you've got three weeks of nothing. Three weeks building up and building up. The tension got extremely high." … Finally Rodeo Royal came, the girls did their riding, and the decision was announced.[528]

In addition to 130 public appearances during a hectic Stampede week, the 1983 trio appeared at more than 200 other events over the year, among them conventions, school visits, small-town rodeos, the Grey Cup in Vancouver and the Tournament of Roses parade in Pasadena. Luckily, Sharon and Marnie were post-secondary students with flexible schedules and secretary-receptionist Shannan had

1983 Queen Shannan Leinweber (centre) with Princesses Marlie Milne and Sharon Dacen. (CSA)

an understanding employer.[529] Although they were grateful for the experience and regarded it as a stepping stone for their careers, Shannan and Marlie expressed relief when the busy year was over, admitting that the hectic schedule had been "a real killer on our social life," and that meeting people "doesn't sound hard… but it really is."[530]

After a disappointing start which saw an unusually low number of applicants, the 1984 campaign ended with record numbers and a banner year. The false start occurred because *Calgary Herald* reporter Richard Hoffman, looking for an interesting angle on the contest, had noticed the rule requiring applicants to be single and to agree not to marry during the year of their reign. An unnamed Stampede worker told him, "It's like the Miss Universe Pageant. They just don't have married women in them," and added somewhat hesitantly, "I guess it comes down to a question of virtue." Writing, "it's difficult to believe that there are no virtuous married people in Calgary," a bemused Hoffman checked with the Stampede's public affairs manager, who surprisingly agreed, saying "we tend to get better candidates with that stipulation in there. They are more virtuous."[531]

The question of virtue aside, Hoffman wondered if he was about to blow the lid off a discrimination case, so he called the Alberta Human Rights Commission.

Disappointingly, from his point of view, it confirmed that the Stampede had the right to dictate the marital status of employees in a contractual arrangement, i.e., the royalty volunteers. Taking another tack, Hoffman asked if the Stampede might be guilty of sex discrimination because royal trios were always female despite the fact that "[t]he contest is, strictly speaking, open to females… and males. Nothing in the contest rulebook distributed by Stampede organizers mentions the requirement of sex." This was deliberate; not wanting to tangle with human rights legislation, the Queen Committee had shied away from a rule specifying gender when the so-called oversight first had been noticed in 1975. At the time, it had decided to rely on the strong likelihood that "anyone aiming for the title of queen or princess is female," and, so far, it had been lucky, and no males had ever challenged the unspoken rule. With sex discrimination a non-starter, Hoffman had to be satisfied with a mildly tantalizing headline for his contest piece: "Virtuous single cowgirls sought."[532]

Although he had set out to promote the contest, the slightly negative tone of Hoffman's article had made the Stampede Queen contest sound a little stuffy and old-fashioned, and it probably put off more than a few potential candidates. Two weeks later, with the closing date looming, the Committee was relieved when the *Herald* ran another piece on the contest, one with a more positive approach. Even the headline was intriguing: "Mamas should let their daughters grow up to be cowgirls." First, Stampede advertising manager, Tim Hansen admitted he was a little worried. "The 1984 Queen of the Big Rodeo contest is short of queenly contestants. It's dragging a bit… We've got about twelve interested so far… it's no banner year. The times are changing." Then 1983 Queen Shannan took reporter John Howse through the contest step by step, and between them they were able to reinforce a few key points in a non-threatening way. "People just like the queen to be able to ride… no one wants a Stampede queen upended off her horse before the afternoon rodeo crowd," and "there's no use being a queen if you're not gung-ho on the old hometown." Shannan made the whole process sound relatively easy and quite doable, reassuring potential candidates. "The key is to be yourself," she said, urging them to "go for it… It's been the best year of my life."[533]

After that positive appeal, the 1984 contest attracted a whopping seventy-three entries. The winners were 20-year-old Pat Brown as Queen and 21-year old Michele Fussell and 22-year-old Monica Perchaluk as Princesses. "It's a great honor and a great experience," said Queen Pat, but the winners soon discovered that "[b]eing a 'goodwill ambassador' for the greatest outdoor show on earth is a demanding full-time job."[534] In the first few months after being crowned, the trio attended fifty functions. Then, as the city geared up for Stampede, the pace accelerated and they started making public appearances "every second day at least," including a visit to the Spokane Lilac Festival. They made approximately fifteen appearances a day over the ten days of Stampede and attended another hundred or so functions over the fall and winter, including the Grey Cup in Edmonton and the Tournament of Roses parade, totalling some 300 public appearances before their reign ended at Rodeo Royal the following March.[535]

By the mid-1980s, Stampede royals definitely were feeling the impact of winning on their personal lives. A legal secretary, Queen Pat was able to use her four weeks of vacation time to cover most of the functions that required her presence, and luckily her employer was good about giving her time off to cover the rest of her queenly duties. Princess Michele took a year off from touring on the equestrian circuit and Princess Monica, after arranging to put her university studies on hold for six months, decided against looking for a summer job. "I could not ask an employer to hire me," she said. "I wouldn't be there."[536] But, as reporter Judy Walters discovered,

223
★

1984 Queen Pat Brown (centre) with Princesses Michele Fussell and Monica Perchaluk. (CSA)

Despite having to radically rearrange their personal lives, the girls do not begrudge the sacrifices they have to make. The honour of serving as goodwill ambassadors for the Calgary Exhibition and Stampede is a once-in-a-lifetime opportunity... They'll likely get to travel... they'll polish their riding and public speaking skills. They'll be coached on personal grooming, poise and makeup, how to walk, sit, stand, get in and out of a car, how to carry a flag, how to walk up to and away from a microphone, how to wave to the crowd from atop a galloping horse, and how to get along... [537]

And get along they did. The *Herald Magazine* published a feature piece on Queen Pat and her Stampede week experiences, but she gave full credit to Princesses Michele and Monica, saying:

I couldn't have done it without [their] help... We were always together; we became good friends over the ten days... Just towards the end we got a little grouchy, but we'd been told there had always been a fight between the queens and princesses towards the end. We set our minds to it and we wouldn't fight. Whenever there was a problem, we'd talk it out. We're still good friends.[538]

Pat also credited their support staff with the trio getting through the busy week harmoniously:

Our main chaperone was Marg Fraser, and Jackie Makenny spelled her off on weekends. They were just super. They were through it before, and knew what they were doing and what we had to go through. They were responsible for keeping us on time, getting us dressed properly for all the functions… We each had seven outfits, some were mix and match, and [Marg] always had in mind what our day's outfits were…

And she organized us in the hotel. We had a huge, almost apartment-like room with a living area and three bathrooms. That was really important for us in the morning…

Another thing that saved us were the drivers. We were chauffeured around all week and it was quite a chore. We'd be in one quarter of the city and have to be across town in 20 minutes. But some of the drivers made it a lot of fun…

It was quite tiring, we were going from 6 am to midnight and not sitting down all day. There were maybe 15 to 20 minutes between functions. It got so we slept in the car every chance we got. Tired or not, we had to keep those smiles on our faces.[539]

Calgary Herald fashion columnist Bernice Huxtable picked up on the fact that Stampede trios now were receiving seven outfits apiece, a big jump from the three that had been provided before Margaret Fraser had taken over the task of dressing royalty in 1976. Now in her ninth season of designing and coordinating royal outfits, Marg had a vision that was strong and sure. "My big thing is to keep the Stampede Western," she told Huxtable. "The girls are the show point of Stampede, the color. They create the image people take home… We don't want them in blue jeans. We want them femininely dressed, fit for action and colorful enough to catch the eyes of spectators perched near the heavens."[540]

This also may have been the motivation behind Marg's 1980 offer to outfit finalists for Rodeo Royal if they lacked suitable attire to make a queenly impression before the competition crowd.[541] No doubt she remembered the fun and satisfaction of helping 1976 competitor Cindy Morres to achieve a more regal look before the finals, an exercise that certainly contributed to Cindy's confidence and possibly her subsequent win. With finalists on display every night during the rodeo, Margaret's offer may have had as much to do with increasing the glamour quotient of the contest finals as shoring up the competitors' confidence, but it was important to her that they all looked like potential queens. As co-owner of Bradley's Western Wear with her brother David, Marg had access to many spare pieces of cowgirl clothing, so it was an easy, but generous, thing for her to help contenders achieve a dressier look for the final part of the competition.

In creating outfits for the royal trio, Marg still worked in polyester, finding it "the most practical fabric for many reasons, mainly because it's washable and it will stretch or shrink as needed and that's crucial because the girls' weights fluctuate as much as 6–8 kilograms during the show." She judged that one of the flashiest outfits in 1984 was in off-white polyester trimmed with turquoise ultrasuede, at a cost of close to $400 (twice that amount today) for four pieces: walking shorts, pants, blouse and short jacket.[542] No doubt it was this outfit that prompted Stampede director Eleanor Bailey to ask the Queen Committee if the colour of the girls' hats could be changed that year, because the white clashed with their cream suits. Sensibly, the committee rejected this suggestion, saying, "It was decided that the white hat is symbolic of Calgary and that the public becomes upset when a color is worn."[543]

Interestingly, Margaret Fraser chose to outfit the 1985 trio in cream as well. After seven weeks of a competition that started with sixty applicants, 20-year-old Karyn Scott was crowned Queen, with 20-year-old Dyanna Browne and 21-year-old Karen Dornan as Princesses. Twenty-five years later, Queen Karyn reminisced fondly about the clothing Marg had designed for the 1985 winners:

The cream outfit was really classy, and we wore them a lot. Both the skirt and the blazer were made of a silk fabric, the blouse a polyester fabric. We had an ostrich belt with our belt buckles from Olsen's that tied it all together. I felt good in this outfit, [it] was a nice classic look that I don't think has gone out of style. My favourite time wearing this outfit was when we were invited backstage at the Kenny Rogers concert and had our photo taken with him. He was wearing a suit that was very similar to mine, just a bit more flashy, with rhinestones all over it.[544]

In addition to describing the royal clothing in detail for readers, Bernice Huxtable's 1984 article revealed just how reliant the Queen Committee had become on the generosity of donors and sponsors for outfitting Stampede royalty. The new belt buckles, created by the Olson Silver and Leather Company of High River, represented a $2,000 donation from Castor Holdings of Montreal (owners of the Calgary Skyline Hotel). The trio had five pairs of boots each

Queen Karyn Scott (right) with Princesses Dyanna Browne and Karen Dornan at the Stampede Indian Village, 1985. (CSA)

to match their wardrobe. At an average cost of $600 per pair, they had been donated by the Alberta Boot Company, Woodward's, Western Outfitters, Boulet of Quebec and the Hondo Boot Company of El Paso, Texas. In all, Marg Fraser calculated that each lucky young royal would end her reign with a wardrobe of Western clothing and accessories worth about $20,000 ($41,000 today), about one-fifth of which had been donated by her own business, Bradley's Western Wear. In addition, all three received Western saddles with unique silver trim and lacings worth about $3,300 in total. Made by Eamor's Saddlery, they were donated by Simpsons-Sears and Associated Grocers, which alternated for several years in providing the queen's saddle and those for the princesses.[545] This arrangement lasted until 1986, when Davidson Enman Lumber took over as saddle sponsor, freeing Sears to focus on supplying luggage for the trio.

As volunteers, Stampede royals were not paid a salary, and they gave a lot of hours in exchange for a small honorarium and being supplied with these and other valuable gifts such as jewellery, watches, sunglasses, cameras and the like. Other donations, being services rather than tangible gifts, were less easy to identify but were of equal importance to the success of the queen program. For example, in the mid-1980s, Shaw GMC Trucks Ltd. began supplying a Suburban for the trio's use. This was to supplement the royal convertible, no longer considered entirely reliable but still in occasional use, particularly for the trio's nightly appearance in the Stampede Park parade.[546] In 1990 the Queen Committee decided to put personalized licence plates on the Suburban to give the ladies a little publicity while they travelled about the city. Finding that the plates ROYALTY and ROYAL3 were already in use, it settled on CSTRIO.[547]

According to donor lists compiled by the Stampede Queen Committee during this period, other big players at the time were Falconer Academy of Modelling, Western Airlines, the Palliser Hotel, Sony of Canada, Konica Canada Ltd. and Henry Birks and Sons Jewellers, but there were several dozen other local businesses that supplied all manner of merchandise and services for reigning queens and princesses. With this level of support, it is not surprising that a considerable amount of Committee time was spent discussing ways of thanking sponsors. In 1980 the young ladies started presenting donors with signed photographs and, later, postcards of themselves as keepsakes. Other strategies included having the girls write thank-you cards, issuing complimentary tickets to Rodeo Royal, giving tangible recognition at that event by displaying donated goods and crediting sponsors in the program, and, as always, allowing trios to participate in sponsors' special events and promotions.[548]

The 1985 trio soon found out why a revised contest rule had specified that candidates "must reside or work within a 40-mile [65-kilometre] radius of Stampede Park."[549] This was a more specific version of the rule that had stated that candidates "must reside in Calgary or the Calgary district," itself an easing of the original 1966 rule stipulating that winners must "be prepared to reside in Metropolitan Calgary."[550] Some years later the distance rule was eased further to allow winners to reside, work or attend school within a 100-kilometre radius of Calgary.[551] As Queen Karyn told a reporter, they had to be able to get into Calgary on very short notice. "It's like a full-time job... The unexpected promotions and last-minute receptions all have to be met with a cheerful 'I'll be there.' You have to drop everything."[552]

By the mid-1980s the Queen Committee was expecting a lot of its royalty – and generally getting it – thanks to its hard work earlier in the decade refining the judging process and fine-tuning rules. Having resolved earlier issues, it anticipated a successful close to the decade, looking ahead to two special years when it anticipated that Stampede royalty would shine: the Stampede's 75th anniversary celebration in 1987 and Calgary's hosting of the XV Winter Olympic Games in 1988. Little did it realize that the next few years would prove to be among the most trying ever faced by the Queen Committee and its members.

CHAPTER 12 ★ 1986–1989

"Stampede trio more than beauty contest winners"

After the *Calgary Herald*'s Richard Hoffman failed to stir up much controversy with his 1984 article suggesting the Stampede was being discriminatory in insisting that contest applicants be single and remain so for the year, the committee probably thought the issue safely dead and buried. Not so. In January 1986 it was raised again by *Herald* columnist Catherine Ford in a scathing piece headed "Stampede rules insulting." The newspaper had received the Queen Committee's usual press release, but instead of a staff reporter writing a nice promotional article, Ford used it as the subject of one of her thrice-weekly columns, taking umbrage at the very idea of the contest and what she considered to be its outdated rules. Skewering relentlessly and at length, Ford wrote:

> There's one week left for the young, pure and presumably virginal to enter the annual Calgary Stampede Queen contest. Why any woman would want to be

1986 Queen Kary Ager (right) with Princesses Kathleen Mackie and Jayne Boyce. (CSA)

Stampede Queen escapes me, but just in case, entries for this year's competition close at the end of January.

For those young women willing to spend the next seven weeks being figuratively poked and prodded like prize cattle, I hope it's at least fun to be lionized and pampered and photographed dewy-lipped and always smiling with every visiting fireman.

I suspect it isn't always. Fun, that is. Surely the Stampede Queen and her princesses must get hot, sweaty and tired, and by the time they've worn out those silly-looking pastel dress-Western outfits, I'd like to think they never even want to look at another horse or another cowboy.

And speaking of those insipid costumes they have to wear, isn't there any satin or silk in this city? Or something that doesn't look like what it is – good, durable, washable, dull polyester? Practicality is one thing anyone wearing the title "queen of" shouldn't have to concern herself about. A little pizzazz in the costume department would make the annual trio look less like dowdy penguins and more like the beauty queens they are.

(No, madam, I don't believe the Stampede Queen is chosen strictly on the basis of her ability to ride a horse and her sparkling personality. I will go so far as to believe that beauty isn't everything, although it's way ahead of whatever's in second place)…

Meanwhile… there's the slight matter of the rules and regulations for this annual event. They are, quite simply, an insult…

Parading around for up to seven weeks being judged on such attributes as an ability to answer inane questions and keep smiling without having crease lines develop permanently in your cheeks is one thing.

Having to attest to your virginity is quite something else. That's the insulting point of this facade. Oh well, they don't really have to prove that they're unsullied, but the application form states "you must never have been married nor have had a child, and you must agree not to marry during your reign." …

Presumably the Stampede Queen could do just as good a job if she were married. … But let's not quibble about that. Let's quibble about this never having been married nonsense. And while we're at it, the unmitigated insult contained in the condition that the entrant has never had a child. It's about time somebody explained that. …

[I]t is an insult to insist that the women who enter a beauty contest be genuinely single and not, under any circumstance, have borne a child. Why? Does this diminish your beauty? Does this make you less of an ambassador for the city?

Does anybody really care? The answer to the latter better be no, nobody really cares, because it says a great deal about the collective state of mind if the citizens of Calgary give one hoot whether the Stampede Queen was a maiden or not. … As there are thousands of virtuous married women in this city, one must assume that singleness isn't the only qualification for the label of "virtuous."

Ah, for a moment there I was almost willing to believe that things had changed in the world of fantasy and fairy tales and dazzling smiles. But no – it's still a world where virtue isn't judged on inner factors such as strength of character, moral fortitude or religious convictions, but on the facade. It's a lot like judging a book by its cover – presumptive, insulting and frequently incorrect.[553]

Interestingly, Ford had raised some of the same points three years before in a column headed "Beauty covered in plastic." In that piece, the target had been the Miss Calgary contest. She hated the black dresses that the young women aged 18 to 24 were required to wear ("too old, too dark") and queried rules that somehow equated having "the integrity to deal with people from all walks of life honestly and generously" with the requirement that entrants be single and "never have had a marriage annulled nor given birth to a child," saying, "They ask for documentation of purity, perhaps?" But, with the daughters of a personal friend competing in the contest, she was relatively mild in her criticism:

Forget all the nonsense about beauty contests being meat markets and insulting to women. (Beauty, like playing hockey, is a God-given talent and if a girl chooses to use her talents, good for her.)

… What fascinates me is what swirls around these young women during such events – over which they exercise no control or authority. (That, in my opinion, is the true insult of such pageants.)

… Who took naturally healthy, glowing skin and plastered it with makeup so that they had all the color of newsprint?

What happened to their hair?

It isn't the fact that a group of beautiful young women would aspire to be Miss Calgary – that's understandable. It is, in the final analysis, an achievement. But by the time they've been customized, they've lost the very kind of appeal which makes them beautiful.[554]

The following year, Ford's predictable response to the announcement that the Miss Universe contest would be coming to Calgary during Stampede week 1984 included a sly little jab: "Can a city which puts its Stampede Queens in those pastel parodies known as Dress Western suits stand the dazzle?"[555] Two years later her opinions had become much harsher and there is no doubt that the Queen Committee considered her 1986 editorial to be an unexpected blow. Traditionally, the local press had tended to view the Stampede as something of a sacred cow, an economic engine so important to the city's local economy and public image that all things Stampede were supported by the media as a matter of course and as an extension of local pride.[556] Of course, columnists like Ford had more leeway than reporters in voicing private opinions, and editors secretly may have rejoiced in printing the odd disrespectful piece calculated to stir up a little controversy.

Although Ford's criticism rankled, the Queen Committee, with just a week left until the contest closed and lots of entries already received, could afford to ignore her editorial. But six former queens and princesses took it upon themselves to retaliate on behalf of the Committee and the Stampede. Several weeks after Ford's column appeared, the *Herald* printed a long letter penned by 1984 Princess

Monica Perchaluk and signed by five other former royals, headed "Stampede trio more than beauty contest winners." Among the many statements she made in support of the contest and the hard work done by winning trios, Monica wrote:

234

> Although I may not agree with all of the rules of the contest, they are there for a reason. Would Ford rather have the trio degraded by snide remarks, probably by the same group of people who are now criticizing this contest, or would she rather have a trio that, although we all admit to being human, are "fresh and young."
>
> As a Stampede princess, I asked why we were not allowed to be married, and the answer I received made a lot of sense: "When you are married you might feel guilty being as busy as we are, and you might resent not being able to give as much time to your family as you might like."
>
> … Instead of putting the winners down, I think the girls should be given some recognition.[557]

As Monica indicated, people frequently queried the never married, no children rule but it was never retracted. The Queen Committee always claimed it was in place to protect young women from taking on something that would be damaging to personal relationships because of the time commitment required of winners.[558] That concern was valid, but, most likely, other forces were at work too, although they may have been subconscious ones as far as the Committee was concerned. This kind of rule was fairly standard for contests that involved choosing a young woman as a representative or goodwill ambassador for a group that might be concerned about public image. Catherine Ford had observed the same restrictions in the rules for Miss Calgary, which were the same as those used for Miss Canada and for the model of them all, Miss America.

As noted by Sarah Banet-Weiser in her study of the Miss America contest, almost from its inception the pageant had insisted on curfews, constant chaperoning and a strict no-alcohol policy to maintain an aura of respectability. By stipulating that contestants must "never [have] been married, never been a mother, and must be of good moral character," pageant rules implied that "in order to be considered a good or proper 'representative,' contestants must not bear evidence of having had sex."[559] Similarly, Patrizia Gentile's study of the Miss Canada contest indicated that marriage (or childbirth)

justified disqualification precisely because it created a dilemma regarding a beauty queen's sexual status…

The role and purpose of the contest chaperone was crucial in this regard because their presence confirmed that measures were in place to not only protect the beauty contestant but to ensure the maintenance of sexual purity.[560]

Although it is doubtful that concerns ever were articulated in these terms, the Queen Committee certainly felt a strong responsibility to maintain the Stampede's family-oriented public image by trying to ensure that the young women who were chosen could never be described as anything but wholesome during their reign as public-relations representatives. Although the never married rule was never retracted, there was a gradual relaxing of the unspoken rules surrounding premarital sexual relations. In 1994 a Committee member suggested adding "you cannot be living common-law" to the contest entry form to eliminate candidates who were circumventing the rule against marriage.[561] By 2002 the attitude of the Committee had moderated to such an extent that a blind eye was turned upon discreet stable relationships and a journalist could report that candidates (and winners) "can live with a boyfriend but it can't be a hush-hush arrangement."[562]

In spite of the controversy caused by Catherine Ford's editorial, the 1986 contest proceeded on track and resulted in a 21-year-old Queen, Kary Ager, with Princesses Jayne Boyce and Kathleen Mackie. One positive thing that seems to have resulted from Ford's editorial was a new look for Stampede trios which started in 1986. Marg Fraser may have felt a little hurt by the criticism, but she took the point and began dressing the ladies in the brighter colours and more feminine styles favoured during the 1980s. Although polyester was still in use because of its durability and stretchiness, she often used softer, prettier fabrics such as rayon, synthetic silk and ultrasuede for outfits that featured gathers and ruffles.

As the 1986 trio's reign was ending, a positive article in the *Herald*'s weekly supplement, *Neighbours*, must have helped soften any resentment the Queen Committee felt toward the newspaper. The article, headed "Stampede queen, princesses hard-working ambassadors," was positive throughout:

Wearing the crown of Stampede royalty is no easy task. The Stampede queen and princesses are not simply three women living out a fairy-tale year of glamor and galas on horseback. They must devote endless hours to put the sparkle into the Stampede message they represent.

Public speaking is practised until voices nearly crack. Hours are spent in a saddle perfecting riding skills. And through it all – smile 'til it hurts, then smile some more. But the rewards make the effort worthwhile.

Acknowledging that "some people are down on the contest," Queen Kary went on to say: "But when you see how happy some people are to meet you, like seniors in nursing homes, you know what you're doing is worthwhile. It's a big commitment, but I'd do it again if I could."[563]

With the recession of the mid-1980s over and Stampede finances back on track, the Queen Committee asked for and received a substantial increase to its annual budget in 1987, bringing the total to nearly double what it had been at the start of the decade. Even so, the Committee increasingly relied upon sponsors to supplement its budget; by decade's end, they were providing one-quarter of the total in the form of donations.[564]

Following a pattern that was by now typical, sixty-one young women sent in applications for the 1987 contest but only forty remained to compete after the introductory meeting. The winners were 23-year-old student Holly Dunn as Queen with Princesses Debbie Simpson and Shaunna Thompson, both 21. All three winners were Calgarians, and Debbie and Shaunna had gone through high school together.

Debbie's mother, Dixie Girletz, had been a queen contest winner, too – a Lady-in-waiting in 1963.[565] A decade after she won as princess, Shaunna gave back to the program by joining the Queen Committee and serving as a long-time member.

Perhaps from a desire to be politically correct, Calgary newspapers shied away from announcing Queen Holly's win as anything out of the ordinary, but the San Francisco *Sun-Reporter* did not hesitate to make the point: "Miss Dunn's reign is both significant and unique. She is the first Black woman to be crowned Stampede Queen in the 75-year history of the Calgary Stampede."[566] Holly had been encouraged to enter the contest by a friend of hers, 1986 Queen Kary Ager.[567] She did not know much about the contest, but assumed when she entered that she did not have much chance of winning because all she had ever seen before were white winners. She had come third in the Miss Calgary contest but decided to give the queen contest a go anyway, mostly so that she could enjoy a few weeks of free riding time.

A city girl who did not own a horse and had never had lessons, Holly loved to ride but her skills were basic compared with some of the other candidates. Having entered the contest "without stars in her eyes," she was very surprised, and more than a little

1987 Queen Holly Dunn (centre) with Princesses Shaunna Thompson and Debbie Simpson. (CSA)

worried that tokenism might be at work, as she made her way successfully through the various levels of the competition. But when she emerged as the winner, she realized she must have exhibited the qualities judges were looking for or they would not have taken a chance on her simply to appear liberal-minded. Reminiscing years later, she hoped her win simply indicated good timing, that "the Stampede was open and ready to choose a Black queen." Because her skin was relatively light, many observers did not realize her background and she was very amused when some of the seniors she visited patted her hand and commented on her lovely tan.[568]

The 1987 trio had a busy year, making over 350 appearances. They were so busy during Stampede week that the Queen Committee considered, but never implemented, the idea of bringing back police escorts so that the group could be whisked more efficiently from function to function.[569] With that kind of workload, Holly decided to put her schooling on hold. She did not have to worry about money, because she was still living at home and expenses connected with performing royal duties were covered by the Queen Committee. Because the honorarium amounts were paid out sporadically, as the need to cover expenses arose, she was not aware that her group was the first to receive a raise since the

late 1970s when the total fund had been raised from $1,200 to $1,500. Although the distribution had been changed in 1981 so that each girl received the same amount, the overall budget line had not increased for nearly a decade.

In the fall of 1987 the Board finally authorized an increase in honorariums and made the raise retroactive to that year's Stampede:

During the past several years additional promotional and other activities have been required from the Queen and Princesses and it was felt that an additional $1,500 should be allocated in the budget for honorarium purposes in helping to cover the additional time that the Queen and Princesses are away from work and/or in incurring extra expenses in performing their duties.[570]

The honorarium budget was doubled to $3,000 for the 1987 trio, $1,000 per girl, but the Board specified that the money continue to be allocated on a discretionary basis, arguing that the payment should not be automatic in case one young lady made more (or less) of a contribution than the others. The Queen Committee could use its judgment in making use of honorarium money to "assist with a shortfall in personal finances" for those unable to make a sufficient income while reigning as a Stampede royal. Although this was considered to be a generous increase, director Dale Main, a former Queen Committee stalwart, felt compelled to remind his fellow Board members that "the amount set aside was very conservative when considering the effort that is required in fulfilling all the duties asked of the Queen and her Princesses."[571]

Not only was the Stampede celebrating its 75th anniversary in 1987, but that year's trio also helped to promote the XV Olympic Winter Games which Calgary was set to host February 13–28, 1988. In honour of that, the Alberta Boot Company made each young lady a pair of periwinkle-blue boots sporting the Games' Olympic rings in pink. In addition to attending the Grey Cup in Vancouver and the Quebec Winter Carnival, the trio went to the Pacific National Exhibition in Vancouver, where they appeared on a float co-sponsored by the Calgary Tourist and Convention Association and the Calgary Olympic Organizing Committee. At the Medicine Hat Exhibition they met Prince Andrew and his wife, Sarah, Duchess of York, who said to Holly, "I really love your crown," and asked if she would like to trade.[572]

Holly had come to the attention of the San Francisco *Sun-Reporter* because her trio was invited to ride in the Black Cowboys' Association Parade in Oakland before making an appearance at the Grand National Rodeo in San Francisco, October 21–25. Until she made that trip, Holly's experience attending the Calgary Stampede had taught her that rodeo and cowboy culture were mainly white activities, so it was a "monumental, eye-opening revelation," and a very affirming experience, for her to participate in the Black Cowboys' parade and learn that she had been mistaken. She "really felt part of it all for once" and savoured the fact that "the shoe was on the other foot," that she was the one who blended with the crowd while her princesses had the novel experience of standing out.[573]

During their five-day stay in the Bay area, the 1987 trio promoted Calgary, the Stampede's 75th anniversary and the upcoming Olympic Games. After more than six months on the job, the team was up to the challenge. "We're given the chance to represent a city we're proud of. We're asked a lot of questions about Calgary, the Stampede and the Olympics, so you have to be very aware of what's going on."[574] Stampede advertising manager Tim Hansen was pleased with their effort, telling the Queen Committee that they had done "a super job and represented the Stampede in a first class manner, as always." Chaperone Jackie Makenny also filed a complimentary report:

The girls were well received not only during the parade but all of the time... We did not have much free time on this trip, but in a way I am glad because I believe the girls realize this is firstly a business trip and not something just for their pleasure. The girls were totally co-operative with me, Tim and others who requested things of them. They were always on time, always looked great and made me proud of them the entire time.[575]

Ever a willing partner in anything affecting the Calgary economy, public image and tourism, the Stampede played a pivotal role during the 1988 Olympics. With the largest public buildings and space within the city limits (including the new Saddledome), and a legion of well-organized volunteers already at hand, it was a natural to help host the massive event and many subsidiary activities and celebrations over the two weeks of the Olympics and for the rest of the year.[576] Nearly fifty former Stampede Queens and Princesses from around the world joined in the massive reunion held during Stampede week called Homecoming '88.

The 1987 trio was still reigning when the Olympics opened in February, so they helped to host the first-ever Olympic Rodeo held in the Stampede Corral, February 22–27. It took the place of Rodeo Royal that year, so the queen contest was moved forward by a month to coincide. Following much the same format as usual, at each of the six performances the six finalists for queen were introduced to the crowd before riding their pattern. They took it in turns each night to present a one-minute prepared welcome speech on behalf of the group. The 1988 trio was crowned during the final performance of the Rodeo '88 Challenge Cup. The winners were 21-year-old Laura Godwin from Millarville as Queen, with 22-year-old Susanne Astley from Springbank and 19-year-old Jennifer Ough from Bragg Creek as Princesses.[577]

A shy girl, Queen Laura found the media focus on the queen a little wearing and speech-making intimidating at times.[578] Aware that the Committee's increased emphasis on media exposure was a challenge for some winners, Committee member Pat Pearson had introduced a day-long camera and media interview training session held in the broadcasting department of the Southern Alberta Institute of Technology.[579] Even so, Laura felt very nervous facing the grandstand crowd, especially her first time, when she found the unexpected feedback from the microphone unnerving. Admitting that this part of her role as queen sometimes "got on her nerves," she was glad to share the spotlight with Susanne and Jennifer. They rotated public speaking duties

1988 Queen Laura Godwin (centre) with Princesses Susanne Astley and Jennifer Ough. (CSA)

whenever they could, and Laura always insisted that they pose together when photographs were requested. Although she had a bigger, flashier crown and usually wore a different-coloured outfit, in her mind they were all equal members of a well-coordinated team and this attitude helped to diffuse any feelings of animosity, even when outsiders insisted on focusing on her. Instead, the group decided to get the most they could out of the experience, and enjoyed being the centre of attention during their visits to shopping mall breakfasts, senior citizens homes, and hospitals ("bringing the Stampede to them if they can't get to us.")[580] One of the most unusual, but hilarious, things they were asked to do that year was to ride live ostriches into the infield one day during the Grand Entry before the Stampede rodeo.

As was by then a long-established custom, the trio's main chaperone during Stampede week was Margaret Fraser, now in her thirteenth year of performing this duty. As with everything she did, Marg approached her job as chaperone with enormous dedication and military precision. Before moving into the Palliser Hotel for Stampede week, Laura, Susanne and Jennifer received a list of handwritten instructions from Marg detailing what to bring. It was framed as if they were about to head out on an exciting journey:

You are about to embark on an 11- or 12-day junket that will take you from the deep southern outskirts to the far northern reaches of Calgary. As with any major trip you'll need your tickets, passports, luggage and a wardrobe that will be suitable for any occasion that might arise – and those invitations are still rolling in.

Your Tickets: those badges that say Stampede Queen, Stampede Princess which were handed out on Badge Day.

Your Passports: Your name tags – both the gold and the red and white.

Luggage – whatever you need to bring in your extras – makeup, extra jeans, lingerie etc.

Wardobe – We will pick most of the clothes up at JoVal on Thursday. However, to double check, this is what you're to bring: all makeup plus the diagram from John Cox (Paint By Number); shampoo–conditioner, rollers, dryer etc. … Clothing: any and all belts you've received… earrings, turquoise boots – what else? red/white blouse, yellow/white blouse, skirt sets, copper–brown-tone skirt and blouse, taupe–cream pants; we'll pick up all the other pieces from JoVal; CASUAL – you might want to throw in a couple of pair of jeans, blouses, sweater… Don't forget your pjs or nitegown etc. …

I'll bring soap and fabric softener.

PS: Any books or magazines you might be reading at present would be good![581]

Margaret's unflagging enthusiasm for the job endeared her to many royals, including Laura, whose attachment to Mother Margaret made her want to give back to the program when her reign ended. In 1990 she inquired about serving on the Queen Committee. Her application was rejected, however, because, at the time, Margaret felt strongly that there should be a gap of more than a few years before former royals were allowed to join the Committee. Her rather curious reasoning was that recently retired royals "might take attention away from the three girls" (i.e., the currently reigning trio). The name of 1986 Queen Kary Ager was rejected at the same Committee meeting for the same reason, although the minutes recorded: "It must be noted that these two girls are great choices, but it was felt necessary to wait just a bit longer before bringing them on."[582] Undeterred, Laura put her name forward again several years later and ended up serving on the Stampede Queen Committee for a number of years in the late 1990s.[583]

One of the jobs Laura took on for the Committee was coordinating the activities of visiting royalty – rodeo queens and princesses from other fairs who visited Calgary during Stampede week and who required some degree of attention as special guests. This job had come under Queen Committee direction in 1988, delegated by the Board "in an effort to improve the relationship between the visiting ladies and the Stampede's own Queen and Princesses."[584] Originally assigned to one of the chaperones on the committee, the task of coordinating members of the Queens' Alumni to assist with hosting and touring these special visitors was managed by Laura during the late 1990s and taken over by the Queens' Alumni Committee itself in the 2000s.

Although the trio did not allow it to dim their joy in winning, the Queen Committee was disturbed by yet another negative editorial from Catherine Ford that appeared immediately following the 1988 contest. Taking another dig at the image of the Stampede's royal trio, in particular the outfits designed by Margaret Fraser, Ford expressed

ennui at Dress Western and pastel polyester. At the boring and predictable farce perpetrated each year in this city when the young and presumably virginal go through the process of being winnowed out until three bland-looking Calgary girls are chosen to parade around for the entire Stampede as the Queen and her Princesses.

They are, I know, nice girls. They're charming, polite, fully dressed and, I am convinced, trained not to flirt, sparkle, glow or otherwise raise the ambient temperature in any room.

Aside from the fact that this annual charade is insulting – let's pretend they're chosen for their horsemanship and niceness, when what we really want is a pretty face and a body that doesn't look like a sack of potatoes in those awful clothes – it's also embarrassing for reasons other than that of feminist values: They have no wattage.[585]

Ford's outburst prompted letters to the *Herald* from 1956 Queen Shirley Willock and from 1974 Queen Happy Barlow, writing on behalf of the Queens' Alumni Association as vice-president. Reminding Ford, and *Herald* readers, of the purpose of the royal trio, Happy wrote: "As figureheads of one of the world's most respected and well-run organizations, they not only uphold the image of the Stampede, but also that of the more than 2,000 volunteers who form the nucleus of this operation. They epitomize the image of classic beauty, good taste and charm."[586] Writing from her home in California, in a letter headed "Rodeo queens don't need more glitz," Shirley suggested: "Maybe if [Ford] got involved in the contest she could share her ideas and be more appreciative of the gals who are dedicated to adding a 'something extra' to our now world-famous Calgary Stampede."[587] Over the next few years, Queen Committee member Pat Pearson, who happened to be a personal friend of Ford's, invited the columnist many times to observe the contest more closely or participate as a celebrity judge, in the hope that she would gain (and express) a more positive perspective. Whether a change of heart would have occurred or not, the hoped-for contest visit never happened.[588]

Ford's dismissive, and potentially damaging, comments in the spring of 1988 could not have come at a worse time for the Queen Committee. It was fighting a turf war with the Stampede Indian Events Committee, which had announced it was planning to choose an Indian princess to represent the Treaty 7 Nations that participated in the Stampede. An Indian princess had first been chosen as a representative by the Indian Village Tipi Owners in 1965 (Gloria Littlelight of the Tsuu T'ina Nation*) but, being informal and unofficial, the position had been filled only sporadically over the years, the last incumbent

---

* Unfortunately, it is beyond the scope of this book to include a complete history of the Indian Princess program, photographs of winners and full descriptions of their activities.

having been the Piikani Nation's Denise Yellowhorn in 1972.[589]

In the fall of 1987, Indian Events Committee member Linda Richards-Kelly suggested reviving the position for 1988, but recommended placing the Indian princess and the competition under official Stampede sponsorship to avoid some of the problems experienced in the past. As she envisaged it, the contest would be open to single young women aged 18–24 who belonged to one of the five tribes in Treaty 7. Judging of the five finalists, one per Nation, would take place on the Wednesday before Stampede at the tipi owners dinner. Each contestant would be interviewed, give a prepared speech, speak a greeting in her native language and demonstrate a traditional skill, such as dancing. Estimating that she required a budget of $5,000 to $6,000, Richards-Kelly predicted that there would be lots of exposure for the winner, an honoured place in the Stampede parade, and prizes including clothing, luggage and a scholarship.[590]

The Indian Events Committee was in favour, viewing an Indian princess as a public-relations tool for the Stampede and a bridge between the Western fair and Aboriginal Albertans, particularly those in Treaty 7.[591] But owing to the relatively autonomous nature of Stampede committees, the idea was not vetted outside of the Indian Events Committee before being implemented. As a result, the memo the Committee circulated in early April 1988 to all Stampede departments, announcing that an Indian princess would be crowned on June 2, took Queen Committee members by surprise. In particular, the Queen Committee took exception to the official-sounding nature of the position, indicated by a line in the memo which read: "Should you wish to have this year's Calgary Stampede Indian Princess appear at any functions you and your committee are involved with, please [call] to arrange bookings."[592]

To chair Marg Fraser and the Queen Committee, this sounded like direct competition for the royal trio, heretofore the only official figureheads available for booking by committees and volunteers planning Stampede-related functions. Hoping to mollify ruffled feelings, Stampede president Gordon Pearce sent a memo to the Board on April 11, reminding other directors that the royal trio gave priority to appearances at Stampede functions and hoped for some consideration in return:

[We] trust that they will be considered… in priority to any other persons performing similar functions from outside the Stampede organization. As we spend a significant amount of money in acquiring qualified girls to represent the Stampede as our Queen and Princesses and as the Committee expends considerable effort in preparing the girls for their jobs, it would only appear appropriate that we utilize them wherever we can as well as giving them the presence and appropriate recognition at such functions. It is worthwhile mentioning that this year all of the girls are accomplished riders.[593]

Even Stampede general manager Don Jacques was surprised when he learned that the Indian Events Committee was planning to choose an Indian princess. Saying "this is the first I have heard [of it]," he raised a number of concerns:

(1) The Queen and Princess Contest is not (as it shouldn't be) exclusive to whites, so... Indians could compete and I'm sure they have in the past. (2) When the Queen and 2 Princesses appear at functions, is not the question going to be asked "Where is the Indian Princess?" (3) If the Indian Princess appears at functions alone, is there not going to be the question "Where are the others?" (4) Will there be confusion in the public's mind relative to the whole subject?[594]

As Jacques had observed, there was no restriction preventing Aboriginal women from competing in the Stampede Queen contest, but over the years, very few had chosen to do so. After Evelyn Eagle Speaker's successful campaign had made her Queen in 1954, just two other native women had tried for the crown, in 1960 and 1961. These unsuccessful attempts had occurred during the Associated Canadian Travellers' sponsorship period, when ticket sales had ruled the campaign. Since the Stampede instituted a more competitive structure in 1964, not a single native woman had entered the contest. But it was also during this period that Indian princess competitions were established and embraced by the Aboriginal community with great enthusiasm.[595] Many young women who won contests on local reserves competed in the Calgary Indian Friendship Centre's Indian Princess Calgary contest and/or the Indian Princess Alberta contest, and some even went on to compete in the Canadian Indian Princess Pageant, all introduced during the mid-1960s. In 1965 the Calgary Stampede Indian Village had joined the trend by choosing Gloria Littlelight as its first Princess.[596] Possibly, participation in these contests had been sufficient to absorb the competitive energy of young Aboriginal women, but Linda Richards-Kelly also offered another explanation for their apparent lack of interest in the Stampede Queen contest: "These girls are not comfortable competing in the Miss Calgary Stampede competition. They have different backgrounds, different points of view and different talents. We thought it would be nice to offer them their own platform."[597]

On May 17 the director responsible for the Queen Committee took the matter to the Board, saying that "activities of a Stampede Indian Princess could be in conflict with the duties defined for the Stampede Queen and Princesses, so it is important that the Indian Princess's duties be specified to avoid a potential conflict." In the discussion that followed, Board members expressed concern that it might be confusing for the public to have yet another Stampede princess, and that it was a duplication of effort and funding for competing committees to hold competitions and solicit sponsorship and bookings.[598]

Concerned that the discussion might be tending toward cancelling the competition, the director responsible for the Indian Events Committee assured the Board that the new princess's duties would be restricted to the Indian Village on the Stampede grounds and to Indian-related activities downtown at Rope Square.[599] With that assurance in place, the Board gave its approval to the Indian Princess contest.

The Queen Committee had to back down and be satisfied, but a press report after the competition caused a little concern because it indicated that the Indian Events Committee might have wider aspirations for its princess than had been declared. Linda Richards-Kelly told *Calgary Herald* reporter Bernice Huxtable that although the Indian Village had chosen princesses in the past, "she's never been involved in the Stampede as a whole. We felt it was important that a native represent the village on a broader scale."[600] Announcing contest winner Gloria Snow of the Stoney/Nakoda Nation as "the first Miss Calgary Stampede Indian Princess," Huxtable identified her as "the first wide-ranging ambassador for Stampede Indian Village" and described her duties as "talking to visitors, visiting exhibits and attending the rodeo and other functions here and in the United States." Seemingly confirming the fact that the Indian princess was now an official Stampede representative, Gloria was crowned with a sterling silver coronet designed by Richards-Kelly and executed by Olson Silver of High River, the same company that had produced new crowns for the Stampede trio in 1979. Gloria's crown was "shaped like a tepee, etched with feathers and banded in silver links," and silver pendants were presented to the remaining contestants, "ovals inscribed with the C and lazy S of the Calgary Stampede." Huxtable pronounced the event "simple and elegant… probably one of the most meaningful pageants mounted in this city."[601]

After the Stampede was over, the Queen Committee grumbled that, in spite of prior assurances that the Indian princess's activities would be restricted to the Indian Village and Rope Square, "this was not always the case."[602] It predicted many areas of conflict ahead, including sponsors, donors, publicity, the use of courtesy cars, and "a duplication of promotional activities by two sets of ambassadors."[603] Emphasizing the importance of the royal trio to the show and its home city, Queen Committee chair Margaret Fraser told the press that "the Stampede queen and princesses are probably the one thing that is identifiable to the city as a whole… [They] represent the volunteer system that makes Stampede what it is."[604]

The matter was discussed at length by the Board on several occasions, but, as the Queen Committee had feared, once the Indian princess competition had occurred successfully in 1988, the Board was reluctant to terminate it, especially as the theme of the 1989 Stampede honoured native people. In a small victory, the Board confirmed that the Stampede Queen and Princesses were the official representatives of the Stampede, and stated for the record that there was nothing preventing Aboriginal women from competing in the queen contest.[605] The Indian Events Committee was forced to remove the word Stampede from the title of its representative,[606] and although she was often referred to informally as the Stampede Indian Princess, the official title remained the Indian Village Princess until 2009.

By the end of the decade, the Queen Committee had survived several bouts of potentially damaging media criticism and a perceived threat to the exclusivity of the royal trio's position within the Stampede family, but there was one long-standing irritant still to be resolved: the variable level of winners' riding ability.

A real bonus for royalty, starting in 1987, had been the Committee's apparent success in convincing the Board to reserve three Stampede-owned horses for the exclusive use of the royal trio. Margaret Fraser felt that this would allow each young woman to form a relationship with a consistent mount, a confidence-builder for less experienced riders, and anticipated that it would enable the trio to attend more rural rodeos "based on their familiarity with the stock that they will ride for these events."[607] However, it did not turn out quite that way. Although Stampede horses were always made available for royal use, there was no consistency from day to day, and the young women usually were given whichever horses happened to be available, "sorrels, paints or Ranch Girl horses."[608] Also, handlers proved reluctant to allow Stampede horses to be transported outside the city, so at out-of-town events the ladies still faced the vexing problem of riding unfamiliar, often unschooled horses that were unused to parades and crowds. It would be another five years, and take a serious accident, before trios had the comfort of riding consistent and familiar stock at most events year round.

The placement of an initial riding test earlier in the queen contest, in the late 1970s, had meant that all serious competitors in the 1980s could ride, but it did not guarantee that finalists, or even winners, could ride well. Reluctant to scare off a potential candidate who had the right personality for the job, contest advertising and the marking scheme used by judges downplayed the importance of good riding skills. Most of the time it had not really mattered, because the bulk of the trio's time had not been on horseback. But during the late 1980s there was a push to do more riding more often as the demand rose for trios to participate in local rodeos and parades. Before the 1988 Stampede even began, Queen Laura and Princesses Susanne and Jennifer had already ridden in parades in Innisfail, High River, Okotoks and Black Diamond. During the 1970s, royalty was

required to ride only about 10 to 15 per cent of the time; by the late 1980s, this requirement had doubled to 20 to 30 per cent.[609]

Many times over the years, the Queen Committee had agonized over "how to improve the quality of riders the contest is attracting" and guarantee that winners were competent horsewomen.[610] Finally, at decade's end, it decided to resolve the problem once and for all by introducing into the 1989 contest a second riding test for semifinalists, the last event before the buffet dinner where the six finalists were announced.[611] By providing three opportunities for contestants to be judged on their riding, and be weeded out if their skills were found lacking, the Queen Committee finally committed to horsemanship as a basic requirement for Stampede royalty.

The winners that emerged from the 1989 contest, all Calgarians, were 19-year-old Bonny Wallace as Queen, with 20-year-old Shelly Ann Fyfe and 21-year-old Mary Ellen Rouleau as Princesses. Although the change of rules had resulted in winners who were accomplished horsewomen, accidents happen, and Princess Mary Ellen broke her pelvis in three places after her horse reared up and fell on her during the warm-up for the Black Diamond parade in early June. As a result, during much of the lead-up to Stampede, the 1989 trio was a duo. Mary Ellen was released

from her wheelchair just in time for Stampede. She joked to reporters about her participation in the parade: "'I'm going to be in a convertible behind the other girls with a sign that says, 'Wounded in Action, Back in the Saddle Soon.'" Gamely "hobbling about on crutches," she soldiered on through the big week by taking frequent rest stops, and headed to Great Falls with the others the very next week to ride in the parade.[612]

When the young ladies gave their mid-year critique to the Queen Committee, they emphasized just how grateful they were to have had each other's support throughout those difficult few months.[613] This no doubt helped the Committee decide to reject a suggestion that had been under consideration for several years: to reduce the number of royal positions to two, or even one, as a cost-cutting measure. Instead, the Committee conceded "that the benefits of having three ladies outweigh the costs," and at the start of a new decade, they committed to continue finding and funding a trio of royal representatives for the Calgary Stampede.[614]

Queen Bonny Wallace (centre) with Princesses Mary Ellen Rouleau and Shelly Ann Fyfe at the Chinook Centre Stampede breakfast, 1989. (CSA)

"The riding has to become second nature"

After struggling during the 1980s to top one million visitors, a record first set in 1976, Stampede attendance plateaued around that mark in the 1990s. The release of the Horizon 2000 expansion plan in 1990 signalled the Board's commitment to physical growth and the development of the Stampede as a year-round tourist attraction.[615] There was also a growing recognition of the need to promote the Stampede to new markets, an initiative that directly impacted the Queen program. The royal trio became busier than ever on-park and off during Stampede week, attending more local and regional fairs and rodeos and being included in several big promotional trips farther afield in Canada and the western U.S. With more than half of their 350 public appearances per year occurring outside of Stampede week, by the end of the decade the time commitment demanded of these queenly volunteers was starting to affect

1990 Queen Kari Griffith (left) with Princesses Dawn Chipchase and Vanessa Gleddie. (CSA)

schooling, careers, personal finances and interpersonal relationships.

The Stampede Queen Committee came into the 1990s with a renewed commitment to providing royalty with real riding skills. This meant that winners could perform more credibly on horseback, but the downside was that contestant numbers declined – just 34 competitors in 1990 compared with 73 in 1984. For some reason, contest advertising still downplayed the requirement, simply listing riding ability as "a definite asset." But potential candidates soon learned differently during the introductory meeting with Committee members. Once they understood the actual level of horsemanship expected, and learned that the scores from the various riding events now rated equally with the marks from interviews and speeches, many contestants were scared off, according to Committee chair Margaret Fraser. Of the thirty-four initial applicants in 1990, twelve pulled out before the contest actually began.[616]

Even so, riding ability was only judged as being

equivalent to other qualities and sometimes judges chose queens and princesses with more potential than actual skill. Although most winners no longer required actual riding lessons, John Finn, the member who had managed all things horse- and riding-related for the Committee since the early 1980s, expected to work with new royalty for a good six to eight weeks before he considered them ready to handle crowds, parades and grand entries on horseback. After 1987 the trio always had Stampede-owned horses to use at events in the city, but if they travelled farther afield, they had to ride borrowed horses, so safety became an important consideration, a point brought home when 1989 Princess Mary Ellen Rouleau got thrown before the Black Diamond parade. Knowing that the number of out-of-town events was rising, Finn gave the judges a precise and clear instruction: "make absolutely sure [the trio] can handle their horses in any situation."[617]

Calgary Herald reporter Anne Crawford attended one of Finn's practice sessions just before the 1990 Stampede. It was his twenty-first session with new Queen Kari Griffith, 20, and Princesses Dawn Chipchase and Vanessa Gleddie, both 21, and they were practising their routine for the Grand Entry before the afternoon rodeo. Finn was playing the role usually performed by announcer Bill Kehler:

"And now, ladies and gentlemen, the lovely Stampede princess Dawwwn Chipchase!" Dawn gallops in at rodeo speed and comes to a back-on-the-haunches halt at the far end of the arena.

"And... our other lovely princess... Vanesssaa Gleddie!" Vanessa charges down the other side of the arena, waving all the way.

"And finally, ladies and gentlemen, ... our very own Stampede Queen... Karrriii Griffith!" Kari gallops in down one side, circles the princesses and brings them back along the other rail.

Single file, head-to-tail, they head full tilt at an angle to the gate. And out they go...[618]

Although the rodeo was just a few days away, Finn was still fine-tuning manoeuvres with the girls and giving crucial advice. "The horses will start lunging in towards that gate... If you don't aim for the far post, they're going to take your knee off on that steel." It was important to practise and practise until the routine was perfect. "When they're riding in the grand entry... they're thinking of so many other things," Finn said. "The riding has to become second nature." He was a tough taskmaster but he knew he was dealing with competent riders who were up to the challenge. The routine included a flying lead change as the group turned for the gate and Kari's horse was giving trouble. When she asked what to do, Finn simply advised, "Just sit down, get your butt down in the saddle."[619]

Potential contestants only had to watch royalty perform daily at the Stampede to realize there was no point in entering the queen contest if they could not ride convincingly at that level – radiating a queenly presence in the saddle no longer was enough. This was quite a change of approach from the early 1960s when the Stampede first became involved in the contest. In 1961 Marie Sharpe, one of the first queens required to pass a riding test, recalled that although she rode in the parade, she did not ride again during all of Stampede week. She and her ladies–in–waiting, who also had to prove they could ride in order to win the contest, were driven around the track in a convertible before being introduced to the crowd from the grandstand stage.[620] Thirty years later, riding ability no longer was window dressing but a real requirement and trios were expected to race into the infield just like traditional American rodeo queens.

Although their winning was predicated upon convincing judges that they could speak well in public and mix and mingle successfully at social events, winners still received weeks of coaching to enhance these qualities and polish their public image. After fifteen years of working with each new trio on makeup and deportment, John Cox left the Committee after the 1990 contest. His many years of teaching "beautification" were recognized by the Queens' Alumni Association when he was made an Honorary Associate in 2001.[621] Patti Falconer, owner of the modelling school that had been donating free classes for winners since the mid-1970s, agreed to pick up the slack and incorporate those areas into weekly sessions for the royalty.[622]

Public speaking was another area that frequently required a little polishing: most contestants had no problem speaking to the contest panel, but it was quite another thing to speak to a crowd of 20,000 or more nightly before the grandstand show, even if the young women took turns performing the duty. Media interviews also could be quite intimidating for some winners. Speech instruction with broadcasting instructor Brian Taylor, and practice sessions before cameras and with microphones at the Southern Alberta Institute of Technology arranged by Committee member Pat Pearson, helped to increase both competence and confidence.[623]

All this support for Stampede royalty occasionally was viewed with envy by those responsible for the Indian Village princess. After the heated discussions of the late 1980s, the Indian Events Committee had restricted the Indian princess's activities mostly to the Indian Village and Rope Square during Stampede week. The Public Affairs department slipped up one year and inadvertently advertised her as the Stampede Indian Princess, but after the Queen Committee registered a protest, the oversight was corrected.[624] In comparison with the Queen Committee, the Indian princess subcommittee had a small budget and few sponsors, so, with one significant addition, the list of gifts received by winners was reminiscent of those given to Stampede Queens two decades before: "a silver belt buckle, a pair of fancy Alberta boots, a handsome Smithbilt hat, a portrait painted by local artist John Langeveld and a complete western outfit from Grand Saddlery of Cochrane." The additional item, first introduced in 1989, was a white, hand-beaded deerskin dress designed by Deanna Starlight. Worth $3,500 (nearly $6,000 today), it was sponsored by the Calgary Police Service with the intention that it would be worn for many years by successive princesses.[625]

The 1989 Indian Village Princess, 23-year-old Elinor Crane from the Tsuu T'ina Nation, appeared content with her winnings and treatment, although her sister later said she had "suppressed her anger when [Elinor] was given negligible prominence in the Stampede parade, and… did not receive promised prizes."[626] The 1990 winner, 17-year-old Heather Meguinis, also from Tsuu T'ina, was more vocal in her complaints. After it was reported by the media that she had resigned partway through Stampede week, she complained of tokenism and discriminatory treatment. She told a reporter that her disillusionment had started at the Stampede's opening night ceremonies:

When she tried [to] take her place at centre stage with other title-holding princesses, a stage director told her to stand off to the side. When I asked him why, he said, "Only our own Stampede princesses go there." … Meguinis said the incident wasn't repeated but it left her in tears. "I'm a First Nations person; why should I be treated as a second class citizen?"

… And the inequity did not stop there. While the Stampede princesses stayed in hotel rooms, her accommodation was a showerless trailer at the Indian Village. "I didn't even get a banner to announce my title." She felt that despite working 16-hour days, her efforts as Indian princess had gone largely unappreciated.[627]

Blaming the opening night incident on miscommunication, Stampede president Bob Church apologized, saying, "It won't happen again, but in no way was it intended to be degrading to the Indian princess." But he also implied that the young woman had been "unprepared for such a large responsibility," and reported that because she had not fulfilled her duties, the Indian Events Committee had replaced her mid-week with Lou Ann Solway of the Siksika Nation. Committee chairman Bruce Starlight blamed the contest's meagre budget rather than open discrimination for many of Heather's complaints,[628] telling *Herald* reporters:

> There was never an actual resignation. One day, she just didn't show up. We had to put someone in her place. We've got to keep our commitments... I came to the conclusion she wasn't prepared. It's tough coming from a reservation atmosphere and into the public eye.[629]

Although some felt Heather's accusations may have been overblown, they were nonetheless embarrassing for the Stampede and the Indian Village. On the positive side, her indignant outburst may have resulted in modestly increased budgets and a greater sensitivity being shown in the treatment of subsequent Indian Village princesses. There seems to have been a gap of a few years, but the contest selected royal representatives for the Indian Village

most years during the 1990s: Lori Ann Wright of the Siksika Nation in 1994; Vada Hoof of the Kainai Nation and Ivy Kim Scott of the Piikani Nation in 1995; Lisa Starlight of the Piikani Nation and Nicole Yellow Old Woman of the Siksika Nation in 1996; Gaylene Weasel Child of the Siksika Nation in 1997; Charity Red Gun of the Siksika Nation in 1998; and Camille Wildman of the Stoney/Nakoda Nation in 1999.

After the media coverage of Heather Meguinis in 1990, Margaret Fraser reported she had received "a number of phone calls in regard to letting the Indian Princess go," and although it had nothing to do with the incident and its aftermath, she was upset that the public thought it had and it somehow reflected badly on the Queen Committee.[630] Unwilling to have it thought they supported discriminatory treatment in favour of the royal trio, chairman Pat Pearson and other Committee members began demonstrating their support for the position by attending the Indian princess's crowning ceremony accompanied by the Stampede royalty, and inviting the Indian princess to attend the crowning of the Stampede queen and princesses in return.[631] By the mid-1990s, relations between the Queen and Indian Events committees had improved to such an extent that the Indian princess was included in some of the training sessions offered to the royal trio, most notably the public speaking and media presence sessions presented by Brian Taylor and Pat Pearson.[632]

The Indian Events Committee was grateful for this assistance and the tacit acknowledgement that its representative had an equally important, if different, role to play on the Stampede's behalf. This new collegiality may have been the encouragement needed for the Committee to try once again in 1996 to expand the Indian princess's role and solicit appearance bookings from other Stampede departments and committees.[633] This time, the Queen Committee offered no objection, and by the end of the decade, the Indian Village princess was making about 120 public appearances during Stampede week alone,[634] quite comparable to the royal trio's Stampede average of ten to fifteen appearances per day.

As for trio appearances other than during the Stampede itself, the Committee had decided in 1990 that it was too expensive, and not particularly productive, to send the trio on big out-of-province promotional trips to the same place year after year.[635] This meant that different trios often had quite different travel experiences, although most usually attended the Grey Cup wherever it was held. In 1990 a request to attend the Quebec Winter Carnival was rejected, but the group went to the Pacific National

Exhibition in Vancouver and Cheyenne Frontier Days in Wyoming. They also were the first trio to attend the National Finals Rodeo in Las Vegas, where they rode in the grand entry one evening and spent two hours each day helping out at the Stampede booth at the convention centre.[636] The Committee skipped a year, but the 1992 trio too went to the NFR in Las Vegas. In addition to the rodeo, that group attended the Cowboy Christmas Show and the Miss Rodeo America Pageant. Over the course of their four-day visit, Marg was proud to report that they had handed out over 400 Stampede brochures.[637]

Having wrestled with various attitude and discipline problems during the 1980s, the Queen Committee in 1991 introduced a letter of understanding for winners to sign which outlined "the commitments and obligations of the Royal Trio during their one-year reign."[638] By signing, candidates acknowledged that they understood the consequences of "disreputable conduct… detrimental to the best interests of the Calgary Stampede." They were reminded that out-of-town travel was a privilege, not an automatic right, and that those who misbehaved or displayed unco-operative attitudes might be disallowed from attending or sent home partway through the event. In extreme circumstances, the ultimate disgrace would be being required to relinquish the title.[639] With these threats ever present, most winners toed the line.

The 1991 winners, Halley Strandquist as Queen and Michel Higginbotham and Alison Ross as Princesses, did not go to the NFR but they had other memorable experiences and came out of their year as lifelong friends.[640] Princess Alison later recalled the trio nearly missing their nightly appearance in the Stampede Park parade one evening because they were so intent on meeting that night's Saddledome headliner, country and western singing star Garth Brooks. Curiously, when they attended Cheyenne Frontier Days in Wyoming several weeks later, they met him again, as well as singer Trisha Yearwood.[641] Although they performed most of the traditional duties of Stampede royalty, the 1991 trio had one job less: having decided the white hat ceremony was outdated, the Queen Committee had begun requesting that "the girls not perform it at the functions they attend."[642] Little did the Committee realize that this so-called outdated ceremony would still be going strong well into the next millennium and would by then be considered by many to be a cherished Calgary tradition!

In 1992, with the contest format down pat and the grooming and training of winning trios running smoothly, the Queen Committee was unprepared for

1991 Queen Halley Strandquist (centre) with Princesses Alison Ross and Michel Higginbotham. (CSA)

further criticism from the media. Just weeks before the Stampede opened, the *Calgary Herald*'s Don Martin wrote a column headed "Stampede royalty

sadly out of touch." He had spoken with the 1992 winners, 24-year-old Queen Shauna Oseen from Lethbridge and Princesses Kate McWhir 23, from Priddis and Sherry Mitchell, 19, from Chestermere Lake. Although Martin liked and respected the three personally, he declared that "their reign as the 46th in the line of royal trios must be the last if the Stampede wants to ride with the times." With the recent demise of a number of beauty contests, including popular national competitions for Miss Canada, Miss Teen Canada, and Miss Grey Cup, Martin pronounced that the time had come to discontinue the Stampede Queen contest.

Conceding he had found the young ladies to be "no dummies," Martin wrote:

They have been coached by a broadcasting instructor in polite, articulate and non-controversial comment. They can recite Stampede pamphlets and exhibition history from memory. They can even ride horses. Of course, insist organizers, it's just strange coincidence all three are knock-'em-dead gorgeous to boot.

1992 Queen Shauna Oseen (centre) with Princesses Kate McWhir and Sherry Mitchell. (CSA)

And that was the source of Martin's complaint: he was convinced that the competition to find civic ambassadors was nothing short of a beauty contest. He did not buy the argument made by organizers, and by the trio themselves, that winners were marked on public speaking and riding, not on beauty as such, as evidenced by the fact that there was no swimsuit competition.

Sorry, ladies, but having judges pick winners from among contestants limited by age (19–24), marital status (single) and alleged virtue (childless) is not a *Jeopardy* talent hunt. It's a beauty pageant. Unattractive women won't compete and judges with the best interests of Stampede promotion at heart wouldn't pick 'em if they did.

Referring to the recent demise of several popular national beauty contests, Martin wrote:

[T]he burial song is always the same – the times they are a-changin' …
Now some argue that cancelling pageants due to alleged sexism is radical feminist overkill. Perhaps. But the Stampede showcases Calgary. It claims to be fighting for survival in a highly competitive tourist market. So any promotional effort which

offends or irritates a large and vocal segment of the population is a very questionable marketing gimmick.

And let's face it. As figureheads for ten days when their public speaking is mostly confined to howdys and exhorting crowds into yelping yahoo, their figure is more important than their heads…

If the title no longer suits the country in the 1990s, how can the Stampede continue judging women to wear its Stetson crown? The Stampede is there to celebrate horse and rider – not the dinosaur.[643]

Although Martin's column must have attracted notice, appearing as it did on the front page of the *Herald*'s City section, there were no follow-up pieces in the ensuing weeks and no irate letters to the editor either supporting or disagreeing with his opinion. Just as had occurred after Catherine Ford's critical op-eds during the late 1980s, the reluctance of the local press to disparage anything Stampede may have kicked in and inhibited comment. In any case, the Committee must have given a collective sigh of relief when a more positive article appeared the very next week. As the trio headed into its busiest season, the *Herald* headlined "No end to royal lineage foreseen." Reporter Eva Ferguson subtly acknowledged Martin's argument, writing:

The Miss Canada Pageant is history. Miss Grey Cup's been turfed too. But a young queen and her princesses are fiercely adamant that the Calgary Stampede's contest of beauty, poise and horsemanship will live as long as the fair. "We don't wear bikinis," they firmly note.

Stampede queen Shauna Oseen and princesses Sherry Mitchell and Kate McWhir say their contest is completely unlike others because there's more than one winner and they have a role like no other. As spokeswomen for Calgary and its western heritage they say their role is not to be looked at, but to be spoken to, to be enjoyed and to educate as any other ambassador – or even royalty for that matter…

"We do a lot of informing. We're always telling people what the city's all about. What Stampede is all about… people feel good about coming up and talking to us."[644]

Ferguson's story also quoted Stampede marketing manager Barry Dane, who emphasized how hard the trio worked on behalf of the event and the city. He added that the Stampede was also looking into getting more men, "like the rodeo cowboys," involved in making public appearances on the grounds as goodwill ambassadors, clearly an attempt to remove the taint of sexism from the role of "bringing Stampede and all its splendor 'to a more personal level.'"[645]

Chair Margaret Fraser and the Queen Committee officially ignored Martin's allegation that the contest was based on superficial attractiveness, but, tellingly, before the 1994 contest, the requirement for applicants to provide their height and weight on the contest entry form was finally dropped.[646]

Perhaps to counteract any lingering negative effects from Martin's article, the Committee put a little extra effort into advertising the 1993 contest. During a media blitz from January 11–18, various members of the 1992 trio appeared on a local program called "Hello Calgary" and in feature spots on local radio and television stations. A news release went out to all media, advertisements were placed in *Horses All* magazine and *Pro Rodeo News*, and, as in other years, Committee members placed posters at Calgary locations such as the University, Southern Alberta Institute of Technology, Mount Royal College, the Foothills Hospital nurses residence, Western wear stores, Western bars, shopping centres and grocery stores. Members also ensured that posters appeared in outlying districts such as Okotoks, Chestermere, High River and Bragg Creek.[647]

However, in spite of this massive advertising campaign, contest numbers were much the same as had become the norm during this period – approximately 35 applicants, about ten of whom dropped out after the introductory meeting.[648] After the usual six-week contest, the winners in 1993 were 22-year-old Erin Moynihan as Queen with Princesses Laura Hughes and Melissa McKay.

John Finn had resigned from the Queen Committee after the 1991 Stampede, after a decade of service. Others stepped in to take his place, but his firm hand in preparing the trio for the rigours and intricacies of riding in grand entries was sorely missed. At a Committee meeting on May 3, 1993, it was revealed that the new trio had received no riding instruction to date, and that the Committee member now in charge "does not feel that there is need for concern at this point."[649] No one questioned the wisdom of that decision at the time, but that blasé statement must have haunted the Committee after two members of the 1993 trio were involved in a "spectacular pile-up" during the grand entry on the opening day of the Stampede rodeo.[650] According to a report in the *Calgary Herald*,

The crowd of several thousand at the Stampede gasped, then fell into a shocked hush when princesses Melissa McKay, Laura Hughes and their horses sprawled in the dirt after colliding head-on at full gallop.

1993 Queen Erin Moynihan (right) with Princesses Melissa McKay and Laura Hughes. (CSA)

The accident happened when the announcer introduced McKay, 20, and Hughes, 22, at the start of the rodeo. Each princess rode into the arena from gates at opposite ends. They raced toward each other while waving and looking at the infield crowd. Noticing at the last moment that they were on a collision course, the two riders veered in the same direction and crashed.

The two were taken to the Holy Cross Hospital for observation and treatment. Hughes was able to return to her duties the next day but it was reported that it was unlikely McKay would return for Stampede activities.[651]

Although Melissa was still receiving treatment for a broken jaw nearly a year after her accident,[652] she had recovered well enough by the fall of 1993 to participate with her trio in various post-Stampede activities. But the accident had a significant long-term impact because the Board finally allowed the Queen Committee to purchase three horses for the exclusive year-round use of Stampede royalty. In addition, the Grand Entry was changed so that the trio entered the arena together, in full view of each other at all times. Succeeding royals had many fond memories of the three "bombproof" bays named Bob and Fred, both purchased in 1993, and Gus, who joined the team in

1994, chosen by the Committee for their calm performance "in front of cheering crowds, parade routes of distraction, pyrotechnics and at times a gruelling schedule under any weather condition imaginable."[653]

With no major accidents to disrupt scheduling, the 1994 royalty had a more predictable year, although it was the first trio in many years to be housed elsewhere than the Palliser Hotel for Stampede week. With Calgary, and consequently the Stampede, experiencing a slight economic downturn, the Queen Committee was forced to trim its budget. The cost of placing the royal party at the Palliser for twelve days each July had been climbing steadily over the years and had caused the Committee some concern. When a new hotel manager declined to offer a better discount, reasoning that the hotel was already losing money by hosting the trio during one of the busiest weeks of the Calgary year, chairman Pat Pearson thanked the Palliser for past services and terminated the long-standing partnership.[654]

Instead, 23-year-old Queen Sonya Dueck, Princesses Tamy Midtdal and Holly Watson and their chaperone stayed in the Radisson Plaza (formerly known as the Four Seasons, later the Calgary Skyline Hotel) right across the street, which became the royal headquarters for the next few years. When the Radisson Plaza changed hands again in 1997

to become a Marriott, and a new manager at the Palliser proved to be more accommodating, royal trios returned to their former home for several years until the nearby Hyatt Regency opened in 2000 and took over as royalty's official accommodation sponsor during Stampede week.

Budget cuts during this period resulted in some streamlining, but with the support of sponsors the 1994 trio still managed to travel out of town: to Cheyenne Frontier Days, the Grey Cup in Vancouver and the National Finals Rodeo in Las Vegas. The group also spent many weekends closer to home attending small-town fairs and rodeos. Well aware of the Stampede's important role in tying Calgary to its rural hinterland, the Committee tried to accommodate as many booking requests as possible each season for the trio to appear at smaller events around southern and central Alberta. Having won their positions partly because of their horse-riding skills, it is not surprising that queens and princesses loved these opportunities to get out of the city and ride like rodeo queens.

267 ⭐

1994 Queen Sonya Dueck (centre) with Princesses Holly Watson and Tamy Midtdal. (CSA)

CHAPTER 14 ✭ 1995–1999

"There's more guts than glamour in being Stampede royalty"

The only downside of the new emphasis on riding during the 1990s was the increase in horse-related accidents that accompanied it. After Princesses Melissa and Laura collided in 1993, the Queen Committee minutes recorded the following understatement: "Marg suggested that once the 1994 trio are selected… a horse safety seminar be put on for them and the committee members."[655] This became standard practice, but with more time being spent around horses, it was not uncommon for even very experienced riders to have minor accidents or near-misses, although most were too insignificant to attract media attention.

One incident in 1995, for example, involved transporting horses rather than riding them. Several weeks before the Stampede began, 24-year-old Queen Allison Boswell from Springbank and Princesses Lisa Eastman, 23, from Calgary and Karina Tees, 21,

Queen Allison Boswell (right) and Princesses Lisa Eastman and Karina Tees making their Grand Entry at the Stampede rodeo, 1995. (CSA)

from the Ponoka area were returning from an event at Griffin Valley Ranch northwest of Calgary. Nearly two decades later, Princess Lisa vividly remembered the group driving home along a slippery gravel road and watching in horror as the horse trailer detached and slid past their vehicle on its side. Luckily, horses Gus, Bob and Fred were uninjured, having been well protected by their thick blankets.[656]

A second mishap for the 1995 trio had more serious consequences. After participating in Alberta Derby Day on the Stampede grounds in late September, the young women were feeling frisky with unspent energy and asked chaperone Margaret Fraser if they could race back to the barns. Uncharacteristically indulgent after twenty years of chaperoning trios, Marg said yes, so off they raced, purposely overshooting their goal so that they could race back. Karina was on the slowest horse, Fred, so the others gave her a head start. They were riding neck-and-neck when Lisa's Gus spotted an open gate and went for it. When she tried to correct him, he hit the fence and went down. With no time to react, Bob plowed into

1995 Queen Allison Boswell (centre) and Princesses Lisa Eastman and Karina Tees with Alberta Premier Ralph Klein. (CSA)

Gus and went down too, knocking Allison unconscious.[657] The panicked horses raced on past an astonished Karina, who eventually caught Bob, while Marg went after Gus.[658] Lisa and Allison were taken to hospital by ambulance and both required extensive surgery, Allison for her knee and Lisa her ankle.

Luckily, it was a slow time of year so the two missed very few public appearances while recovering from their injuries. Back to work fulfilling official duties within a few weeks, Lisa recalled them being a rather unusual looking trio with two members hobbling along on crutches.[659] Not surprisingly, this escapade resulted in yet another rule being added to the list that subsequent royalty were required to acknowledge and follow: no horseplay.[660]

Aside from that, 1995 was a significant year because Princess Karina was the first ever Stampede royal with a disability. Deaf since birth, her positive personality and her riding and communications skills had enabled her to win out over sixteen other serious candidates in the queen contest, and to win the Miss Rodeo Canada contest in 1998. After being named Stampede Princess, Karina told a reporter that she "want[ed] to be an inspiration to others with disabilities."[661] Luckily the 1995 trio was a harmonious and supportive group. Allison and Lisa were several years older, and Karina's disability brought out their protective, big-sisterly instincts. Karina recalled feeling free to be herself with them and was happy to follow their lead. They learned basic signing and used it during their nightly greeting to the grandstand crowd, two taking turns signing while the third spoke.[662] Sensitive to the fact that crowded or noisy situations made it more difficult for Karina to lip-read, the group usually stayed close together and assisted each other in answering questions or responding to comments.[663] Afterwards, Queen Allison speculated that an important factor in the bonding of the 1995 trio, and in its effectiveness as a team, had been the very fact that they could not take it for granted that all had heard and understood equally in any given situation. With communication having to be face-to-face, they were forced to slow down and make sure that "everyone was on the same page and marching in the same direction" before making decisions and moving forward.[664]

While the others were recovering from their injuries, Karina attended a special event on her own that could not have included them in any case. In October she was paired with a deaf child for a one-day trip to Disneyland called "Dreams Take Flight" that was organized by Air Canada on behalf of 132 children with disabilities.[665] In November all three rode together in the Grey Cup parade in Regina and a few weeks later headed off with chaperone Dorothy Kennedy to attend the National Finals Rodeo in Las Vegas.

By the mid-1990s the royal trio was making well over 350 public appearances annually. Honorariums to cover extraordinary expenses were still at $1,000 per girl (the amount introduced in 1987), but the size of the wardrobe had increased, a necessity for young women now expected to appear on behalf of the Stampede every few days all year long. As Alanna Mitchell of *The Globe and Mail* reported after interviewing the 1995 trio,

Each of the royal three will go through a dozen white Stetsons during the year. The hats, with silver crown affixed, must be worn each time the Queen and Princesses appear, including when they eat and ride. In addition, each of the three has seven outfits "built" for them, as their handlers say, a total cost of between $8,000 and $9,000 [$11,000 to more than $12,000 today]. They have another ten or so ready-to-wear outfits, five pairs of leather cowboy boots and a custom-made belt buckle."[666]

A very welcome solution to Marg Fraser's annual headache of rounding up extra pairs of boots in addition to those provided by the Alberta Boot Company and additional pieces of clothing to supplement the girls' custom-made outfits had presented itself in the early 1990s when Lammle's Western Wear offered "to supply all the ready-made western wear along with all of the cowboy boots… also… all of the colored Wranglers… for 3–5 years."[667] This trial proved successful for both parties, and Lammle's sponsorship became an ongoing commitment.

The 1996 royalty, Queen Kari Hames and Princesses Jody Hooker and Shilo Johanson, were the first to wear elegant new crowns created by the Olson Silver Company of High River. The former crowns, first presented in 1979, had become worn after years of cleaning and use – the top of the queen's crown had actually broken off in 1993. The Queens' Alumni, composed as it was of dozens of former queens and princesses who had worn the heavy old crowns with their outdated and irritating clasps, agreed it was time to make a change, but the group was disconcerted to learn from chairman Pat Pearson that the Queen Committee had proceeded with the project without asking for input.[668] The Stampede Board had long ago approved the Committee's three-year plan requiring the capital budget to cover the cost of replacing the royal crowns,[669] and with no need for additional funding the Committee had not even considered consulting the Alumni on the matter.

"Alike in every aspect… to reflect the equality of the titles,"[670] the new crowns were another attempt to reinforce the Committee's belief in the equality and interchangeability of the three royal positions, a process that had begun fifteen years earlier with the equalization of honorariums and the introduction of saddle prizes for princesses. Made of sterling silver and ten-karat gold, the crowns were equal in size and lighter to wear. Aside from bearing different titles, they were "identically and intricately engraved," the only perceptible difference being that the queen's crown included two synthetic rubies. Before the old crowns were turned over to the Stampede's Historical

Committee for preservation, Olson's engraved the inside band of them with the names of the former queens and princesses who had worn them over the previous seventeen years.[671]

In spite of being sidelined during their creation, the Alumni Committee was happy with the new crowns and what they represented. But it was disappointed when its request to participate in the 1996 crowning ceremony, the first to use the new crowns, was politely but firmly rejected by the Queen Committee.[672] This was a blow, because that year, alumni were looking for ways to celebrate a proud history. In 1990 the Stampede Historical Committee had invited the group to set up a display of royal memorabilia during Stampede week. The display, which included a selection of photographs, outfits and saddles from former queens and princesses, was a popular success and became an annual tradition. The group had continued its role of assisting during Stampede week by hosting in the Brand Room, judging displays for the Promotional Committee and escorting visiting rodeo queens. Its year-round efforts on behalf of special-needs children also had continued, with the introduction of the first Christmas Special event in 1994. At the end of the decade it would add the annual "4 the Kids Gala" to fundraise on behalf of organizations working with special-needs children.[673] But in

1996, what the Alumni Committee wanted to celebrate was fifty years of Stampede royalty.

The Associated Canadian Travellers had promoted Doreen Richardson as the Stampede's first queen because she was the first to have won the contest they introduced in 1947. For many years, the Stampede had thought of Sharon Patterson as its first queen because she was the first to be chosen in 1964 using Stampede rules only (i.e., no ticket sales). However, once the Queens' Alumni Association was formed in 1972, the group successfully convinced the Stampede and the media that Patsy Rodgers's historic appointment in 1946 had been the true start of the Stampede Queen tradition. Patsy was good friends with the other founding members, Merle Stier and Donna Thomson, and she had been involved in the Alumni since its inception. She had been considered a mentor and an inspiration for generations of queens and princesses as they performed their jobs and retired to join the Alumni. Following a request from the group,[674] the special contribution of the "Queen Mum" was recognized during the 1996 Stampede when Patsy was designated an honorary parade marshal and led more than fifty former queens and princesses in a special Stampede Queens section of the parade.

With the 50th anniversary as a focus, 1996 was a

1996 Queen Kari Hames (right) with Princesses Jody Hooker and Shilo Johanson. (CSA)

big year to be a royal according to Queen Kari, who had entered the contest with the encouragement of her mother's best friend, 1975 Queen Barb Howard. A slightly greater number of candidates than usual – forty – had competed for the crown that year. Because her grandfather owned J. Vair Anderson Jewellers, Kari was amused when she received a valuable watch from long-time sponsor Henry Birks and Sons. That experience later prompted her family's company to supplant Birks as a major royalty sponsor.[675]

Also in 1996, Marg Fraser designed fancy dress outfits to go along with the new crowns: floor-length sequined gowns in purple for the queen and pink for the princesses. Telling the Queen Committee that the usual red and white name badges would clash, Marg ordered a second set in black and gold for formal occasions.[676]

The 1996 trio found themselves well supported by the Alumni during the Stampede. When they made their nightly welcome speech before the grandstand show, they were joined on the stage by a huge colour party of former royals. The group included Patsy Rodgers, who also gave a short prepared speech each night. Although it was an intense year of "living in each other's back pockets," the trio made it work by playing off each other's strengths when dealing with the public. In addition, Queen Kari helped to emphasize the equality of the threesome by declining to ride ahead of the other two and ignoring some of other traditional queenly protocols still in effect.[677]

Chatting with *Herald* reporter Wendy Dudley at Rodeo Royal just as their reign was ending, the group recounted some of the touching, embarrassing and downright harrowing moments that had helped them to bond as a team. Kari remembered toppling from her rearing horse outside the Rodeo Royal arena: "I ended up right underneath him. I got back up to ride him but his bridle was broken." She got on another horse and made her entry seconds later, "proving there's more guts than glamour in being part of Stampede Royalty." Shilo recalled her discomfort after being asked on radio whether she rode English or Western. Her innocent reply, "Oh I can go both ways," prompted amused reaction from strangers for many days to come. Jody's parents were overseas for the year, so she was grateful to find support and a substitute family in the Stampede and her royal sisters. "Everyone took me in under their wing." Perhaps it was that feeling of warmth and community that prompted Jody to join the Stampede Queen Committee several years after her reign ended.[678]

For the 1996 contest, the Queen Committee had developed a set of questions for judges to use while interviewing candidates. This provided welcome structure and consistency and was well received by the judges, so for the 1997 contest the Committee came up with eleven impromptu questions for judges to ask during the speech contest. These proved especially helpful to so-called celebrity judges who provided a little publicity for the contest during the late 1990s by assisting regular community judges. After the candidates finished their one-and-a-half to two-minute prepared speeches, they were asked an impromptu question requiring a thirty-second answer to see how well they handled themselves talking off script. The questions included such real-life scenarios as "You are a finalist in this year's competition at Rodeo Royal. Your horse dumps you in the rodeo arena. How will you react and what will you do?" "As the Stampede Queen or Princess, you are a part of a team comprised of two other girls and a chaperone. How would you pave the way to a good working relationship with the group?" and "As a Stampede Queen or Princess, you will represent the City of Calgary on many occasions. Aside from the Stampede, what other aspects of Calgary would you promote to the travelling public?"[679]

After the semifinalists had been pared down to six finalists, the Queen Committee met with the group to do a final run-through on the rules and regulations for the Rodeo Royal portion of the contest and

1997 Queen Holly Cartwright (centre) with Princesses Karin Hunter and Tina Maynard. (CSA)

to make sure successful candidates really understood and were prepared to abide by the Committee's expectations for the reigning year ahead. The finalists drew for riding position and for who was to speak each time, and a group photograph was taken for the Rodeo Royal program and to hand out to the press. The short biographies finalists provided were to be incorporated into the script used by radio personality and contest emcee Bill Kehler. While candidates were being prepared for the final judging, a Committee member worked with the outgoing trio on speeches for a farewell party scheduled for the Saturday night so that the president's reception on the Sunday could focus on the incoming trio.[680]

The three young ladies who navigated successfully through the intricacies of the 1997 contest were 21-year-old Holly Cartwright as Queen, with 20-year-old Tina Maynard and 21-year-old Karin Hunter as Princesses. The winners were on message right from the start: immediately after being crowned at Rodeo Royal, Queen Holly said, "I'm a history buff, so I want people around the world to understand how important this way of life is. Calgary is Cowtown and I love it." Added Princess Tina, "The Stampede is the heart of this city."[681]

From an old foothills country family, Queen Holly had grown up on the EP Ranch, famously owned by the Prince of Wales (later known as King Edward VIII). Coincidentally, her first riding instructor was Bruce Debnam from Millarville, who had been introduced at the February 1997 meeting of the Queen Committee as the person "who will be looking after the horses and riding program for this year."[682] In fact, Debnam enjoyed his role so much that he stayed on, gradually involving two friends, Tony Patterson and Tony Peacock, in "the care, conditioning and transport of the royal steeds" for the next decade. Their dedication was recognized by the Queens' Alumni Association in 2010 when all three were made Honorary Associates.[683]

Reacting to Catherine Ford's negative comments in the late 1980s that the outfits worn by royal trios were dull and that their look lacked "wattage," Margaret Fraser started using brighter colours and more varied fabrics and patterns. During the 1990s she was influenced by the clothing she saw contestants wearing at the Miss Rodeo America pageants in Las Vegas. She started giving Stampede royals a flashier look, using shinier fabrics and incorporating lots of sequins and sparkles. She wanted the trio to stand out, to be identified easily and from a distance as royalty, but some observers thought that she overdid the look. According to 1996 Queen Kari, the young ladies in her trio had "seven or eight full sequin outfits" as well as a number of sequined tops to pair with Wrangler jeans in every colour.[684] Those in the know were careful never to refer to the outfits worn by rodeo queens as "costumes" (because of that word's implication that the wearer was acting or practising make-believe),[685] but sometimes Margaret's creations during this period veered rather close to that. When the 1997 trio headed to the Pendleton Round-Up and the Houston Livestock Show and Rodeo, Holly, Tina and Karin realized that the glitzy Vegas look Marg had given them was out of step with what was being worn in the real rodeo world. "The only three people in sequins, many people asked, 'What are you?'"[686]

Although their year was very busy – in addition to the above-named shows, the 1997 trio also attended the Grey Cup in Edmonton – this trio's Stampede week was slightly less intense because the Queen Committee had backed off slightly on bookings for 1997. With two fewer appearances per day, the team was able to get to all booked events while still maintaining its schedule.[687] Similarly, as the decade came to a close and a new one began, the Committee started to decline bookings if it judged that the events were too commercial or of no real benefit to the Stampede (for example, if a business simply wanted three pretty girls to act as hostesses for an

event).[688] Mid-day bookings for short appearances were also rejected because it was unfair for royals who were employed to have to make up hours of time at work or get docked a half-day's pay to make a thirty-minute to one-hour public appearance.[689] The Committee even declined several bookings from within the Stampede family because the requests had come in with less than 48 hours' notice even though the events themselves had been planned for months. This was considered insufficient time for the young women to notify employers of an absence.[690]

With the start of another three-year budget period looming in 1998, the Queen Committee did a little soul-searching, asking questions such as: "Should we solicit bookings? How do we reach new markets? Should out-of-town trips, e.g., National Finals Rodeo, be an annual event – are dollars well spent?" and, in terms of booking priorities, "does a Stampede sponsor take precedence over an 'on Park' Stampede event?" (an important consideration, with sponsorship revenues representing nearly one-third of the Committee's total annual budget by the late 1990s).[691] Margaret Fraser also raised the issue of the honorariums paid to Stampede royalty, noting that the last increase, from $500 to $1,000 per girl, had occurred a decade before, in 1987. She proposed another doubling, and the Committee agreed, gradually increasing

1998 Queen Kathryn Larter (right) with Princesses Stacey Cross and Erin Thompson. (CSA)

contest closed with "a record-low number of contestants… the lowest number of contestants to compete in the last 23 years." Just twenty young women applied – half the number of the previous year – and, of those, seven dropped out after the introductory meeting, leaving just thirteen to compete. Committee chairman Jim Gathercole told the *Calgary Herald*, "We're disappointed and we'll have to take a look at what we're doing." Mulling that a review of the contest's profile in the community might be in order, Gathercole suggested, "Part of the problem could be critics who claim the competition is little more than a beauty contest… But it's not… Beauty is just one small segment of it." Shaunna Thompson, a 1987 princess now on the Queen Committee, suggested the royalty program needed to include the public more. "We are in the '90s so there probably is a problem with perceptions," she said. "But if people came out to watch the competition, they would then know just what it takes." Several Committee members blamed the low numbers on the time commitment involved for volunteers. As contest emcee Bill Kehler said, "It's a sign of the times… Many women no longer have the time to sacrifice their jobs or a year of university to become part of the trio."[693]

The Committee spent some time at its next meeting addressing the issue of low numbers with questions

the amount over the next three years until it reached $2,000 per girl in 2000.[692]

The 1998 Committee was shocked when that year's

1999 Queen Christie Fath (centre) with Princesses Kari Lammle and Tara Wesner. (CSA)

sage counsel. "Contest numbers have always been cyclic. There are always highs and lows."[695] In fact, by the next year, numbers had rebounded to thirty-five, considered normal for that period.

Even with fewer initial competitors, the 1998 contest experience was much the same as ever for those who eventually emerged victorious: 21-year-old Kathryn Larter from Olds as Queen, and Stacey Cross and Erin Thompson as Princesses. Queen Kathryn found her win especially sweet because it occurred exactly fifty years after her grandmother, Shirley Kemp, had won as a Stampede Lady-in-waiting in 1948.[696] Representing the Stampede was a much bigger job for Kathryn than it had been in her grandmother's day, but the trio was up to the challenge, and chaperone Elaine McKay was happy to report, after an intense summer of public appearances, that the queen and princesses' performances had been "excellent."[697]

Just before the 1999 Stampede, Queen Christie Fath, 22, and Princesses Tara Wesner and Kari Lammle, both 21, travelled to the western United States on a promotional trip that included a parade in Livingston, Montana, and rodeos in Red Lodge, Montana, and Cody, Wyoming. The royal trio rode in a televised parade with the Cody rodeo committee, and Queen Christie rode in the grand entry with

such as, "Do we need to take any new approaches? How can we increase numbers? Were the posters well distributed?"[694] But mostly, Committee members were philosophical, trusting Margaret Fraser's

Miss Rodeo America, Miss Rodeo Wyoming and the Cody Stampede Queen. Over four days, the Calgary group distributed hundreds of Stampede brochures and posters. Chaperone Margaret Fraser was thrilled with the outstanding reception given to the group. "Common reaction was the disbelief that the Calgary Stampede would actually attend these three 'small' shows."[698]

Like most trios of this period, the group travelled to celebrations in many small towns over the year, including events in Medicine Hat, Claresholm, Vulcan and Red Deer. That fall and winter, they attended the Grey Cup in Vancouver and the National Finals Rodeo and Miss Rodeo America Pageant in Las Vegas. Margaret Fraser accompanied the group to Las Vegas and was their main chaperone during Stampede week. By then in her twenty-fourth year of chaperoning trios, Margaret was rarely perturbed by anything, though it had become something of a tradition for the young women to try to rattle her famous composure. Nicknamed "the bun on the run" by her young charges, there was an annual competition to capture a picture of her with her hair out of its neat and customary bun (1995 Princess Lisa Eastman earned that particular prize),[699] and always lots of mild practical joking.[700] As Princess Tara later recalled,

the 1999 trio was no different… We borrowed some blackout paint from some "clown friends," and between the end of the parade and meeting up again with Margaret, the three of us blacked out various teeth and pretended to have travelled the entire parade that way. Absolutely unfazed, Margaret promptly announced that we were off to the Rodeo Office for our accreditation photos! So the joke was on us as we frantically scraped black paint off our teeth in time for the photo![701]

As the 1990s were coming to a close, the Queen Committee was still wrestling with one last nagging problem. It had resolved the issue of horsemanship before the decade began, and although it tinkered with rules occasionally, it was satisfied with the basic structure of the contest, which had been running smoothly for years. But there seemed to be no solution to the fact that some years were more stressful than others because some trios simply did not get along. The two main chaperones during this period, Dorothy Kennedy (1990–1998) and Elaine McKay (1995–2004) were good-natured, loved their charges and made light of any difficulties, but the Committee chairman through the latter half of the 1990s, Jim Gathercole, frequently helped to chaperone out-of-town trips, so he knew first-hand some of the challenges faced by trios and chaperones alike. At his instigation, the Committee finally decided in 1997 to address some of the issues and reinforce expectations:

> We need to stress that all bookings are important and they will be attended by all three ladies. A meeting should be held prior to Stampede to reiterate the system of "Protocol" that should be adhered to, and to review guidelines by which the Royal Trio are to approach their year as a queen or princess… Each member of the RT will be instructed to call the chaperone in case they become unavailable for a function. They should not leave it to the other ladies to call the chaperone. Chaperones are encouraged to report to the Chairman any ongoing problems with the RT.[702]

An important factor leading to difficult interpersonal relations for some trios was the ongoing differentiation in the treatment of the queen and the princesses. Certainly there had been great strides made during the 1980s, when honorariums had been equalized and the media and event-hosting organizations had been encouraged to pay equal attention to all members of the trio. But although they were more subtle, distinctions still existed, and the Queen Committee had come into the 1990s knowing that more still needed to be done. In 1990 Queen Kari Griffith had struggled with the fact that her saddle had been more decorated and worth "about twice as much" as those presented to the princesses. She had received a television, while they only got radios. She usually wore a different colour, had a more impressive crown, and her belt buckle had gold on it, so it was worth a lot more too. All three girls had been (tastefully) photographed for the *Calgary Sun*'s SUNSHINE Girl page, but only Kari's photograph actually ran. She had a very solid relationship with her princesses, who understood that these distinctions were not her fault, but it would have taken superhuman effort for princesses not to have felt occasional resentment.[703]

By the end of the decade, the royal crowns looked more equivalent but little else had changed. A big part of the problem was that the Queen Committee was still sending a mixed message to winners, sponsors and the media. While the Committee's meeting minutes recorded their good intentions with statements such as "We need to stress with each new trio that the Stampede will always treat the three girls as equals," their continuing support for differentiation was revealed by the very next sentence: "It should be emphasized that the Queen is in fact the Queen and will ride ahead of the Princesses in all parades and will generally be in the centre of photographs, escort the winners on stage for presentations, etc."[704] The fact that no one on the Committee found these statements contradictory was telling, but part of the problem was rooted in how the royal trio was chosen. The Stampede Queen contest was in fact a contest, and everyone who entered competed to win. The tricky part was figuring out how to help the young women who did not earn the top title overcome their very natural disappointment and move from being competitors to co-operators for the good of the team.

Judges tried hard each year to identify three young women who could work together well, but there were no guarantees, and results varied year by year depending upon the personalities and circumstances of those who were chosen. One year, a chaperone might report that "problems still revolve around [the trio's] lack of an interpersonal relationship"; the next year, that the trio was "a delight to work with"; and the year after, that "there were some personality conflicts as usual."[705] Of course, it did not help that no matter what was said, human nature dictated that the media and event organizers still wanted to focus on the queen as the perceived top position. It took a strong, generous queen to insist that the group be viewed as a team, with princesses given equal media time and recognition. But it was not always in the

queen's power to advocate for equality. The 1999 trio encountered exactly the same hurtful scenario as that faced by the 1990 group, when the *Calgary Sun* took photographs of all three winners for its SUNshine Girl feature page but only published the picture of the queen.[706]

Underlying tensions were always very wearing for the groups that experienced them, and they frustrated and exasperated Committee members and chaperones as well. Reflecting back on their reigning years, many former royals remembered the challenge of being thrown together with two other young women, often from very different backgrounds and with very different attitudes and personalities. Three is an awkward number at the best of times, but these young ladies had to spend a very intense year together, most of it in the public eye. Luckily, even the most divisive of trios usually took their job as Stampede figureheads seriously and managed to present a harmonious front during public appearances.[707] But for some, having to get through the year with an unhappy or dysfunctional group was the only blight on an otherwise remarkable experience and was remembered by a few former royals as far more challenging than anything else they ever faced during a year of incredible personal growth and development.[708]

CHAPTER 15 ★ 2000-2007

"An egalitarian royalty: all for one and one for all"

The Calgary Stampede entered the twenty-first century with a renewed sense of direction and optimism. After stalling at the 1.1 million mark throughout the 1990s, attendance in 2000 finally topped the 1988 Olympic year record of 1.2 million. Highpoints over the first decade or so included the celebration of the Alberta Centennial in 2005 and the Stampede's own Centennial in 2012, an extravaganza that attracted a record 1.4 million visitors. In 2004 the Board announced an updated 15-year development and expansion plan. This was followed in 2007 with the launch of a new master brand that omitted the word Exhibition from general usage while promising a renewed focus on traditional rural concepts such as community, western values and pride of place in an attempt to link with the past while resonating with larger and more diverse audiences in the future.[709]

These changes affected the royalty program insofar as they coloured the message conveyed by the royal

2001 Queen Maria Heintz (front) with Princesses Alison Collins and Lisa McNiven. (CSA)

trio on behalf of the Stampede, but other developments later in the decade had a more significant impact. After more than forty years, the queen contest was forced to change its timing and several key elements of its format because of changes to its host event, Rodeo Royal. Around the same time, a push from the Board brought the Indian princess and the royal trio closer together. As the queen contest entered its sixth decade, a new emphasis on youth development led to significant changes in the competition and the entire program.

But these changes were to challenge the Queen Committee much later in the decade. In 2000 its main concern was to address two problems left over from the 1990s: how to attract more competitors to the queen contest, and how to ensure that all three winners felt equally valued as part of the team.

In 1994 chairman Pat Pearson had floated the idea of changing the Committee's name "to something that represents both the Queen and Princesses."[710] Although the idea of a name change had gone nowhere at the time, it seemed to get Committee members thinking about the psychological import-ance of names and naming. Prior to that time, the Committee had always referred to the queen and princesses collectively as "the queens," but after the mid-1990s, its collective descriptor of choice became a more inclusive term that had been in occasional use by the Committee since 1963: the royal trio.

At a meeting on November 16, 2000, the issue of renaming the Queen Committee was raised again. Jim Gathercole, who had succeeded Pat Pearson as chair, told members that the implied emphasis on the queen in the name of the Committee "neglects the standing of the Princesses, when we tell them they are of equal status." He suggested changing the name to the Royal Trio Committee.[711] The matter was tabled at the next meeting, but, with Margaret Fraser and several others opposed, the matter was quietly dropped. Margaret strongly believed in the importance of Stampede royalty maintaining its tie with Western heritage and history. Retaining the Committee's original name was, for her, a matter of history and tradition, just as the titles Queen and Princess kept alive the rodeo queen tradition in a way that a more modern-sounding term like Royal Ambassador never could.[712]

The November 16 meeting was important for another reason. There had been a long-standing rule disallowing unsuccessful finalists from ever entering the contest again. The measure had been introduced in 1972 to prevent candidates who had previously made it into the final five from having an unfair advantage over those going through the contest for the first time, particularly in the final riding events at Rodeo Royal. During the 1970s and '80s, when there were always lots of candidates each year for the queen contest (a high of 73 in 1984), preventing finalists from running again had not caused any problems. By the mid-1990s, however, it was apparent that applicant numbers were in decline. In 1996 Committee members questioned the wisdom of a policy that annually saw three good candidates lost to the contest forever, but Margaret Fraser argued against dropping the rule. She had heard stories of young women who had reached the finals, sometimes several times, but never emerged as winners, and she felt this had been very hard on them emotionally, knowing at least one who had succumbed to depression after trying and failing three times. Margaret was very strong-willed and persuasive, so the matter was dropped.[713]

Four years later, with the number of contestants descending to historic lows, the Committee real-ized it could no longer afford to lose these strong contenders year after year. At the November 16, 2000, meeting, chairman Jim Gathercole initiated a long-overdue discussion on the topic. Margaret, soon realizing that change was inevitable, suggested that former finalists be required to wait at least a year before re-entering the contest. Committee members were divided but most rejected the idea that judges might have lingering impressions in favour of a former finalist. Pointing out that "their job is to judge the contestant in relation to a new year's group," most members expressed faith in the fundamental idea that "each year has to be judged according to the contestants who enter, not who was there the year before." The motion brought forward by Gathercole and Pat Pearson, "that we allow unsuccessful finalists to run again," was passed by a narrow margin and plans were made to open up the 2001 contest by "contact[ing] past finalists who may still be eligible."[714]

Meanwhile, the 2000 edition had attracted a fairly typical thirty-three entries in a contest that saw 19-year-old Jolene Brewster of Sundre crowned as Queen, with 21-year-old Corie David from Langdon and 22-year-old Calgarian Shannon Reid as Princesses. Jolene, from a well-known historical family in the Banff area, was rather shy and introverted but she pushed herself through the public speaking events because she wanted so badly to win for herself and her cheering family. (When she made the semifinals, her excited parents flew her sister

2000 Queen Jolene Brewster (left) with Princesses Corie David and Shannon Reid. (CSA)

home from Australia and her grandparents back from Arizona to watch her compete.) When she fumbled after losing her place in her notes for her prepared speech, she thought her contest was over. She reflected later, though, that perhaps the judges had liked the way she picked herself up and carried on rather than losing her head and giving up, since that was a true reflection of the kind of incident sure to dog a royal during a year of impromptu speeches and unforeseen glitches. Her calm aplomb held her in good stead again later in her reign, in a mishap during the Grey Cup parade in Calgary. When her horse shied violently upon encountering something startling along the route, Jolene fell off and "landed on her head." The horse bolted, but Jolene picked herself up and hopped onto the next float, smiling and waving through the pain like a true professional.[715]

The winners in the 2001 contest, all from rural backgrounds, were Maria Heintz as Queen, with 22-year-old Lisa McNiven from Vulcan and 23-year-old Alison Collins from Okotoks as Princesses. A magazine piece on the trio indicated that the media were finally getting the message. "Heintz, who scored slightly higher in the contest, is the queen, but the traditional hierarchy has little practical meaning. This is an egalitarian royalty: all for one and one for all."[716] In addition to local trips and attending the Grey Cup

in Montreal, this lucky trio was part of a business and cultural promotional trip to Hong Kong.

Just after they were crowned, the lady who had sewn the trio's custom outfits for many years was hurt in an accident. Margaret Fraser ended up ordering outfits from Manuel to supplement items she could sew herself. Queen Maria later recalled Margaret pinning the ladies into their unfinished shirts just before they dashed off to join the Stampede parade. Maria loved the gold and black parade shirt handmade by Margaret, but it was the gorgeous wardrobe of ready-made clothing – classic Manuel jackets and complementary jeans – that proved to be the envy of previous winners.[717]

One of the competitors in the 2002 contest was 2001 Princess Alison's younger sister, 20-year-old Karen Collins, and it was she who became the next Queen. Her Princesses were 19-year-old Calgarian June-Marie Innes and 23-year-old Natalie Havens from Balzac. Natalie had also competed in the 2000 contest, and thus was the first successful competitor to be crowned after the rules were changed to allow finalists to run again. June-Marie was the youngest of the group, but it was the fact that she was the only city girl that made her feel like a bit of an outsider at first until the group had a chance to bond. Forewarned by Committee members and chaperones that successful

2002 Queen Karen Collins (centre) with Princesses June-Marie Innes and Natalie Havens. (CSA)

advice to be true that in any given situation there was always one member who could show leadership and keep the team together, and it was not always the same individual in every case. Team-building eventually led to lifelong friendships.[718]

The 2002 trio made only two big trips, to the Grey Cup in Edmonton and the National Finals Rodeo in Las Vegas, but they were featured in a local film by Lorna Thomas Productions called *Pretty Ladies, Fast Horses: Cowgirls of the Twenty-first Century*. The documentary, which traced a year in the life of a few "exceptional Canadian cowgirls," followed Karen, Natalie and June-Marie through the six-week royalty contest to their March crowning at Rodeo Royal, and then checked back with them as their reign was ending.[719]

Queen Karen said she felt she came into her year with an advantage, having watched her older sister reign the year before: "[I] knew what I was getting myself into and what it was all about."[720] Just as well, because members of the royal trio were required to handle many different, often challenging situations while staying "perpetually perky... impeccably groomed, patient, sensitive and well-mannered."[721] During the training period, they were given some pointers on how to handle themselves in difficult situations and how to answer sensitive questions.

team-building would depend largely on attitude and the willingness to make things work, they found the

Mostly, it was a matter of using common sense, keeping emotions under control, and thinking through responses before voicing them. However, the on-the-job training could be tough, especially at the beginning of a reign before new royals had become adept at dealing with unwelcome comments. Princess June-Marie, doing her first live telephone interview at her first Stampede breakfast, was shocked by the radio announcer's so-called jocular opening gambit, "How do you hide your purging at a Stampede breakfast?" She knew he was just trying to be "funny" and get a rise, riffing on that old chestnut of the beauty contest theme, but she was nevertheless quite taken aback and very offended by his question. Buying herself a little recovery time, she responded, "Excuse me?" and when he repeated the question, she laughed it off, and just as she had been taught to do, successfully redirected the interview to become the usual promotional piece for the Stampede.[722]

After following the 2002 trio around for a day during the Stampede, *Calgary Herald* reporter Deborah Tetley provided her readers with a snapshot of the experience, at the same time laying bare some of the constraints and frustrations of the job:

> A lot's expected of the queen and princesses… There are rules of conduct that accompany the year-long gig – some written, others simply understood – and curly locks and full makeup are two of them.
>
> The rest of the protocol is less materialistic in theory, but much more image-oriented. For example, Calgary Stampede queens and princesses can't be married or have children during their March to March reign. They can live with a boyfriend but it can't be a hush-hush arrangement. They can't drink alcohol or smoke while on duty…
>
> The ladies can never say no to a photo request, are forbidden from expressing religious or political opinions and are cautioned to avoid confrontational situations with the hundreds of people they glad-hand daily. "That's why we come across as ditzy sometimes," says… princess Natalie Havens. "Sometimes we just have to smile and nod even when someone is rude or snubs us." …
>
> There's no question the women love their tenure. However, they all agree some days try their patience, namely when urban cowboys practise their "stud" routine… "We just say, 'It was so nice to meet you. Have a nice time at the Stampede,'" says queen Karen Collins. "We walk away because we don't want to get into a situation with them."
>
> Havens says the only thing worse than a drunk man or an obnoxious "groupie" is the jealous, overprotective woman on his arm. "I always approach

the women first and try to shake their hands," she says. "I never make eye contact with her man unless she doesn't snub us. And the women snub us a lot... Our feelings get hurt a lot."[723]

In addition to keeping the trio on schedule, and assisting with wardrobe or makeup malfunctions, part of the chaperone's job was to steer the young women through these tricky situations and to prevent them from getting into any trouble. By 2002 Margaret Fraser was on her twenty-seventh set of royal ambassadors, and nothing could faze her. "Been there, done that," she told a reporter who described her as "a kind of Mother Superior to the young ladies."[724] With more than 350 events to attend over the course of the year, most trios had two or three chaperones spelling each other off. Affectionately known to some of her young charges as "Queen Mum," longtime chaperone Elaine McKay's duties were typical. Mother of 1993 Princess Melissa McKay, she enjoyed playing the role of surrogate mother to young royals: "Keeping the women out of the sun, making sure they are eating and keeping hydrated, and offering emotional support."[725]

The winners of the 2003 contest were three small-town girls, 21-year-old Trina Percival as Queen, with 22-year-old Kelly Ashbacher and 23-year-old

2003 Queen Trina Percival (centre) with Princesses Kelly Ashbacher and Shannan Martindale. (CSA)

Shannan Martindale as Princesses. By their own admission this threesome amused themselves over their year by playing pranks whenever they met barrel man Dennis Halstead at local rodeos and during Rodeo Royal. "It made our year so memorable to outprank the ultimate prankster."[726] Generally, chaperones were indulgent with trios' displays of high spirits as long as things did not get out of hand and imperil either the young ladies' personal safety or the Stampede's public image as a family event. Although the role remained much the same, it was shortly after this period that chaperones were renamed "advisors." Deciding that the word "chaperone" had an old-fashioned connotation, the Committee reasoned that their function was not so much to supervise their bright and capable young charges, but to offer advice and support when required, especially when a firm hand was needed to deal with pushy event organizers or rowdy admirers.[727]

Although the next year started much the same as any other, 2004 ended up being a controversial time for the royalty program. At the end of Rodeo Royal, 19-year-old Amy Smith was crowned Queen with 21-year-old Breanna Ernst and 22-year-old Brianna Hamblin* as Princesses. Breanna had graduated from Olds College and was working, but the other two were still in school, Amy in her second year at

*No relation to the author.

2004 Queen Amy Smith (centre) with Princesses Breanna Ernst and Brianna Hamblin. (QAC)

Mount Royal College and Brianna (Brie) just finishing a science degree at the University of Lethbridge.[728] The trio's year went like clockwork until Brie learned she had been accepted into the Western College of Veterinary Medicine at the University of Saskatchewan. Spaces at veterinary colleges were scarce at the time – it was her second time applying – so she was thrilled to be accepted, "one step closer to fulfilling her lifelong goal of becoming a veterinarian."[729] Unwilling to pass up this opportunity, Brie decided to resign from her position as Princess after the Stampede was over so she could devote all her time that fall and winter to attending school.

Understandably the Queen Committee was upset and annoyed by Brie's decision. As far as the Committee was concerned, by signing her letter of understanding, she had entered into a contract and committed herself to a year of voluntary service on behalf of the Stampede. The feeling was that she should not have entered the contest or accepted the crown knowing she had applied for schooling that would start midway through her term, or, conversely, that she should have deferred her schooling so that she could follow through on her commitment to the Stampede.[730] As it was, Amy and Breanna had to complete the year as a duo, travelling to the Grey Cup in Ottawa, the Western Fairs Association Convention in Reno and the National Finals Rodeo in Las Vegas. Many former queens and princesses sympathized with the Committee's position but were uncomfortable with the action taken: Brie was stripped of her "title, saddle, buckle and crown."[731]

Although she had completed nearly half of her term, including the most demanding and important few months surrounding the Stampede, her name was deleted from the official listing of Stampede royalty. This was the first and only time such drastic

action had been taken, although there had been a few occasions in the past when royals had come close to being asked to relinquish their title or had resigned before ending their reign for various personal reasons (usually to marry). The Committee's action led to a long, at times heated, discussion at a Queens' Alumni Committee meeting, but ultimately the group decided to "follow the example set by the Queen Committee and honour only the two remaining royalty" in terms of recognition and Association membership.[732] However, the decision remained controversial* and, even a decade later, continued to provoke strong opinions pro and con whenever discussed by Alumni.[733]

Normally, retiring queens and princesses became automatic members of the Queens' Alumni, a ready-made group of like-minded friends, bonded by shared experiences and training:

Who else knows the boot-busting fatigue of Stampede, appearing at hundreds of events for as

*Interestingly, when the Alumni celebrated the Stampede's Centennial in 2012 by producing a scrapbook-style *Memory Book*, Amy and Breanna specifically requested that their year be represented by a picture of all three crowned royals, including Brie. In the caption, they explained without rancour how 2004 had come to be known as the year with a duo instead of a trio.

little as 15 minutes each before being bundled off to the next function by the always-hovering chaperone? Who else knows the patience, charm, and diplomacy necessary to be able to handle public speeches, skittish horses, and occasionally, skittish people?[734]

Coming off an intense year of Stampede promotion, many former royals also joined the Alumni Committee, to stay involved in Stampede affairs by giving back to the organization, to maintain connections recently forged with others in the Stampede family and to find a new outlet for their training and talents by working with and for children with disabilities.

The influx of new blood each year had resulted in a steady growth of Committee membership: by the mid-2000s, more than half the Association membership was also active on the Committee.[735] But there was a wide range of commitment and activity levels. In 2001 the Committee had rebranded its activities for special-needs children as Giddy-Up events. Having added new events every few years throughout the 1980s and 1990s, by the 2000s, Committee members were hosting four big events each year that required a lot of volunteer time: the Giddy-Up Gala, Giddy-Up Rodeo, Giddy-Up Grits and Giddy-Up Christmas (with Giddy-Up Aggie Days to follow later in the decade). Uneven levels of participation had led to an increasingly unbalanced workload, and by mid-decade some active Committee members were starting to feel burned out.[736]

In 2004 the group decided to deal with this problem by introducing a points system "to keep track of volunteer participation and identify clear expectations." Volunteers received points for attending meetings, serving on subcommittees and assisting at special events, and the Stampede required volunteers to accumulate a certain number of such points each year in order to maintain their volunteer status.[737] With this system in place, the Queens' Alumni Committee continued its support of special-needs children, although the focus reverted to organizing special events rather than fundraising when the Giddy-Up Gala was discontinued in 2008 after raising a stellar $1.2-million-plus for local special-needs organizations and programs during its ten-year history.[738]

In addition to these volunteer activities, in 2006 the Alumni marked the sixtieth anniversary of Patsy Rodgers's appointment as the Stampede's first queen. As part of the Homecoming event, seventy former

Calgary Stampede Queens' Alumni Association 60th Anniversary celebration, 2006. (CSA)

CS Queens' Alumni — CALGARY STAMPEDE QUEENS' ALUMNI — 60th Anniversary

July 3, 2006

royals participated in the Stampede parade that year, sporting matching saddle pads and serapes decorated with braided sparkles. In 2008 the group celebrated the election of one of its own to the Stampede board of directors: 1976 Princess Wynne Anderson. That same year, eighty-six former queens, princesses and ladies-in-waiting, plus seven former Indian princesses, rode in the parade behind 2008 Stampede parade marshal Patsy Rodgers. In 2011 the Alumni honoured deceased members by unveiling a commemorative bronze called "Forever Remembered," created by Didsbury sculptor Sandy Farr with finishing details by her daughter, silversmith Shawna Whiteside.* When the Stampede celebrated its Centennial in 2012, the Queens' Alumni were recognized officially as one of ten iconic groups deemed to be "instrumental and significant to Stampede history." Of the ninety-seven former royals who participated in that year's Homecoming event, fifty-six dressed in vintage cowgirl outfits and rode horses or carriages in the Stampede parade. As a special project to mark the occasion, the Alumni privately produced

a history titled *The Queens' Alumni Memory Book: Celebrating the Stampede's Centennial in 2012*, edited by former Stampede princesses Tara Wesner (1999) and Whitney Wilkie (2011).[739]

By the 2000s the Queens' Alumni had named quite a number of Honorary Associates, with more being added nearly every year. In addition to those mentioned previously, long-time contest emcee Bill Kehler was recognized in 2003, and long-serving Queen Committee supporters Jim Gathercole and Bob Cairns received the nod in 2003 and 2012 respectively. Ron Gillis had been recognized in the 1990s for his help during trips to the Grey Cup and the Quebec Winter Carnival; more recent chaperones Dorothy Kennedy and Elaine McKay were honoured in 2004 and 2009 respectively. In addition, a number of individuals who had helped the Alumni ride as a colour party in the annual parade were recognized over the years: Lee Thompson in 1983, Dennis Hoffman in 1996, Tom Magnusson in 2006 and John Scott in 2011.[740]

While the Alumni occupied itself with these activities over the decade, its numbers were augmented by the royalty contest continuing to generate new trios year after year. The 2005 contest attracted twenty-four entrants, six of whom dropped out after the initial briefing session revealed that the winning trio would

*At the time of its unveiling there were 11 names of deceased alumni inscribed on little plaques circling the wooden base of the bronze. Along with retired crowns and other royal memorabilia, it is customarily displayed during the Stampede in the Queens' Alumni section of Western Showcase.

be expected to be available to make some 400 public appearances: 150 during Stampede week and another 250 over the rest of the year.[741] Proving the effectiveness of the Committee's strategy of letting finalists run again, 20-year-old Lauren MacLennan emerged as Queen after having competed twice before. After she won, she told a reporter: "This year, I felt I was ready. I know a few of the past queens and I did a lot of research. I am prepared for this."[742]

Twenty-year-old Coleen Crowe and 19-year-old Justine Milner were named as Princesses. It was an especially exciting win for Coleen because her mother, Leslie MacDonald, had been Stampede Queen in 1971.

Leslie had become a founding member of the Queens' Alumni Association just as her reign was ending, and after she retired as Queen, she stayed involved in the program. She served as a royalty chaperone from 1973 to 1983 and worked for the Queen Committee as a horsemanship judge for over thirty years. This long involvement earned her the honour of becoming a Stampede Life Member in 2000.[743] Over the years, Leslie recruited and/or gave invaluable advice and support to many contest competitors, but her daughter Coleen's win was understandably special, and she told a local reporter proudly, "She's done an outstanding job. She's very prepared."[744]

2005 Queen Lauren MacLennan (centre) with Princesses Justine Milner and Coleen Crowe. (QAC)

In 2005, Alberta's Centennial year, there were special events in Calgary all year long, many of which involved the Stampede or Stampede representation. The royal trio was extra busy, attending more functions than usual (the projected 400 appearances that had scared off one-quarter of the contest applicants). One of the highlights was the trio's being presented to Queen Elizabeth at a state dinner held on May 24, an honour which required Queen Lauren and Princesses Justine and Coleen to attend a three-day crash course in royal etiquette.[745]

Perhaps it was because of the great number of high-profile public events during the Alberta Centennial year, but 2005 saw an interesting development for Stampede royalty. Ever since it had begun sponsoring an Indian Village princess in 1988, the Indian Events Committee had acceded to Queen Committee wishes and restricted its princess's activities mainly to the Indian Village and to Indian-related activities downtown during the Stampede. The Indian princess usually made more than 120 public appearances during the busy Stampede week, but sometimes she also attended Aboriginal events out of town during the pre- and post-Stampede season. Before 2005 her schedule rarely overlapped with that of the royal trio, except when they met for daily appearances at the rodeo and grandstand show.[746]

But during the Alberta Centennial year, the four royal representatives frequently found themselves at the same events, and introduced in almost the same breath, as the Stampede royalty. By midsummer, Lauren could tell the *Cochrane Eagle* that she and the princesses, and Indian Village Princess Lana Waterchief of the Siksika Nation, had "spent quite a bit of time" together, with the result that they had "all become close friends."[747] It would be another few years before official policy caught up, but 2005 marked an important first step in changing the

relationship between the Stampede's royal trio and its Indian princess.

Sadly, tragedy struck the Queen Committee in 2005 with the death of Margaret Fraser. Only 58, she had been in declining health for more than a year as she battled cancer, but she had been loath to give up her committee responsibilities. In addition to losing a devoted and passionate colleague, Committee members suddenly found themselves bereft of the knowledge, guidance and leadership of a woman many, including long-time member Pat Pearson, considered to be "the backbone of the Committee."[748] In addition to being an active volunteer with the Queen Committee for thirty years, and chairing it from 1986 to 1993, she had literally done everything relating to the royal trio at one time or another: "buckle design, bookings, chaperoning, sponsorship management, travel arrangements, outfit design and fabrication..." The Queens' Alumni Association had expressed their appreciation by making her an Honorary Associate in 1993. The Stampede made her a Life Member in 2005, just a week before she passed away, and she was awarded an Alberta Centennial Service Medal posthumously the same year.[749]

2006 Queen Cheryl Dafoe (centre) with Princesses April Kanderka and Teri Murray. (CSA)

Although the loss of Margaret was deeply felt and truly mourned, the queen program was well established and did not falter as Committee members rallied to take on new challenges and forge new directions. In 2006 Rodeo Royal was moved from late March to late April, so the 2005 trio had a slightly longer reign than most – thirteen months. The new winning team, chosen from among twenty-four competitors, was 23-year-old Queen Cheryl Dafoe with Princesses April Kanderka, also 23, and Teri Murray, 19. Like other trios during this period, the 2006 group attended the Grey Cup in Winnipeg, the Canadian Finals Rodeo and the National Finals Rodeo in Las Vegas. Even though it was considered to be an ordinary year, with no special celebrations, their busy schedule of promoting the Stampede involved, once again, close to 400 public appearances.

The young ladies chosen in 2007 from a field of twenty-eight were 20-year-old Amanda Kochan as Queen, with 24-year-old Caia Morstad and 21-year-old Amanda Byrne as Princesses. Cochrane-area resident Amanda Kochan had gained some insight into royal duties while appearing at the 2006 Stampede as a Ranch Girl, helping to open the daily rodeo by riding into the arena in formation while carrying a flag. In addition to the usual annual events, the 2007 trio went on a promotional trip to Florida and attended the 400th anniversary of the Quebec Winter Carnival.[750]

Unbeknownst to them, these would be the last trio to be chosen and to serve as royalty according to the pattern set down more than forty years before, when the Stampede first had become involved in the annual contest to choose its Queen.

2007 Queen Amanda Kochan (centre) with Princesses
Caia Morstad and Amanda Byrne. (QAC)

CHAPTER 16 ★ 2008–2014

"A walking, talking poster for the Stampede"

After the 2007 contest, the Queen Committee decided to take a bold step and make some changes, although, for the first time in more than forty years, the changes did not simply involve revisions to the rules. As had been the case for many years, an eligible applicant still had to be a female between the ages of 19 and 24. She had to be "a passport-carrying Canadian citizen who has lived in Alberta at least a year, and must never have been married nor had a child. She also must not have a criminal record and be a least a high school graduate."[751] In addition, the entry form stipulated that she "must agree to reside within a 100-kilometre radius of Stampede Park. Place of employment or educational institution must also meet this requirement… Must possess a current, valid Alberta driver's licence and have full access to a vehicle." The form inquired about hobbies, interests, education and place of employment, and then asked prospective applicants to outline in 500 words or less "the reason why you would like to be a member of the Royal Trio."[752]

Still satisfied with these basic rules, what the Committee was wrestling with in the winter of 2007–2008 was changing the timing of the contest. Ever since 1964, when the Stampede had first insisted on judging candidates on horsemanship and other desirable qualities, the queen contest had culminated with finalists competing at a spring riding event on the Stampede grounds. Initially that event had been the Calgary Spring Horse Show, later called the Calgary International Horse Show. The switch to Rodeo Royal in 1972 had meant moving the contest date forward from May to March, but that had been welcomed because it allowed more preparation time for winners before they headed into the busy pre-Stampede season. In 2006, however, when Rodeo Royal was pushed back a month, to late April, the Committee and the incoming trio had felt the impact on training.

2008 Royalty Transition Team: Lauren MacLennan, Caia Morstad, Justine Milner, Amanda Byrne, Coleen Crowe, Trina Percival. (CSA)

In November 2007 the Stampede announced that Rodeo Royal would become a fall event in 2008, and would be given a new name, the Canadian Rodeo Tour Championship. In February 2008 the Queen Committee confirmed that it would continue to harmonize its activities with Rodeo Royal by also making the switch to become a fall event.[753] Starting in the fall of 2008 the contest to choose the next year's trio would run through September, culminating with the crowning on the final night of the Canadian Rodeo Tour Championship in early October. Interestingly, the Stampede's press release announcing the change referred to the Committee as the Royal Trio Committee, a name that had been proposed by chairman Jim Gathercole in 2001 but never adopted. Whether this was deliberate or in error, the Queen Committee must have realized that this period of change was an ideal time to make a long-contemplated – some would say long overdue – change of name. By the time the Stampede started the following July, it had adopted a more inclusive sounding name: Royalty Committee.

Having made the decision to change the timing of the contest, the only problem for the Committee was accomplishing the actual switchover from a spring to a fall event. It was important to have a queen and princesses for the 2008 Stampede, but the Committee was reluctant to run two contests in a single year, in March–April for the 2008 trio and then again in September–October to choose winners for 2009. In any case, it seemed unfair to ask a trio to reign for only six months instead of the usual year. Coming up with a creative solution, the Committee invited former winners to apply for the job of covering the six-month gap between reigns in 2008. Some young ladies had moved away or were not interested in serving again or, having since married, no longer qualified for the job. But six were recruited: 2007 Princesses Caia Morstad and Amanda Byrne agreed to stay on and were joined by former Queen Trina Percival (2003), and the entire team from 2005: Queen Lauren MacLennan and Princesses Justine Milner and Coleen Crowe. Known as the Stampede 2008 Royalty Transition Team, this experienced group shared all the usual duties of representing the Stampede from April through to October of 2008.[754]

While this period of transition was occurring, Stampede president George Brookman followed up on his announcement that the Stampede's theme for 2008 would be to honour its own history and traditions, by naming the first Stampede Queen, Patsy Rodgers, as the 2008 parade marshal. A contingent of eighty-six former Stampede queens, princesses and ladies-in-waiting, along with seven former Indian princesses, all of whom were designated honorary parade marshals, accompanied the 82-year-old Patsy as she rode along the parade route waving to the crowd from an open, white carriage.[755] Asked to say a few words each night before the grandstand show, Patsy was a little nervous until she discovered that her short speech would be prerecorded. To her relief, all she had to do each evening was turn up in advance to have stage makeup applied, including sparkly false eyelashes, then mouth along convincingly as her speech played over the loudspeaker. She thoroughly enjoyed all the special activities held during her week in the limelight, particularly the President's Reception, when nearly a hundred former and reigning royals gathered for a commemorative photograph. After standing back and watching the group assemble, she inquired where they wanted her to sit, and was placed centre-front, perched on the knee of Calgary Member of Parliament and Prime Minister of Canada Stephen Harper.[756]

The February 2008 press release that announced the shift in timing for both the royalty and the Indian princess competitions revealed another change as well: that both programs were now considered to be part of the Calgary Stampede Foundation's youth development initiatives. Established in 1994, the Foundation is mandated "to preserve and promote our Western traditions, culture and heritage through charitable giving as well as promoting and advancing character-building youth programs."[757] In the 2008 announcement, Royal Trio Committee chair Deb Ward noted that "the Royal Trio and Indian Princess are an integral part of the Calgary Stampede's youth programs. Both the competition and the year-long reigns help to build knowledgeable young women who will continue to be an asset to our community." Ivy Kim Scott-Friesen, 1995 Indian Village Princess and chair of the Indian princess competition, added, "The Indian Princess has been a great ambassador for Indian Village and a role model in her community for over 15 years. Each princess is able to teach others about her traditions, giving visitors a greater understanding of native culture."[758]

Clearly, both committees had experienced a subtle shift in thinking. No longer simply viewing the purpose of their programs as being the identification and training of suitable public-relations representatives for the Stampede, henceforth their contests and programs would be promoted to young women as educational opportunities and vehicles for personal growth and development. This fundamental change in orientation was reinforced in the final statement of the 2008 news release:

The Calgary Stampede invests almost $2-million annually into youth programs, including the Calgary Stampede Showband, Youth Speech and Debate, Stampede Talent Search, Stampede Royalty and the Indian Princess. Each of the youth programs at Stampede Park encourages hard work and dedication to help transform today's youth into the leaders of tomorrow.[759]

Shifting to a fall contest meant that future royal trios and Indian princesses would end their year with the Stampede and its aftermath, rather than having it fall midway through their reign. Also, it would give new royals a much longer training period during the relatively quiet post-Stampede fall months. In addition to bringing the royalty and Indian princess programs more into line with Stampede youth development guidelines by boosting their educational components, the timing of the training would ensure that new royals were up to speed and ready to go when things started building again toward the next Stampede in the new year. Additionally, the royal year would follow the school year, hopefully making the commitment more attractive to young women pursuing post-secondary degrees because they could take an entire year off if they wished rather than disrupt their education two years in a row.[760]

The Indian princess had been joining the royal trio in some aspects of their training for more than a decade, but her full inclusion in the new training program reflected another significant change made during this period of transition. In 2008 the Stampede Board finally made the long overdue decision to upgrade the role and status of the Indian Village princess to more closely resemble that of the royal trio. Except for 2000, when the Indian Events Committee had experimented with having five young women, one from each of the Treaty 7 Nations, share the role of representing the Indian Village during Stampede week, the Indian princess contest had run smoothly during the 2000s, with one princess chosen each year from 2001 through 2007: Tiffany Andy of the Piikani Nation (2001); Chrissy Snow of the Stoney/Nakoda Nation (2002); Natasha Calfrobe Ayoungman of the Siksika Nation (2003); Marcie Meguinis of the Tsuu T'ina Nation (2004); Lana Waterchief of the Siksika Nation (2005); Nicole Weasel Head of the Piikani Nation (2006); and Livia Many Wounds of the Tsuu T'ina Nation (2007).

Although most of these winners had been identified by the words Calgary Stampede Indian Princess beaded onto their crowns (the word "Village" having disappeared from the crowns after 2002), technically, these young women had represented only the

Indian Village, not the wider Stampede. That limited interpretation of the role changed dramatically when the Stampede Board, led by 2007–2008 president George Brookman, decided it was time to capitalize on the great public-relations potential of the position by making the Indian princess a fully acknowledged Stampede representative equivalent in every way to the royal trio. Initially, Brookman suggested that the two contests and programs merge into one committee handling all Stampede royalty, but their differing mandates and traditions made this impractical. Instead, the newly named Royalty Committee and the Indian Princess Competition subcommittee of the Indian Events Committee agreed to work more closely together in areas where co-operation and harmonized procedures made sense: training, publicity, bookings, and sponsors.[761]

Within a very short time, the Indian princess and the royal trio were appearing at functions together 60 to 70 per cent of the time, although they still maintained separate and well-defined identities on behalf of the Stampede. Whereas the queen and princesses represented the Stampede's commitment to promoting Western heritage and values, the Indian princess represented the Stampede's long relationship with the Treaty 7 Nations.[762] Just as she had always done, the Indian princess still served as a liaison between local native people and the Stampede, but now the job became year round and broadened beyond the confines of the Indian Village and Stampede week, and she became an envoy from the native community to the general public via the Stampede. To reflect this wider vision and responsibility, in 2009 the position was officially renamed the Stampede Indian Princess.[763]

Ever since 1990, when there had been complaints about differential treatment, the Stampede and various sponsors had been giving support and official gifts to the Indian princess – clothing, jewellery, and the like – but now, sponsorship, prizes and honorariums were equalized with the royal trio. More importantly, after 2008 the four royal winners were pictured together on the annual promotional postcards produced by the Stampede, and all four were included in news releases, media reports and interview opportunities. Although the titles Queen, Princess, Royal Trio and Indian Princess still were very much in use, often the foursome were described in news releases and by the media in more inclusive terms, such as the Stampede Royalty or the Royal Team.

Aside from these changes, the competition to choose the Indian princess stayed much the same and was still restricted to young women from the five Treaty 7 Nations in partnership with the Stampede at the Indian Village (the Tsuu T'ina, Piikani, Stoney/ Nakoda, Kainai and Siksika). As always, the contest had a different focus from the one that chose royal trios. In addition to demonstrating horsemanship and public speaking ability, contestants were judged on knowledge of their culture and a native language, plus demonstration of a traditional skill such as dancing. Judges represented each of the five tribes of Treaty 7, the Stampede, contest sponsors and the wider community.

The contest itself, which previously had occurred in June with the official crowning at the Indian Village during Stampede week, was moved in 2008 to the third week of September to harmonize with the new timing of the contest for Stampede Queen and Princesses so that all four royals could reign together over the same period.[764] Just as had happened with the royal trio, no new Indian princess was chosen in 2008 as the contest transitioned from a spring event to a fall one. Instead, four former Indian princesses shared the role of representing the Stampede and the Indian Village during that transition year: Ivy Kim Scott-Friesen (1995), Nicole Yellow Old Woman (1996), Gaylene Weasel Child (1997) and Livia Joy Many Wounds (2007).[765]

The first winner after these changes had been made was Nikkole Heavy Shields, 19, of the Kainai Nation, who was crowned 2009 Stampede Indian Princess on September 21, 2008. A fancy dancer, Nikkole was pictured "twirling in a vibrant rainbow of colour" in *Together We Dance*, a painting by Vilem Zach that was reproduced for the 2011 Stampede poster.[766] Before the transition period, recent Indian Village princesses had made roughly 150 appearances per year, mainly during June and July. The Stampede Indian Princess's expanded role after 2008 meant that the number of annual public appearances increased rapidly. As the first incumbent after the change, Nikkole made about 250 appearances in 2009. Demonstrating that she fully understood her role, she told a reporter, "It's about sharing the rich culture with other people… They're interested in the dancing. They're interested in how, since 1912, that bond between the Indian village and the Stampede is still preserved."[767]

Meanwhile, with the Royalty Transition Team handling the 2008 Stampede, the Royalty Committee organized the 2009 contest. Except for the August 22 closing date, and five, instead of the previous six, intense weeks of competition, the 2009 contest closely followed the established format. On October 5, 2008, the final night of the Canadian Rodeo Tour Championship, the winners for 2009 were announced: 23-year-old Kerri Williamson

2009 Queen Kerri Williamson (left) with Princesses Kateri Cowley and Tara Sergerie. (CSA: MARC BINKLEY PHOTOGRAPHY)

from Millarville as Queen, with 22-year-old Kateri Cowley from Exshaw and 23-year-old Tara Sergerie from Okotoks named as Princesses. Fast-tracking the bonding process, the winners already knew each other very well: Kerri and Tara had grown up competing against each other in 4-H contests, and were studying nursing together at Mount Royal College, while Tara and Kateri had worked together as horse wranglers and stunt doubles on the set of the made-in-Alberta television series *Heartland*.[768] It was Kateri's second run at the crown, as she had been a finalist previously, and Tara had won Miss Rodeo

Canada in 2007. Tara had been inspired to enter the contest after growing up hearing stories about being a Stampede royal from her mother, 1976 Queen Cindy Morres.[769]

The 2009 winners began their training just three days after the royalty contest ended, and they spent the next six weeks being "polish[ed] up a lot," in the words of Princess Kateri, a real-life working cowgirl who told a reporter after the crowning ceremony, "Right now, I'm [just] a rough, tough cowgirl."[770] In addition to polishing up their public image, training sessions traditionally focused on helping winners improve their public speaking, media and communication skills (including, in this modern age, sessions on social media). But now the training period also included several weeks of instruction about the history of the Stampede and its vision for the future.[771] In 2007 Stampede general manager Vern Kimball had announced the Stampede's new direction while introducing the new corporate master brand. Although the rural population of Alberta had declined to less than 20 per cent, and the Calgary Stampede was dropping the word Exhibition from general usage, Kimball noted that the incorporation of the organization's "C lazy S" brand into the new logo was in recognition of the fair's agricultural roots, and "represents our commitment to preserve and promote the unique values of the Stampede and our community – Western hospitality, integrity, commitment to community and pride of place."[772]

Given this mandate, it was important that royalty be able to articulate the Stampede's history and vision and that they emerge from their training period prepared to deliver a consistent message: that the Stampede was dedicated to the preservation and promotion of Western heritage and values.[773] With the Indian princess now part of the royal team, the implicit message was also one of friendship and co-operation between native people and the broader community as represented by the Stampede. This new direction coloured not only the content of royalty training sessions but also the choice of winning candidates. As Royalty Committee chair Jody Hooker (Stampede Princess, 1996) emphasized before the 2011 contest:

> The judges will be looking for the contestants that embody the Stampede values of integrity, pride of place, western hospitality and commitment to community. The winning trio will receive self-development training to help them act as official ambassadors of the Stampede – promoting western heritage and values to the community and to people around the world.[774]

With this shift in emphasis, from having royalty simply promoting the Stampede and its rodeo, to having royals perform a broader mandate, that of representing and promoting the values that the Stampede espoused, while also functioning as positive role models for young women,[775] it became increasingly important for the Royalty Committee to choose the right candidates for the job. Although horse-loving native Calgarians still succeeded occasionally, winners during the 2000s more often tended to come from a rural or small-town ranching or farming background, personifying the kind of Western heritage, culture and mindset articulated and promoted as part of the Stampede experience. No longer interested simply in finding good riders who could communicate well, or good communicators with acceptable riding skills, judges were tasked with identifying mature young women who could do both well while serving as believable spokeswomen and role models for the Stampede brand.

This shift in thinking was reflected in the choice of winners during the 2000s and in statements made by them after they won. Before entering the contest, 2002 Queen Karen Collins, a self-described farm girl from Okotoks, was given some deceptively simple winning advice from her sister, 2001 Princess Alison Collins: "Just be yourself."[776] Reflecting on her 2000 win, Banff-area ranch-girl-turned-Queen Jolene Brewster concluded that judges were not looking for "polished perfection," but for a real person, an individual whose "open, friendly, approachable nature could be enhanced with training to become a walking, talking poster for the Stampede."[777] Confirming her commitment to ranch life, 2009 Princess Kateri Cowley, who grew up on the Rafter Six Ranch near Exshaw, said that "[b]eing a cowgirl isn't an outfit, it's a lifestyle."[778] Princess Janelle Phillips (2010), from semi-rural Springbank on the outskirts of Calgary, told 2011 contest hopefuls: "Be yourself… Go in there, be proud of who you are, be proud of where you come from."[779] 2011 Stampede Indian Princess Eva Meguinis's advice to her successor was to "stay positive and be herself."[780] In 2011 Queen Jenna Lambert summed up the accumulated wisdom when she stated quite simply, "I am the Stampede Queen, but I am also myself – it's one and the same."[781]

Right after their training period was done, 2009 winners Kerri, Kateri, Tara and Nikkole headed off to Montreal with the 2009 Calgary Grey Cup Committee. As was customary during this kind of promotional event, the young ladies wore their full royal regalia whenever they were out in public, causing quite a splash whenever they ventured out to do a little shopping or sightseeing.[782] Before a five-day promotional trip to Toronto the following March, they received new pairs of custom-made boots from the Alberta Boot Company, a sponsor of the royal trio since the 1980s and now of the Indian princess as well. Confirming her new equality with the other royals, the *Calgary Herald* reported that "for the first time, the Indian princess was also given her own pair." Made of royal blue and brown eel-skin, Nikkole's boots were considered by company president Tim Gerwing to be "a cut above."[783]

From the 2009 contest on, the royal year took on a new pattern and pacing. After the crowning in early October, there followed six (later, eight) weeks of intense training, culminating in the first big assignment of the royal year, the Grey Cup in late November. In the new year, the number of events and appearances built toward a crescendo and an intensely busy Stampede week. After a relatively quiet summer, the royals would help with the contest in September, crown the winners in early October and then continue with their lives. Losing the first few months of the royal year to training, and the last month to a focus on the next contest, meant that many more functions had to be fitted into the eight or nine months leading up to the Stampede and immediately following it, because overall numbers of public appearances had risen steadily during the decade, from about 400 in 2000 to well over 450 by 2010 for the royal trio, and from about 150 per year in the early 2000s to approximately 350 by 2010 for the Indian princess.

With such a heavy schedule, it was more important than ever that winners of the royalty contest be able to get along and function as a team during their reign, and have the goodwill and flexibility to incorporate a fourth member, the Indian princess, when required. Luckily, contest judges became quite adept at getting it right during the 2000s, consistently choosing harmonious trios year after year. Perhaps it was the increased emphasis during the contest on determining potential team dynamics before naming winners and team leaders. Perhaps there was better mentoring from previous winners in the Queens' Alumni Association, so that potential candidates had a more accurate idea of the commitment required and the pitfalls to be avoided. Certainly, many winners in the 2000s referenced a friend or family member who had competed successfully in a previous contest and had given them much-needed support throughout their own competition and reign.

Perhaps the longer training period allowed different personalities a better opportunity to meld as a team with a common purpose before the group was exposed to the demands of travel and public appearances. One winner speculated that the incorporation of the Indian princess into the team had made a difference; four was a better number to work with than three, and her presence made it clearer that everyone had their own identity and brought something different and unique to the team.[784] Perhaps the Royalty and Indian Events Committees simply got better at insisting on a team approach from sponsors, function organizers and the media, and this diffused potentially irritating situations before they could occur. Following their own advice, Royalty Committee members began working with queens and princesses during the training period to ensure that each individual had an area of specialization for public speaking, and that speaking duties were shared and rotated whenever possible.[785]

No doubt all these factors were important, but another essential ingredient may have been that, generally speaking, winners in the 2000s tended to be older, with more life experience. The official age range for entrants was still 19–24, but very few of those chosen after 2000 were 19 or even 20; most were 21 or older. This shift occurred because of the important decision taken by the Queen Committee at the beginning of the decade that allowed previous contest finalists to run again. With that in mind, judges could safely pass over younger contestants with good potential in favour of more mature candidates, knowing that if they truly were interested in the job, these good candidates likely would enter the contest again when they were slightly older and better able to take on the demands of being a royal representative.[786] To thank finalists for their efforts, and encourage future participation, those who made the top six received Calgary Stampede pendants and were given outfits, hats and custom-made boots during meetings with sponsors. They also helped to represent the Stampede at several events, mimicking the kind of work that winners would encounter.[787]

The 2010 royal team typified the trend toward older winners: from an initial field of twenty-four, the winning trio was 21-year-old Katie Rochon from Calgary as Queen, with Princesses Janelle Phillips, 24, from Springbank and Kristie Rougeau, 21, from Cluny. Similarly, Stampede Indian Princess Sahvanne Weasel Traveller from the Piikani First Nation was 23. A highlight for this group was attending the XXI Olympic Winter Games in Vancouver as Stampede representatives. Additionally, the 2010 Royal Trio was the first to sport a different look on horseback. Ever since 1993, when the Queen Committee had begun purchasing stock for the exclusive use of royalty, all the horses had been bays. As the original three, Fred, Gus and Bob, retired, they were replaced

2010 Queen Katie Rochon (centre) with Princesses Kristie Rougeau and Janelle Phillips. (QAC)

by three other bays, Levi in 1999, Ned in 2002 and Bud in 2006. In 2010 the Royalty Committee decided that a more regal look was needed, "to set the ladies apart from the crowd," so three new mounts were acquired: a dun movie horse called Hawk, and two palomino rope horses named Snoopy and Kansas.[788]

The 2011 competition, which began with just sixteen contestants, saw several significant changes in format because of a change in circumstances. After just two years, the Stampede announced in 2010 that it was discontinuing the Canadian Rodeo Tour Championship. For the first time in more than forty-five years, queen contest finalists no longer had a rodeo venue for their final riding competition. Chair Jody Hooker and the Royalty Committee were forced to plan this part of the competition, and the subsequent crowning ceremony, as stand-alone events. The ensuing discussions prompted Committee members to rethink other aspects of the contest and program, ultimately resulting in other significant philosophical changes.[789]

Following the formal identification in 2008 of the royalty program as part of the Stampede's larger youth development initiative, the Royalty Committee had become a more important factor. In recognition of this, an attempt had been made to make the panel more robust by nearly doubling its size to twenty-four members.[790] In the past, Margaret Fraser had insisted that even a gap of two or three years was still too brief to allow a former royal to join the Queen Committee, but 2010 Princess Janelle Phillips was welcomed onto the expanded Royalty Committee right after she retired, her recent experience as a royal being viewed positively as a valuable asset.[791] In addition to other community volunteers, Janelle joined two other former royals on the Committee: 1987 Princess Shaunna Thompson, who had been serving for more than a decade, and 1996 Princess Jody Hooker, who had joined several years earlier.

Accompanying its improved status, the Royalty Committee also was given a bigger baseline budget, although the understanding was that it would continue to rely, as before, on donations of cash and of goods and services to fund the bulk of its operations.[792] With that in mind, the Committee was encouraged to focus its efforts on enhancing and developing reciprocal relationships with sponsors. By 2012, five Committee members were dedicated to this task, formerly the responsibility of a single individual. Although the number of sponsors had remained fairly constant since the mid-1980s (around forty), over the years the level of their support had increased dramatically. When the Stampede Queen Committee had begun in 1966, a few corporate sponsors supplemented its annual budget of less than $5,000 by contributing items worth, at most, a few thousand dollars. By 2012, according to chair Dana Tremblay, donations from sponsors accounted for "a great majority" of the Committee's overall budget, which had increased more than fifty times in value over the intervening sixty-five years. As a result, it was not surprising that by 2012, up to half of the time spent by royal trios making public appearances was related in some way to thanking sponsors for their contributions to the royalty program or to the Stampede itself.

Naturally, there also was a new emphasis on the program's potential for educational outcomes. The Committee's revised mission and mandate became to "preserve western heritage and values on behalf of the Calgary Stampede through a sustainable development program of three young women who embody, promote and share these traditions." The Committee proposed to accomplish this goal by offering "a fair and objective judging process for public relation[s] focused, equestrian based young women by facilitating contest events and venues for the annual selection of the trio," and by providing "knowledge, training, development and support of the Royal Trio for the delivery and presentation of Stampede's key messages, values and heritage as year-long ambassadors to the Calgary Stampede."[793]

In a bid to increase the educational value of the contest, judges' comments were relayed anonymously to competitors through feedback forms introduced in 2010 by Committee member Dana Tremblay.[794] This enabled all contestants to learn from the experience by being informed of their areas of strength and areas to develop (though not their actual marks). Unsuccessful competitors who wished to try again now knew where best to concentrate their efforts (for example, on riding or public speaking). Even the winners received feedback forms and were encouraged to choose three areas of development to work on during the first, training part of their year. The royalty contest was still a competition, but now it was one that adhered to the philosophy of nurturing winners as well as potential winners.

The educational component of the royalty program was further enhanced in 2010 with two new opportunities for reigning royalty. Long-time Committee member Pat Pearson introduced a concept he had become familiar with while working at SAIT Polytechnic (formerly Southern Alberta Institute of Technology). The Prior Learning Assessment initiative provided retiring royals with a document outlining the learning and development accomplished during their reign. It could be presented to a post-secondary institution at the time of registration to earn potential course credits.[795]

The second educational enhancement instituted in 2010 was an interesting return to a prize offered to many early Stampede royals but not seen since the mid-1970s: a sponsor-funded program through which retiring royals were offered a $1,500 scholarship for post-secondary training, to be used within the year following their reign. As well as demonstrating the royalty program's mandated commitment to youth development and personal growth, these new initiatives aimed at making a year of volunteer

315
★

service for the Stampede more attractive for potential applicants.[796]

In spite of these philosophical and practical changes, the contest itself remained much the same, with just a bit of minor tweaking. It still consisted of three rounds of competition. In the initial round, contestants were evaluated at four official events: a contestant mixer (new in 2009), brief preliminary interviews with a panel of five judges, a first riding event, and two speeches, one impromptu and one prepared from topics relating to the Stampede that they had drawn during the contestant mixer the week before. After these events, the field was reduced to ten semi-finalists who were assessed during three events: an informal dinner, a second riding event following a riding clinic (new in 2010) and a formal cocktail reception. The six finalists who emerged from the second round faced a lengthy in-depth interview with three judges, followed by several formal dinners and participation in an event similar to the kind of function customarily attended by Stampede royalty (for example, Bingo Night at the Alberta Children's Hospital). Impromptu speaking featured prominently during third-round activities, which also included Parents' Night and a traditional pancake breakfast. The contest culminated with the final riding competition and a crowning event where finalists

interacted with sponsors, judges, volunteers and the media before three winners were announced.[797]

As always, it was only the marks earned during the final two rounds of the competition that determined the winners. And, as had been the case for some thirty years, judges' marks were sent to an outside accounting firm for tabulation, although Committee members usually looked over the results and questioned obvious inconsistencies.[798] With the number of judges hovering around thirty by the 2000s, uneven marking had become something of a problem, so the Royalty Committee decided in 2010 to reduce the number "to gain a more consistent and comprehensive evaluation of the contestants." After the streamlining process, fifteen to seventeen judges, some known and some hidden, followed candidates throughout the five weeks of competition, using benchmark descriptions to "evaluate each contestant on a set of competencies… presence, interpersonal competencies, teamwork, communication, horsemanship, commitment and time management, passion and work ethic, and western values and integrity."[799]

Although the Committee's ultimate goal was to reintroduce a stand-alone riding and crowning event at Stampede Park once the much-anticipated Agrium Western Event Centre opened in 2014, in the

2011 Queen Jenna Lambert (centre) with Princesses Whitney Wilkie and Stephanie Gray. (CSA)

Twenty-one-year-old Queen Jenna Lambert from Calgary was joined by 21-year-old Whitney Wilkie from Priddis and 24-year-old Calgarian Stephanie Gray as Princesses. Crowned after her second run at the title, Princess Stephanie said, "I came back here with more heart, and feel I gave it 150 per cent."[801] Interestingly, in view of the Committee's hard work in trying to ensure that winners felt they were part of a team effort, when a reporter from her hometown newspaper, the Okotoks *Western Wheel*, asked Whitney after her win if she was disappointed in not being named Queen, she replied, "Of course not… We all get treated the same and we all get the same opportunities."[802]

The fourth member of the royal team in 2011 was 24-year-old Eva Meguinis from the Tsuu T'ina First Nation, crowned a week earlier by judges from Calgary and Treaty 7 in a ceremony that culminated the Stampede Indian Princess contest. For the first time, in the start of a new tradition, the Indian princess was included in the saddle sponsorship program long enjoyed by the royal trio. In recognition of the increased presence and time commitment demanded of her position, Eva received a richly tooled saddle handcrafted by Eamor's Saddlery.[803] She was fortunate in being the only member of the royal team chosen to be presented to Prince William and his

meantime, the two events had to be held separately, for practical reasons. For the 2011 competition, finalists competed in a day-long final riding competition at the Okotoks Agricultural Society's indoor Hebson Arena on October 2, 2010. For their first two riding events, candidates had been given reining patterns to follow, but for this final event, the six finalists were allowed to choreograph a pattern to their own choice of music, an opportunity they really enjoyed. The next day, winners were crowned after an event held at the BMO (formerly Roundup) Centre at Stampede Park.[800]

wife, Catherine, Duchess of Cambridge, during their whirlwind visit to Calgary and the 2011 Stampede.[804]

Although she was now considered to be an official part of the royal team, and appeared often enough with the royal trio for the young women to consider that a real friendship had developed, the Indian princess's main role still was to act as the Stampede's ambassador to and from native communities, "representing her people and their long heritage as part of the Stampede." Over the course of her year, the Indian princess attended many Aboriginal events on her own – summer powwows and the like – but she also had an important role as a liaison with the non-Aboriginal community, "a stepping stone between the cultures." As Princess Eva quickly learned, "It's kind of crazy how much people don't know about natives… You have to have an open mind to be in this role. You can't get offended. A lot of people don't know anything about you or your culture other than from the movies… Calgary is a city that is surrounded by five tribes, so people need to understand the history of their city."[805]

Despite the Royalty Committee's hope that a fall start to the royal year would help to attract more competitors, contest numbers declined steadily through the 2000s, most years attracting fewer than two dozen candidates. Even the 2012 royalty contest in September 2011 attracted only twenty-four, despite the advertised cachet of reigning during the Stampede's Centennial year. That year, the Committee began promoting the contest in early June, hoping that the greater visibility of royalty during the Stampede might attract more contestants. Sadly, it did not, and the next year saw an even greater decline once the excitement surrounding the Centennial had passed (just a dozen candidates competed in September 2012 for the 2013 crowns). Committee members and other observers remained philosophical, reasoning that contest numbers always had been variable, and even if overall interest in the contest was in a period of decline, the quality of individual contenders was higher than ever.[806]

Curiously, even though actual contestant numbers were down, the Royalty Committee sometimes received a "deluge" of applications during the 2000s.[807] The problem was that many of the initial applicants did not meet contest criteria, particularly with respect to riding ability. For many years, the application form had warned that "competent riding ability is a necessity," but many applicants overstated their qualifications, or simply ignored the requirement, assuming that beauty or personality would carry them through. According to Committee member Sandy Tidswell, the final straw for the Royalty

Committee came when a young man sent in an application on behalf of a girlfriend who had never even sat a horse.[808]

Although winners spent only 20 to 30 per cent of their time riding during their reign, it was essential that serious contenders demonstrate adequate skill.[809] Genuine concern for rider safety following several serious mishaps during the initial phase of the competition dovetailed with new standards for rider and animal safety adopted by the Stampede in 2009, and prompted the Committee to come up with a simple but effective weeding strategy in 2010. All future applicants were required to prove their riding competence in advance by providing "a signed letter of reference from a bona fide equestrian trainer attesting to your equestrian skills and abilities," or a three-minute video "demonstrating a mount–dismount, walk, trot, lope and figure eight on a horse of your choice."[810]

The 2012 contest saw a repeat of the format used in 2011, with the final riding event occurring in Okotoks and the crowning luncheon held the next day at the BMO Centre. The lucky Centennial Queen was 22-year-old Candice Lee from Springbank, bouncing back to win on her third try after two unsuccessful attempts in 2009 and 2010. Realizing she was now a walking advertisement for the Royalty Committee's strategy of allowing finalists to re-enter the contest, Candice said, "I want girls to know it doesn't always happen on the first time and to go back because you could be the perfect fit the next year."[811]

Queen Candice was joined by 23-year-old Princesses Danielle Gariepy from Rockyford and Jessica Manning from Longview. Although she had grown up on the outskirts of Calgary, Candice did not have a rural background, so she was glad to be able to pass ranching and agriculture-related questions to her two princesses during interviews.[812] She felt that being able to say "it's not my area of expertise" and redirect attention to one of the others was a technique that helped to build the team and emphasize to outsiders that every member held a unique and valuable place within the group. In fact, this had become an important leadership skill for queens. Candice's successor, 2013 Queen Jessica Williams, recalled absorbing exactly the same lesson during her training period, that the harmony of the team largely depended upon the queen's willingness and ability to "shift the spotlight."[813] Assuming, probably correctly, that there had been very little significant difference in their marks during the contest, that it was "just luck if you come out as Queen or Princess," the 2012 trio moved forward quickly after crowning by adopting the attitude that "it was no longer about you

2012 Queen Candice Lee (centre) with Princesses Danielle Gariepy and Jessica Manning. (CSA)

320
☆

was Stampede Indian Princess Amelia Crowshoe, 23, of the Piikani First Nation, chosen to "serve as a role model and ambassador for all Treaty 7 First Nations people and the Indian Village."[814] During the Stampede's Centennial year, the four members of the royal team travelled to the Grey Cup in Vancouver, and partnered with Travel Alberta and the Canadian Tourism Commission to promote visiting Alberta, Canada and "the biggest Stampede ever" during trips to Washington, Berlin and Anaheim, California.[815] Asked what it was like "travelling in a posse of white cowgirl princesses," Amelia testified to the close relationships now being fostered by the solid team-building efforts of the Royalty and Indian Events Committees:

We go everywhere. We have such a great connection. We're sharing a once-in-a-lifetime moment, so it's not work for us. When you're having a bad day these girls support you, as they know what you're going through. I miss them when we're not together.

That said, since the Indian princess finally was allowed to represent the Stampede nationally and internationally, Princess Amelia's busy year of well over 350 public appearances also saw a number of solo excursions, including promotional trips to

individually, but about everyone, the team; you're all just a small part of the Stampede puzzle." The young women also remembered feeling very well supported during their training period and subsequent reign by members of the Royalty Committee, with whom the girls formed individual bonds, and with their advisors, the modern equivalent of chaperones.

The fourth member of the 2012 team, "bring[ing] the cultural aspect to the Stampede royalty program,"

Memphis and China, where she memorably jingle-danced along the Great Wall.[816]

Princess Jessica of the 2012 royals had an unusual connection to the event that year. Her aunt was 1962 Queen Donna Thomson, so Jessica had grown up hearing tales about being a royal during the Stampede's golden jubilee year. She thought it might be fun, and somehow fitting, to be a royal exactly fifty years after her aunt and during another celebratory year, the Stampede Centennial. Comparing notes afterward, they could see that, in its essentials, the job had not changed: representing the Stampede still kept royals busy during Stampede week and involved them the rest of the year in attending small-town rodeos, appearing at special events for local organizations and sponsors, and visiting schools, children's hospitals and seniors' residences. But they laughed over the difference that fifty years had made in the time commitment required. Whereas Donna had made eight to ten appearances daily during the six days of Stampede, and another dozen or so over the rest of the year, Jessica and her trio had attended a dizzying seventeen to twenty-two functions every day during a ten-day Stampede week plus an astounding 350 more appearances through the year, for a whopping total of 550.[817] Although this number may have been inflated in 2012 by Stampede

2013 Queen Jessica Williams (centre) with Princesses Catherine Morneau and Danielle Kakoschke. (CSA)

Centennial celebrations, the Royalty Committee realized that this level of commitment was asking far too much of volunteers. Wisely, they decided to relieve the pressure by streamlining future bookings and capping the number at a more reasonable level. As a result, the next royal trios, 2013 Queen Jessica Williams and Princesses Danielle Kakoschke and Catherine Morneau, and 2014 Queen Danica Heath and Princesses Stephanie Patterson and Shannon Black, were scheduled to make one hundred fewer personal appearances, for a still impressive but much more manageable annual total of 450.[818] As had been the norm for the past several years, the Stampede Indian Princesses for 2013, Amber Big Plume of the Tsuu T'ina Nation, and 2014's Carly Weasel Child of the Siksika Nation were scheduled to make 350 appearances during their year-long reigns.

Whereas each new Indian princess received her own uniquely beaded crown that indicated her year of service, the royal trio always handed their crowns on to the next winning queen and princesses. While it was discussing other changes in 2010, the Royalty Committee decided to update the trio's crowns to bring them into compliance with the Stampede's master brand, which had been introduced a few years earlier. Because the crowns were considered to be legacy items, this process took a while. First there was a lengthy consultation with stakeholders, including the Queens' Alumni. Using this feedback, a small group of women, including Royalty Committee member and 1987 Princess Shaunna Thompson and 1988 Queen Laura Godwin, worked on the design, taking into consideration "concerns of weight, height, functionality and presentation." As in 1996, the new crowns were made of sterling silver and 14-karat gold, intricately engraved, and alike in every aspect except for bearing different titles and sporting synthetic rubies in the queen's crown. Crafted by Becker Buckles of Airdrie, the crowns took eight months to create but were ready for presentation to the Centennial trio, Queen Candice and Princesses Danielle and Jessica.[819]

Although they could not keep their crowns, by 2012, the young women volunteering as the Stampede royal trio were receiving some very nice tangible rewards. Among the gifts and services from more than forty different sponsors were many from local donors who had supported the royalty program for more than twenty-five years: Lammle's Western Wear, Shaw GMC, Eamor's Saddlery, Alberta Boot Company, Patti Falconer Agencies, Sears Canada, Associated Grocers and Davidson Enman Lumber. In addition to receiving many valuable items to keep – watches, jewellery, cameras, luggage, "tons of makeup," half a dozen pairs of boots and some forty-five Western outfits[820] – queens and princesses had their incidental and travel expenses covered during their year of service. Honorariums had increased over the decade to reflect the greater time commitment asked of the volunteers and the increased cost of living. In 2000 each member of the royal trio was eligible to receive $2,000 to help cover expenses; by 2012 this amount had risen to just over $3,000. And, with the new focus on education, a royal who wished to continue her schooling could exit her year with an additional $1,500 in the form of a scholarship. With similar rewards for the Indian princess, it is not surprising that the Stampede continued to be successful year after year in attracting four new, enthusiastic young volunteers to function as its royal team.

But most former queens and princesses agree that it was not the concrete rewards so much as the intangibles that, in retrospect, made their volunteer year so worthwhile and personally fulfilling. Retiring royals always reported finishing their reigns with increased self-confidence and improved communication and public-relations skills. With the new emphasis in the royalty program on personal growth and development, modern royals also felt they had benefited personally and professionally from the mentoring and networking opportunities afforded by a year of working closely with the officials, volunteers and sponsors that made up the elite Stampede family. Best of all, in the opinion of many, retiring queens and princesses gained a wide circle of like-minded friends and a new direction for their talents and training on behalf of the Stampede by becoming automatic lifelong members of a strong, supportive sisterhood, the Queens' Alumni Association.

Queen Danica Heath (right) with Princesses Shannon Black and Stephanie Patterson, 2014. (CSA)

AFTERWORD

Looking back and moving forward

By the time the Calgary Stampede celebrated its centennial in 2012, nearly two hundred young women had served as royal representatives in the sixty-six years since Patsy Rodgers had been selected as the first Stampede Queen. After Patsy's historic appointment in 1946, the Stampede had stepped back for more than a decade, relying on the Associated Canadian Travellers to choose the Queen of the Stampede on its behalf. Starting in 1947 the ACT sponsored an annual contest to select a queen and ladies-in-waiting based on the number of tickets or votes each candidate had sold during a fundraising campaign. As time went on, and the Stampede began to realize the promotional value of its royalty, it became discouraged by the variable nature of the candidates produced by a vote-based contest. Interested in finding representatives with demonstrated riding ability and the right kind of skill set to suit what had become more of a public-relations job than simply a prize, Stampede officials decided to become more

directly involved in the contest. As of 1959 the ACT had been required to supplement ticket sales with tests for horsemanship and other desirable qualities; by 1964, ticket sales had been eliminated in favour of a contest based solely on proven ability; and in 1966 a Stampede committee took over the contest entirely.

As the control and direction of the contest evolved, so too did the job required of winners. Early queens and ladies-in-waiting during the ACT period served during a six-day Stampede that rarely saw more than six to eight appearances per day. After Stampede week, queens may have made another half-dozen or so appearances over the rest of their reigning year, but with public focus very much on the queen, some ladies-in-waiting never attended another function after the Stampede ended. With the shift to Stampede control in the mid-1960s, queens and princesses were expected to play a bigger role in representing and promoting the show and its host city. As the Stampede extended to nine days, then ten, the total number of annual appearances climbed to 150 by the early 1970s and to 200 by the end of the decade. Travel outside

Alberta several times a year to promote Calgary and the Stampede became the norm, and the Queen Committee began to require a year-round commitment from all members of the royal team. The next decades saw a steady rise in the annual number of public appearances: 300 during the 1980s, 350 in the 1990s, 450 in the 2000s and an astonishing 550 during the Stampede's 2012 Centennial year.

Over the years, the Queen Committee had concentrated on honing the contest and program devised by the ACT during the last years of its sponsorship. Although minor modifications frequently occurred, there was very little change made to the basic structure of the contest and the rules governing winners during the first forty years of Stampede control. From the beginning, judges evaluated candidates' horsemanship at a series of riding events and assessed their suitability for the promotional aspects of the job during formal and informal social and public speaking events. Over the years, the testing area that saw the most change was horsemanship. Although there never was any doubt that a certain level of riding competence was desirable, both from the standpoint of safety and to maintain the credibility of royalty as representatives of a horse-based show, the Queen Committee struggled to determine how to rate this requirement in relation to other skills. It

went from demanding riding ability in preference to all other qualities during the 1960s, to de-emphasizing it almost out of existence during the 1970s and early 1980s, to finally achieving a more balanced middle ground as the contest entered the 1990s.

In comparison, most other testing areas evolved in a more straightforward manner. However, the Committee struggled for some years to determine the best approach for identifying winners who could work together as a harmonious team during an intense year of pressure in the public eye. Part of the problem was the tradition of uneven recognition and compensation that originated during the ACT period, when the focus was very much on the queen as the winner of the contest. After the Stampede took over, the Queen Committee began promoting all three winners as part of a public-relations team. But the queen, as leader, was still treated as the focus of the team and rewarded with better prizes and more public recognition. This caused a problem for some trios because princesses were expected to give equal time and effort but were not compensated accordingly. The solution lay in equalizing their compensation and insisting that sponsors and the media recognize all members of the team equally, but it took the Committee many years to achieve this goal. By the 2000s, though, the issue had been resolved, enabling all royal volunteers to be viewed, and, more importantly, to view themselves, as full and equal members of the team.

As various elements of the contest were fine-tuned over the years, the Queen Committee remained clear about its goal: to find three young women who could ride reasonably well and had the right combination of personality and interpersonal skills to form a solid team able to handle the pressures and promotional aspects of the job. This was the strength of the Stampede Queen contest, and a major reason why it survived when others lost favour during the late 1980s and early 1990s. Of course, it helped that it was part of the Stampede, and therefore benefited from the positive public image usually accorded all things Stampede by Calgarians and the local media. And it did make some effort to move with the times and remain relevant to new generations of contestants (for example, in recent years, dressing royalty in outfits that more closely follow current fashion trends and relaxing rules governing behaviour to allow for discreet common-law relationships). But it also was the fact that contestants were, in effect, being auditioned for the job of representing the Stampede that helped distinguish it from other contests. Although it shared some elements with traditional beauty contests – winners were judged on qualities such as personality and poise, they had to demonstrate certain talents, such

as public speaking, and they received valuable prizes – the requirement that the winning trio be competent horsewomen and be willing to dedicate a year of personal time to volunteering for the Stampede lifted it far beyond the realm of the usual beauty contest and allowed the Committee to market it to entirely different audiences. Although critics were correct in that unattractive young women were unlikely to win, candidates never were judged on personal appearance alone and there never was anything like the bathing suit and evening gown competitions typical of most beauty contests. Demonstrated skills far outweighed appearance in the marking schemes used by judges, and ultimately the ability to ride creditably, to mix and mingle with crowds, to speak in public with ease and to work as part of a team were considered to be far more valuable assets from the Stampede's point of view than mere beauty.

Aside from the minor tweaking of rules and procedures over the years, the queen contest underwent its greatest periods of change during the mid-1960s, when it evolved from a ticket sales competition to a contest based on judged categories, and the late 2000s, when new directions set by the Stampede had a significant impact on the format and orientation of the program. After more than forty years as a spring competition, in 2008 it followed the lead of its host, Rodeo

Royal, to become a fall event. That same year saw a number of other important changes, including a new name for the Queen Committee, now the more inclusive-sounding Royalty Committee. Revisions were made to the contest and the royalty training period to bring the program into line with the educational and development goals of the Stampede's youth programs. At the same time, the program was positively influenced by the inclusion of the Calgary Stampede Indian Princess as a full and acknowledged member of the royal team. In addition, a new focus during competition and training emphasized the importance of harmonizing royalty's public image and message with the Stampede's new brand emphasis on Western heritage and values. More changes occurred in 2010, as the Royalty Committee continued to enhance the educational aspects of the program and took on a new challenge when the demise of the Canadian Rodeo Tour Championship forced it to start producing standalone events for contest finalists.

Although the Stampede still looms large in the Calgary mindset and economy, in recent years it has attempted to reconnect with its rural roots and audience by focusing on its historic role in promoting and preserving Western culture and lifestyle. This change in focus, in conjunction with the Royalty Committee's renewed commitment to horsemanship over the past few decades, likely explains the modern

trend for the majority of contest winners to come from rural or small-town backgrounds. No longer simply a public-relations team inviting the world to visit Calgary and its famous show, royal representatives now must exhibit other, less tangible qualities in addition to the long-time standards of being intelligent, looking attractive, having an open, pleasing personality and being able to communicate fluently and ride a horse with confidence and ease. Twenty-first-century royals also must embody, and be able to project convincingly, the traditional Western values now being espoused as part of the Stampede mandate: integrity, pride of place, Western hospitality and commitment to community. With these qualities in mind, the ideal royal representative for the Stampede has become a lively, intelligent, friendly and confident young woman from a rural or small-town background who loves to ride and has deep Western roots.

Curiously, this description brings the Stampede Queen program full circle, as it corresponds exactly with the candidate chosen by Jack Dillon all those years ago, when he was asked in 1945 to select a rodeo queen for the Calgary Stampede. Without benefit of judges, contest or committee, Jack knew intuitively that the very best representative of the Stampede and what it stood for would be ranch-bred, horse-loving, pretty and personable young Patsy Rodgers from Bottrell, Alberta.

APPENDIX

Stampede Royalty, 1946–2014

	QUEEN	LADY-IN-WAITING	LADY-IN-WAITING
1946	Patsy Rodgers		
1947	Doreen Richardson	Eva Brewster	
1948	Gloria Klaver	Margaret Forsgren	Shirley Kemp
1949	Merle Stier	Marion Birchall	Inez Melby
1950	Eileen Beckner	Ann Dutchak	Gussie MacDonald
1951	Marion McMahon	Shirley Clark	June Dewhirst
1952	Sherry Moore	Donna Christie	Helen Smith
1953	Edith Edge		
1954	Evelyn Eagle Speaker	Kay Dench	Peggy Fisher
1955	Mary Ellen Jones	Joan Johnston	Elaine Kent
1956	Shirley Willock	Kay Marshall	Carolyn Schoeppe
1957	Marquitta Elton	Karen Downey	Kay Larsen
1958	Jennie Chow	Beverly Haeh	Isabella Hamilton
1959	Julie Akkerman	Doreen Wynne	Margaret Powell
1960	Margot Turney	Judy Taylor	Gail Leonard
1961	Marie Sharpe	Lynn Puckett	Sharon Taylor
1962	Donna Thomson	Linda Rennells	Frances Reeder
1963	Frances Swann	Beryl Edge	Dixie Girletz
1964	Sharon Patterson	Gail Henry	Gwenda Marshall
1965	Donna Israelson	Frances Chamberlain	Mary MacDonald

	QUEEN	PRINCESS	PRINCESS
1966	Betty Wright	Lorraine McLean	Ann Neilson
1967	Patsy Allan	Bonnie MacGregor	Candace Smith
1968	Diane Leech	Heather Lawrence	Arlene Weidner
1969	Carol Burns	Patricia Johnston	Winnifred Reid
1970	Vicky Hayden	Cheryl Going	Lynn Boake
1971	Leslie MacDonald	Wendy Copithorne	Shirley Inkster
1972	Patti Girling	Diane Wallace	Dawn MacLean
1973	Suzanne Randle	Bettie Knight	Joan Horne
1974	Happy Barlow	Karin Kraft	Sis Thacker
1975	Barbara Howard	Stacy Kirk	Chris Wigle
1976	Cindy Morres	Wynne Anderson	Carol Ovans
1977	Gillian Newman	Brenda Orr	Sylvia Wittmoser
1978	Dawne Van Wart	Judy Shaw	Patti Stephens
1979	Pam Jonassen	Shauna Harrington	Brenda Warden
1980	Jodi Merriman	Audrey Collins	Dawn Pringle
1981	Cathy Robinson	Diane Hamilton	Barb Penner
1982	Michelle Williamson	Jenny Baillod	Penny Watt
1983	Shannan Leinweber	Sharon Dacen	Marlie Milne
1984	Pat Brown	Michele Fussell	Monica Perchaluk
1985	Karyn Scott	Dyanna Browne	Karen Dornan
1986	Kary Ager	Jayne Boyce	Kathleen Mackie
1987	Holly Dunn	Debbie Simpson	Shaunna Thompson
1988	Laura Godwin	Susanne Astley	Jennifer Ough
1989	Bonny Wallace	Shelly Ann Fyfe	Mary Ellen Rouleau
1990	Kari Griffith	Dawn Chipchase	Vanessa Gleddie
1991	Halley Strandquist	Michel Higginbotham	Alison Ross

	QUEEN	PRINCESS	PRINCESS
1992	Shauna Oseen	Kate McWhir	Sherry Mitchell
1993	Erin Moynihan	Laura Hughes	Melissa McKay
1994	Sonya Dueck	Tamy Midtdal	Holly Watson
1995	Allison Boswell	Lisa Eastman	Karina Tees
1996	Kari Hames	Jody Hooker	Shilo Johanson
1997	Holly Cartwright	Tina Maynard	Karin Hunter
1998	Kathryn Larter	Stacey Cross	Erin Thompson
1999	Christie Fath	Kari Lammle	Tara Wesner
2000	Jolene Brewster	Corie David	Shannon Reid
2001	Maria Heintz	Lisa McNiven	Alison Collins
2002	Karen Collins	June-Marie Innes	Natalie Havens
2003	Trina Percival	Kelly Ashbacher	Shannan Martindale
2004	Amy Smith	Breanna Ernst	Brianna Hamblin
2005	Lauren MacLennan	Coleen Crowe	Justine Milner
2006	Cheryl Dafoe	April Kanderka	Teri Murray
2007	Amanda Kochan	Caia Morstad	Amanda Byrne
2008	Lauren MacLennan	Coleen Crowe	Justine Milner
	Trina Percival*	Caia Morstad*	Amanda Byrne*
2009	Kerri Williamson	Kateri Cowley	Tara Sergerie
2010	Katie Rochon	Janelle Phillips	Kristie Rougeau
2011	Jenna Lambert	Whitney Wilkie	Stephanie Gray
2012	Candice Lee	Danielle Gariepy	Jessica Manning
2013	Jessica Williams	Danielle Kakoschke	Catherine Morneau
2014	Danica Heath	Stephanie Patterson	Shannon Black

*Royalty Transition Team

1 Max Foran, "The Stampede in historical context," c. 1 in *Icon, Brand, Myth: The Calgary Stampede*, edited by Max Foran (Edmonton: AU Press, 2008), 3–6; Foran, "More than partners: The Calgary Stampede and the City of Calgary," c. 6 in ibid., 148–149.

2 Fred Kennedy, *The Calgary Stampede Story* (Calgary: T. Edwards Thonger, 1952), 123.

3 James Gray, *A Brand of Its Own* (Saskatoon: Western Producer Prairie Books, 1985), 120.

4 Ibid., Appendix 1.

5 "Record crowds view parade and opening of Stampede," *Calgary Herald* (henceforth *CH*), Jul 9, 1945.

6 Kennedy, *The Calgary Stampede Story*, 133.

CHAPTER 1, 1946

7 Jean Leslie, "Once a Queen, always a Queen," *Herald Magazine*, Jul 3, 1988, 26.

8 Dorothy Robertson, research notes, 1996, reported in "Dublin, Texas, Rodeo History," n.d., Texansunited.com, accessed Mar 23, 2012, www.texansunited.com/dublin/dublin-texas-rodeo-history; see also "History of the Dublin Rodeo," linked from Vernon L. Williams, ed., "The Dublin Rodeo Home Page," Abilene (Texas) Christian University History Department, Feb 15, 2000, accessed Jul 23, 2013, www.acu.edu/academics/history/dublin/dubhome.htm.

9 Joan Burbick, *Rodeo Queens and the American Dream* (New York: Public Affairs, 2002), 86; Renée M. Laegreid, "Performers prove beauty and rodeo can be mixed: The return of the cowgirl queen," *Montana: The Magazine of Western History* 54, no. 1 (Spring 2004), 44–46.

10 Renée M. Laegreid, *Riding Pretty: Rodeo Royalty in the American West* (Lincoln: University of Nebraska Press, 2006), 2.

11 Ibid., 124; Laegreid, "Performers prove beauty," 47.

12 Laegreid, *Riding Pretty*, 16.

13 Patsy Rodgers Henderson scrapbook, 1946–2011. Much of the information relating to Patsy Rodgers's life and experiences as Stampede Queen was gathered from scrapbooks in her possession and during interviews with the author Mar 17 and 21, 2012.

14 Leslie, "Once a Queen."

15 Ibid.

16 "Calgary girl to lead great New York rodeo," *Albertan*, May 18, 1946.

17 Biographical notes on Patsy Rodgers, ca. Apr 1946, Henderson scrapbook, loose.

18 "Alberta girl in New York rodeo," *Windsor Daily Star*, Jun 27, 1946.

19 "Calgary girl is selected 'Miss Canada' in New York rodeo," *CH*, May 16, 1946.

20 "Calgary girl to lead," *Albertan*, May 18, 1946.

21 Lorne Stout, "Calgary honored," *Canadian Cattlemen* 9, no. 1 (Jun 1946), 46.

22 Ibid.

23 "Calgary girl to lead," *Albertan*, May 18, 1946.

24 Marta Gold, "Legwork reveals GWG story," *CH*, Aug 28, 2012.

25 "Cowgirl from Canada arrives in Cowtown: To join Dublin rodeo," Henderson scrapbook, [12].

26 "As Canada's rodeo queen arrived in Lethbridge," *Lethbridge Herald*, Jul 4, 1946.

27 "'Wildest rodeo I have seen' says Madison Square Garden manager," *Lethbridge Herald*, Jul 5, 1946.

28 "Enjoys rodeo and plans to return," *Lethbridge Herald*, Jul 6, 1946.

29 Leslie, "Once a Queen."

30 "8,000 at flower show: Patsy Rodgers crowned," *Albertan*, Aug 27, 1946.

31 "'Miss Canada' visits city en route to New York," Henderson scrapbook, [11].

32 Ibid., "Cowgirl from Canada arrives in Cowtown," 12.

33 "Ranch girls sponsor Garden rodeo," *Nashua [New Hampshire] Telegraph*, Oct 25, 1948.

34 Flyer, Henderson scrapbook, [14].

35 "Ranch girls," *Nashua Telegraph*, Oct 25, 1948.

36 Abilene Christian University, "History of the Dublin Rodeo."

37 "Cowgirls off to rodeo at MSG," Henderson scrapbook, [13].

38 "A Big Hello to East from West," ibid., [17].

39 Henderson, interview.

40 Leslie, "Once a Queen."

41 Monica Andreeff, "Royal roots," *Avenue Magazine* (Jul/Aug 2001), 27.

42 Henderson, interview.

43 Robin Summerfield, "Glory days," *CH*, Jul 6, 2000.

44 Leslie, "Once a Queen."

45 Andreeff, "Royal roots," 27.

46 Jack Gaver, "Up and down Broadway," *Beaver Daily Times*, Sep 27, 1946.

47 Cindy Morres Sergerie, "Patricia 'Patsy' Rodgers: A brief biography…," unpublished manuscript, 2011.

48 "Rodeo 'Sponsor Girls,'" Henderson scrapbook, [23].

49 "Patsy Rodgers of Calgary and Ona Mae Clark," *Daytona Beach Morning Journal*, Oct 26, 1946.

50 "Patsy Rogers back from Cinderella trip," *Albertan*, Nov 13, 1946.

51 Stacy Keach to Patsy Rodgers, Oct 21, 1946, Henderson scrapbook, [15].

52 "Patsy Rogers back," *Albertan*, Nov 13, 1946.

53 Christmas card, Henderson scrapbook, [6].

54 Miscellaneous clippings, Henderson scrapbook, [26, 27].

55 "Patsy Rogers back," *Albertan*, Nov 13, 1946.

56 Henderson interview.

57 Miscellaneous clippings, Henderson scrapbook, [28, 29].

58 "Patsy Rogers back," *Albertan*, Nov 13, 1946.

CHAPTER 2, 1947–1949

59 Marilyn McLean, "ACT celebrates anniversary at convention in Calgary," *Herald Magazine*, May 20, 1961.

60 "Foothills Flares," *ACT Magazine*, Feb 1945.

61 Ibid., Nov 1945; "Foothills Footnotes," *ACT Magazine*, Feb, Jun, Sep 1946.

62 "Calgary's biggest Stampede sets many new records," *CH*, Jul 13, 1946.

63 McLean, "ACT celebrates."

64 Joan Dixon and Tracey Read, *Celebrating the Calgary Exhibition and Stampede* (Canmore: Altitude, 2005), 36.

65 Gray, *A Brand of Its Own*, 65.

66 Renée Laegreid, *Riding Pretty*, 2; Laegreid, "Performers prove beauty," 47.

67 Sarah Banet-Weiser, *The Most Beautiful Girl in the World: Beauty Pageants and National Identity* (Berkeley: University of California Press, 1999), 41–42.

68 Patrizia Gentile, "Queen of the Maple Leaf: A history of beauty contests in Twentieth Century Canada" (PhD dissertation, Queens University, 2006), 27, 29.

69 Renée Laegreid, *Riding Pretty*, 124, 127

70 "Stampede to have 'Queen,'" *CH*, Apr 18, 1947.

71 CSA, Board and Executive Minutes, CS.99.106, Box 1, Minute Book No. 2, Memo of meeting of Parade Committee, May 14, 1947.

72 "Stampede to have 'Queen,'" *CH*, Apr 18, 1947.

73 "Vote for your favorite in the Stampede Queen contest," *Albertan*, May 31, 1947.

74 "Doreen Richardson, Queen of Stampede," *CH*, Jul 4, 1947; "Doreen Richardson wins Stampede Queen title," *Albertan*, Jul 5, 1947.

75 "Doreen Richardson Wins," *Albertan*, Jul 5, 1947.

76 "Doreen Richardson, Queen," *CH*, Jul 4, 1947.

77 Robert M. Seiler and Tamara P. Seiler, "The Social Construction of the Canadian Cowboy: Calgary Exhibition and Stampede posters, 1952–1972," c. 12 in *Icon, Brand, Myth: The Calgary Stampede*, edited by Max Foran (Edmonton: AU Press, 2008), 303, 309.

78 Andreeff, "Royal roots," 25.

79 "Stampede Queen will wear bright Western costume," *CH*, Jul 5, 1947.

80 "Greatest Stampede opens," *CH*, Jul 7, 1947.

81 "First Queen receives her crown," *Albertan*, Jul 9, 1947.

82 "Foothills Footnotes," *ACT Magazine*, Aug 1947.

83 "Queen attends rodeo," *Cardston News*, Jul 24, 1947.

84 "Miss Doreen Richardson, Queen of the Calgary Stampede," in Glenbow Library newspaper clipping file "Calgary Exhibition and Stampede – Stampede Queens etc." (hereafter Glenbow clipping file), ca. Jul 1947.

85 "Stampede Queen going to U.S.," *CH*, Sep 9, 1947.

86 "Your 1961 – 15th annual Stampede Queen contestants," Glenbow clipping file, ca. May, 1961.

87 "Attention service clubs and community organizations," *CH*, Feb 14, 1948.

88 "Help elect your favorite!" Glenbow clipping file, ca. May 1948.

89 "City Clerk to count Stampede Queen ballots," *CH*, Jun 19, 1948.

90 "Feature attraction at the cowboy ball," *CH*, Jul 14, 1944.

91 "Help elect your favorite!" Glenbow clipping file, ca. May 1948.

92 "Calgary Stampede Queen to be selected by tally," *Edmonton Journal*, Jun 4, 1948.

93 Ibid.

94 "Colorful film version of Stampede," *CH*, Jun 7, 1948; "Queens parade on chuckwagon," *CH*, Jun 18, 1948.

95 "The Stampede Queen," *ACT Magazine*, Jul 1949.

96 "Hi, Pardner!" Glenbow clipping file, ca. May 1949.

97 "The Stampede Queen," *ACT Magazine*, Jul 1949.

98 "Stampede Queen result confirmed," *CH*, Jun 20, 1949.

99 "Mrs. Merle Stier wins Stampede Queen title," *CH*, Jun 16, 1949; "The Stampede Queen," *ACT Magazine*, Jul 1949.

100 "Mrs. Merle Stier wins," *CH*, Jun 16, 1949

101 Frank Dabbs, *Branded by the Wind: The life and times of Bill Herron* (Calgary: Marjorie A. Herron, 2001), 170.

102 Gray, *A Brand of Its Own*, 124.

103 "Stampede Queen title won by Mrs. M. Stier," *Albertan*, Jun 16, 1949.

104 "1949 Stampede under way," *CH*, Jul 11, 1949; "Record crowd sees parade," *Albertan*, Jul 12, 1949.

105 "1949 Stampede under way," *CH*, Jul 11, 1949.

106 Inez Melby Shaver, interview with author, Feb 5, 2013.

107 Naomi Barenholtz, "Debits and credits," *CH*, Jul 15, 1949.

108 "Foothills Flares," *ACT Magazine*, Aug 1949.

109 Ibid.

CHAPTER 3, 1950–1953

110 Gray, *A Brand of Its Own*, 131, 144.

111 Kennedy, *Calgary Stampede Story*, 1.

112 Gray, *A Brand of Its Own*, 136–137.

113 "Stampede Queen event is boon to charity," *CH*, Jun 16, 1954.

114 "Miss Calgary Stampede contest," Glenbow clipping file, ca. May 1950.

115 "Foothills Flares," *ACT Magazine*, Jul 1950.

116 Eileen Beckner Lockwood, interview with author, Nov 29, 2012.

117 "Busy week scheduled for Stampede Queen," *CH*, Jul 6, 1950.

118 Foran, "More than partners," 153, 155, 166–167.

119 "Ridpath Hotel dedication seen by several hundred," *Spokane Daily Chronicle*, Apr 5, 1952.

120 "Mrs. June Dewhirst," *Saskatoon Star-Phoenix*, Jun 4, 1957.

121 "Windsor Park 'Queen' to reign at Stampede," *CH*, Jun 21, 1951.

122 "Stampede Queen draws winning ticket for kin," *CH*, Jul 11, 1951.

123 "Corral Calls," *ACT Magazine* Aug 1951.

124 "Calgary Queen to be feted," *CH*, Jun 12, 1952.

125 Sherry Moore Bronfman, interview with author, Oct 27, 2012.

126 "Stampede Queen Sherry Moore," *CH*, Jul 12, 1952.

127 "Queen stars in street dance," *CH*, Jul 9, 1952.

128 "Heap big time for all: Stampede Queen Sherry Moore and Sarcee Chief" *CH*, Jul 8, 1952.

129 "Stampede Queen event is boon to charity," *CH*, Jun 16, 1954.

130 "Cochrane ranch girl 1953 Stampede Queen," *CH*, Jun 24, 1953.

131 Karla Reinhard, "Former Stampede Queen, Edith Edge enjoys 'the ranch life,'" *Cochrane Eagle*, Apr 4, 2012.

132 "Cochrane ranch girl," *CH*, Jun 24, 1953.

133 "All eyes were on Edith Edge of Cochrane," *CH*, Jul 6, 1953.

134 "1953 Stampede Queen made Indian Princess," *CH*, Jul 17, 1953.

135 "Cochrane ranch girl," *CH*, Jun 24, 1953.

136 "Stampede Queen wins Las Vegas dream trip," *CH*, Jul 8, 1953.

137 "LasVegasLynn," "The Fabulous Flamingo Hotel History in the 1950s," *Classic Las Vegas* (blog), Sep 23, 2007, accessed Jul 28, 2013, http://is.gd/tvRCkk.

138 "Stampede Queen wins Las Vegas dream trip," *CH*, Jul 8, 1953.

139 Burbick, *Rodeo Queens*, 108.

140 "Stampede Queen back from Hollywood trip," *CH*, Nov 13, 1953.

141 "Stampede 'sweetheart' leaves for Hollywood," *CH*, Nov 2, 1953.

CHAPTER 4, 1954

142 "Corral Calls," *ACT Magazine*, Feb 1954.

143 Ibid., Apr 1954.

144 Burbick, *Rodeo Queens*, 86

145 Susan Joudrey, "The Expectations of a Queen: Identity and race politics in the Calgary Stampede," c. 7 in *The West and Beyond: New Perspectives on an Imagined Region*, Alvin Finkel et al., eds. (Edmonton: AU Press, 2010), 137.

146 Evelyn Eagle Speaker Locker, interview with author, Apr 6, 2012.

147 "Indian Princess in contest," *CH*, Apr 17, 1954.

148 Gentile, "Queen of the Maple Leaf," 97–98.

149 Locker, interview.

150 Joudrey, "Expectations of a Queen," 140.

151 CSA, Board and Executive Minutes, CS.99.106, Box 1, Minute Book No. 2, Minutes, Apr 8, 1954.

152 Joudrey, "Expectations of a Queen," 139.

153 Locker, interview.

154 CSA, Minutes, Apr 8, 1954.

155 "Thousands jam roads as new theatre opens," *CH*, Jul 17, 1953.

156 "Tonight only! Special Indian Tribal ceremony," *CH*, Apr 22, 1954.

157 "Tribes adopt Indian Princess," *Albertan*, Apr 23, 1954.

158 Locker, interview.

159 "First time in history of Western show: Indian girl is voted 1954 Stampede Queen," *CH*, Jun 22, 1954.

160 Ibid.

161 Burbick, *Rodeo Queens*, 102–104.

162 Locker, interview.

163 Glenbow Archives, Philip H. Godsell fonds, M-433-71, Godsell to Mike Eagle Speaker, Jan 5, 1955.

164 "She should wear her native dress," *CH*, Jun 25, 1954.

165 "Princess Wapiti's dress," *CH*, Jun 25, 1954.

166 "Wapiti costume debated," *CH*, Jun 28, 1954.

167 "During Stampede week: Indian Queen to wear native costume twice," *CH*, Jun 29, 1954.

168 "Not part way: Indian dress all week," *CH*, Jun 29, 1954.

169 DAR, William D. Dowell and Harry Hutchcroft, letters to the editor, *CH*, Jun 29, 1954.

170 Philip G. Godsell, "The queen's dress," *CH*, Jun 30, 1954.

171 Joudrey, "Expectations of a queen," 145–146.

172 John Freeborn, "1954's Miss (Poor-little-mixed-up) Calgary Stampede," editorial cartoon, *Albertan*, Jul 3, 1954.

173 Joudrey, "Expectations of a queen," 147.

174 "Stampede Queen's costume settled," *Albertan*, Jul 3, 1954.

175 W.G. Cochrane, "The ACT viewpoint," *CH*, Jul 3, 1954.

176 "Stampede Queen's costume settled," *Albertan*, Jul 3, 1954.

177 Locker, interview.

178 "Indian Princess gets beautiful new costume," *Albertan*, Jul 3, 1954.

179 "Many thanks," *Albertan*, Jul 5, 1954.

180 "A triumphal appearance," *Albertan*, Jul 6, 1954.

181 "Calgarians on Monday saw Princess Wapiti," *CH*, Jul 6, 1954.

182 "Big moment for Indian maiden," *Albertan*, Jul 8, 1954.

183 "This is one of the proudest moments of my life," *CH*, Jul 7, 1954.

184 "Wapiti to visit Las Vegas," *CH*, Jul 7, 1954.

185 "Stampede Queen leaves for U.S. goodwill tour," *CH*, May 4, 1955.

186 Locker, interview.

187 "Wins job on merit," *Albertan*, Jun 6, 1955.

188 Joudrey, "Expectations of a Queen," 149.

CHAPTER 5, 1955-1958

189 Gray, *A Brand of Its Own*, 137.

190 Ibid., 139.

191 Foran, "The Stampede in historical context," in *Icon, Brand, Myth*, 8.

192 Gray, *A Brand of Its Own*, 139–140.

193 "Vote for your favorite candidate," Glenbow clipping file, ca. May 1955.

194 "Gruelling grind for Queen candidates," *CH*, May 26, 1955.

195 "Ponoka girl wins crown," *Albertan*, Jun 22, 1955.

196 "Ponoka girl's Stampede victory 'like a dream,'" *CH*, Jun 22, 1955.

197 "Gruelling grind," *CH*, May 26, 1955.

198 Rosemary Wood, "Calgary Stampede Queen prepares for gala week," *CH*, Jul 9, 1955.

199 "Ponoka girl's Stampede victory," *CH*, Jun 22, 1955.

200 Wood, "Queen prepares," *CH*, Jul 9, 1955.

201 Ibid.

202 "Gruelling grind," *CH*, May 26, 1955.

203 "Pert and pretty," *Albertan*, Jun 20, 1956.

204 Don Cumming, "'For pete's sake!' said Queen Shirley," *Albertan*, Jun 21, 1956.

205 Ibid.

206 "Busy Stampede schedule for Queen Shirley Willock," *CH*, Jul 6, 1956.

207 Shirley Willock Bertoli, interview with author, Oct 18, 2012.

208 "Allergy nearly bests Miss Stampede," *CH*, May 28, 1957.

209 "To Las Vegas," unidentified clipping in scrapbook kept by Shirley Willock Bertoli, ca. May 1957.

210 "10th Queen now chosen," *CH*, Jun 26, 1957.

211 "July means Stampede," *Albertan*, ca. Jul 2, 1957.

212 Joy Van Wagner, "Stampede snapshots," *CH*, Jul 12, 1957.

213 "130,000 jam city streets for big parade spectacle," *CH*, Jul 8, 1957.

214 "10th Queen now chosen," *CH*, Jun 26, 1957.

215 "Second-day show figures decline," *CH*, Jul 10, 1957.

216 "Calgary Calls," *ACT Magazine*, Jan 1958.

217 "ACT gives $12,113," *CH*, Dec 8, 1958.

218 Van Wagner, "Stampede snapshots," *CH*, Jul 12, 1957; "12th Stampede Queen wins in race of 33," *CH*, Jul 5, 1958.

219 Van Wagner, "Stampede snapshots," *CH*, Jul 12, 1957.

220 "'China doll' ends her Calgary reign," *Star Weekly*, Jul 4, 1959.

221 For example, "Calgary's 1958 Stampede Queen," *Saskatoon Star-Phoenix*, Jun 27, 1958; "Chinese Rodeo Queen," *Montreal Gazette*, Jun 28, 1958.

222 "12th Stampede Queen wins in race of 33," *CH*, Jul 5, 1958.

223 Van Wagner, "Stampede snapshots," *CH*, Jul 12, 1957.

224 Henderson, interview.

225 Peter Degenstein, interview with author, Oct 18, 2012..

226 Hazel Walters, "Parade criticized," *CH*, Jul 14, 1958.

227 "'China doll,'" *Star Weekly*, Jul 4, 1959.

228 "Julie Akkerman 13th Stampede Queen," *CH*, Jul 4, 1959.

229 "Parade of queens," *CH*, May 19, 1959.

230 "Sports car replaces phone booth," unidentified clipping in scrapbook kept by Margaret Powell Clark, ca. May 1959.

231 "Julie Akkerman Stampede Queen," *CH*, Jun 25, 1959.

232 "Mayor's daughter: Julie reigns as Stampede Queen," *Albertan*, Jun 25, 1959.

233 "Rodeo Queens' receive briefing," *CH*, Oct 5, 1959.

234 "Let's help make this a 'winning' smile!" unidentified clipping in Clark scrapbook, ca. May 1959.

235 Margaret Powell Clark, interview with author, Oct 23, 2012.

236 "Life the same despite contest," *CH*, Mar 27, 1963.

237 Clark, interview; "An evening to remember," unidentified clipping in Clark scrapbook, ca. Jul 1959.

238 "Candidates to appear 'on stage,'" *Albertan*, May 24, 1960.

239 "Calgary Calls," *ACT Magazine*, Jul 1960.

240 "Candidates to appear 'on stage,'" *Albertan*, May 24, 1960; "Your 1961 – 15th annual Stampede Queen contestants," Glenbow clipping file, ca. May, 1961.

241 Margot Turney DeMeo, interview with author, Dec 9, 2012.

242 "Tartans and kilts form colorful contrast to debutantes' frothy white gowns at ball," *CH*, Jun 4, 1955; "Hello again, Margot!" *Ottawa Citizen*, Jun 25, 1960.

243 "Players rehearse English comedy," *CH*, Mar 22, 1960.

244 "Calgary Calls," *ACT Magazine*, Aug 1960.

245 "City girl gets crown of Stampede Queen," *CH*, Jun 29, 1960.

246 DeMeo, interview.

247 Gray, *A Brand of Its Own*, 146.

248 Ibid.

249 Foran, "The Stampede in historical context," in *Icon, Brand, Myth*, 7–9.

250 Gray, *A Brand of Its Own*, 146.

251 Jane Croft, "Former queen departs," *South Side Mirror*, Jul 18, 1963.

252 "Calgary folk to be aboard initial flight," *Spokane Daily Chronicle*, May 16, 1960.

253 Dave Cobb, "15,000 watch as airliner brings jet age to Calgary," *CH*, Jan 16, 1961.

254 "Odds listed, hotel lobbies cleared," *CH*, Nov 23, 1960.

255 John Hopkins, "Stampede Queen true Calgary envoy," *CH*, Apr 9, 1977.

256 "Your 1961 – 15th annual Stampede Queen contestants," Glenbow clipping file, ca. May, 1961.

257 "Calgary Calls," *ACT Magazine*, Jan 1961.

258 "Calgary Calls," *ACT Magazine*, Aug 1961.

259 Pat Campbell, "Stampede Queen for 1961 accomplished horsewoman," Glenbow clipping file, ca. Jun 1961.

260 Marie Sharpe O'Bertos, interview with author, Nov 15, 2012.

261 "Marie Sharpe Queen," *Albertan*, Jun 29, 1961.

262 "Saddle trip await[s] '62 Stampede Queen," *CH*, Mar 13, 1962.

263 "Calgary Calls," *ACT Magazine*, Jun 1962.

264 "'62 Queen judging Thursday," *CH*, Jun 27 1962.

265 Bill Stavdal, "Cowboy's daughter to reign as Jubilee Stampede Queen," *CH*, Jun 29, 1962.

266 Donna Thomson Brasso, interview with author, Jan 8, 2013.

267 "Black Diamond girl is Stampede Queen," *CH*, Jul 7, 1962.

268 Gray, *A Brand of Its Own*, 149.

269 Lawrie Kergan, "Hectic preparations are over; now the fun is about to start," *CH*, Jul 7, 1962.

270 Brasso, interview.

271 Ibid.

272 CSA, CS.99.106, Box 2, Minute Book No. 3, Minutes, Feb 26, 1963.

273 "Ticket sales, not ability to decide Stampede Queen," *CH*, Apr 1, 1963.

274 Ibid.

275 Degenstein, interview.

276 Denny Layzell, "Queen Contest aids many organizations," *CH*, May 4, 1963.

277 Degenstein, interview

278 "Calgarian named Stampede Queen," *CH*, Jul 4, 1963.

279 Frances Swann Anderson, interview with author, Nov 19, 2012.

280 Bonnie McCachen, "Stampede activities keep Queen busy," *CH*, Jul 11, 1963.

281 Johnny Hopkins, "Johnny Hopkins… reports," *CH*, Apr 15, 1964.

282 Anderson, interview.

283 Hopkins, "Johnny Hopkins… reports," 1964.

CHAPTER 7, 1964–1966

284 Degenstein, interview.

285 CSA, Board and Executive Minutes, CS.99.106, Box 2, Minute Book No. 3, Letter from ACT Calgary Club attached to Minutes, Jan 31, 1964.

286 CSA, CS.99.106, Box 2, Minute Book No. 3, Minutes, Feb 6, 1964.

287 Ibid., Mar 19, 1964.

288 "Stampede Queen rules changed: Popularity tickets out," *CH*, Mar 26, 1964.

289 "1964 ACT Stampede Queen contest: NO ticket sales," *CH*, Mar 30, 1964.

290 Ibid.

291 "Calgary Club," *ACT Magazine*, Apr 1964.

292 Robert Donahue, "Wild replies fail to unfreeze poker faces of 'Queen' judges," *CH*, Apr 24, 1964.

293 Ibid.

294 Gray, James. *A Brand of Its Own*, 154, 156.

295 "Stampede expects 18 Queen entries," *CH*, Mar 30, 1965.

296 "Stampede Queen candidates demonstrate riding style," *CH*, Apr 12, 1965.

297 "Horsemanship key to Stampede Queen," *CH*, May 7, 1964.

298 "Queen contestants," *CH*, Apr 22, 1963.

299 Johnny Hopkins, "Johnny Hopkins… reports," *CH*, Apr 15, 1964.

300 "Winner of a number of horse show and girl rodeo trophies," *Albertan*, May 11, 1964; Doug Sagi, "'Wise Patch' raised Sharon to 1964 Stampede Queen," *CH*, May 12, 1964.

301 Gwenda Marshall Davies, interview with author, Nov 22, 2012.

302 Linda Curtis, "Stampede Queen has attractive outfits," *Albertan*, Jul 6, 1964.

303 "Queen couture: The fashion and influence of Calgary Stampede Queens through the decades," *Western Horse Review*, Jul–Aug 2012, 28–33.

304 CSA, CS.99.106, Box 2, Minute Book No. 3, Minutes, Feb 25, 1965.

305 Ibid; "Calgary Club," *ACT Magazine*, Aug 1965.

306 Marilynn Hehr, "Didsbury girl, 20, Stampede Queen," *CH*, May 10, 1965.

307 "Stampede Queen candidates demonstrate riding style," *CH*, Apr 12, 1965.

308 Ibid.

309 CSA, CS.99.106, Box 2, Minute Book No. 3, Minutes, Oct 19, 1966.

310 Frank Hutton, "180,000 watch parade kick off Stampede," *Edmonton Journal*, Jul 5, 1965.

311 "Calgary Club," *ACT Magazine*, Apr 1966.

312 Ibid., May 1966.

313 Ibid., Jul 1966.

314 CSA, CS.99.106, Box 2, Minute Book No. 3, Minutes, Oct 19, 1966.

315 "Calgary Club," *ACT Magazine*, Oct 1966.

316 CSA, Committee Minutes, CS.99.106, Box 3, Queen Committee, Minutes, Dec 14, 1966.

317 "Miss Stampede crowning set for last day of horse show," *CH*, Mar 1, 1966.

318 Ibid.

319 Degenstein, interview.

320 "Miss Stampede crowning," *CH*, Mar 1, 1966.

321 "Capital seeks Stampede title," *CH*, Apr 4, 1966.

322 "Edmonton girl 'Queen' finalist," *CH*, Apr 23, 1966.

323 "Stampede Queen," *CH*, May 13, 1966.

324 "1966 Stampede Queen," *CH*, May 9, 1966.

325 "Miss Stampede moving here," *CH*, May 20, 1966.

326 "Young oil steno is Queen of 1966 Stampede," *CH*, Jul 9, 1966.

327 Olive Elliott, "Calgary getting over Miss Stampede shock," *Edmonton Journal*, Jul 14, 1966.

328 "Calgary's rose float fund nearing $15,000 objective," *CH*, Dec 24, 1966.

329 CSA, CS.99.106, Box 2, Minute Book No. 3, Minutes, Nov 2, 1966.

CHAPTER 8, 1967–1969

330 Foran, "More than partners," in *Icon, Brand, Myth*, 151.

331 Joan Plastow Langford, interview with author, Jan 13, 2013.

332 Tara Wesner and Whitney Wilkie, eds., *The Queens' Alumni Memory Book: Celebrating Stampede's Centennial in 2012* (Calgary: Heritage Makers, 2012), "Honorary Associates."

333 CSA, CS.99.106, Box 3, Queen Committee, Minutes, Dec 14, 1966.

334 "Stampede new sponsor for 'Stampede Queen,'" *CH*, Feb 11, 1967; "Stampede Queen contest," *CH*, Feb 18, 1967.

335 CSA, CS.99.106, Box 3, Queen Committee, Minutes, Dec 14, 1966.

336 Degenstein, interview.

337 Langford, interview.

338 CSA, CS.99.106, Box 3, Queen Committee, Minutes, Dec 14, 1966.

339 Johnny Hopkins, "Johnny Hopkins," *CH*, Feb 25, 1972.

340 CSA, CS.99.106, Box 3, Queen Committee, Minutes, Dec 14, 1966.

341 Ibid., Minutes, May 1, 1967.

342 Ibid., Minutes, Feb 9, 1967.

343 Ibid., Minutes, Apr 4, 1967.

344 Ibid., Minutes, ca. Mar 1967.

345 Ibid., Minutes, Feb 9, 1967.

346 "Preliminary tests run for Queen candidates," *CH*, Apr 17, 1967.

347 Ibid.

348 CSA, CS.99.106, Box 3, Queen Committee, Minutes, May 1, 1967.

349 Edythe Humphrey, "'67 Stampede Queen crowned," *CH*, May 8, 1967.

350 Bonnie MacGregor Thompson, interview with author, Nov 27, 2012.

351 Ibid.

352 CSA, CS.99.106, Box 3, Queen Committee, Minutes, Dec 14, 1966.

353 Thompson, interview.

354 "Calgary Club," *ACT Magazine*, Apr 1967.

355 Cheryl Larson, "7 Stampede Queens recall old memories," *CH*, Apr 3, 1967.

356 Eva Reid, "Socially Speaking: Stampede socially," *Albertan*, Jul 15, 1967.

357 Don Thomas, "Alberta ropes hearts at Expo," *CH*, Oct 7, 1967.

358 CSA, CS.99.106, Box 2, Minute Book No. 3, Minutes, Nov 9, 1967.

359 CSA, CS.99.106, Box 3, Queen Committee, Minutes, Dec 14, 1966.

360 "Stampede royalty to be declared at March rodeo," *CH*, Jan 10, 1972.

361 "Stampede Queen entries close," *Albertan*, Mar 4, 1970.

362 Vern Simaluk, "Ranch-girl turned 'city slicker' likely to be Stampede Queen," *CH*, Mar 28, 1968.

363 CSA, CS.99.106, Box 2, Minute Book No. 3, Minutes, Feb 8, 1968.

364 Ibid., Minutes, Sep 10, 1968.

365 Gray, *A Brand of Its Own*, Appendix 1.

366 "Stampede is dream fulfilled for Calgary's Diane Leech," *CH*, Jul 2, 1968.

367 Arlene Weidner, interview with author, Nov 21, 2012; Thompson, interview.

368 Beth Raugust, "Western wear expert designs Queen's garb," *CH*, Jun 18, 1968.

369 "Queen's chaperone finds life hectic," *CH*, Jul 10, 1968.

370 Ibid.

371 Elaine Seskevich, "A day in the life of Stampede royalty," *CH*, Jul 10, 1970.

372 Weidner, interview.

373 Tom Keyser, "Well, we adored him once," *CH*, Mar 1, 1984.

374 "Grey Cup invasion set," *CH*, Nov 26, 1968.

375 CSA, CS.99.106, Box 3, Queen Committee, Minutes, May 24, 1968.

376 "Stampede Queen aspirants sought," *CH*, Jan 25, 1969.

377 "What it means to be the Stampede Queen," *CH*, Jan 25, 1969.

378 Dave Mabell, "She's Queen for a year, but busy reign soon over," *Albertan*, ca. Jul 1969.

379 "Busy timetable for Stampede Queen," *CH*, Jul 7, 1970.

380 Langford, interview.

381 "Stampede Queen, Princesses work hard for royal treatment," *CH*, Jul 3, 1969.

382 Lynne Rach, "Miss Stampede spreads word – with feeling," *CH*, Feb 4, 1970.

CHAPTER 9, 1970–1974

383 Gray, *A Brand of Its Own*, Appendix 1.

384 Margrit Eichler and Marie Lavigne, "Women's movement," in *The Canadian Encyclopedia*, Historica-Dominion Institute, 2012 www.thecanadianencyclopedia.com/articles/womens-movement, accessed Feb 23, 2013.

385 Naomi Lakritz, "After turmoil of 1960s, the '70s were groovy," in "100 Years of Calgary Stampede, Part VII: The 1970s," *CH*, Jun 13, 2012, CC20–21.

386 Foran, "The Stampede in historical context," in *Icon, Brand, Myth*, 10–11.

387 Edythe Humphrey, "Stampede Queen contest now open," *CH*, Feb 10, 1970.

388 Linda Curtis, "Queen's reign nears end," *Albertan*, Jan 18, 1972.

389 Seskevitch, "A day in the life," *CH*, Jul 10, 1970.

390 "Busy time-table for Stampede Queen," *CH*, Jul 7, 1970.

391 Seskevich, "A day in the life."

392 "Choosing the reigning monarch is a weighty matter indeed," *CH*, Mar 15, 1971.

393 Leslie MacDonald Crowe, interview with author, Nov 21, 2012.

394 Monica Andreeff, "Royal roots," *Avenue Magazine*, Jul/Aug 2001, 27.

395 "Stampede royalty," *CH*, Jul 8, 1971.

396 Andreeff, "Royal roots," 27, 29.

397 "Stampede rodeo king wanted," *CH*, Jul 16, 1971.

398 CSA, Board and Executive Minutes, CS.99.106, Box 2, Minute Book No. 5, Minutes, Oct 20, 1971.

399 Nancy Bissell, "For Stampede royalty, humor's just a miscue away," *CH*, Jun 24, 1984.

400 Donna Thomson Brasso, "History of the Calgary Stampede Queens' Alumni," unpublished manuscript, 1996.

401 CSA, Board and Executive Minutes, CS.99.106, Box 2, Minute Book No. 5, Minutes, Nov 8, 1971.

402 Ibid.

403 Eva Reid, "Eavesdrop with Eva," *Albertan*, Jan 14, 1972; Linda Curtis, "Where are all the Queens?" *Albertan*, May 25, 1972.

404 CS Queens' Alumni Committee, "Queens' Alumni Association History," n.d. www.stampedequeensalumni.com (Oct 25, 2012).

405 CSA, Committee Minutes, CS.99.106, Box 10, Women's World (Creative Living) Committee, Minutes, Dec 13, 1978.

406 CS Queens' Alumni, "Association history."

407 "Stampede royalty to be declared at March rodeo," *CH*, Jan 10, 1972.

408 Johnny Hopkins, "Johnny Hopkins," *CH*, Feb 25, 1972.

409 Ibid., Jul 14, 1972.

410 Crowe, interview.

411 Elaine Brown, "The parade's over for another queen," *CH*, Jan 26, 1973.

412 "Stampede Queen contestants halved," *CH*, Feb 19, 1973.

413 "Stampede hopefuls show equestrian skills," *CH*, Mar 12, 1973.

414 Philip Cohen, "Miss Pot o' Gold," *Albertan*, Jul 10, 1972.

415 "Blonde rodeo competitor named Stampede Queen," *CH*, Mar 26, 1973.

416 Joan Horne Sveen, interview with author, Dec 14, 2012.

417 Sveen, interview.

418 "Stampede seeking queen, 2 princesses," *CH*, ca. Jan 1974.

419 Happy Barlow, interview with author, Dec 15, 2012.

420 Happy Barlow, "Queens uphold more than Stampede's image," *CH*, Apr 18, 1988.

421 Barlow, interview.

CHAPTER 10, 1975–1979

422 "Queens for a year," *CH*, Mar 24, 1975.

423 Barry Nelson, "'75 Stampede Queen could be a prince," *CH*, Nov 16, 1974.

424 "Calgary's young men fail to make Queen bid," *CH*, Jan 17, 1975.

425 Bob Shiels, "Queen recruiting begins," *CH*, Dec 11 1975.

426 Barbara Howard Denoon, interview with author, Nov 20, 2012.

427 Ibid.; Foran, "More than partners," in *Icon, Brand, Myth*, 164.

428 Sveen, interview.

429 "There's a world of excitement for you as the 1975 Calgary Stampede Queen" (advertisement), *CH*, Dec 14, 1974.

430 "There's a world of excitement for you as the 1976 Calgary Stampede Queen" (advertisement), *CH*, Jan 3, 1976.

431 CSA, CS.99.106, Box 2, Minute Book No. 3, Minutes, Feb 8, 1968.

432 Denoon, interview.

433 CSA, Committee Minutes, CS.99.106, Box 10, Queen Committee, Minutes, Nov 21, 1979.

434 Ibid.

435 Joan Plastow Langford, interview with author, Jan 13, 2013.

436 Cindy Morres Sergerie, interview with author, Dec 13, 2012.

437 Pat Pearson, interview with author, Feb 4, 2013.

438 Catherine Butlin, "Western gear that is fit for a queen," *CH*, Jul 12, 1979.

439 Linda Curtis, "Royalty didn't mind losing sleep," *Albertan*, Jul 15, 1979.

440 Calgary CSA, CS.99.106, Box 10, Queen Committee, Listing prepared by Margaret Fraser, 1976.

441 Shiels, "Queen recruiting begins."

442 "Horse-loving Irricana girl, 20, chosen 1964 Stampede Queen," *CH*, May 11, 1964; CSA, CS.99.106, Box 3, Queen Committee, Minutes, May 24, 1968.

443 Sandy Young Tidswell, interview with author, Dec 15, 2012; Pearson, interview.

444 CSA, CS.99.106, Box 10, Queen Committee, Information for judging interviews, 1976.

445 Ibid.

446 John Hopkins, "John Hopkins," *CH*, Mar 26, 1976.

447 Sergerie, interview.

448 "Queen couture," *Western Horse Review* (Jul–Aug 2012), 30.

449 Sergerie, interview.

450 CSA, CS.99.106, Box 10, Queen Committee, Minutes, Sep 27, 1976.

451 Pearson, interview.

452 "Hint of summer: Stampede Queen search launched," *CH*, Jan 6, 1977.

453 John Hopkins, "Stampede Queen true Calgary envoy," *CH*, Apr 9, 1977.

454 "Stampede caravan to visit big shopping centres," *CH*, Jul 7, 1977.

455 "Andrew shys Stampede date," *CH*, Jul 9, 1977.

456 "Prince told to 'shut up,'" *Montreal Gazette*, Jul 11, 1977.

457 Pearson, interview.

458 CSA, CS.99.106, Box 10, Queen Committee, Minutes, Jan 10, 1978.

459 Eva Reid, "Eavesdrop with Eva: Sweethearts of the Stampede," *Albertan*, Jul 13, 1978.

460 CSA, CS.99.106, Box 10, Queen Committee, Minutes, Apr 17, 1978.

461 Linda Curtis, "The end of the trail," *Albertan*, Feb 4, 1979.

462 Ibid.

463 Ibid.

464 Peter Calamai, "Prince Andrew 'so-so' at disco," *Ottawa Citizen*, Aug 8, 1978.

465 Linda Curtis, "Taking the royal ride," *Albertan*, Jul 15, 1978; Curtis, "The end of the trail."

466 Curtis, "The end of the trail."

467 Curtis, "Taking the royal ride."

468 CSA, CS.99.106, Box 10, Queen Committee, Minutes, Apr 17, 1978.

469 Ibid.

470 Ibid., Jun 28, 1978.

471 Bissell, "Humor's just a miscue away."

472 Wesner and Wilkie, *Memory Book*, "1979."

473 Bissell, "Humor's just a miscue away."

474 CS Queens' Alumni Committee, "History of the Crowns," n.d., accessed Oct 25, 2012, www.stampedequeensalumni.com.

475 CSA, CS.99.106, Box 10, Queen Committee, Minutes, Oct 11, 1977; Jan 10, Apr 17, 1979.

476 Bernice Huxtable, "Royalty rides out," *CH*, Jul 10, 1984.

CHAPTER 11, 1980–1985

477 Valerie Fortney, "Wild Ride: Decade brought great highs, lows," in "100 Years of Calgary Stampede, Part VIII: The 1980s," *CH*, Jun 13, 2012, Special Keepsake Edition, DD3–5.

478 Foran, "More than partners," in *Icon, Brand, Myth*, 149–152, 166–167.

479 Colin S. Campbell, "The Stampede: Cowtown's sacred cow," in *Stampede City: Power and politics in the West*, ed. Chuck Reasons (Toronto: Between the Lines, 1984), 106–113 passim.

480 Dave Margoshes, "Search for the Stampede Queen narrows to five contenders: Judges seek salesperson for the city," *CH*, Feb 25, 1980.

481 CSA, CS.99.106, Box 10, Queen Committee, Minutes, Apr 17, 1978.

482 Ibid., Contest brochure, 1981.

483 "Sweethearts of the rodeo," *CH*, Feb 9, 1980.

484 Margoshes, "Search for the Stampede Queen."

485 CSA, CS.99.106, Box 10, Queen Committee, Minutes, Apr 30, 1980.

486 Linda Curtis, "Royalty has no time for horse-play," *Albertan*, Jul 13, 1980.

487 Brasso, "History."

488 CSA, CS.99.106, Box 10, Queen Committee, Contest brochure, 1981.

489 Ibid., Minutes, Jan 4, 1981.

490 Ibid., Contest brochure, 1982.

491 Ibid., Minutes, Jan 4, 1981.

492 Ibid., Minutes, Nov 10, 1986.

493 Ibid., Minutes, Dec 13, 1989.

494 Curtis, "Royalty has no time."

495 CSA, CS.99.106, Box 10, Queen Committee, Contest brochure, 1981.

496 Ibid., Minutes, Jan 4, 1981.

497 Ibid., Minutes, Nov 16, 1983.

498 Ibid., Minutes, Apr 5, 1984.

499 "A tip of the hat," *CH*, Mar 23, 1981; "They shoe horses, don't they?" *Calgary Sun*, Stampede ed., 1981.

500 Cathy Robinson Ladiges, interview with author, Nov 27, 2012.

501 Ibid.

502 Barb Penner Colborne, interview with author, Nov 18, 2012.

503 Opinions expressed to author during interviews with former Stampede royalty, Mar 17, 2012–Feb 5, 2013.

504 Joanne Blain, "Only in Calgary, you say: Britain gets taste of Stampede," *CH*, Jul 2, 1981.

505 CSA, CS.99.106, Box 10, Queen Committee, Minutes, Jun 16, 1981.

506 Ibid., Minutes, Nov 21, Dec 11, 1979.

507 Ibid., Minutes, May 11, 1981.

508 Ibid., Minutes, Dec 9, 1981.

509 Ibid., Minutes, Dec 11, 1979.

510 Langford, interview with author, Jan 13, 2013.

511 CSA, CS.99.106, Box 10, Queen Committee, Minutes, May 12, 1988.

512 CSA, Committee Minutes, CS.99.138, Box 8, Queen Committee, Minutes, Apr 10, Jul 22, 1991.

513 Pearson, interview.

514 Opinions expressed to author during interviews with former Stampede royalty from Mar 17, 2012, to Feb 5, 2013.

515 CSA, CS.99.106, Box 10, Queen Committee, Notes by Margaret Fraser, Mar 21, 1983.

516 Ibid., Minutes, Jan 15, 1980.

517 Ibid., Notes by Margaret Fraser, Mar 21, 1983.

518 Phyllis Leppa, "The hat does fit," *Alberta Rural Month*, Jul 1983, 14–20.

519 CSA, CS.99.106, Box 10, Queen Committee, Minutes, Oct 28, 1981.

520 Kate Zimmerman, "Stampede royalty gets fitted for fete," *CH*, Jul 8, 1982; Bernice Huxtable, "Royalty rides out," *CH*, Jul 10, 1984.

521 CSA, CS.99.106, Box 10, Queen Committee, Budget, 1975–1976.

522 Ibid., Minutes, Sep 23, 1981.

523 Zimmerman, "Stampede royalty."

524 CSA, CS.99.106, Box 10, Queen Committee, Minutes, Nov 30, 1982.

525 Zimmerman, "Stampede royalty."

526 CSA, CS.99.106, Box 10, Queen Committee, Minutes, Oct 28, Dec 15, 1981.

527 Ibid., Minutes, Nov 30, 1982.

528 Leppa, "The hat does fit."

529 Nancy Bissell, "Rigorous days ahead for Stampede royalty," *CH*, Jul 7, 1983.

530 Dena Townsend, "Days long but exciting for past Stampede royalty," *CH*, Jul 5, 1984.

531 Richard Hoffman, "Virtuous single cowgirls sought," *CH*, Jan 9, 1984.

532 Ibid.

533 John Howse, "Mamas should let their daughters grow up to be cowgirls," *CH*, Jan 20, 1984.

534 Judy Walters, "As long as he saw her ride in Stampede Parade," Glenbow clipping file, n.p., n.d. [ca. Jul 1984].

535 Dena Townsend, "Little rest for Stampede royalty," *CH*, Jun 24, 1984.

536 Walters, "As long as he saw her ride."

537 Ibid.

538 "Pat Brown, 1984 Stampede Queen," *CH Magazine*, Jun 30, 1985.

539 Ibid.

540 Huxtable, "Royalty rides out."

541 CSA, CS.99.106, Box 10, Queen Committee, Minutes, Mar 12, 1980.

542 Huxtable, "Royalty rides out."

543 CSA, CS.99.106, Box 10, Queen Committee, Minutes, Jun 12, 1984.

544 "Queen couture," *Western Horse Review*, Jul–Aug 2012, 31.

545 Huxtable, "Royalty rides out."

546 CSA, CS.99.106, Box 10, Queen Committee, Minutes, Aug 18, 1987.

547 CSA, CS.99.138, Box 8, Queen Committee, Minutes, May 31, Jun 25, 1990.

548 Ibid., Minutes, Nov 21, 1979; Jan 27, Mar 27, 1987.

549 CSA, Committee Minutes, CS.99.106, Box 1, Queen Committee, Entry form, ca. 1985.

550 Shiels, "Queen recruiting begins"; CSA, CS.99.106, Box 2, Minute Book No. 3, Minutes, Dec 22, 1966.

551 CS Royalty Committee, "2013 Calgary Stampede Queen and Princess Application Form," 2012, accessed Jul 26, 2012, http://corporate.calgarystampede.com/upload/media_element/32/01/2013_application_form.pdf.

552 Roman Cooney, "Stampede Queen is busy," *CH*, Jun 23, 1985.

CHAPTER 12, 1986–1989

553 Catherine Ford, "Stampede rules insulting," *CH*, Jan 23, 1986.

554 Catherine Ford, "Beauty covered in plastic," *CH*, Jun 13, 1983.

555 Catherine Ford, "Here's the law for cowboy cads," *CH*, Mar 20, 1984.

556 Foran, "The Stampede in historical context," in *Icon, Brand, Myth*, 10–11.

557 Monica Perchaluk, "Stampede trio more than beauty contest winners," *CH*, ca. Feb 1986.

558 Pearson, interview.

559 Banet-Weiser, *The Most Beautiful Girl*, 26, 38, 51.

560 Gentile, "Queen of the Maple Leaf," 103.

561 CSA, CS.99.106, Box 5, Queen Committee, Minutes, Apr 13, 1994.

562 Deborah Tetley, "Beneath the royal facade," *CH*, Jul 14, 2002.

563 "Stampede queen, princesses hard-working ambassadors," *CH Neighbours*, May 20–26, 1987.

564 CSA, CS.99.106, Box 10, Queen Committee, Budget questionnaire, ca. Jul 1986.

565 "Princesses at ease on horses," *CH*, Jul 2, 1987.

566 "Oakland Lassos Calgary Stampede Queen," San Francisco *Sun-Reporter*, Oct 23, 1987.

567 Holly Dunn, interview with author, Nov 19, 2012.

568 Ibid.

569 CSA, Board and Executive Minutes, CS.99.106, Box 5, Shannon File 5, Minutes, Jul 14, 1987.

570 CSA, CS.99.106, Box 5, Shannon File 5, Minutes, Oct 13, 1987.

571 Ibid.

572 Holly Dunn, interview.

573 Ibid.

574 "Stampede queen, princesses hard-working," *CH Neighbours*, May 20–26, 1987.

575 CSA, CS.99.106, Box 10, Queen Committee, Reports, Dec 2, 1987.

576 Dixon and Read, *Celebrating the Calgary Exhibition and Stampede*, 44.

577 "Rodeo Queen crowned," *CH*, Feb 26, 1988.

578 Laura Godwin Dunn, interview with author, Dec 14, 2012.

579 CSA, CS.99.106, Box 10, Queen Committee, Minutes, Nov 10, 1987.

580 Dena Townsend, "Queen and princesses hitch up their smiles," *CH*, Jun 30, 1988.

581 CSA, CS.99.106, Box 10, Queen Committee, Memo from Margaret Fraser, Jul 1988.

582 CSA, CS.99.138, Box 8, Queen Committee, Minutes, Feb 5, 1990.

583 Laura Dunn, interview.

584 CSA, CS.99.106, Box 10, Queen Committee, Minutes, Aug 30, 1988.

585 Catherine Ford, "Clinic churns out rodeo queens," *CH*, Mar 31, 1988.

586 Barlow, "Queens uphold more."

587 Shirley Willock Symonds, "Rodeo queens don't need more glitz," *CH*, Jun 5, 1988.

588 Pearson, interview.

589 Tammy Kneller (CS Indian Events Committee, Indian Princess Sub-Committee), Correspondence with author, Mar 13, 14, 2012.

590 CSA, Committee Minutes, CS.99.138, Box 4, Indian Events Committee, Minutes, Oct 21, 1987.

★

591 Ibid., Minutes, May 9, 1988.

592 CSA, CS.99.106, Box 10, Queen Committee, Memo from Indian Events Committee, ca. early Apr 1988.

593 CSA, CS.99.106, Box 5, Queen Committee, Memo, Apr 11, 1988.

594 CSA, CS.99.138, Box 4, Indian Events Committee, Memo, May 2, 1988.

595 Gentile, "Queen of the Maple Leaf," 95–102.

596 "Shy Sarcee girl is first Stampede Princess," *Albertan*, Jul 10, 1965.

597 Bernice Huxtable, "Indian princess pageant meaningful, elegant," *CH*, Jun 14, 1988.

598 CSA, CS.99.106, Box 5, Shannon File 5, Minutes, May 17, 1988.

599 Ibid.

600 Huxtable, "Indian princess pageant."

601 Ibid.

602 CSA, CS.99.106, Box 10, Queen Committee, Minutes, Aug 30, 1988.

603 CSA, CS.99.106, Box 5, Queen Committee, Minutes, Sep 20, 1988.

604 Townsend, "Queen and princesses."

605 CSA, CS.99.106, Box 5, Shannon File 5, Minutes, Nov 14, 1988.

606 CSA, Board and Executive Minutes, CS.99.106, Box 5, Shannon File 6, Minutes, Jan 17, 1989; CS.99.138, Box 8, Queen Committee, Minutes, Jun 25, 1991.

607 CSA, CS.99.106, Box 5, Shannon File 5, Minutes, Apr 7, 1987.

608 Wesner and Wilkie, *Memory Book*, "The Other Royal Trio."

609 Jennifer Worley, "Stampede Royalty," *Calgary Sun*, Jul 7, 1989.

610 CSA, CS.99.106, Box 10, Queen Committee, Minutes, Apr 18, 1988.

611 CSA, CS.99.106, Box 5, Shannon File 6, Minutes, Jan 10, 1989.

612 Mark Miller, "Feisty princess awaits big day," *Calgary Sun*, Jun 26, 1989; Chris Dawson, "Stampede Royalty," *CH*, Jul 14, 1989; Dena Townsend, "Wheelchair-bound princess won't be left on sidelines," *CH*, Jun 29, 1989.

613 CSA, CS.99.138, Box 8, Queen Committee, Minutes, Oct 19, 1989.

614 CSA, CS.99.106, Box 10, Queen Committee, Minutes, Aug 18, 1987; CS.99.138, Box 8, Queen Committee, Minutes, Jan 7, 1991.

CHAPTER 13, 1990–1994

615 CS Corporate Communications, "Chronological history of the Calgary Stampede," ca. 2009, accessed Mar 27, 2012, http://corporate.calgarystampede.com/about/stampede-history/chronological-history.html.

616 Anne Crawford, "Queens prepped in hazards on horseback," *CH*, Jul 5, 1990.

617 Ibid.

618 Ibid.

619 Ibid.

620 O'Bertos, interview.

621 Wesner and Wilkie, *Memory Book*, "Honorary Associates."

622 CSA, CS.99.138, Box 8, Queen Committee, Minutes, May 9, 1990.

623 CSA, Committee Minutes, CS.99.138, Box 2, Queen Committee, Minutes, Apr 6, 1992.

624 CSA, CS.99.138, Box 8, Queen Committee, Minutes, Jun 25, 1991.

625 Bernice Huxtable, "Indian princess's dress gesture of friendship," *CH*, Jul 11, 1989.

626 Lana Michelin, "Indian Village princess quits, claiming bias," *CH*, Jul 13, 1990.

627 Ibid.

628 Ibid.

629 Susan Mate and Sheldon Alberts, "Natives replaced AWOL princess," *CH*, Jul 14, 1990.

630 CSA, CS.99.138, Box 8, Queen Committee, Minutes, Aug 20, 1990.

631 CSA, CS.99.138, Box 2, Queen Committee, Minutes, May 20, 1992, May 3, 1993.

632 CSA, CS.99.138, Box 4, Indian Events Committee, Minutes, May 19, 1994; CSA, Committee Minutes, CS.99.106, Box 5, Queen Committee, Minutes, Sep 8, 1994.

633 CSA, CS.99.138, Box 4, Indian Events Committee, Minutes, Jun 4, 1996.

634 Ibid., Minutes, Sep 26, 1996.

635 Ibid., Minutes, Jan 10, 1990.

636 Ibid., Minutes, Sep 26, 1990.

637 CSA, CS.99.138, Box 2, Queen Committee, Minutes, Minutes, Dec 15, 1992.

638 CSA, CS.99.138, Box 8, Queen Committee, Minutes, May 1, 1991.

639 Ibid., Minutes, Apr 10, 1991.

640 Tara Wesner Linton, interview with author, Jul 31, 2012.

641 Alison Ross, "My Stampede: Friends in low places," posted in 2012 http://my.calgarystampede.com/friends-in-low-places.html, accessed Jul 28, 2012.

642 CSA, CS.99.138, Box 8, Queen Committee, Minutes, Oct 23, 1990.

643 Don Martin, "Stampede royalty sadly out of touch," *CH*, Jun 19, 1992.

644 Eva Ferguson, "No end to royal lineage foreseen," *CH*, Jun 28, 1992.

645 Ibid.

646 CSA, CS.99.138, Box 2, Queen Committee, Minutes, Nov 22, 1993.

647 Ibid., Minutes, Feb 1, 1993; CS.99.138, Box 8, Queen Committee, Minutes, Jan 10, 1990.

648 CSA, CS.99.138, Box 2, Queen Committee, Minutes, Feb 1, 1993.

649 Ibid., Minutes, May 3, 1993.

650 "'Princesses' injured in Stampede pile-up." *Toronto Star*, Jul 13, 1993.

651 "Stampede princesses injured in accident," *CH*, Jul 13, 1993.

652 CSA, CS.99.106, Box 5, Queen Committee, Minutes, Jun 16, 1994.

653 Wesner and Wilkie, *Memory Book*, "The Other Royal Trio."

654 Pearson, interview; CSA, CS.99.138, Box 2, Queen Committee, Minutes, Nov 22, 1993.

CHAPTER 14, 1995–1999

655 CSA, CS.99.138, Box 2, Queen Committee, Minutes, Sep 20, 1993.

656 Lisa Eastman, interview with author, Oct 31, 2012.

657 Lisa Eastman, correspondence with author, Mar 26, Apr 2, 2013.

658 Karina Tees Geleynse, correspondence with author, Feb 16, 2013.

659 Eastman, interview.

660 CSA, CS.99.106, Box 5, Queen Committee, Minutes, Oct 23, 1995.

661 Alanna Mitchell, "Queen puts pretty face on Stampede," *The Globe and Mail*, Jul 8, 1995.

662 Allison Boswell Wright, interview with author, Dec 18, 2012.

663 Eastman, interview.

664 Wright, interview.

665 CSA, CS.99.106, Box 5, Queen Committee, Minutes, Oct 23, 1995.

666 Mitchell, "Queen puts pretty face on Stampede."

667 CSA, CS.99.138, Box 2, Queen Committee, Minutes, Nov 19, 1992.

668 Ibid., Minutes. Nov 16, 1995.

669 Ibid., Minutes, Apr 1, 1996.

670 CS Queens' Alumni Committee, "History of the Crowns."

671 CSA, CS.99.106, Box 5, Queen Committee, Minutes, Apr 1, 1996.

672 Ibid., Minutes, Jan 8, Feb 13, 1996.

673 CS Queens' Alumni Committee, "Queens' Alumni Committee History."

674 CSA, CS.99.106, Box 5, President's file: Queens' Alumni Association, Leslie Crowe to Bob Dinning, ca. Feb 1996.

675 Kari Hames Beermann, interview with author, Nov 27, 2012.

676 CSA, CS.99.106, Box 5, Queen Committee, Minutes, Apr 1, 1996.

677 Beermann, interview.

678 Wendy Dudley, "Stampede royals bid farewell to limelight," *CH*, Mar 22, 1997.

679 CSA, CS.99.106, Box 5, Queen Committee, Minutes, Feb 10, 1997.

680 Ibid., Minutes, Mar 10, Apr 7, 1997.

681 Jason Van Rassel, "Triple Crown: Stampede Royalty start reign," *Calgary Sun*, Mar 24, 1997; Wendy Dudley, "Legends smile down on Holly," *CH*, Mar 24, 1997.

682 CSA, CS.99.106, Box 5, Queen Committee, Minutes, Feb 10, 1997.

683 Wesner and Wilkie, *Memory Book*, "Honorary Associates."

684 Beermann, interview.

685 Burbick, *Rodeo Queens*, 110.

686 Wesner and Wilkie, *Memory Book*, "1997."

687 CSA, CS.99.106, Box 5, Queen Committee, Minutes, Aug 19, 1997.

688 Ibid., Minutes, Aug 26, 1999.

689 Ibid., Minutes, Apr 30, 2001.

690 Ibid., Minutes, May 8, 2000.

691 Ibid., Minutes, Sep 17, 1997.

692 Ibid., Minutes, Apr 22, 1997.

693 Wendy Dudley, "Low numbers turn out for Stampede Queen contest," *CH*, Feb 23, 1998.

694 CSA, CS.99.106, Box 5, Queen Committee, Minutes, Mar 9, 1998.

695 Dudley, "Low numbers."

696 "Family royalty (Kathryn Larter crowned Queen of the Calgary Stampede)," *Alberta Report* 25, no. 16 (Apr 6, 1998), 37.

697 CSA, CS.99.106, Box 5, Queen Committee, Minutes, Oct 27, 1998.

698 Ibid., Minutes, Aug 26, 1999.

699 Eastman, interview.

700 Wesner and Wilkie, *Memory Book*, "Honorary Associates: Margaret Fraser."

701 Ibid., "1999."

702 CSA, CS.99.106, Box 5, Queen Committee, Minutes, Sep 30, 1997 [emphasis in the original].

703 Kari Griffith, interview with author, Dec 14, 2012.

704 CSA, CS.99.106, Box 5, Queen Committee, Minutes, Sep 30, 1997 [emphasis in the original].

705 Ibid., Minutes, Nov 18, 1997; Oct 27, 1998; Aug 26, 1999.

706 Wesner, interview.

707 CSA, CS.99.106, Box 5, Queen Committee, Minutes, Nov 19, 1992, Aug 26, 1999.

708 Opinions expressed to author during interviews with former Stampede royalty, Mar 17, 2012–Feb 5, 2013.

CHAPTER 15, 2000–2007

709 Foran, "The Stampede in historical context," in *Icon, Brand, Myth*, 16.

710 CSA, CS.99.106, Box 5, Queen Committee, Minutes, Apr 13, 1994.

711 Ibid., Minutes, Nov 16, 2000.

712 Pearson, interview.

713 CSA, CS.99.106, Box 5, Queen Committee, Minutes, Apr 1, 1996.

714 Ibid., Minutes, Nov 16, 2000.

715 Jolene Brewster, interview with author, Nov 16, 2012.

716 Andreeff, "Royal roots," 21.

717 "Queen couture," *Western Horse Review* (Jul–Aug 2012), 33.

718 June-Marie Innes, interview with author, Dec 14, 2012.

719 *Pretty Ladies, Fast Horses: Cowgirls of the Twenty-first Century*, Lorna Thomas Productions, 2000, accessed Jul 26, 2012, www.lornathomasproductions.com/cowgirls.htm.

720 Linda Slobodian, "Born to ride and destined to reign," *CH*, Jun 29, 2002.

721 Deborah Tetley, "Beneath the royal facade," *CH*, Jul 14, 2002.

722 Innes, interview.

723 Tetley, "Beneath the royal facade."

724 Slobodian, "Born to ride."

725 Tetley, "Beneath the royal facade."

726 Wesner and Wilkie, *Memory Book*, "2003."

727 Pearson, interview.

728 University of Lethbridge, "The Notice Board: U of L student one of Calgary Stampede's 2004 Royal Trio," posted Mar 28, 2004, accessed Aug 3, 2012, www.uleth.ca/notice/display.html?b=4&s=1209.

729 University of Lethbridge, "Crowning achievements: Brie Hamblin," *2004 Community Report* (2004), 22.

730 Sandy Young Tidswell, interview with author, Dec 15, 2012.

731 CS Queens' Alumni Committee, Minutes, Feb 10, 2005.

732 Ibid.

733 Interviews with Eastman, Linton; Wesner and Wilkie, *Memory Book*, "2004."

734 Andreeff, "Royal roots," 22.

735 CS Queens' Alumni Committee, "History of the Calgary Stampede Queens' Alumni [Draft]," 2007.

736 CS Queens' Alumni Committee, Minutes, Mar 11, 2004.

737 Ibid.

738 CS Queens' Alumni Committee, "Giddy-Up Gala Retires – 2008," n.d., accessed Feb 16, 2013, http://is.gd/juOXjB.

739 Wesner and Wilkie, *Memory Book*, "History of the Stampede Queens' Alumni Association and Committee"; "Forever Remembered."

740 Ibid., "Honorary Associates."

741 Sean Myers, "Stampede's new royal trio riding tall in the saddle," *CH*, Mar 21, 2005.

742 Ibid.

743 Crowe, interview.

744 Sheena Read, "Crowe named princess," *Nanton News*, Mar 23, 2005.

745 Ibid.

746 "Indian Princess crowned," *CH*, Apr 18, 2005.

747 Sarah Junkin, "Tired queen rides on," *Cochrane Eagle*, Jul 20, 2005.

748 Pearson, interview.

749 Wesner and Wilkie, *Memory Book*, "Honorary Associates"; Sean Myers, "Fraser was 'mother' to Stampede queens," *CH*, Nov 3, 2005.

750 Pam Doyle, "Stampede Queen… has Canmore connection," *Canmore Leader*, Apr 25, 2007.

CHAPTER 16, 2008–2012

751 Renato Gandia, "Calgary Stampede in search of 2013 royalty," *Calgary Sun*, Jun 7, 2012, accessed Aug 10, 2013, www.calgarysun.com/2012/06/07/calgary-stampede-in-search-of-2013-royalty.

752 CS Royalty Committee, "2013 application form."

753 "Stampede Royalty to be crowned in the fall," Stampede press release, Feb 1, 2008, accessed Aug 3, 2013, http://news.calgarystampede.com/files/Documents_news/stampede_royalty_to_be_crowned_in_the_fall.pdf.

754 Kristen Odland, "Royalty makes a return," *CH*, Jun 6, 2008.

755 Wesner and Wilkie, *Memory Book*, "History of the Stampede Queens' Alumni Association and Committee."

756 Henderson, interview; scrapbook.

757 "100 Year Birthday Gift: Philanthropist, rancher and businessman Bill Siebens gifts historic Alberta ranching property to the Calgary Stampede Foundation," Stampede press release, Jun 19, 2012, accessed Feb 16, 2013, http://news.calgarystampede.com/News/Latest-News/Release-Details/2012/-100-Year-Birthday-Gift-Philanthropist-rancher-and-businessman-Bill-Siebens-gifts-historic-Alberta-ranching-property-to-the/default.aspx.

758 "Stampede Royalty to be crowned in the fall," Stampede press release, Feb 1, 2008, accessed Feb 16, 2013, http://news.calgarystampede.com/files/Documents_news/stampede_royalty_to_be_crowned_in_the_fall.pdf,.

759 Ibid.

760 Odland, "Royalty makes a return."

761 Pearson, interview.

762 Dana Tremblay, interview with author, Feb 6, 2013.

344
★

763   Kneller, correspondence.

764   Anne Garnett (CS Indian Events Committee, Indian Princess Sub-Committee), correspondence with author, Mar 14, 2012.

765   "Piikani woman returns as Stampede Indian Princess," *The Regional* (southern Alberta multi-newspaper supplement), Jul 2, 2008.

766   Shawn Logan, "Stampede poster unveiled," *Calgary Sun*, Jul 14, 2010.

767   Katy Anderson, "Stampede Indian Princess crowned," *CH*, Sep 28, 2009.

768   Katy Anderson, "New Stampede royalty take reins," *CH*, Oct 6, 2008.

769   Sergerie, interview.

770   Rob Alexander, "Valley cowgirl crowned Stampede princess," *Rocky Mountain Outlook*, Oct 9, 2008.

771   Robert Rooney, "Royal ambassadors," *Stephen* [magazine] (Fall 2001), 46–47.

772   Foran, "The Stampede in historical context," in *Icon, Brand, Myth*, 17.

773   "Centennial Stampede Queen and Princesses crowned," Stampede press release, Oct 2, 2011, http://news.calgarystampede.com/News/Latest-News/Release-Details/2011/Centennial-Stampede-Queen-and-Princesses-crowned-/default.aspx, accessed Feb 16, 2013.

774   "Let the competition begin," Stampede press release, Sep 10, 2010 http://news.calgarystampede.com/News/Latest-News/Release-Details/2010/Let-the-competition-beginthe-search-is-on-for-the-2011-Stampede-Queen-and-Princesses/default.aspx, accessed Feb 16, 2013.

775   Rooney, "Royal ambassadors," 46.

776   Slobodian, "Born to ride."

777   Brewster, interview.

778   Alexander, "Valley cowgirl."

779   Sara Francis, "Living her dream," *Cochrane Times*, Jul 14, 2010.

780   Clara Ho, "Dream comes true for Stampede Indian Princess," *CH*, Sep 19, 2011.

781   Angela Sengaus, "Mount Royal Stampede Queen," Mount Royal University Newsroom, Jun 30, 2011, accessed Jul 28, 2012, www.mtroyal.ca/AboutMountRoyal/MediaRoom/Newsroom/stampedeQueen2011.htm.

782   Valerie Fortney, "'Royals' make splash in Montreal," *CH*, Nov 21, 2008.

783   Alexis Bevan, "These boots are made for Stampede royalty," *CH*, Mar 14, 2009.

784   Jessica Manning, interview with author, Jan 10, 2013.

785   Tremblay, interview.

786   Tidswell, interview.

787   Manning, interview.

788   Wesner and Wilkie, *Memory Book*, "The other royal trio."

789   Ibid., "The Queen contest origins and history."

790   Tremblay, interview.

791   CSA, CS.99.138, Box 8, Queen Committee, Minutes, Feb 5, 1990; Janelle Phillips, interview with author, Nov 20, 2012.

792   Tremblay, interview.

793   Wesner and Wilkie, *Memory Book*, "The Queen contest origins and history."

794   Tremblay, interview.

795   Pearson, interview.

796   Wesner and Wilkie, *Memory Book*, "The Queen contest origins and history."

797   Ibid.

798   Pearson, interview.

799   Wesner and Wilkie, *Memory Book*, "The Queen contest origins and history."

800   Manning, interview.

801   Lea Storry, "MRU student crowned 2011 Stampede queen," *CH*, Oct 4, 2010.

802   John Barlow, "Priddis gets its princess," (Okotoks) *Western Wheel*, Oct 13, 2010.

803   Wesner and Wilkie, *Memory Book*, "Saddles."

804   Pearson, interview.

805   Rooney, "Royal ambassadors," 47.

806   Interviews with Crowe, Ladiges, Pearson, Tidswell.

807   Gandia, "Calgary Stampede in search."

808   Tidswell, interview.

809   Tremblay, interview.

810   CS Royalty Committee, "2013 application form."

811   Bryce Forbes, "Stampede royalty unveiled," *CH*, Oct 3, 2011.

812   Candice Lee, interview with author, Jan 12, 2013.

813   Jessica Williams, interview with author, Jan 14, 2013.

814   Ho, "Dream comes true."

815   Pat Kolafa, "Calgary Stampede Centennial Princess hails from Rockyford," *Drumheller Mail*, May 23, 2012.

816   Jody Robbins, "Meet the 2012 Stampede Indian Princess," Vacay.ca, posted Jul 14, 2012, accessed Apr 22, 2013, http://vacay.ca/2012/07/meet-the-2012-calgary-stampede-indian-princess.

817   Interviews with Brasso, Manning.

818   Tremblay, interview.

819   Wesner and Wilkie, *Memory Book*, "The crowns."

820   Manning, interview.

PRIMARY MATERIALS

Bertolli, Shirley Willock. Reminiscences; copies of scrapbook items, 1956–1957, 2012.

Brasso, Donna Thomson. "History of the Calgary Stampede Queens' Alumni." Unpublished manuscript, 1996.

————. "Memories," 2012.

Calgary Public Library. Newspaper clipping files. "Calgary Exhibition and Stampede: Queens."

Calgary Stampede Archives. Calgary Exhibition and Stampede. Board, Executive and Committee Minutes, 1945–2001. CS.99.106.

————. Calgary Exhibition and Stampede. Committee Minutes, 1987–2000. CS.99.138.

Calgary Stampede Corporate Communications. "Chronological History of the Calgary Stampede," ca. 2009. http://corporate.calgarystampede.com/about/stampede-history/chronological-history.html (Mar 27, 2012)

Calgary Stampede Historical Committee. "Calgary Stampede History," ca. 2010. http://historical.calgarystampede.com/calgary-stampede-history.html (Mar 27, 2012)

Calgary Stampede Queens' Alumni Committee. "Calgary Stampede Queens' Alumni," 2012. http://www.stampedequeensalumni.com (Jul 30, 2012)

Calgary Stampede Queens' Alumni Committee. "History of the Calgary Stampede Queens' Alumni Association and Calgary Stampede Queens [sic] Alumni Committee [Draft]," 2007.

Calgary Stampede Queens' Alumni Committee. Minutes, 1990–2012.

Calgary Stampede Royalty Committee. "Frequently asked questions." 2012 http://www.csqueenandprincesses.com (Oct 1, 2012)

————. "History and purpose of the program." http://www.csroyalty.com/faqs.html (Mar 14, 2013)

Clark, Margaret Powell. Reminiscences; copies of scrapbook items, 1959–1960, 2012.

Glenbow Archives. Philip H. Godsell fonds. M-433.

Glenbow Library. The Associated Canadian Travellers' Magazine, 1945–1967.

————. Newspaper clipping files. "Calgary Exhibition and Stampede: Stampede Queens, etc."

Henderson, Patsy Rodgers. Scrapbooks; photographs, 1946–2012.

Sergerie, Cindy Morres. "Patricia 'Patsy' Rodgers: A brief biography…" Unpublished manuscript, 2011.

INTERVIEWS AND CORRESPONDENCE WITH AUTHOR

Anderson, Frances Swann. Interview, Nov 19, 2012.

Barlow, Happy. Interview, Dec 15, 2012.

Beermann, Kari Hames. Interview, Nov 27, 2012.

Benoit, Aimee. Correspondence, Jan 24, 2012–Apr 20, 2013.

Bertolli, Shirley Willock. Interview, Oct 18, 2012.

Brasso, Donna Thomson. Interview, Jan 8, 2013. Correspondence, Jan 9, Apr 4, 2013.

Brewster, Jolene. Interview, Nov 16, 2012.

Bronfman, Sherry Moore. Interview, Oct 27, 2012.

Clark, Margaret Powell. Interview, Oct 23, 2012.

Colborne, Barb Penner. Interview, Nov 18, 2012.

Crowe, Leslie MacDonald. Interview, Nov 21, 2012.

Davies, Gwenda Marshall. Interview, Nov 22, 2012; Apr 17, 2013.

Degenstein, Peter. Interview, Oct 18, 2012.

DeMeo, Margot Turney. Interview, Dec 9, 2012.

Denoon, Barbara Howard. Interview, Nov 20, 2012.

Dunn, Holly. Interview, Nov 19, 2012.

Dunn, Laura Godwin. Interview, Dec 14, 2012.

Eastman, Lisa. Interview, Oct 31, 2012. Correspondence, Jul 20, 2012–Apr 2, 2013.

Garnett, Anne. Correspondence, Mar 14, 2012.

Geleynse, Karina Tees. Correspondence, Feb 16, 2013.

Griffith, Kari. Interview, Dec 14, 2012.

Henderson, Patsy Rodgers. Interviews, Mar 17, 21, 2012.

Innes, June-Marie. Interview, Dec 14, 2012

Johnsen, Lisa McNiven. Correspondence, Mar 6, 2013.

Kneller, Tammy. Correspondence, Mar 13, 14, 2012.

Ladiges, Cathy Robinson. Interview, Nov 27, 2012. Correspondence, Feb 23, 2013.

Langford, Joan Plastow. Interview, Jan 13, 2013.

Lee, Candice. Interview, Jan 12, 2013.

Linton, Tara Wesner. Interviews, Jul 31, 2012; Jan 31, 2013. Correspondence, Feb 7, Apr 29 and May 7, 2013.

Locker, Evelyn Eagle Speaker. Interview, Apr 6, 2012.

Lockwood, Eileen Beckner. Interview, Nov 29, 2012.

Manning, Jessica. Interview, Jan 10, 2013.

O'Bertos, Marie Sharpe. Interview, Nov 15, 2012.

Pearson, Pat. Interview, Feb 4, 2013.

Phillips, Janelle. Interview, Nov 20, 2012.

Sergerie, Cindy Morres. Interview, Dec 13, 2012.

Shaver, Inez Melby. Interview, Feb 5, 2013.

Sveen, Joan Horne. Interview, Dec 14, 2012.

Thompson, Bonnie MacGregor. Interview, Nov 27, 2012. Correspondence, Feb 23, 2013.

Tidswell, Sandy Young. Interview, Dec 15, 2012.

Tremblay, Dana. Interview, Feb 6, 2013.

Weidner, Arlene. Interview, Nov 21, 2012. Correspondence, Feb 25, 2013.

Williams, Jessica. Interview, Jan 14, 2013.

Wright, Allison Boswell. Interview, Dec 18, 2012.

BOOKS

Banet-Weiser, Sarah. *The Most Beautiful Girl in the World: Beauty Pageants and National Identity.* Berkeley: University of California Press, 1999.

Burbick, Joan. *Rodeo Queens and the American Dream.* New York: Public Affairs, 2002.

Campbell, Colin S. "The Stampede: Cowtown's sacred cow." In *Stampede City: Power and politics in the West*, edited by Chuck Reasons, 103–120. Toronto: Between the Lines, 1984.

Dabbs, Frank. *Branded by the Wind: The life and times of Bill Herron.* Calgary: Marjorie A. Herron, 2001.

Dixon, Joan, and Tracey Read. *Celebrating the Calgary Exhibition and Stampede: The Story of the Greatest Outdoor Show on Earth.* Canmore: Altitude, 2005.

Foran, Max. "More than partners: The Calgary Stampede and the City of Calgary." Chapter 6 in *Icon, Brand, Myth: The Calgary Stampede*, edited by Max Foran, 147–174. Edmonton: AU Press, 2008.

———. "The Stampede in historical context." Chapter 1 in *Icon, Brand, Myth*, edited by Max Foran, 1–19. Edmonton: AU Press, 2008.

Gentile, Patrizia. "Queen of the Maple Leaf: A history of beauty contests in twentieth-century

Canada." PhD dissertation, Queens University, 2006.

Gray, James. *A Brand of Its Own: The 100 year history of the Calgary Exhibition and Stampede.* Saskatoon: Western Producer Prairie Books, 1985.

Joudrey, Susan. "The Expectations of a Queen: Identity and race politics in the Calgary Stampede." Chapter 7 in *The West and Beyond: New Perspectives on an Imagined Region*, edited by Alvin Finkel et al., 133–155. Edmonton: AU Press, 2010.

Kennedy, Fred. *The Calgary Stampede Story.* Calgary: T. Edwards Thonger, 1952.

Laegreid, Renée M. *Riding Pretty: Rodeo Royalty in the American West.* Lincoln: University of Nebraska Press, 2006.

Seiler, Robert M., and Tamara P. Seiler. "The Social Construction of the Canadian Cowboy: Calgary Exhibition and Stampede posters, 1952–1972." Chapter 12 in *Icon, Brand, Myth*, edited by Max Foran, 293–323. Edmonton: AU Press, 2008.

Wesner, Tara, and Whitney Wilkie, eds. *The Queens' Alumni Memory Book: Celebrating Stampede's Centennial in 2012.* Calgary: Heritage Makers, 2012.

SELECTED ARTICLES SIGNED (IN DATE ORDER WHERE SAME AUTHOR)

Alexander, Rob. "Valley cowgirl crowned Stampede princess." *Rocky Mountain Outlook*, Oct 9, 2008.

Anderson, Katy. "New Stampede royalty take reins." *Calgary Herald*, Oct 6, 2008.

———. "Stampede Indian Princess crowned." *Calgary Herald*, Sep 28, 2009.

Andreeff, Monica. "Royal roots." *Avenue Magazine*, Jul/Aug 2001, 20–29.

Barenholtz, Naomi. "Debits and credits." *Calgary Herald*, Jul 15, 1949.

Barlow, Happy. "Queens uphold more than Stampede's image." *Calgary Herald*, Apr 18, 1988.

Barlow, John. "Priddis gets its princess." (Okotoks) *Western Wheel*, Oct 13, 2010.

Bevan, Alexis. "These boots are made for Stampede royalty." *Calgary Herald*, Mar 14, 2009.

Bissell, Nancy. "Rigorous days ahead for Stampede royalty." *Calgary Herald*, Jul 7, 1983.

———. "For Stampede royalty, humor's just a miscue away." *Calgary Herald*, Jun 24, 1984.

Blain, Joanne. "Only in Calgary, you say: Britain gets taste of Stampede," *Calgary Herald*, Jul 2, 1981.

Brown, Elaine. "The parade's over for another queen." *Calgary Herald*, Jan 26, 1973.

Butlin, Catherine. "Western gear that is fit for a queen." *Calgary Herald*, Jul 12, 1979.

Calamai, Peter. "Prince Andrew 'so-so' at disco." *Ottawa Citizen*, Aug 8, 1978.

Campbell, Bruce. "Mother Margaret honored by Stampede, Little Britches Rodeo." *High River Times*, Nov 9, 2005.

Carefoot, Stacey. "Calgary Stampede: The first queen." *Our World*, Jun 2001, 8–9.

Cochrane, W.G. "The ATC [sic] viewpoint." *Calgary Herald*, Jul 3, 1954.

Cohen, Philip. "Miss Pot o' Gold." *Albertan* (Calgary), Jul 10, 1972.

Cooney, Roman. "Stampede Queen is busy." *Calgary Herald*, Jun 23, 1985.

Crawford, Anne. "Queens prepped in hazards on horseback." *Calgary Herald*, Jul 5, 1990.

Cumming, Don. "'For pete's sake!' said Queen Shirley," *Albertan*, Jun 21, 1956.

Curtis, Linda. "Stampede Queen has attractive outfits." *Albertan*, Jul 6, 1964.

———. "Queen's reign nears end." *Albertan*, Jan 18, 1972.

————. "Where are all the Queens?" *Albertan*, May 25, 1972.

————. "Taking the royal ride." *Albertan*, Jul 15, 1978.

————. "The end of the trail." *Albertan*, Feb 4, 1979.

————. "Royalty didn't mind losing sleep." *Albertan*, Jul 15, 1979.

————. "Royalty has no time for horseplay." *Albertan*, Jul 13, 1980.

Dawson, Chris. "Stampede Royalty." *Calgary Herald*, Jul 14, 1989.

Donahue, Robert. "Wild replies fail to unfreeze poker faces of 'Queen' judges." *Calgary Herald*, Apr 24, 1964.

Doyle, Pam. "Stampede Queen… has Canmore connection," *Canmore Leader*, Apr 25, 2007.

Dudley, Wendy. "Stampede royals bid farewell to limelight." *Calgary Herald*, Mar 22, 1997.

————. "Legends smile down on Holly." *Calgary Herald*, Mar 24, 1997.

————. "Low numbers turn out for Stampede Queen contest." *Calgary Herald*, Feb 23, 1998.

Elliott, Olive. "Calgary getting over Miss Stampede shock." *Edmonton Journal*, Jul 14, 1966.

Ferguson, Eva. "No end to royal lineage foreseen." *Calgary Herald*, Jun 28, 1992.

Forbes, Bryce. "Stampede royalty unveiled." *Calgary Herald*, Oct 3, 2011.

Ford, Catherine. "Beauty covered in plastic." *Calgary Herald*, Jun 13, 1983.

————. "Here's the law for cowboy cads." *Calgary Herald*, Mar 20, 1984.

————. "Stampede rules insulting." *Calgary Herald*, Jan 23, 1986.

————. "Clinic churns out rodeo queens." *Calgary Herald*, Mar 31, 1988.

Fortney, Valerie. "H.R. resident creator of lovely Stampede outfits." *Eagleview Post*, Jul 12, 1988.

————. "'Royals' make splash in Montreal." *Calgary Herald*, Nov 21, 2008.

————."Wild ride: Decade brought great highs, lows." In "100 Years of Calgary Stampede, Part VIII: The 1980s." *Calgary Herald*, Jun 13, 2012, Special Keepsake Edition, DD3–5.

Francis, Sara. "Living her dream." *Cochrane Times*, Jul 14, 2010.

Freeborn, John. "1954's Miss (Poor-little-mixed-up) Calgary Stampede." Editorial cartoon. Calgary *Albertan*, Jul 3, 1954.

Gandia, Renato. "Calgary Stampede in search of 2013 royalty." *Calgary Sun*, Jun 7, 2012, accessed Aug 10, 2013, www.calgarysun.com/2012/06/07/calgary-stampede-in-search-of-2013-royalty.

Gaver, Jack. "Up and down Broadway." *Beaver Daily Times*, Sep 27, 1946.

Gerson, Jen. "Calgary Stampede: A defiant last stand of the politically incorrect." *National Post*, Jul 4, 2012. Accessed Apr 22, 2013. http://news.nationalpost.com/2012/07/04/calgary-stampede-a-defiant-last-stand-of-the-politically-incorrect,.

Godsell, Philip G. "The Queen's dress." *Calgary Herald*, Jun 30, 1954.

Gold, Marta. "Legwork reveals GWG story: Writer pens history of jeans maker." *Calgary Herald*, Aug 28, 2012.

Guttormson, Kim. "Battling beyond its boundaries." In "100 Years of Calgary Stampede, Part IX: The 1990s." *Calgary Herald*, Jun 13, 2012, Special Keepsake Edition, DD12–13.

Hehr, Marilynn. "Didsbury girl, 20, Stampede Queen." *Calgary Herald*, May 10, 1965.

Ho, Clara. "Dream comes true for Stampede Indian Princess." *Calgary Herald*, Sep 19, 2011.

Hoffman, Richard. "Virtuous single cowgirls sought." *Calgary Herald*, Jan 9, 1984.

Hopkins, John. "John Hopkins." *Calgary Herald*, Mar 26, 1976.

Hopkins, John. "Stampede Queen true Calgary envoy." *Calgary Herald*, Apr 9, 1977.

Hopkins, Johnny. "Johnny Hopkins… reports." *Calgary Herald*, Apr 15, 1964.

Howse, John. "Mamas should let their daughters grow up to be cowgirls." *Calgary Herald*, Jan 20, 1984.

Humphrey, Edythe. "'67 Stampede Queen crowned." *Calgary Herald*, May 8, 1967.

————. "Stampede Queen contest now open." *Calgary Herald*, Feb 10, 1970.

Hutton, Frank. "180,000 watch parade kick off Stampede." *Edmonton Journal*, Jul 5, 1965.

Huxtable, Bernice. "Royalty rides out." *Calgary Herald*, Jul 10, 1984.

————. "Indian princess pageant meaningful, elegant." *Calgary Herald*, Jun 14, 1988.

————. "Indian princess's dress gesture of friendship." *Calgary Herald*, Jul 11, 1989.

Jeffery, Yvonne. "Coming of Age." In "100 Years of Calgary Stampede, Part IV: The 1940s." *Calgary Herald*, Jun 13, 2012, Special Keepsake Edition, BB21–22.

Junkin, Sarah. "Tired queen rides on." *Cochrane Eagle*, Jul 20, 2005.

Kergan, Lawrie. "Hectic preparations are over; now the fun is about to start." *Calgary Herald*, Jul 7, 1962.

Keyser, Tom. "Well, we adored him once." *Calgary Herald*, Mar 1, 1984.

Kolafa, Pat. "Calgary Stampede Centennial Princess hails from Rockyford." *Drumheller Mail*, May 23, 2012.

Laegreid, Renée M. "Performers prove beauty and rodeo can be mixed: The return of the cowgirl queen." *Montana: The Magazine of Western History* 54, no. 1 (Spring 2004): 44–55.

Lakritz, Naomi. "After turmoil of 1960s, the '70s were groovy." In "100 Years of Calgary Stampede, Part VII: The 1970s." *Calgary Herald*, Jun 13, 2012, Special Keepsake Edition, CC20–21.

Larson, Cheryl. "7 Stampede Queens recall old memories." *Calgary Herald*, Apr 3, 1967.

"LasVegasLynn." "The Fabulous Flamingo Hotel History in the 1950s." *Classic Las Vegas* (blog), Sep 23, 2007. Accessed Jul 28, 2013, http://is.gd/tvRCkk.

Layzell, Denny. "Queen contest aids many organizations." *Calgary Herald*, May 4, 1963.

Leppa, Phyllis. "The hat does fit." *Alberta Rural Month*, Jul 1983, 14–20.

Leslie, Jean. "Once a Queen, always a Queen." *Calgary Herald Magazine*, Jul 3, 1988, 26.

Logan, Shawn. "Stampede poster unveiled." *Calgary Sun*, Jul 14, 2010.

Lyle, Dannie. "Former Queens of Stampede leading busy, varied lives." *Calgary Herald*, Jul 9, 1958.

Mabell, Dave. "She's Queen for a year, but busy reign soon over." *Albertan*, ca. Jul 1969.

Margoshes, Dave. "Search for the Stampede Queen narrows to five contenders: Judges seek salesperson for the city." *Calgary Herald*, Feb 25, 1980.

Martin, Don. "Stampede royalty sadly out of touch." *Calgary Herald*, Jun 19, 1992.

Mate, Susan, and Sheldon Alberts. "Natives replaced AWOL princess." *Calgary Herald*, Jul 14, 1990.

McCachen, Bonnie. "Stampede activities keep Queen busy." *Calgary Herald*, Jul 11, 1963.

McLean, Marilyn. "ACT celebrates anniversary at convention in Calgary." *Calgary Herald Magazine*, May 20, 1961.

Michelin, Lana. "Indian Village princess quits, claiming bias." *Calgary Herald*, Jul 13, 1990.

Miller, Mark. "Feisty princess awaits big day." *Calgary Sun*, Jun 26, 1989.

Mitchell, Alanna. "Queen puts pretty face on Stampede." *The Globe and Mail*, Jul 8, 1995.

Myers, Sean. "Stampede's new royal trio riding tall in the saddle." *Calgary Herald*, Mar 21, 2005.

———. "Fraser was 'mother' to Stampede queens." *Calgary Herald*, Nov 3, 2005.

Nelson, Barry. "'75 Stampede Queen could be a prince." *Calgary Herald*, Nov 16, 1974.

Odland, Kristen. "Royalty makes a return." *Calgary Herald*, Jun 6, 2008.

Perchaluk, Monica. "Stampede trio more than beauty contest winners." *Calgary Herald*, ca. Feb 1986.

Rach, Lynne. "Miss Stampede spreads word – with feeling." *Calgary Herald*, Feb 4, 1970.

Raugust, Beth. "Western wear expert designs Queen's garb." *Calgary Herald*, Jun 18, 1968.

Read, Sheena. "Crowe named princess." *Nanton News*, Mar 23, 2005.

Reid, Eva. "Socially Speaking: Stampede socially." *Albertan* (Calgary), Jul 15, 1967.

———. "Eavesdrop with Eva." *Albertan*, Jan 14, Jul 12, 1972.

———. "Eavesdrop with Eva: Sweethearts of the Stampede." *Albertan*, Jul 13, 1978.

Reinhard, Karla. "Former Stampede Queen, Edith Edge enjoys 'the ranch life,'" *Cochrane Eagle*, Apr 4, 2012.

Robbins, Jody. "Meet the 2012 Stampede Indian Princess." Vacay.ca, posted Jul 14, 2012. http://vacay.ca/2012/07/meet-the-2012-calgary-stampede-indian-princess/ (Apr 22, 2013).

Rooney, Robert. "Royal ambassadors." *Stephen* [magazine], Fall 2011, 46–47.

Sagi, Doug. "'Wise Patch' raised Sharon to 1964 Stampede Queen," *Calgary Herald*, May 12, 1964.

Sengaus, Angela. "Mount Royal Stampede Queen." Mount Royal University Newsroom, Jun 30, 2011. Accessed Jul 28, 2012, www.mtroyal.ca/AboutMountRoyal/MediaRoom/Newsroom/stampedeQueen2011.htm.

Seskevich, Elaine. "A day in the life of Stampede royalty." *Calgary Herald*, Jul 10, 1970.

Seskus, Tony. "The Golden Age." In "100 Years of Calgary Stampede, Part V: The 1950s." *Calgary Herald*, Jun 13, 2012, Special Keepsake Edition, CC5–6.

Shiels, Bob. "Queen recruiting begins." *Calgary Herald*, Dec 11 1975.

Simaluk, Vern. "Ranch-girl turned 'city slicker' likely to be Stampede Queen." *Calgary Herald*, Mar 28, 1968.

Slobodian, Linda. "Born to ride and destined to reign." *Calgary Herald*, Jun 29, 2002.

Stavdal, Bill. "Cowboy's daughter to reign as Jubilee Stampede Queen." *Calgary Herald*, Jun 29, 1962.

Storry, Lea. "MRU student crowned 2011 Stampede queen." *Calgary Herald*, Oct 4, 2010.

Stout, Lorne. "Calgary honored." *Canadian Cattlemen* 9, no. 1 (Jun 1946): 46.

Summerfield, Robin. "Glory days." *Calgary Herald*, Jul 6, 2000.

Symonds, Shirley Willock. "Rodeo queens don't need more glitz." *Calgary Herald*, Jun 5, 1988.

Tetley, Deborah. "Beneath the royal facade." *Calgary Herald*, Jul 14, 2002.

———. "Building toward a bright future." In "100 Years of Calgary Stampede, Part X: The 2000s." *Calgary Herald*, Jun 13, 2012, Special Keepsake Edition, DD19–20.

Thomas, Don. "Alberta ropes hearts at Expo." *Calgary Herald*, Oct 7, 1967.

Townsend, Dena. "Little rest for Stampede royalty." *Calgary Herald*, Jun 24, 1984.

———. "Days long but exciting for past Stampede royalty." *Calgary Herald*, Jul 5, 1984.

———. "Queen and princesses hitch up their smiles," *Calgary Herald*, Jun 30, 1988.

———. "Wheelchair-bound princess won't be left on sidelines." *Calgary Herald*, Jun 29, 1989.

Van Rassel, Jason. "Triple Crown: Stampede Royalty start reign." *Calgary Sun*, Mar 24, 1997.

Van Wagner, Joy. "Stampede snapshots." *Calgary Herald*, Jul 12, 1957.

———."1958 Stampede Queen just what job requires." *Calgary Herald*, Jun 27, 1958.

Varadi, Zoltan. "Race, representation and the rodeo." *Fast Forward Weekly*, Jul 7, 2012. Accessed Apr 22, 2013, www.ffwdweekly. com/calgary-blogs/culture/2012/07/13/ race-representation-and-the-rodeo-1101.

Volmers, Eric. "Not your grandpa's Stampede." In "100 Years of Calgary Stampede, Part VI: The 1960s." *Calgary Herald*, Jun 13, 2012, Special Keepsake Edition, CC14–15.

Walters, Hazel. "Parade criticized." *Calgary Herald*, Jul 14, 1958.

Walters, Judy. "As long as he saw her ride in Stampede Parade." Glenbow clipping file, n.p., n.d. [ca. Jul 1984].

Wood, Rosemary. "Calgary Stampede Queen prepares for gala week." *Calgary Herald*, Jul 9, 1955.

Zimmerman, Kate. "Stampede royalty gets fitted for fete." *Calgary Herald*, Jul 8, 1982.

SELECTED ARTICLES UNSIGNED (IN DATE ORDER)

ACT Magazine. "Foothills Flares." Feb 1945.

———. "Foothills Footnotes." Feb, Jun, Sept 1946.

———. "Foothills Footnotes." Aug 1947.

———. "The Stampede Queen." Jul 1949.

———. "Foothills Flares." Aug 1949.

———. "Foothills Flares." Jul 1950.

———. "Corral Calls." Aug 1951.

———. "Corral Calls." Feb, Apr 1954.

Albertan (Calgary). "Calgary girl to lead great New York rodeo." May 18, 1946.

———. "8,000 at flower show: Patsy Rodgers crowned." Aug 27, 1946.

———. "Patsy Rogers back from Cinderella trip." Nov 13, 1946.

———. "Vote for your favorite in the Stampede Queen contest." May 31, 1947.

———. "Doreen Richardson wins Stampede Queen title." Jul 5, 1947.

———. "Tribes adopt Indian Princess." Apr 23, 1954.

———. "Stampede Queen's costume settled." Jul 3, 1954.

———. "Big moment for Indian maiden." Jul 8, 1954.

———. "Shy Sarcee girl is first Stampede princess." Jul 10, 1965.

Calgary Herald. "Feature attraction at the cowboy ball." Jul 14, 1944.

———. "Calgary girl is selected 'Miss Canada' in New York rodeo." May 16, 1946.

———. "Calgary's biggest Stampede sets many new records." Jul 13, 1946.

———. "Stampede to have 'Queen.'" Apr 18, 1947.

———. "Doreen Richardson, Queen of Stampede." Jul 4, 1947.

———. "Stampede queen will wear bright western costume." Jul 5, 1947.

———. "Greatest Stampede opens." Jul 7, 1947.

———. "Stampede Queen going to U.S." Sep 9, 1947.

———. "Attention service clubs and community organizations." Feb 14, 1948.

———. "Colorful film version of Stampede." Jun 7, 1948.

———. "Queens parade on chuckwagon." Jun 18, 1948.

———. "City Clerk to count Stampede Queen ballots," Jun 19, 1948.

———. "Mrs. Merle Stier wins Stampede Queen title." Jun 16, 1949.

———. "1949 Stampede under way." Jul 11, 1949.

———. "Busy week scheduled for Stampede Queen." Jul 6, 1950.

———. "Stampede Queen draws winning ticket for kin," Jul 11, 1951.

———. "Calgary Queen to be feted." Jun 12, 1952.

———. "Heap big time for all: Stampede Queen Sherry Moore and Sarcee Chief: Cameras keep clicking, Indians keep dancing: A Mardi Gras with feathers." Jul 8, 1952.

———. "Queen stars in street dance." Jul 9, 1952.

———. "Stampede Queen Sherry Moore." Jul 12, 1952.

———. "Cochrane ranch girl 1953 Stampede Queen." Jun 24, 1953.

———. "All eyes were on Edith Edge of Cochrane." Jul 6, 1953.

———. "Stampede Queen wins Las Vegas dream trip." Jul 8, 1953.

———. "1953 Stampede Queen made Indian Princess." Jul 17, 1953.

———. "Thousands jam roads as new theatre opens." Jul 17, 1953.

———. "Stampede 'sweetheart' leaves for Hollywood." Nov 2, 1953.

———. "Stampede Queen back from Hollywood trip." Nov 13, 1953.

———. "Indian Princess in contest." Apr 17, 1954.

———. "Stampede Queen event is boon to charity: $50,000 raised since 1947." Jun 16, 1954.

———. "First time in history of Western show: Indian girl is voted 1954 Stampede Queen." Jun 22, 1954.

———. "She should wear her native dress." Jun 25, 1954.

———. "Princess Wapiti's dress." Jun 25, 1954.

———. "Wapiti costume debated," Jun 28, 1954.

———. "Not part way: Indian dress all week." Jun 29, 1954.

———. "During Stampede week: Indian Queen to wear native costume twice." Jun 29, 1954.

———. "Calgarians on Monday saw Princess Wapiti," Jul 6, 1954.

———. "Gruelling grind for Queen candidates." May 26, 1955.

———. "City Chinese chosen '58 Stampede Queen." Jun 25, 1958

———. "Ticket sales, not ability to decide Stampede Queen." Apr 1, 1963.

———. "Stampede Queen rules changed: Popularity tickets out." Mar 26, 1964.

———. "1964 ACT Stampede Queen contest: NO ticket sales." Mar 30, 1964.

———. Horsemanship key to Stampede Queen." May 7, 1964.

———. "Stampede new sponsor for 'Stampede Queen.'" Feb 11, 1967.

———. "13 Stampede Queens to ride in parade." Mar 11, 1967.

———. "Queen's chaperone finds life hectic." Jul 10, 1968.

———. "Stampede royalty to be declared at March rodeo." Jan 10, 1972.

Calgary Stampede. "Stampede Royalty to be crowned in the fall." Press release, Feb 1, 2008. Accessed Aug 3, 2013, http://news.calgarystampede.com/files/Documents_news/stampede_royalty_to_be_crowned_in_the_fall.pdf.

———. "100 Year Birthday Gift: Philanthropist, rancher and businessman Bill Siebens gifts historic Alberta ranching property to the Calgary Stampede Foundation." Press release, Jun 19, 2012. Accessed Feb 16, 2013, http://news.calgarystampede.com/News/Latest-News/Release-Details/2012/-100-Year-Birthday-Gift-Philanthropist-rancher-and-businessman-Bill-Siebens-gifts-historic-Alberta-ranching-property-to-the/default.aspx.

Cardston News. "Queen attends rodeo." Jul 24, 1947.

Daytona Beach Morning Journal. "Patsy Rodgers of Calgary and Ona Mae Clark." Oct 26, 1946.

Edmonton Journal. "Calgary Stampede Queen to be selected by tally." Jun 4, 1948.

Lethbridge Herald. "As Canada's rodeo queen arrived in Lethbridge." Jul 4, 1946.

———. "Enjoys rodeo and plans to return." Jul 6, 1946.

———. "'Wildest rodeo I have seen' says Madison Square Garden manager." Jul 5, 1946.

Montreal Gazette. "Chinese rodeo queen." Jun 28, 1958.

Nashua [New Hampshire] Telegraph. "Ranch girls." Oct 25, 1948.

The Regional (southern Alberta multi-newspaper supplement). "Piikani woman returns as Stampede Indian Princess." Jul 2, 2008.

Saskatoon Star-Phoenix. "Mrs. June Dewhirst." Jun 4, 1957.

Spokane Daily Chronicle. "Ridpath Hotel dedication seen by several hundred." Apr 5, 1952.

Star Weekly (Toronto). "'China doll' ends her Calgary reign." Jul 4, 1959.

Sun-Reporter (San Francisco). "Oakland lassos Calgary Stampede Queen." Oct 23, 1987.

Western Horse Review. "Queen couture: The fashion and influence of Calgary Stampede Queens through the decades." Jul–Aug, 2012, 28–33.

Windsor Daily Star. "Alberta girl in New York rodeo." Jun 27, 1946.

Index

Abercrombie, Helen 34
Aboriginal Stampede royalty 69–73, 246–247. *See also* variously Eagle Speaker, Evelyn; Indian Princesses; Indian Village Princess
age of queen candidates. *See* Stampede Queen program: contestants, requirements for: age
Ager, Kary 231, 235, 236, 243, 330
Akkerman, Julie 107, 109–111, 116, 156, 157, 208, 329
Alberta Boot Co. 239, 311, 322
Alexander, Percy 181, 210
Allan, Patsy 149, 155, 173, 330
Anderson, Art 175
Anderson, Wynne 193, 194, 208, 296, 330
Andy, Tiffany 306
Ashbacher, Kelly 291, 331
Associated Canadian Travellers (ACT)
  fundraising by 34–38, 42–43, 62, 69, 90
  history of 33–34
  Stampede Queen contest, and 34–38, 46, 66, 90, 117–118, 124–125, 131–134, 140–141, 147, 153–154, 273. *See also* Stampede Queen Committee: transition from ACT to Stampede control
Associated Grocers 218, 228, 322
Astley, Susanne 240, 241, 330
Autry, Gene. *See also* Colborn, Everett C.
  as Stampede parade marshall, 1946 18
  Patsy Rodgers and 29–30
  World Championship Rodeo, and 13, 22–23
Bailey, Alex 149, 151, 154, 163, 176, 178
Baillod, Jenny 219, 220, 330
Baker, Wilf 149
Barenholtz, Naomi 51
Barlow, Happy 183, 184, 244, 330

beauty contests 35, 290. *See also* the various "Miss" contests respectively
  feminist criticism of 205–206, 231–235, 244, 261–263. *See also* feminism
  Stampede Queen event distinguished from 83, 134, 169–170, 206, 279, 327
Becker Buckles 322
Beckner, Eileen 53, 54, 56, 91, 116, 156, 329
Bestwick, Mel 188
Big Plume, Amber 322
Bill, Alan 76, 78
Birchall, Marion 47, 48, 49, 329
Blackburn, Les 202
Black Cowboys' Association (U.S.) 239
Blackfoot. *See* Siksika First Nation
Black, Shannon 321, 323, 331
Black Stampede royalty 236–237. *See also* Dunn, Holly
Bloods. *See* Kainai First Nation
Boake, Lynn 169, 171, 172, 173, 330
Boothby, Marion 66
boots. *See* Stampede Queen program: clothing, boots, regalia
Boston Garden. *See* World Championship Rodeo: Boston Garden, 1946
Boswell, Allison 269, 331
Boyce, Jayne 231, 235, 330
Bradley's Western Wear 190, 226, 228. *See also* Fraser, Margaret
Brewster, Eva 39, 40, 329
Brewster, Jolene 287, 311, 331
Brookman, George 304, 307
Browne, Dyanna 226, 227, 330
Brown, Ian 149
Brown, Pat 223, 224, 330
Burns, Carol 163, 165, 166, 330
Butler, Sibyl 153, 161–162, 171

Byrne, Amanda 300, 301, 303, 304, 331
Cairns, Bob 296
Calfrobe Ayoungman, Natasha 306
Calgary Elks Club No. 4 70
Calgary Exhibition and Stampede
  "Exhibition" dropped 285
  origins 11–12
Calgary Grey Cup Committee 116, 311
Calgary Horticultural Society Flower Show 21
Calgary International Horse Show 154, 173
  supplanted by Rodeo Royal as queen contest culmination, 1972 178, 303. *See also* Rodeo Royal: renamed, changed to fall event, 2008
Calgary Jaycees (Junior Chamber of Commerce) 170
Calgary Skyline Hotel 227, 265
Calgary Spring Horse Show. *See* Calgary International Horse Show
Calgary Stampede
  economic impact of 206
  origins of. *See* Calgary Exhibition and Stampede: origins
Calgary Stampede (film). *See* Hollywood and movies
Calgary Stampede Foundation 305. *See also* Stampede Royalty Committee: Calgary Stampede youth initiatives
Calgary Tourist and Convention Association 146, 185, 239
Camden, George 34, 36, 41
Canadian Indian Princess Pageant 246. *See also* Indian Princesses
Canadian Rodeo Tour Championship 304, 308, 328. *See* prior to 2008, Rodeo Royal
  discontinuance of, 2010 313–314

Caravan Committee 196, 213
Cartwright, Holly 276, 277, 331
Chamberlain, Frances 138, 329
Cheyenne Frontier Days 14, 176, 258, 267
Chipchase, Dawn 253, 254, 330
Chow, Jennie 102, 103, 105, 107, 109, 329
Christie, Donna 60, 329
Clark, Dave. *See* Dave Clark Five
Clark, Shirley 57, 59, 91, 329
clothing. *See* Stampede Queen program: clothing, boots, regalia
Cochrane, W. Gordon 83
Cohen, Martha 178
Colborn, Everett C. 26. *See also* Autry, Gene
  influence on origin of Stampede Queen program 13–17
Collins, Alison 285, 288, 310, 331
Collins, Audrey 205, 207, 330
Collins, Karen 288, 289, 290, 310, 331
Copithorne, Wendy 175, 330
Cowley, Kateri 308, 309, 311, 331
Cox, John 165, 166, 173, 195, 196, 201, 242, 255
Cozart, Mona 178
Crane, Elinor 256
Creative Living Committee 177, 208
Crosby, Bing 67, 90, 115
Cross, James B. 17, 20, 21
Cross, Stacey 279, 280, 331
Crowchild, Daisy 83
Crowe, Coleen 297, 303, 304, 331
crowns. *See* Stampede Queen program: clothing, boots, regalia: crowns
Crowshoe, Amelia 320
Dacen, Sharon 220, 221, 330
Dafoe, Cheryl 298, 300, 331
Dan, Gary 165, 201

352

D'Arcy, Jerry   149, 151, 154, 163
Dave Clark Five   140
David, Corie   287, 331
Davidson Enman Lumber   228, 322
Debnam, Bruce   277
Degenstein, Peter   117, 131, 138, 140, 147, 149, 150, 151, 153
Dench, Kay   69, 72, 75, 329
Dewhirst, June   57, 59, 181, 329
Dillon, Jack   7
   influence on origin of Stampede Queen program   13–17, 20–21, 34, 328
   with Patsy Rodgers in New York   28
Disney, Walt   90, 140
Dornan, Karen   226, 227, 330
Dowell, William D.   80
Downey, Karen   100, 101, 329
Dublin, Texas. See World Championship Rodeo
Dueck, Sonya   265, 267, 331
Dunham, Randy   180, 181, 196, 210
Dunn, Holly   236–239, 237, 330
Dutchak, Ann   53, 54, 329
Dutton, Merv (Red)   112
Eagle Speaker, Evelyn   69–87, 85, 102, 103, 112, 246, 329. See also Princess Wapiti
Eagle Speaker, Mike   71, 76
Eamor's Saddlery   118, 121, 175, 228, 317, 322
Eastman, Lisa   269, 281, 331
Edge, Beryl   127, 128, 329
Edge, Edith   62, 64, 69, 86, 91, 111, 127, 157, 329
education. See Stampede Queen program: educational aspects
Edworthy, George   17, 20, 21, 54
Edworthy, Myrle   20
Egan, Pat   30
Elton, Marquitta   99, 100, 101, 156, 329
Ernst, Breanna   292, 331
Falconer Academy of Modelling   228. See also Patti Falconer Agencies
Farley, Joan   44

Fath, Christie   280, 331
feminism   39, 48, 64, 93, 169–170, 187, 205–207, 231–233, 261–262. See also beauty contests: feminist criticism of; Stampede Queen program: contestants, requirements for: marital/parental status
Finn, Frank   147, 149, 152, 153
Finn, John   210, 254, 263
First Nations
   and Stampede Queen candidates   71–75
   participation in Stampede   11, 70, 245–248
   terminology   11
Fisher, Peggy   69, 75, 329
Ford, Catherine   231–235, 243–244, 262, 277
Forsgren, Margaret   45, 46, 329
Fraser, Margaret   192
   chaperone, as   191, 200, 202, 225, 242–243, 269, 281, 291
   contestants' riding ability, and   210
   Honorary Associate of Stampede Queens' Alumni Assn., 1993   298
   passing of, 2005   298
   Stampede Life Member, 2005   298
   Stampede Queen Committee, and   190–191, 242, 245, 248, 257, 263, 280, 286–287, 314
   Stampede royalty couture, and   190–192, 225–228, 235, 243–244, 275, 277–278, 288
   urban royals, and   211–212
   Western traditionalism, and   286
Fraternal Order of Eagles   21
Freeborn, John   82
Fussell, Michele   223, 224, 330
Fyfe, Shelly Ann   249, 251, 330
Gainor, Les   102
Gariepy, Danielle   319, 320, 331
Gathercole, Jim   279, 281, 286, 287, 296, 304
Gillis, Ron   296
Girletz, Dixie   128, 236, 329

Girling, Patti   178, 179, 181, 330
Girls Town   33–34, 38, 48, 141
Gleddie, Vanessa   253, 254, 330
Godsell, Philip   76, 78, 81
Godwin, Laura   240, 241, 242, 243, 322, 330. See also Stampede Queen Committee: hosting visiting rodeo royalty
Going, Cheryl   169, 171, 172, 173, 330
Gow, Jack   112, 117, 124, 127, 136, 147, 149, 150, 151, 153, 183
Gow, Orpha   155, 160
   chaperone, as   127
   Stampede royalty clothing design, and   136–137, 151
Grand Saddlery   256
Gray, Stephanie   317, 331
Great West Garment Co. (GWG)   18
Grey Cup   50–51, 116–117, 162, 239, 258
Griffith, Kari   253, 254, 282, 330
Griffith, Wilbur   136, 154
Haeh, Beverly   105, 329
Hall, Tom   149
Halstead, Dennis   292
Hamblin, Brianna   292–293, 331
Hames, Kari   272, 274, 331
Hamilton, Diane   210, 211, 213, 330
Hamilton, Isabella   105, 138, 329
Hamilton, Isabelle   105
Hannah, Jim   34, 36
Harrington, Shauna   201, 203, 330
Harris, Phil   90
Hatchwear Uniform Co.   190
Havens, Natalie   288, 289, 290, 331
Hayden, Vicky   169, 171, 172, 173, 330
Hays, Harry   56, 116, 117, 146
Heath, Danica   321, 323, 331
Heavy Shields, Nikkole   308, 311
Heintz, Maria   285, 288, 331
Helldorado Days   87, 98
Hendel, Ed   100
Henry, Gail   131, 136, 329

Herron, Bill   162
   iconic white hat, and   17, 50, 54
Higginbotham, Michel   259, 330
Historical Committee   273
Hoffman, Dennis   296
Hollywood and movies   64, 69, 72, 75, 84, 87, 89, 92, 98, 111, 114
   Calgary Stampede (film)   44
   cultural influence on Stampede   39, 41, 66
   Patsy Rodgers and   28, 31
   Pretty Ladies, Fast Horses (documentary)   289
   promo visits to by Stampede Queens   66–67
Holtkamp, Elfreda   160, 160–161
honorariums. See Stampede Queen program: honorariums
Hoof, Vada   257
Hooker, Jody   272, 274, 310, 314, 331
Hope, Bob   90
Hopkins, Johnny   129, 135, 178, 193, 195
Horne, Joan   181, 182, 189, 330
horses and riding   48, 50–51, 54, 60, 64. See also Stampede Queen program: requirements for contestants: riding skill
   accidents   251, 263, 265, 269–270
   riding instruction   253–255
   Stampede-owned stock reserved for royalty use   248–249, 265, 313
Howard, Barbara   187, 188, 275, 330
Hudson's Bay Co.   127, 153, 163
Hughes, Laura   263, 264, 331
Hunter, Karin   276, 277, 331
Hutchcroft, Harry   81
"Indian." See First Nations: terminology
Indian Princess Alberta/Calgary/ Canada   246
Indian Princesses   87, 255–259, 296, 304, 305, 306–308, 311, 313, 317, 322, 328. See also Indian Village Princess

as integral part of royal team   305–308, 320

cultural trope, as   71–72

early history of   11

honorary title granted by First Nations   43, 56, 70

Stampede Queen Committee, and   244–248

Indian Village Princess. *See also* Indian Princesses; Stampede Indian Events Committee; Stampede Indian Village; Treaty 7 Nations: Stampede Indian Events Committee and

controversy over breadth of mandate   247–248, 255–256

expansion of role   258, 298, 306–307, 318

"Village" gone from crowns after 2002   306

parity with royal trio for gifts, sponsorships etc.   307, 317

transition to fall event, 2008, and   307–308

treatment of at official events, 1990   256–257

Inkster, Shirley   175, 330

Innes, June-Marie   288, 289, 331

Israelson, Donna   138, 153, 157, 160, 329

Jacques, Don   246

Jenkins, Bob   178

Johanson, Shilo   272, 274, 331

Johnson, Doug   146, 154

Johnston, Joan   91, 93, 329

Johnston, Patricia   163, 165, 166, 330

Jonassen, Pam   201, 203, 330

Jones, Mary Ellen   89, 91, 93, 107, 157, 329

Jones, Mrs. Everal   175

Kainai First Nation   11, 70, 72–73

Kakoschke, Danielle   321, 331

Kanderka, April   298, 300, 331

Kehler, Bill   254, 277, 279, 296

Kemp, Shirley   45, 46, 280, 329

Kennedy, Charles   116, 117

Kennedy, Dorothy   271, 281, 296

Kent, Elaine   91, 93, 329

Kirk, Stacy   187, 188, 330

Klaver, Gloria   45, 46, 51, 156, 329

Knight, Bettie   181, 182, 330

Kochan, Amanda   300, 301, 331

Kraft, Karin   183, 184, 330

Lambert, Jenna   311, 317, 331

Lammle, Kari   280, 331

Lammle's Western Wear   272, 322

Langeveld, John   256

Langford, Joan Plastow. *See* Plastow, Joan

Larsen, Kay   100, 101, 329

Larter, Kathryn   279, 280, 331

Las Vegas, Nev.   69, 87, 92, 98, 111. *See also* Schiller, Abe

declining interest in as prize trip   114

Lawrence, Heather   158, 160, 162, 330

Leach, Ken   66, 87, 98, 111

Lebbert, Lyle   64

ACT Queen Committee, and   54, 69

Princess Wapiti regalia controversy, and   78

Lee, Candice   319, 320, 331

Leech, Diane   158, 160, 162, 330

Lee, Harold   99

Leinweber, Shannan   217, 220, 221, 330

Leonard, Gail   114, 329

Leslie, Jack   56, 162

Lethbridge rodeo   18–20

Linder, Herman   18

Linderman, Bill   24, 25

Patsy Rodgers, and   20–21, 24

Littlelight, Gloria   245, 247

Longmoor, Val   202

Love, H. Gordon   122

MacDonald, Gussie   53, 54, 329

MacDonald, Leslie   173, 175, 210, 330

chaperone, as   179, 183, 213–214, 297

horsemanship judge, as   180, 297

Stampede Life Member, 2000   297

MacDonald, Mary   138, 183, 188, 329

MacEwan, Grant   56, 99, 127

MacGregor, Bonnie   149, 155, 160, 330

Mackay, Don   54, 56, 62, 67, 99, 146

Mackie, Kathleen   231, 235, 330

MacLean, Dawn   179, 330

MacLennan, Lauren   297, 303, 304, 331

Maclin Motors Ltd.   160

Madison Square Garden. *See* World Championship Rodeo

Magnussen, Karen   180

Magnusson, Tom   296

Main, Dale   149, 239

Makenny, Jackie   225, 240

Manning, Jessica   319, 320, 321, 331

Many Wounds, Livia   306, 308

Markus, Marg   191

Marshall, Gwenda   131, 136, 329

Marshall, Kay   97, 329

Martindale, Shannan   291, 292, 331

Martin, Don   259

Martinson, Peter   83

Maynard, Tina   276, 277, 331

McCallum, Hiram (Buck)   50

McKay, Elaine   280, 281, 291, 296

McKay, Melissa   263, 264–265, 291, 331

McLean, Lorraine   144, 146, 156, 330

McMahon, Marion   57, 59, 329

McNiven, Lisa   285, 288, 331

McWhir, Kate   261, 262, 331

Meguinis, Eva   311, 317–318

Meguinis, Heather   256, 257

Meguinis, Marcie   306

Melby, Inez   48, 49, 179, 329

Merriman, Jodi   205, 207, 330

Midtdal, Tamy   265, 267, 331

Miller, Jack M.   38, 45

Milne, Marlie   220, 221, 330

Milner, Justine   297, 303, 304, 331

Miss America contest   35, 234

Miss Calgary contest   17, 206, 211, 234.

criticism of   232–233

Stampede royalty as stepping stone to   111

"Miss Canada". *See also* Rodgers, Patsy: not initially recognized as first Stampede Queen

media misunderstanding first Stampede Queen as   17, 20, 22, 28–29

Miss Canada pageant

discontinuance of   206, 262

feminist criticism of   234–235

launch of   35

Stampede royalty as stepping stone to   111

Miss Pot o' Gold contest   170

Miss Rodeo America contest   98, 124, 138, 258, 277, 281

Miss Rodeo Canada contest   64, 109, 124, 271, 309

Miss Universe contest   222, 233

Mitchell, Sherry   261, 262, 331

Moore, Sherry   60, 70, 329

Morneau, Catherine   321, 331

Morres, Cindy   193, 194, 226, 309, 330

Morstad, Caia   300, 301, 303, 304, 331

Moynihan, Erin   263, 264, 331

Murray, Teri   298, 300, 331

National Finals Rodeo (U.S.)   258, 267, 271, 281, 289, 293, 300

Neilson, Ann   144, 146, 330

Newman, Gillian   196, 197, 208, 330

O'Connor, Ed   173, 176

Olson Silver and Leather Co.   184

Olympic Rodeo   240

Orr, Brenda   196, 197, 330

Oseen, Shauna   261, 262, 331

Ouellet, Bill   120–121, 124, 133

Ough, Jennifer   240, 241, 330

Ovans, Carol   193, 194, 330

Pacific National Exhibition   239, 258

Paget, Ken   125

Palliser Hotel   97, 100, 111, 123, 127, 156, 195, 265

Parsons, Irv   131, 137, 140, 147, 149

Patterson, Sharon   131, 135, 138, 157, 273, 329

Patterson, Stephanie 321, 323, 331
Patterson, Tony 277
Patti Falconer Agencies 322. *See also* Falconer Academy of Modelling
Peacock, Tony 277
Pearce, Gordon 245
Pearson, Pat 197, 240, 244, 255, 257, 258, 285, 298, 315
Peigan. *See* Piikani First Nation
Pendleton (Oregon) Round-Up 35, 36, 39, 41, 42, 278
 Aboriginal royalty, and 70
 pioneers of rodeo royalty idea 14
Penner, Barb 210, 211, 213, 330
Perchaluk, Monica 223, 224, 234, 330
Percival, Trina 291, 303, 304, 331
Phillips, Janelle 311, 313, 314, 331
Piikani First Nation 11, 72–73, 313, 320
Plastow, Joan 149–150, 165, 176, 178, 215
Pollard, Bill 48
Postlethwaite, Don 187, 195
Powell, Margaret 109, 111, 113, 329
Princess Wapiti. *See also* Eagle Speaker, Evelyn
 controversy over regalia 75–86
 naming of 72–73
Pringle, Dawn 205, 207, 330
prizes. *See* Stampede Queen program: prizes, gifts
Puckett, Lynn 109, 118, 329
Pullar, W. 83
Quebec Winter Carnival 163, 183, 239, 258, 300
Queen contest. *See* variously under Stampede Queen program
Queen for a Day 67, 98
Queens' Alumni Association. *See* Stampede Queens' Alumni Association
Randle, Suzanne 181, 182, 330
Red Gun, Charity 257
Reeder, Frances 123, 329
Reid, Shannon 287, 331

Reid, Winnifred 163, 165, 166, 330
Rennells, Linda 122, 123, 329
requirements for contestants. *See* Stampede Queen program: contestants, requirements for
Richards-Kelly, Linda 245, 247
Richardson, Doreen 33, 37, 38–39, 40, 41, 44, 45, 156, 273, 329
 Patsy Rodgers, and 33, 273
Riley & McCormick Ltd. 17, 41
Robinson, Cathy 210, 211, 330
Rochon, Katie 313, 331
rodeo queen tradition. *See also* Hollywood and movies: cultural influence on Stampede
 Aboriginal people, and 69–70
 Black people, and 239
 feminism, and. *See* beauty contests: feminist criticism of
 function of 20, 35–36
 origin 13–14
 Stampede royalty and 286
Rodeo Royal
 1st Rodeo Royal Special, 1987 208
 influence on queen contest scheduling 177–178, 240, 285, 300, 328
 origin as queen contest culmination, 1972 208–209
 renamed, changed to fall event, 2008 303–304. *See now* Canadian Rodeo Tour Championship
Rodgers, Patsy 7, 15, 16, 18, 29, 156, 176, 194, 208, 328, 329
 60th anniversary of appointment 296
 Bill Linderman, and 20–21, 24
 Gene Autry, and 29–30
 Hollywood offers, and 28, 31
 named first Stampede Queen 14–15
 not initially recognized as first Stampede Queen 17, 20, 33, 273
 Stampede 1946, and 17–21
 Stampede parade, and 31, 296, 304–305

Stampede Queens' Alumni Assn., and 31, 273
 U.S. media, and 26–30
 World Championship Rodeo, at 21–30
Rodgers, William Jasper (Jappy) 14
Ross, Alison 259, 330
Rougeau, Kristie 313, 331
Rouleau, Mary Ellen 249, 251, 254, 330
Royalty Transition Team, 2008 304, 331
Running Bull 59
Russell Sporting Goods 72
Sarcee. *See* Tsuu T'ina First Nation
Schiller, Abe 66, 87, 93, 98, 111, 114
Schoeppe, Carolyn 97, 329
scholarships. *See* Stampede Queen program: scholarships
Scott, Ivy Kim 257, 305, 308
Scott, John 296
Scott, Karyn 226, 227, 330
Sears Canada 322. *See also* Simpsons-Sears Ltd.
Sergerie, Tara 308, 309, 331
Sharpe, Marie 118, 136, 156, 157, 255, 329
Shaw GMC 228, 322
Shaw, Judy 198, 330
Sherman, Mabel 97
Siksika First Nation 11, 43, 72–73, 298
Simpson, Debbie 236, 237, 330
Simpsons-Sears Ltd. 118, 121, 127, 136, 140, 153, 163, 175, 218, 228. *See also* Sears Canada
Smith, Amy 292, 331
Smithbilt Hats 17
Smith, Candace 149, 155, 330
Smith, Helen 60, 91, 329
Snow, Chrissy 306
Snow, Gloria 247
sponsors, sponsorship. *See* Stampede Queen program: sponsors and sponsorship
Stampede Indian Events

Committee 244–248, 306–307, 312, 320. *See also* Indian Village Princess
 extent of Indian Village Princess functions 255–256, 258, 298, 306–307
Stampede Indian Princess. *See* variously, Indian Princesses, Indian Village Princess, Stampede Indian Events Committee
Stampede Indian Village 70, 247. *See also* Indian Village Princess
Stampede Queen Committee 303, 304, 312, 313, 314, 326, 327, 328. *See after* 2008, Stampede Royalty Committee
 bookings policy changes 278
 chaperone function redefined 292
 finances, and 220, 236, 265, 267
 former royals, and 243
 hosting visiting rodeo royalty 243. *See also* Godwin, Laura
 inaugural members of 149–151
 Margaret Fraser and 190–192, 210, 242, 263, 280, 286–287
 mixed messaging on royalty: 1+2? or team of 3? 216–218, 282–283, 285–286, 288. *See also* generally, Stampede Queen program: functioning of royalty as team
 reserved riding stock, obtaining 248–249, 265
 response to a Princess quitting midway 292–293
 Stampede Indian Events Committee, relations with 244–248, 257–258, 298
 Stampede Queens' Alumni Assn., relations with 272–273
 transition from ACT to Stampede control 140–141, 147, 149–154, 190
 transition to fall event, 2008, and other changes 303–306
Stampede Queen program 328. *See also* generally, Stampede Queen Committee

355
★

clothing, boots, regalia   41, 93–94, 175, 225–227, 239, 271–272, 272, 322

belt buckles   21, 41, 136, 183, 256, 272, 282

as symbol of office   293

couture of   190–192, 225–228, 277–278. *See also* Fraser, Margaret; Gow, Orpha; Holtkamp, Elfreda

criticism of   231–233, 243–244

crowns   146, 202–203, 272–273, 293, 322

Indian Princess coronet   247–248

status of princesses, and   202–203

silver spurs   21

contestants, fluctuating numbers of   69, 125, 192, 205, 222, 263, 279–280, 318

letting unsuccessful finalists run again   286–288, 297

resulting in older contestants   312–313

contestants, requirements for

age   142, 152, 183, 303, 312–313. *See also* Stampede Queen program: contestants, fluctuating numbers of: letting unsuccessful finalists run again: resulting in older contestants

conduct   215–218, 258–259

function of chaperones   291–292

driver's licence, access to vehicle   195, 303

gender   187, 222–223, 303

high school graduate   209, 303

marital/parental status   48, 152, 189, 208–209, 222, 231–235, 303. *See also* Stampede Queen program: contestants, requirements for: time commitment

no criminal record   209, 303

presentability, poise, public speaking   154, 178, 195–196, 255, 289–291, 309–310

residency, citizenship   142–144, 151–152, 209, 229, 303

riding skill   50–51, 60, 152, 154, 180–181, 193, 200–201, 207, 209–211, 249,

253–255, 318–319, 326. *See also* horses and riding: riding instruction

time commitment   56, 198–199, 223–225, 253, 292–293, 297, 311–312, 321–322. *See also* Stampede Queen program: functions of royalty.

2008 rescheduling, and   306

as rationale for marital/parental status requirement   234.

contestants, rural or urban origin of   90–92, 211, 310–311

contest procedure   36–38, 42–46, 48, 152–154, 177–178, 210–211, 326–328

advertising for   197–198

criticism of   54, 57, 205

judging of contestants   124, 154, 170–171, 192–193, 214–215, 220–221, 275–277, 316

group dynamics   214, 216–218, 220, 282–283. *See also* Stampede Queen program: functioning of royalty as team

judges' anonymous feedback to contestants   315

"the Red Book" manual   195

criticism of generally   231–233, 259, 261–262

educational aspects   315–316. *See also* Stampede Queen program: scholarships

functioning of royalty as team   199–200, 214–218, 224–225, 271, 275, 281–283, 288, 292–293, 312, 319–320, 326. *See also* Stampede Queen Committee: mixed messaging on royalty: 1+2? or team of 3?; Stampede Queen program: contest procedure: judging of contestants: group dynamics

specifically as trio   251

functions of royalty   235–236. *See also* Stampede Queen program: contestants, requirements for: time commitment

out-of-province promotional travel   42, 56, 92, 98–99, 116–117, 175–176, 213, 239–240, 258, 267, 280–281, 320. See

also, e.g., Grey Cup, Quebec Winter Carnival, National Finals Rodeo

public relations team, as   206–208, 240, 242, 271, 311–312

honorariums   189–190, 218, 228, 238–239, 271, 278–279, 322

prizes, gifts   43, 66, 92, 195, 218, 228, 317, 322

scholarships   315–316, 323

conflation with honorariums   189, 218

sponsors and sponsorship   42–43, 90–91, 190, 227–228, 272, 275, 278, 314, 322

parity for Indian Princesses, 2008   307. *See also* Indian Princesses: as integral part of royal team

Stampede Queens' Alumni Association

50th anniversary of queen program   273, 275

60th anniversary of queen program   294

countering negative press   244

membership   208, 323

origin of, 1972   176–177, 273

Patsy Rodgers and   31, 273

Stampede Queens' Alumni Committee, and   294

Stampede Queens' Alumni Committee

50th anniversary of Queen program   273, 275

60th anniversary of Queen program   294–295, 296

Honorary Associates   296

honouring deceased members   296

hosting visiting rodeo royalty   243. *See also* Stampede Queen Committee: hosting visiting rodeo royalty

origin of, 1980   208

response to a Princess quitting midway   292–293

Stampede Queen Committee, relations with   208, 272–273

Stampede Queens' Alumni Assn., and   294

Stampede volunteering and   208, 273, 294

year-round functioning of   273

Stampede Royalty Committee   316, 318, 319, 320, 321, 322, 328. *See also* Stampede Queen Committee

budget increased   314

Calgary Stampede youth initiatives   305–306, 314–316

expanded public relations mandate for royals   310

former royals admitted to panel   314

inception with new name   304

Royalty Transition Team, and   308

Stampede Indian Events Committee, and   307

"Stampeder Special" to Grey Cup football game in Toronto, 1948   50

Starlight, Bruce   257

Starlight, Lisa   257

Stephens, Patti   198, 330

Stier, Merle   47, 53, 54, 109, 154, 156, 176, 177, 273, 329

Stoney/Nakoda First Nation   11, 59, 64–65, 72–73, 247

Strandquist, Halley   259, 330

Swann, Frances   125, 127, 128, 156, 329

Sykes, Rod   189

Taylor, Brian   255, 258

Taylor, Judy   114, 329

Taylor, Sharon   118, 329

Tees, Karina   269, 331

Thacker, Sis   183, 184, 330

The Bay. *See* Hudson's Bay Co.

Thompson, Erin   279, 280, 331

Thompson, Lee   296

Thompson, Shaunna   236, 237, 279, 314, 322, 330

Thomson, Donna   121, 122, 123, 156, 157, 176, 177, 178, 273, 321, 329

tiaras. *See* Stampede Queen program: clothing, boots, regalia: crowns

time commitment. *See* Stampede Queen program: contestants, requirements for: time commitment travel. *See* Stampede Queen program: functions of royalty: out-of-province promotional travel

Treaty 7 Nations   11, 72–74. *See also* Kainai, Piikani, Siksika, Stoney/ Nakoda and Tsuu T'ina nations respectively; various topics under First Nations

Stampede Indian Events Committee and   244–248, 306–307

Tremblay, Dana   314, 315

Trudeau, Pierre Elliott   162

Tsuu T'ina First Nation   11, 43, 46, 56, 60, 72–73, 317

Turney, Margot   113, 114, 116, 118, 157, 173, 329

Van Wart, Dawne   198, 330

Wallace, Bonny   249, 251, 330

Wallace, Diane   179, 330

Ward, Betty   43

Ward, Deb   305

Warden, Brenda   192, 201, 203, 330

Waterchief, Lana   298, 306

Waterton Lakes Jamboree   84

Watson, Holly   265, 267, 331

Watt, Penny   219, 220, 330

Weadick, Guy   34, 143

advocate for First Nations participation in Stampede   70

founding of Stampede, 1912   11

Weasel Child, Carly   322

Weasel Child, Gaylene   257, 308

Weasel Head, Nicole   306

Weasel Traveller, Sahvanne   313

Webster, George   35

Weidner, Arlene   158, 160, 162, 330

Welden, Don   149

Wesner, Tara   280, 281, 296, 331

Western movies. *See* Hollywood and movies: cultural influence on Stampede

white hat as icon   54, 67, 146, 226, 259. *See also* Herron, Bill; *See also* Mackay, Don

Wigle, Chris   187, 188, 330

Wildman, Camille   257

Wilkie, Whitney   296, 317, 331

Williams, Jessica   319, 321, 331

Williamson, Kerri   308, 309, 331

Williamson, Michelle   219, 220, 330

Willock, Shirley   95, 96, 97, 99, 114, 244, 329

Wittmoser, Sylvia   196, 197, 330

women in rodeo   13. *See also* rodeo queen tradition

Woodward's   163

World Championship Rodeo   13, 16–18. *See also* Autry, Gene; Colborn, Everett C.; "Miss Canada"

Boston Garden, 1946   29–30

Dublin, Texas, 1946   21–23

Madison Square Garden, NYC, 1946   23–28

Patsy Rodgers at   16–17, 21–31

wages paid to "sponsor girls"   25

Wright, Betty   142, 143, 144, 146, 147, 151, 153, 155, 156, 157, 180, 208, 330

Wright, Lori Ann   257

Wynne, Doreen   109, 111, 177, 329

Yellowhorn, Denise   245

Yellow Old Woman, Nicole   257, 308

357

About the Author

Jennifer Hamblin has an MA in history from McMaster University and a Master of Library Science from the University of Toronto. She works as a librarian and archivist at Calgary's Glenbow Museum. In her spare time, she enjoys researching and writing about interesting Alberta women. She has penned a number of articles for *Alberta History* and is the co-author of *The Diva and the Rancher: The Story of Norma Piper and George Pocaterra* (Rocky Mountain Books, 2006). She and her husband, Tony, live in Calgary and are the proud parents of two grown-up children, Lindsay and Graham.